I0885031

Management Strategies for Sustainability, New Knowledge Innovation, and Personalized Products and Services

Mirjana Pejic-Bach
University of Zagreb, Croatia

Çağlar Doğru
Ufuk University, Turkey

A volume in the Advances in Logistics, Operations, and Management Science (ALOMS) Book Series

IGI Global
PUBLISHER of TIMELY KNOWLEDGE

Published in the United States of America by
IGI Global
Business Science Reference (an imprint of IGI Global)
701 E. Chocolate Avenue
Hershey PA, USA 17033
Tel: 717-533-8845
Fax: 717-533-8661
E-mail: cust@igi-global.com
Web site: http://www.igi-global.com

Copyright © 2022 by IGI Global. All rights reserved. No part of this publication may be reproduced, stored or distributed in any form or by any means, electronic or mechanical, including photocopying, without written permission from the publisher.
Product or company names used in this set are for identification purposes only. Inclusion of the names of the products or companies does not indicate a claim of ownership by IGI Global of the trademark or registered trademark.

Library of Congress Cataloging-in-Publication Data

Names: Pejić-Bach, Mirjana, editor. | Dogru, Caglar, 1983- editor.
Title: Management strategies for sustainability, new knowledge innovation, and personalized products and services / Mirjana Pejic-Bach, and Caglar Dogru, editors.
Description: Hershey, PA : Business Science Reference, [2022] | Includes bibliographical references and index. | Summary: "This reference book brings together the emerging topics of digital transformation, new knowledge innovation, sustainability, personalized products and services, advances in information technologies, new management strategies and digital practices in human resources and new forms of work"-- Provided by publisher.
Identifiers: LCCN 2021043056 (print) | LCCN 2021043057 (ebook) | ISBN 9781799877936 (hardcover) | ISBN 9781799877943 (paperback) | ISBN 9781799877950 (ebook)
Subjects: LCSH: Information technology--Management. | Sustainable development. | Knowledge management.
Classification: LCC HD30.2 .M36136 2022 (print) | LCC HD30.2 (ebook) | DDC 658.4/038--dc23
LC record available at https://lccn.loc.gov/2021043056
LC ebook record available at https://lccn.loc.gov/2021043057

This book is published in the IGI Global book series Advances in Logistics, Operations, and Management Science (ALOMS) (ISSN: 2327-350X; eISSN: 2327-3518)

British Cataloguing in Publication Data
A Cataloguing in Publication record for this book is available from the British Library.

All work contributed to this book is new, previously-unpublished material.
The views expressed in this book are those of the authors, but not necessarily of the publisher.

For electronic access to this publication, please contact: eresources@igi-global.com.

Advances in Logistics, Operations, and Management Science (ALOMS) Book Series

John Wang
Montclair State University, USA

ISSN:2327-350X
EISSN:2327-3518

MISSION

Operations research and management science continue to influence business processes, administration, and management information systems, particularly in covering the application methods for decision-making processes. New case studies and applications on management science, operations management, social sciences, and other behavioral sciences have been incorporated into business and organizations real-world objectives.

The **Advances in Logistics, Operations, and Management Science** (ALOMS) Book Series provides a collection of reference publications on the current trends, applications, theories, and practices in the management science field. Providing relevant and current research, this series and its individual publications would be useful for academics, researchers, scholars, and practitioners interested in improving decision making models and business functions.

COVERAGE

- Marketing engineering
- Finance
- Risk Management
- Production Management
- Services management
- Information Management
- Networks
- Computing and information technologies
- Decision analysis and decision support
- Political Science

IGI Global is currently accepting manuscripts for publication within this series. To submit a proposal for a volume in this series, please contact our Acquisition Editors at Acquisitions@igi-global.com or visit: http://www.igi-global.com/publish/.

The Advances in Logistics, Operations, and Management Science (ALOMS) Book Series (ISSN 2327-350X) is published by IGI Global, 701 E. Chocolate Avenue, Hershey, PA 17033-1240, USA, www.igi-global.com. This series is composed of titles available for purchase individually; each title is edited to be contextually exclusive from any other title within the series. For pricing and ordering information please visit http://www.igi-global.com/book-series/advances-logistics-operations-management-science/37170. Postmaster: Send all address changes to above address. Copyright © 2022 IGI Global. All rights, including translation in other languages reserved by the publisher. No part of this series may be reproduced or used in any form or by any means – graphics, electronic, or mechanical, including photocopying, recording, taping, or information and retrieval systems – without written permission from the publisher, except for non commercial, educational use, including classroom teaching purposes. The views expressed in this series are those of the authors, but not necessarily of IGI Global.

Titles in this Series

For a list of additional titles in this series, please visit: http://www.igi-global.com/book-series/

Key Factors and Use Cases of Servant Leadership Driving Organizational Performance
Maria Pressentin (International School of Management, France)
Business Science Reference • © 2022 • 315pp • H/C (ISBN: 9781799888208) • US $215.00

Handbook of Research on Innovative Management Using AI in Industry 5.0
Vikas Garg (Amity University, Greater Noida, India) and Richa Goel (Amity University, Noida, India)
Business Science Reference • © 2022 • 351pp • H/C (ISBN: 9781799884972) • US $295.00

Contemporary Challenges for Agile Project Management
Vannie Naidoo (University of Kwa-Zulu Natal, South Africa) and Rahul Verma (Delhi University, India)
Business Science Reference • © 2022 • 354pp • H/C (ISBN: 9781799878728) • US $225.00

Cases on Optimizing the Asset Management Process
Vicente González-Prida (University of Seville, Spain & National University of Distance Education, Spain) Carlos Alberto Parra Márquez (University of Seville, Spain) and Adolfo Crespo Márquez (University of Seville, Spain)
Business Science Reference • © 2022 • 457pp • H/C (ISBN: 9781799879435) • US $215.00

Handbook of Research on Current Trends in Asian Economics, Business, and Administration
Bülent Akkaya (Manisa Celal Bayar University, Turkey) Kittisak Jermsittiparsert (Henan University of Economics and Law, China) and Ayse Gunsel (Kocaeli University, Turkey)
Business Science Reference • © 2022 • 497pp • H/C (ISBN: 9781799884866) • US $295.00

Logistics and Supply Chain Management in the Globalized Business Era
Lincoln C. Wood (University of Otago, New Zealand) and Linh N.K. Duong (University of the West of England, Bristol, UK)
Business Science Reference • © 2022 • 413pp • H/C (ISBN: 9781799887096) • US $225.00

Managerial Issues in Digital Transformation of Global Modern Corporations
Thangasamy Esakki (Poompuhar College (Autonomous), India)
Business Science Reference • © 2021 • 323pp • H/C (ISBN: 9781799824022) • US $195.00

IGI Global
PUBLISHER of TIMELY KNOWLEDGE

701 East Chocolate Avenue, Hershey, PA 17033, USA
Tel: 717-533-8845 x100 • Fax: 717-533-8661
E-Mail: cust@igi-global.com • www.igi-global.com

Editorial Advisory Board

Beatriz Casais, *University of Minho, Portugal*
Marisa R. Ferreira, *Polytechnic Institute of Porto, Portugal*
Maria Jesus Garcia Garcia, *University of Valencia, Spain*
Antonios Kargas, *National and Kapodistrian University of Athens, Greece*
Carina Silva, *Polytechnic Institute of Porto, Portugal*

Table of Contents

Detailed Table of Contents

Economic and technological developments that took place the last 30 years have resulted in a new form of industrial revolution, widely known as Industry 4.0 (I4.0). Researchers and professionals worldwide try to foresee and contribute to its development, while the COVID-19 pandemic acted as an accelerator and revealed that changes arising under Industry 4.0 will affect a wide variety of working-life aspects. Among these aspects, skills and competencies needed under I4.0 are expected to change. The current chapter uses the European Skills, Competences, Qualifications, and Occupations (ESCO) database to identify which are the most valuable skills and competencies in the time being, when European businesses are taking part in the so-called digital transformation, part of Industry's 4.0 evolution. The most significant skills and competencies will be presented alongside with an analysis on existing research on the relationship between I4.0 and new skills/competencies needed.

A recommendation system is a significant part of artificial intelligence (AI) to help users' access information at any time and from anywhere. Online product recommender systems are widely used to recommend products based on consumers' preferences. The traditional recommendation algorithms of recommendation engines do not meet the needs of users in the AI environment when exposed to large amounts of data resulting in a low recommendation efficiency. To address this, a personalized recommendation system was introduced. These personalized recommendation systems (PRS) are an important component for ecommerce players in the Indian e-commerce aspects. Since personalized recommendations are becoming increasingly popular, this study examines information processing theory with respect to personalized recommendations and their impact on user satisfaction. Further, relationships between the variables were examined by conducting regression analysis and found a positive correlation exists between personalized product recommendation and user satisfaction.

Climate change, pollutants, sustainable development, and public health have become increasingly more relevant issues that continuously get addressed and discussed by governments and entities all over the globe. Through the adoption of policies and recyclable methods, they hope to encourage and aid the responsible consumption of natural resources so as to reduce the creation of waste. Furthermore, the generation of sustainable communities is encouraged so as to safeguard and protect the population's health against the risks associated with different types of pollutants. To support SMEs in the adoption of sustainable practices, this chapter aims to introduce, guide, and provide some useful tools that can then be utilized by readers and professionals operating within SMEs to maximize the effectiveness of their sustainability approaches and tools while also providing knowledge on how the implementation of sustainable practices could be integrated within their businesses.

Big data and artificial intelligence (AI) technologies have changed how we live, how we work, and how we organize businesses. Thus, it is no surprise that it is also changing how we manage human resources (HR). For HR leaders, digital transformation is a very hot topic, having the potential to create high value for businesses. First,

HR can transform all functions, processes, and systems by leveraging digital platforms and applications. Second, HR can lead business digitalization, enabling a compelling employee experience where a digital culture, a digital workplace, and digital management are welcomed. To provide a more pragmatic perspective, this chapter discusses digitalization of HR with big data and artificial intelligence (AI) technologies and identifies key digital HR strategies and roles needed to sustain the digital transformation. Also, this chapter presents the advantages of digital HR and the basic pitfalls HR faces in the digital transformation of HR.

Many businesses around the world have begun to take advantage of digital technology in recent years. Making use of digital technology enables one to do things in less time, need fewer employees, reduce costs, use information and resources effectively, produce the most products with the least resources, and consequently, increase the profitability of the enterprises. The shipping sector is one of the building blocks of the maritime industry. It aims to increase its profitability by digitizing in today's increasingly competitive conditions. In recent years, digital twin (DT) technology has been used extensively for the digitalization of the sector. This chapter introduces the current and potential uses of DT technology in ship operations and management and gives an idea about how DT technology will create an opportunity to develop the shipping sector.

The industry's internet of things (IoT) applications have drawn significant research attention in recent decades. IoT is a technology in which intelligent objects with sensors-enabled RFID tags, actuators, and processors communicate information to cater to a meaningful purpose in the industry. This way, IoT technology aims to simplify the distributed data collection in industrial practice, sharing and processing information and knowledge across many collaborating partners using suitable enterprise information systems. This chapter describes new methods with grounded knowledge representation techniques to address the needs of formal information modeling and reasoning for web-based services. The chapter presents a framework, apparel business decentralized data integration (ABDDI), which uses knowledge

Preface

It is unquestionable that the world is in such a transition from old one to a new form. Digital transformation in every function of management will be the comparative advantages of organizations over the others by creating innovative organizations competitive core capabilities. From manufacturing to education, in every business sector there is a shift from traditional way of doing business to a brand-new understanding. In today's ever-changing business environment, managers and employees need essential capabilities in order to reach organizational goals and to survive. Among these capabilities innovativeness take the lead. In this digitalized era, it is obvious that old school firms and organizations will not survive due to changing demands and business strategies.

Nothing will be same with the past decade for sure. The upcoming era necessitates digital transformation in all of the institutions of government and non-profit sector as well as profit organizations. Among them companies should take the lead in digital transforming by carrying all of their procedures to a digitalized media since in this modern society needs and wants of end-users have been changed. New developments in information technologies provide the essential base for digital transformation. This will provide time-effectiveness, lowered costs, perfect timing and efficiency in personalized products and services. Furthermore, not only governmental agencies but also, private organizations need to employ sustainability practices without loosing a second since our world needs them more than any time. In today's world, digital transformation and sustainability management practices are the two main legs of a business context. From a sustainable perspective, a more specific way of supplying services to customers appear to be the personalized services. Proactive organizations have started to apply strategies for the personalized services using various sources of consumer data in order to be successful in presenting personalized services. From another perspective, it is obvious that, digital transformation is well positively related to the personalized services.

Therefore in this globalization and digitalization era, digital transformation, sustainability practices and personalized services are getting more and more critical. In today's change-oriented and complex business environment, both entrepreneurs and leaders have to keep up with the latest developments around them. In this book, with the valuable contributions of the authors, latest data and research on the issues in sustainability, digital transformation in the new World, and practices of personalized services in the organizations are present.

In this context, we can give brief descriptions of the chapters, which are present in this reference book.

In Chapter 1, it is aimed to contribute to the digital transformation literature by using European Skills, Competences, Qualifications and Occupations (ESCO) database. Throughout this chapter, the effects of Industry 4.0 evolution on digital transformation and companies' generating new skills and competences are discussed.

In Chapter 2, personalized product recommendation and user satisfaction theory are explained and discussed. Product recommendation is put forth as a significant part of artificial intelligence and personalized service. This is achieved by conducting a quantitative research. According to the research, positive correlation between personalized product recommendation and user satisfaction was found.

Chapter 3 discusses the sustainability tools and practices in businesses to highlight the latest sustainability approaches. In this chapter, it is aimed to introduce useful sustainability tools for small and medium sized enterprises.

Chapter 4 sets forth the link between digital transformation and human resources management in the organizations. While analyzing this connection, the effects of big data and artificial intelligence are examined. Furthermore, in this chapter, the key digital human resources strategies and roles are discussed so as to ease and sustain the digital transformation.

In Chapter 5, digital transformation is analyzed in a specific industry that is maritime industry. Since the digital twin technology has been used extensively for the digitalization of the maritime sector, this chapter introduces the current and potential uses of digital twin technology in ship operations and management.

Chapter 6 presents a framework for digital transformation processes in the industry. This is achieved by providing information on internet of things and Apparel Business Decentralized Data Integration which uses knowledge representation methods and formal languages to explain the necessary business activities.

In Chapter 7, the relationships among organizational culture, knowledge and innovation in organizations are explained theoretically. According to this chapter, in order to provide a sustainable atmosphere in the organizations, supportive organizational climate is needed to create knowledge and innovation.

Chapter 8 contributes to the sustainability literature by providing insights on renewable energies and its applications in the urban environment in Spain. This is based on the necessity for the orient urban structures, homes and buildings under premises that are as respectful as possible with the environment in Spain.

In Chapter 9, a multi-objective mathematical model is developed for the simultaneous examination of potentially influential factors, including those claimed to be neglected by the mirroring hypothesis. According to the results obtained in this chapter, it is put forth that modular product architecture does not necessarily lead to supplier disintegration, but that its effect is contingent on a firm's priorities.

In Chapter 10, a special case of a Portuguese company is examined and explained in order to underline the ever-changing business environment of today's world. The need for digital transformation practices is underlined while examining this case study.

Chapter 11 provides a framework for the open innovation initiatives in the management field and information technologies. According to this chapter, an enterprise should choose the suitable concepts and practices from interdisciplinary areas so as to be successful in open innovation initiatives.

In Chapter 12, new management strategies for product innovation and personalization are discussed. According to the chapter, by acquiring personal consumer data from the social media, personalized services have been possible for companies in the modern business life.

A tremendous contribution is intended to make to the contemporary research on these subjects by collecting the most up to date research findings and combining these with the theoretical framework. The most popular contemporary topics in digitalization in management fields and sustainability will provide valuable insight for understanding today's business organizations operating in a global, dynamic, and complex environment. Each separate chapters of the book handles an up-to-date topic, mostly on the basis of sustainability and technological advances. This book will fill a critical gap by providing management strategies for sustainability and personalized services from the perspective of digital transformation.

The target audience is intended to be scholars from universities all over the world, as well as the undergraduate and graduate students studying at the fields of sustainability, information technologies, digitalization, digital transformation, business administration, innovation, organizational behavior, human resources management, marketing, personalized services, and management information systems. Furthermore, the professional managers, specialists, consultants, educationalists, and the employees of especially social organizations around the world, are in the scope of the target audience of this reference book.

Consequently, we thank to all of the chapter authors for their diligent work, and we wish everyone would benefit from this peer-reviewed scientific book.

Mirjana Pejić-Bach
University of Zagreb, Croatia

Çağlar Doğru
Ufuk University, Turkey

Chapter 1
Recognizing Skills and Competencies Required Under Industry 4.0's Framework for Achieving Business Digital Transformation

Antonios Kargas
https://orcid.org/0000-0001-6157-1761
National and Kapodistrian University of Athens, Greece

Andreas Giannakis
National and Kapodistrian University of Athens, Greece

Iraklis Foukas
National and Kapodistrian University of Athens, Greece

ABSTRACT

Economic and technological developments that took place the last 30 years have resulted in a new form of industrial revolution, widely known as Industry 4.0 (I4.0). Researchers and professionals worldwide try to foresee and contribute to its development, while the COVID-19 pandemic acted as an accelerator and revealed that changes arising under Industry 4.0 will affect a wide variety of working-life aspects. Among these aspects, skills and competencies needed under I4.0 are expected to change. The current chapter uses the European Skills, Competences, Qualifications, and Occupations (ESCO) database to identify which are the most valuable skills and competencies in the time being, when European businesses are taking part in the so-called digital transformation, part of Industry's 4.0 evolution.

DOI: 10.4018/978-1-7998-7793-6.ch001

Copyright © 2022, IGI Global. Copying or distributing in print or electronic forms without written permission of IGI Global is prohibited.

The most significant skills and competencies will be presented alongside with an analysis on existing research on the relationship between I4.0 and new skills/ competencies needed.

INTRODUCTION

Modern business environment seems to be transformed rapidly under COVID-19 era. Digital forms of working and cooperation are used heavily, while more and more industries face the necessity of transforming their traditional operations and product / service development in a more digital and "online – connected – to – customers" manner. Even though the concept of Industry 4.0 gained lot of attention during the last 10 years, only after recent pandemic crisis its implementation seem to touch sectors other than manufacturing as a "current" need – rather than a trend of change in the future.

Existing studies seem to be more oriented to technological factors, while emphasis is put on businesses' readiness and on maturity models for a successful implementation. Aspects of Industry 4.0 most commonly mentioned (Baur & Wee, 2015) during research are (indicatively): machine flexibility, predictive maintenance, human – robot collaboration, remote monitoring and control, real time supply chain optimization. Statistical process control, digital quality management, data driven design to value and demand prediction, concurrent engineering, virtually guided self-service etc. All these aspects take for granted how human factor will react to changes needed, even though less significant changes (e.g. teleworking, massive use of P.C. and mobile devices in everyday life) took years to be globally implemented and failures occurred in several cases.

Undoubtedly, the forthcoming changes will fully affect the workforce of all sectors, while several studies already report the transformation of the labor – market, moving employers' interest from low-skills jobs to new ICT-based ones. Moreover, there is a growing interest on new skills development and the necessary training procedure required for existing employees, in order to better fit in teleworking conditions and Industry's 4.0 technological changes.

Current chapter aim to highlight the challenges emerged under these conditions. Moreover, changes in labor market will be revealed via existing literature and an initiatory analysis of the relationship between "Industry 4.0 and digital skills recognized as significant for its implementation" will be conducted. The analysis will be based on existing literature, while a well – known database will be used to evaluate most significant digital skills required for Industry 4.0, namely:

European Skill / Competency Qualification and Occupation (ESCO).

The ESCO classification identifies and categorizes skills, competences, qualifications and occupations relevant for the EU labor market and education and training. It systematically shows the relationships between the different concepts. The proposed dataset is established in European Union era, while its purpose is to interconnect three (3) significant pillars of labor market, namely:

1. Occupations, involving 2942 occupations, clustered into 10 major categories involving:
    a. Armed forces occupations,
    b. Managers,
    c. Professionals,
    d. Technicians and associate professionals,
    e. Clerical support workers,
    f. Service and sales workers,
    g. Skilled agricultural, forestry and fishery workers,
    h. Craft and related trades workers,
    i. Plant and machine operators and assemblers,
    j. Elementary occupations.
2. **Skills and competencies**. The skills pillar of ESCO contains 13,485 concepts structured in a hierarchy which contains four sub-classifications. Each sub-classification targets different types of knowledge and skill/competence concepts:
    a. Knowledge,
    b. Skills,
    c. Attitudes and values,
    d. Language skills and knowledge.
3. **Qualifications**, where skills and competencies can be connected with a formal outcome of an assessment and validation process which is obtained when a competent body determines that an individual has achieved learning outcomes to given standards.

Selected occupations coming from "Professionals" categories are analyzed in terms of skills and competencies, in order to evaluate the most significant ones. The outcome of the analysis is compared with literature review regarding technical (hard) and non – technical (soft) skills / competencies. The proposed results can contribute to the development of effective management strategies and knowledge innovation regarding human resource transformation according to Industry's 4.0 needs. The analysis presented could benefit both researchers and managers. Moreover, decision makers in the business environment can use the proposed results to reorganize internal factors in order to faster develop employees' skills and competencies according to digital transformation procedures and to adopt more rapidly / successfully values and principles related with the Fourth Industrial Revolution.

In the following sections, a literature review of Industry 4.0 and how it is expected to transform labour market is conducted, while in the main focus of the chapter the European Skills, Competences, Qualifications and Occupations dataset is presented, alongside with research methodology and proposed results. It follows the "solutions and recommendations" section, as well as future research and conclusions.

BACKGROUND

Even though Industry 4.0 started from a pure technological position, soon enough its meaning and importance expanded to several sectors, services and business operations. Industry's 4.0 initial aim was to achieve the integration between various technological elements in order to develop operational systems capable to custom predictions about demand, to plan production of products and to control business outcomes for reaching foreseen targets (Industrial Internet Consortium, 2013). First operational scenarios included sensors, actuators and microprocessors posed to everyday objects and products (smart objects) capable to transmit big data in real time to cloud, developing the so – called Internet of Things (IoT) in order to (a) redesign custom products according to customers' needs and (b) redesign business' operations according to information gathered in terms of production, marketing, sales / purchase, maintenance, after sales services e.t.c. (Wahlster, 2013).

Such an approach indicates that Industry 4.0 and its implications will affect not only manufacturing and production but moreover not – traditional economic activities (Kargas & Varoutas, 2020) as well as every business operation where internet and embedded systems will facilitate the procedure of integrating physical objects, human actors, intelligent machines, production lines and processes (Schumacher et al., 2016). The new business era of Industry 4.0 involves (a) keeping mass production most significant elements (Petrelli, 2017), (b) reaching customers' needs with big data in real time, (c) use the information gathered to transform business processes and operations (Kagermann et al., 2013) and (d) to meet mass customization on demand targeting to enrich customers' consuming "experience" as a whole. Authors recognize that Industry 4.0 involves human resource development in terms of new skills and competencies, not – merely related with technological tools (Schallock et al., 2018).

The forthcoming transformation of working life under Industry 4.0 has been already mentioned by various researchers (Cantoni & Mangia, 2019; Gebhardt et al., 2015; Jaschke, 2014; Prifti et al., 2017), in terms of transformed processes, business models and technologies (Acatech, 2016), as well as in terms of new job requirements describing unique and specialized skills' set (Grzelczak et al., 2017; Kergroach, 2017). It is not only a matter of degree of education that will gain significance among labour workforce but moreover, the new job profiles will be enriched with a wide range of skills / competencies (Acatech, 2016; Atiku, 2019; Kagermann et al., 2013; Sackey & Bester, 2016; Smit et al., 2016), while their quality and the overall qualifications of the workforce will most probably play a significant role on economy's development and to innovation's creation (Benešová & Tupa, 2017; Mavrikios et al., 2018).

Scholars have pointed out the existence of a gap between skills needed under Industry 4.0 and skills developed at the current time (Shvetsova & Kuzmina, 2018), as a result of that it is missing a clear awareness of job requirements under Industry 4.0 (Maisiri et al., 2019). Researchers from different fields try to answer the question of which skills and competencies are most valuable at the current phase of digital transformation that will successfully lead to Industry 4.0. Moreover, various models / tools to reveal these skills / developments are presented. In (Imran & Kantola, 2018) three approaches are combined in order to answer this question, namely (a) sociotechnical system theory, (b) competence-based view and (c) competence models of the Evolute approach. Existing research reveals that skills requirements under Industry 4.0 significantly differ regarding changes occurred in industry during previous years (Prifti et al., 2017). For example, constant technological advances require life-long learning capabilities, interdisciplinary understanding is needed, alongside with behavioural skills and discipline knowledge (Prifti et al., 2017).

In (Cotet et al., 2017) a psychological evaluation system alongside with the Big Five personality traits (OCEAN model) are used in order to map the capacities necessary for selection of human resources able to work in the environment of Industry 4.0. According to this study, employees should have general skills / competencies, not related only with technical and technological parameters. More specifically, when the research focuses on top management, characteristics such as interpersonal skills, confidence/motivation, ethics/integrity and critical thinking play a more significant role (Foutty, 2019). In (Adolph et al., 2014) are discussed competencies regarded as vital for production unden Industry 4.0 environment, including ability to reshape processes, flexibility, agility in problem solving and self-learning.

From a different point of view, there is interest on changing technical skills in the context of Industry 4.0, in order to reach faster at a good maturity level (Pinzone et al., 2017), while in the project it was used qualitative information coming from manufacturing stakeholders. In (Kravcik et al., 2018), authors are focusing in SMEs as an economic sector with unique characteristics and difficulties to cope with Industry 4.0, so that to facilitate planning and monitor of digital transformation and skills' development among employees. Difficulties are mainly related with limited resources, financial pressures and the lack of dedicated IT departments (Fenton et al., 2019).

Research on SMEs is important because in most economies, especially in smaller countries, manufacturing is not advanced enough to research and develop Industry's 4.0 technologies, while gaining a competitive advantage in European or Global level is much more difficult (Kargas et al., 2020; Laitsou et al., 2020). In such cases, companies find it difficult to relate Industry 4.0 with their domain and their business strategy (Erol, Schuhmacher, et al., 2016), leading to failures regarding digital transformation and employees' skills / competencies development. Relevant uncertainty seem to exist (in a smaller degree) even in manufacturing sector (Schumacher et al., 2016), where Industry 4.0 changes have been associated with increased complexity in both macro and micro level (Schuh et al., 2014)

Even though differences may occur between different sectors, SMEs and large manufactures, there are also large similarities in skills / competencies needed in all environments, especially in terms of soft skills (Gudanowska et al., 2018; World Economic Forum, 2016). Under these circumstances, recognizing skills / competencies and developing training programs is of high importance in order employees to adapt to Industry 4.0 requirements (Lorenz et al., 2015; Zinn, 2015). In (Perini et al., 2017) a training analysis model is proposed, capable to define employees' skills level, while (Fitsilis et al., 2018) describe the dimensions of knowledge and skills necessary to Industry 4.0 and propose their model capable to assess the knowledge gaps existing in a company. Erol et. al. (Erol, Jäger, et al., 2016) studied existing literature to propose competencies needed in order to deliver a scenario-based learning concept for students. Following these perspectives technical and academic institutions rearrange their programs to deliver not – only theoretical knowledge but moreover practical skills, soft skills, values, entrepreneurship capabilities and other competencies (Selamat et al., 2017).

Existing analysis of research on skills and competencies needed in Industry 4.0, revealed an existing, on-going dispute on the subject, recognizing the need for new skills and competencies for every field of economic activity. At the same time, it was revealed that there is a growing need to specify which skills and competencies seem more valuable at the current point in order to facilitate companies reach their digital transformation's goals. This is the topic where current chapter contributes significantly by analyzing European Skills, Competences, Qualifications and Occupations database.

MAIN FOCUS OF THE CHAPTER

European Skills, Competences, Qualifications and Occupations (ESCO)

European Skills, Competences, Qualifications and Occupations (ESCO) is a European multilingual **classification of Skills, Competences and Occupations**. European Commission and its services initially launched ESCO in 2010 as a project aiming to identify and categorize skills, competences, qualifications and occupations relevant for the EU labour market and education and training. The whole project was open to any interested stakeholder in order to reach as broad consultation as possible.

The first demo version (ESCO v0) released on 2013, stating the beginning of testing phase which led to a full version (ESCO v1) in 2017. ESCO 1.1 is planned by European Commission to be released by the end of 2021, marking the end of the three-year period that Member States had to map or adopt ESCO according to the Eures Regulation.

Nowadays, ESCO provides descriptions of 2942 occupations and 13.485 skills linked to these occupations, translated into 27 languages (all official EU languages plus Icelandic, Norwegian and Arabic). The relationships between occupations, skills, competencies and qualifications are constantly under negotiation / consultation with an extended network of stakeholders whose origins are coming from distinct countries, while they cover a wide are related with people, education, training, labour market, e.t.c. More precisely stakeholders participating to the proposed classification include:

- employment services,
- providers of job boards, social media, HR software or career guidance services,
- social partners,
- education and training organisations,
- statistical organisations, researchers and big data analysts,
- skills councils and networks.

Moreover, ESCO aim to support job mobility across Europe and therefore a more integrated and efficient labor market, by offering a "common language" on occupations and skills that can be used by different stakeholders on employment and education and training topics. ESCO is organized in three pillars:

- The **occupations pillar** containing 2 942 occupations with each one described with a unique profile containing a description, scope note and definition, as well as the knowledge, skills and competences required for this occupation on a European scale. Knowledge, skills and competences are distinguished in two distinct categories, namely essential and optional.

- The **knowledge, skills and competences pillar** containing about 13,500 knowledge, skills and competence concepts, in a hierarchical framework containing four distinct sub-classifications:
    - Knowledge,
    - Skills,
    - Attitudes & values,
    - Language skills and knowledge.
- The **qualifications pillar** reflecting the qualifications needed by employers, public and private employment services, learners, workers, jobseekers, education and training providers and other actors.

The relationship / interconnection between the 3 pillars is presented in figure 1, revealing how an occupation can be related with various skills / competencies, leading to one or more qualifications needed. Moreover, it is presented how an occupation can be connected with skills and competencies from different groups, developing a complex map for labour market's skills and competencies aspects.

Figure 1. Relationship between ESCO's pillar
Source: European Commission (European Commission, 2013)

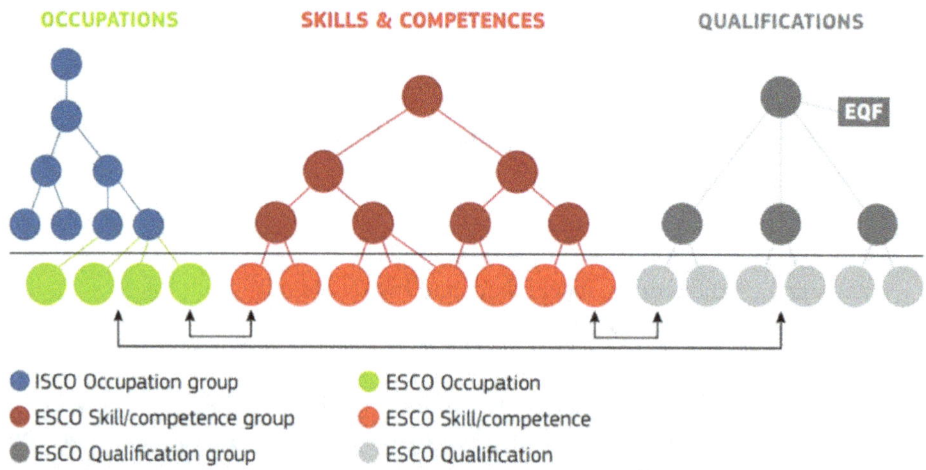

Overall, this three-layered structured approach allows ESCO to organize terminology for the European labor market and the education/training sector in a consistent, transparent and usable way. ESCO runs under Directorate General Employment, Social Affairs and Inclusion (DG EMPL), while it is available (as an open tool) in an online portal and can be consulted free of charge. Finally, the importance laid on ESCO by European Commission is recognized by its contribution on the "Europe 2020" strategy and the "New Skills Agenda for Europe".

ESCO is directly linked with the International Standard Classification of Occupations (ISCO-08), serving (the latter) as the hierarchical structure for the occupations pillar (of the former). More precisely, according to Figure 2 each occupation is directly associated with one of ISCO-08's unit group, revealing that ESCO provides information and data about occupations in the lower possible level (a new fifth – level of analysis) of the proposed hierarchical structure, ensuring a more detailed analysis.

Figure 2. Occupation hierarchy in ESCO using ISCO-08
Source: ESCOpedia (European Commission, 2021a)

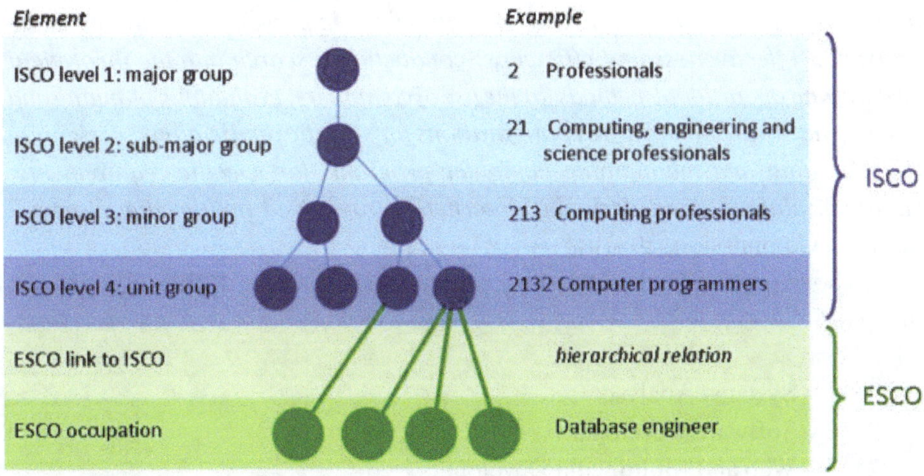

Methodology

The research was based on the occupation pillar and the occupations under Category 2, "**Professionals**". The proposed category was selected as the most relevant to ICT – Based Jobs, while according to ESCO in this category it is included occupations related with scientific concepts and theories, developing stock of knowledge and engaging / teaching about the foregoing. Occupations in this major group are classified into five (5) major sub – groups including:

- 21 – Science and Engineering Professionals
- 22 – Health Professionals
- 23 – Teaching Professionals
- 24 – Business and Administration Professionals
- 25 – Information and Communications Technology Professionals
    - 251 – Software and Applications Developers and Analysts,
    - 252 – Database and Network Professionals.
- 26 – Legal, Social and Cultural Professionals

Authors, decided to specify their research on the major sub-group 25 - **Information and communications technology professional**, as a result its strong and direct relationship (compared with the other sub – groups) with both Industry 4.0 and digital transformation. Moreover, to deepen their research, author enlightened skills, competencies and knowledges for the minor sub – group 251 – **Software and Applications Developers and Analysts**, which seem more appropriate according to the describe of tasks provided by ESCO: "*researching information technology use in business functions and identifying areas in which improvements could be made to maximize effectiveness and efficiency; conducting research into the theoretical aspects of and operational methods for the use of computers; evaluating, planning and designing hardware or software configurations for specific applications; designing, writing, testing and maintaining computer programs for specific requirements; evaluating, planning and designing Internet, Intranet and multimedia systems.*" (European Commission, 2021b).

The above – mentioned minor sub – group consists of five distinct unit groups, namely:

- 2511 – Systems Analysts
- 2512 – Software Developers
- 2513 – Web and Multimedia Developers
- 2514 – Applications Programmers
- 2519 – Software and Applications Developers and Analysts Not Elsewhere Classified

Each unit group contains a variety of occupations, as it is presented in Table 1. In total, the minor sub – group 251 – Software and Applications Developers and Analysts, its unit groups and the containing occupations, consist of **704 unique skills**, which can be categorized as follows:

- **358 Essential skills and competences,**
- **149 Optional skills and competences,**
- **197 Optional Knowledge.**

Table 1. Occupations under 251 category's unit groups

2511	2512	2513	2514	2519
ICT research consultant	user interface developer	web developer	industrial mobile devices software developer	ICT disaster recovery analyst
ICT system architect	software analyst	search engine optimisation expert	ICT application configurator	ICT quality assurance manager
integration engineer	software architect	user interface designer	numerical tool and process control programmer	data quality specialist
green ICT consultant	software developer	web content manager	ICT application developer	ICT test analyst
IT auditor		digital games developer		ICT auditor manager
ICT system integration consultant				software tester
enterprise architect				
ICT business analyst				
ICT system analyst				
data analyst				
data scientist				
user experience analyst				
ICT system developer				
ICT business analysis manager				
computer scientist				
embedded system designer				
ICT intelligent systems designer				
ICT consultant				

Source: ESCO (European Commission, 2021b)

Results

As far as the 704 unique skills (358 Essential skills and competences, 149 Optional skills and competences, 197 Optional Knowledge) are concerned, results indicate that emphasis is given mainly on "Essential skills and competencies" (with a percentage up 50,85%), followed by "Optional Knowledge" (with a percentage up to 27,98%), while "Optional Skills" and competencies is less required category (with a percentage of 21,16%). Figure 3 presents the categorization of unique skills, revealing that most occupations of the under – analysis category put emphasis on "Essential skills and competencies" as required characteristics.

Figure 3. Categorization of required unique skills

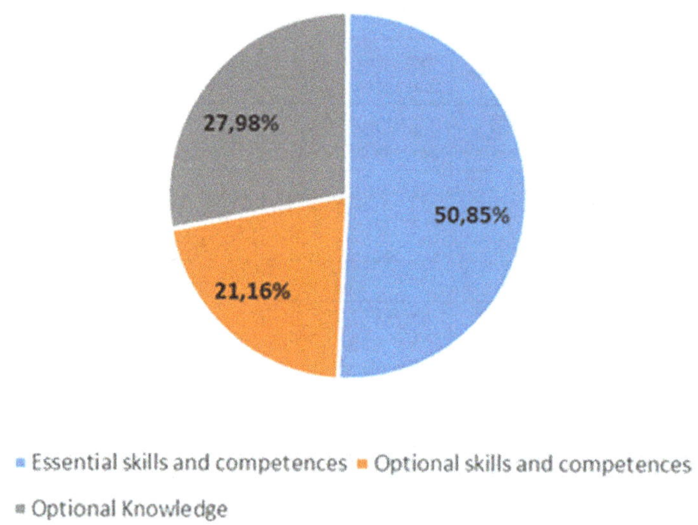

As it is presented in Figure 4, most of these unique skills (89,14%) have a rate of appearance 1 – 5 times (it appear in 1-5 different occupations), while there exist skills that have a maximum appearance rate of 11 – 15 times (a percentage of 3,32% of the total unique skills). Authors further concentrated their analysis is this particular category of unique skills.

The analytic frequency of appearance per category of required unique skills is presented in Table 2, while a detailed list of skills and competencies, both essential and optional, for the ones with a frequency of appearance 6-10 times are (Box 1, 2, 3) and the ones with a frequency of appearance 11-15 times (Box 4, 5, 6) is given in Appendix 1.

Figure 4. Frequency of appearance

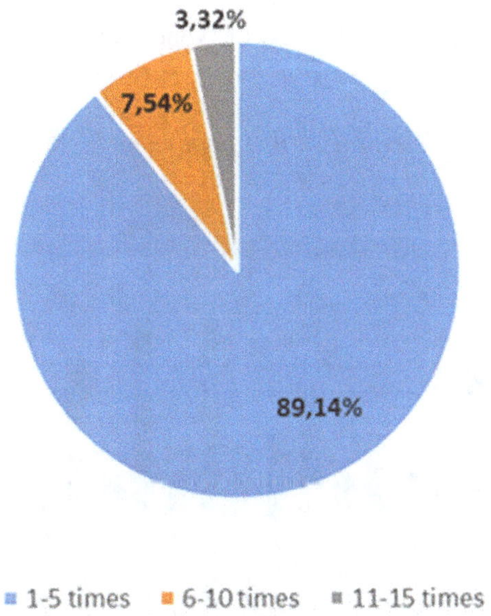

Table 2. Frequency of Appearance per Category of required unique skills

	Frequency of Appearance			
	1-5 times	**6-10 times**	**11-15 times**	**Total**
Essential skills and competences	331	21	6	358
Optional skills and competences	131	17	1	149
Optional Knowledge	129	12	15	197

As far as occupations and skills / competencies with a frequency of appearance over 11 – 15 times, the next figures present most significant results. More precisely, Figure 5 presents the relationship between the occupations and the essential skills competencies. The graph consists out of 26 distinct occupations, related with ESCO's minor sub – group 251 – Software and Applications Developers and Analysts, which are presented according to the 6 essential skills and competencies (presented to the bottom layer of Figure 5). A more detailed presentation is given to Table 4 of Appendix 3.

Regarding optional skills and competences, there is only one such characteristic, namely "use object – oriented programming", with a frequency of occurrence in category 11-15 times. The above – mentioned optional skill is appearing in 11 occupations presented in Figure 6. Optional skills and competences is the less effective category, appearing less times in the various occupations in the minor sub – group 251 – Software and Applications Developers and Analysts. A more detailed presentation is given to Table 5 of Appendix 2.

Figure 5. Occupations - Essential skills / competencies with a 11-15 frequency of appearance

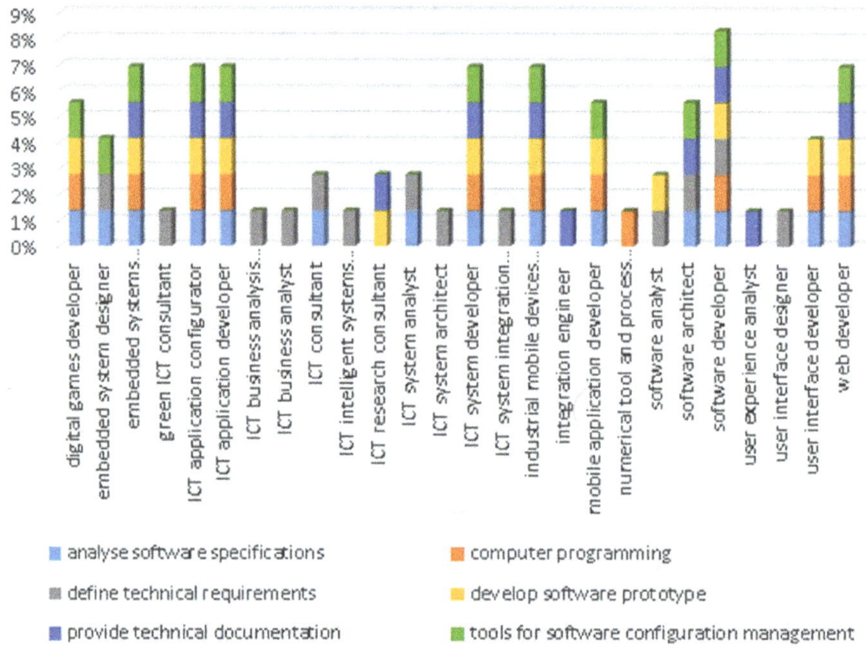

Optional knowledge is the second category in terms of importance, after essential skills and competences when there exists a frequency of appearance over 11 – 15 times. Figure 7 presents the relationship between the occupations and the optional knowledge. The graph consists out of 33 distinct occupations, related with ESCO's minor sub – group 251 – Software and Applications Developers and Analysts, which are presented according to the 15 optional knowledges (presented to the bottom layer of Figure 7). A more detailed presentation is given to Table 6 of Appendix 2.

Results revealed most significant skills and competences per category presented above, when there exists a frequency of appearance over 11 – 15 times. These unique skills seem to be the drivers for implementing Industry 4.0 and digital transformation among organizations. The proposed categories and most significant skills / competencies:

- Essential skills and competences
  - develop software prototype – frequency of occurrence 12,
  - define technical requirements – frequency of occurrence 13,
  - analyze software specifications – frequency of occurrence 14.
- Optional skills and competences
  - use object-oriented programming – frequency of occurrence 11.
- Optional Knowledge
  - XQuery – frequency of occurrence 15,
  - MDX – frequency of occurrence 15,
  - LDAP – frequency of occurrence 15.

Figure 6. Occupations - Optional skills and competences with a 11-15 frequency of appearance

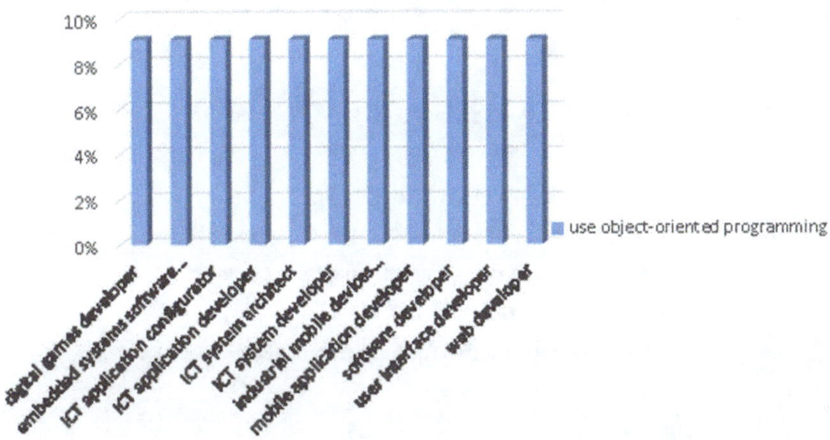

As far as occupations is concerned, results indicate that **software developer** is the occupation that requires most of 3 categories of skills / competencies. More precisely, it requires all essential skills / competencies (6 the number), all optional skills (1 the number) and most optional knowledges (10 out of 15 the number). It can be assumed that "software developer" occupation is the most representative for the ESCO's minor sub – group 251 – Software and Applications Developers and Analysts.

Moreover, Table 3 provides the rest of most important occupations in terms of the ones with the most of essential skills and competencies – optional skills and competencies – optional knowledge. It is a total of 6 distinct occupations gathering at least 5 essential skills and competencies, one optional skill / competency and a variety of 6 to 10 optional knowledges. Alongside with software developer, these occupations create a list of widespread occupations that can act as drivers through digital transformation and Industry 4.0 implementation.

Figure 7. Occupations - Optional Knowledge with a 11-15 frequency of appearance

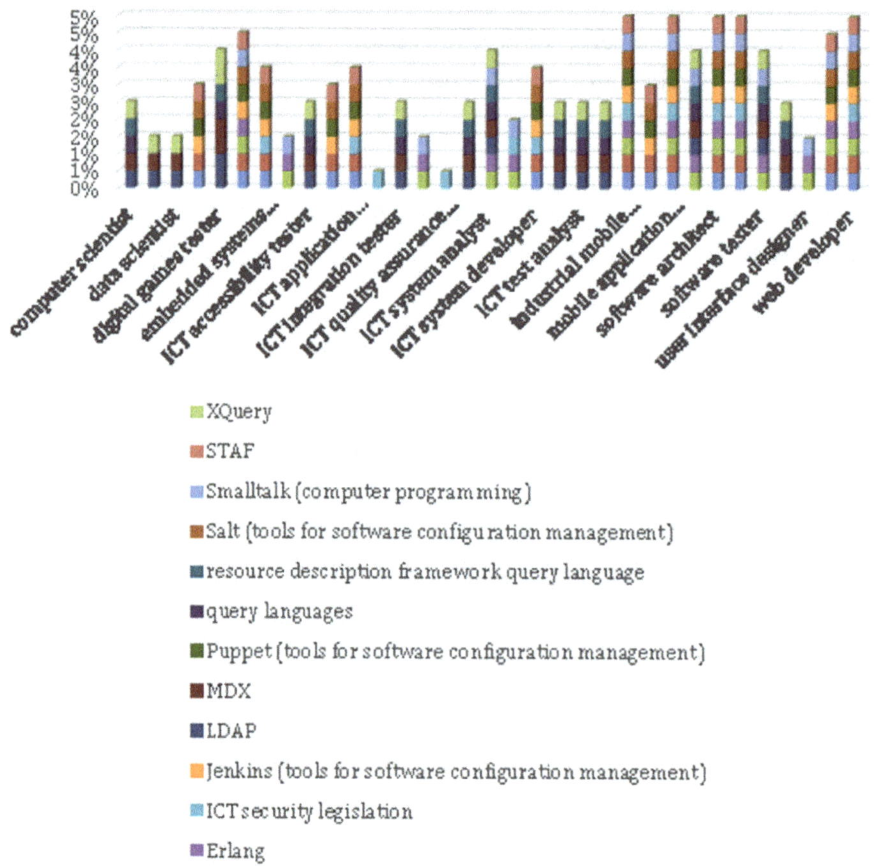

SOLUTIONS AND RECOMMENDATIONS

Recognizing skills and competencies, required under Industry 4.0 framework or agreed as necessary for digital transformation, is an ongoing research procedure. Moreover, the direction that required skills and competencies will take is related with the type of work performed (Beier et al., 2017), as well as with the degree of digitization (Cimini et al., 2020; Grenčíková et al., 2020) or robotization (Beier et al., 2017) that will take place. Results presented in current chapter are consistent with the results indicated in international literature. Existing literature proposes various divisions of skills and competencies, while most notable are:

- technical, personal, social (Liboni et al., 2019),
- hard (professional) and soft (social) (Liszka et al., 2019).

Table 3. List of 6 occupations with most unique skills and competencies

Occupations	Essential skills and competences	Optional skills and competences	Optional Knowledge	Grand Total
ICT system developer	5	1	7	13
ICT application configurator	5	1	6	12
ICT application developer	5	1	7	13
embedded systems software developer	5	1	7	13
web developer	5	1	10	16
industrial mobile devices software developer	5	1	10	16

The skills and competencies presented in the previous section are mainly related with the technical and hard categories. More precisely, current study proposes that most valuable, essential skills and competencies are (a) capability to **analyze software specifications**, (b) abilities on **defining technical requirements** and (c) capabilities on **developing software prototypes**. Moreover, results indicate that (d) **using object-oriented programming** is also required frequently but mainly as an optional skill / competency. Proposed results are consistent with several studies proposing as important skills and competencies: IT and technology affinity (Acatech, 2016; Erol, Jäger, et al., 2016; Gebhardt et al., 2015; Hartmann & Bovenschulte, 2013; Hoberg et al., 2017; Lorenz et al., 2015), product service offerings (Acatech, 2016; Hoberg et al., 2017; Zinn, 2015), digital security, including data and network (Acatech, 2016; Grega & Kornecki, 2015; Hoberg et al., 2017; Wang et al., 2012; Zinn, 2015), knowledge about mobile technologies (Hoberg et al., 2017) and embedded systems and sensors (Grega & Kornecki, 2015), knowledge on network technology and M2M communication (Acatech, 2016; Erol, Jäger, et al., 2016; Gebhardt et al., 2015; Wang et al., 2012; Zinn, 2015), possessing knowledge of robotics and artificial intelligence (Acatech, 2016; Hartmann & Bovenschulte, 2013; Lorenz et al., 2015), modelling and programming knowledges (Erol, Jäger, et al., 2016; Kortuem et al., 2013; Lorenz et al., 2015), knowledge about cloud computing and cloud architectures (Acatech, 2016; Hoberg et al., 2017; Wang et al., 2012), DB knowledge (Hoberg et al., 2017), big data and data analysis and interpretation (Acatech, 2016; Erol, Jäger, et al., 2016; Hoberg et al., 2017; Lorenz et al., 2015; Zinn, 2015).

Of course, ESCO is concentrating on formal skills and competencies, related with job finding and occupations, leading study to a more technological (hard – professional) analysis. This can be characterized as the main limitation of the research, being less enlighten in social and personal aspects required under Industry 4.0 framework. Existing literature supports the importance of such elements, including (among others):

- ability to work under pressure (Ejsmont, 2021)
- adaptability (Kiesel & Wolpers, 2015; Xia, 2011),
- analytical skills (Erol, Jäger, et al., 2016; Hartmann & Bovenschulte, 2013; Lorenz et al., 2015),
- capability of working in interdisciplinary environments (Acatech, 2016; Gebhardt et al., 2015; Grega & Kornecki, 2015; Kiesel & Wolpers, 2015; Lorenz et al., 2015),
- cognitive abilities (Prifti et al., 2017),
- collaboration willingness (Acatech, 2016; Kiesel & Wolpers, 2015),
- compromising (Erol, Jäger, et al., 2016) and negotiating (Prifti et al., 2017),
- creativity (Erol, Jäger, et al., 2016; Stocker et al., 2014; Xia, 2011),
- critical thinking (Xia, 2011),
- decision making (Acatech, 2016; Kagermann et al., 2013; Kortuem et al., 2013; Smit et al., 2016),
- emotional intelligence (Prifti et al., 2017),
- flexibility (Erol, Jäger, et al., 2016),
- innovative attitude (Acatech, 2016; Stocker et al., 2014),
- intercultural competency (Erol, Jäger, et al., 2016; Guo, 2015; Xia, 2011),
- leadership skills (Acatech, 2016; Lorenz et al., 2015; Smit et al., 2016),
- lifelong learning abilities (Maisiri et al., 2019),
- literacy (Guo, 2015),
- maintaining customer relationships and creating business networks (Acatech, 2016; Hoberg et al., 2017),
- optimization abilities (Acatech, 2016; Gebhardt et al., 2015),
- presentation ability (Prifti et al., 2017),
- problem solving (Acatech, 2016; Erol, Jäger, et al., 2016; Gebhardt et al., 2015; Smit et al., 2016; Xia, 2011),
- project management skills (Grimheden & Törngren, 2014; Mäenpää et al., 2015), manage complexity skills (Acatech, 2016; Erol, Jäger, et al., 2016) and management ability in general (Smit et al., 2016),

- teamwork (Erol, Jäger, et al., 2016; Grega & Kornecki, 2015; Kiesel & Wolpers, 2015; Xia, 2011),
- technical communication (Erol, Jäger, et al., 2016; Xia, 2011).

The above – mentioned analysis indicate that "soft" skills (non – technical skills) are increasingly gain attention from researchers and professionals, while many of them cannot be automated, leading to the need for a balanced mixed between both hard and soft skills (Maisiri et al., 2019). Moreover, under Industry 4.0 framework it is expected to be reached a strong interaction between man – machine leading to increased need for employees with skills / competencies such as technical communication, emotional intelligence, innovative attitude, critical thinking and creativity. Such an approach wide opens the dialogue regarding "interdisciplinary and multidisciplinary" in skills development as a valuable asset for achieving productivity under Industry 4.0 era.

Technical skills and programming skills, such as the proposed by current study, is expected to keep their great significance at least until digital transformation of businesses and organizations reach a sufficient maturity level. Most probably, the proposed skills / competencies will keep their importance afterwards as well, even though priorities may change, and even more technical skills increase their significance (e.g. artificial intelligence).

Research on Industry 4.0 and employees' required skills / competencies reveal a strong tendency to reform educational institutions, so that to cope with industry's needs and to offer an enlarged variety of skills to their candidates. The term "Education 4.0", seem to gain more and more attention, following the perspectives and the dispute originating from Industry's 4.0 framework.

FUTURE RESEARCH DIRECTIONS

Taking into account that Industry 4.0 is an ongoing procedure where sudden and essential changes can occur, researchers should put emphasis on understanding and foresee aspects related with employees' skills and competencies. For example, COVID-19 changed significantly our thinking about everyday working life and led to the implementation of a series on new operational and business logics to both private and public organizations. Teleworking, increased demand for internet speed, cloud services, tele – cooperation platforms become a necessity, while what is characterized as primary skills / competencies changed dramatically.

Future research could firstly deepen research and our understanding on the topic, while secondly it could broaden databases used for research analysis. Apart from ESCO database used in current chapter, there are similar databases which could provide additional information. Such bases are (a) Occupational Information Network (O*NET) located in U.S.A., (b) ICT Body of Knowledge (ICT – BoK) mainly concentrating on e-Skills for ICT Professionals and ICT Professionalism in general, (c) data coming from Council of European Professional Informatics Societies (CEPIS) putting emphasis on information sciences and professionals' skills / competencies. All these institutions / datasets gather information from their social / professional stakeholders, trying to provide knowledge to every – interested party about needs and prerequisites of specific professions (varied from "some profession" up to "every" profession in European or U.S.A. level).

Consequently, it is needed to wide – open our understanding about skills and competencies that most probably will be needed under Industry 4.0 era, in order to develop innovation, personalized products / services and moreover to implement management strategies capable to bring sustainability. Already Generation Y (Millennials) and the followed Generation Z has reshaped how companies do business and recruit personnel – e.g. employer branding techniques(Kargas & Tsokos, 2020), while a new approach is already developed regarding teleworking. Such changes, reshape management strategies while business sustainability is more and more based on digital means for conducting traditional economic activities such as (indicatively): producing / serving, promoting, delivering, purchasing, socializing with customers, competing e.t.c.

CONCLUSION

Results presented alongside with existing literature reveal that Industry 4.0 gains the interest of researchers and professionals. Even though this interest is constantly growing, the impact of I4.0 on employees' required skills and competencies is still under investigation. This is due to the fact that there exist significant differences from sector to sector, as well as differences to digitization and robotization degree that can be applied. Moreover, it should be taken into account the difficulty of research on the proposed topic as a result of its dual nature, incorporating both technical and non – technical skills / competencies.

Current research supports conducting research, especially in the field of technical categories of skills / competencies. By analyzing a well – known and acceptable database, ESCO database, results provide an insight in most valuable, technical, skills and competencies of specific IT professions. Research conducted revealed a dataset of 704 unique skills, out of which ESCO characterizes (a) 358 of them as essential skills and competences, (b) 149 of them as optional skills and competences and (c) 197 of them as optional knowledges. Results indicate that "**Essential skills and competencies**" is the most important characteristic for most occupations under research. More specifically, research detect three (3) distinct required skills / competencies as most valuable, namely: (a) capability to **analyze software specifications**, (b) abilities on **defining technical requirements** and (c) capabilities on **developing software prototypes**. Moreover, results indicate that (d) using **object-oriented programming** is also required frequently but mainly as an optional skill / competency.

Proposed skills and competencies contribute to existing results from previous studies and moreover come to support the idea that under Industry 4.0 framework should exist a tight human-machine collaboration. All required skills and competencies proposed in current research contribute towards this direction. Moreover, it is accepted that Industry 4.0 increase significantly the level of skills complexity required in the workforce of the future (Maisiri et al., 2019), while current research de-escalates in some degree this complexity.

ACKNOWLEDGMENT

This research received no specific grant from any funding agency in the public, commercial, or not-for-profit sectors.

REFERENCES

Acatech, D. A. D. T. (2016). *Kompetenzentwicklungsstudie Industrie 4.0*. https://docplayer.org/24401230-Kompetenzentwicklungsstudie-industrie-4-0.html

Adolph, S., Tisch, M., & Metternich, J. (2014). Challenges and approaches to competency development for future production. *Journal of International Scientific Publications–Educational Alternatives*, *12*(1), 1001–1010.

Atiku, S. O. (Ed.). (2019). *Human capital formation for the fourth industrial revolution* (1st ed.). IGI Global.

Baur, C., & Wee, D. (2015). *Industry 4.0 is more than just a flashy catchphrase. A confluence of trends and technologies promises to reshape the way things are made*. https://www.mckinsey.com/business-functions/operations/our-insights/manufacturings-next-act

Beier, G., Niehoff, S., Ziems, T., & Xue, B. (2017). Sustainability aspects of a digitalized industry – A comparative study from China and Germany. *International Journal of Precision Engineering and Manufacturing-Green Technology, 4*(2), 227–234. doi:10.1007/s40684-017-0028-8

Benešová, A., & Tupa, J. (2017). Requirements for Education and Qualification of People in Industry 4.0. *Procedia Manufacturing, 11*, 2195–2202. doi:10.1016/j.promfg.2017.07.366

Cantoni, F., & Mangia, G. (Eds.). (2019). *Human resource management and digitalization* (1st ed.). Routledge.

Cimini, C., Boffelli, A., Lagorio, A., Kalchschmidt, M., & Pinto, R. (2020). How do industry 4.0 technologies influence organisational change? An empirical analysis of Italian SMEs. *Journal of Manufacturing Technology Management, 32*(3), 695–721. doi:10.1108/JMTM-04-2019-0135

Cotet, G. B., Balgiu, B. A., & Zaleschi, V.-C. (2017). Assessment procedure for the soft skills requested by Industry 4.0. *8th International Conference on Manufacturing Science and Education – MSE 2017 "Trends in New Industrial Revolution,"* 1–8. 10.1051/matecconf/201712107005

Ejsmont, K. (2021). The Impact of Industry 4.0 on Employees—Insights from Australia. *Sustainability 2021, 13*(6), 3095. doi:10.3390/su13063095

Erol, S., Jäger, A., Hold, P., Ott, K., & Sihn, W. (2016). Tangible Industry 4.0: A Scenario-Based Approach to Learning for the Future of Production. *Procedia CIRP, 54*, 13–18. doi:10.1016/j.procir.2016.03.162

Erol, S., Schuhmacher, A., & Sihn, W. (2016). Resource Efficiency for Global Competitiveness. *International Conference on Competitive Manufacturing (COMA)*, 495–500. http://publica.fraunhofer.de/documents/N-382579.html

European Commission. (2013). *ESCO European Classification of Skills/Competences, Qualifications and Occupations. The first public release.* doi:10.2767/76494

European Commission. (2021a). *ESCO - ESCOpedia.* https://ec.europa.eu/esco/portal/escopedia/Occupations_pillar

European Commission. (2021b). *ESCO - Occupations - Software and applications developers and analysts.* https://ec.europa.eu/esco/portal/occupation?uri=http%3A%2F%2Fdata.europa.eu%2Fesco%2Fisco%2FC251&conceptLanguage=en&full=true#&uri=http://data.europa.eu/esco/isco/C251&treeSelection=C2,C25,C251

Fenton, A., Fletcher, G., & Griffiths, M. (Eds.). (2019). *Strategic digital transformation : a results-driven approach* (1st ed.). Routledge. doi:10.4324/9780429020469

Fitsilis, P., Tsoutsa, P., & Gerogiannis, V. (2018). Industry 4.0: Required personnel competences. *Industry 4.0, 3*(3), 130–133.

Foutty, J. (2019, January 23). Aspire to Lead in Industry 4.0? Hone Your Soft Skills. *The Wall Street Journal*. https://deloitte.wsj.com/articles/aspire-to-lead-in-industry-4-0-hone-your-soft-skills-01548295337

Gebhardt, J., Flensburg, E.-U., & Neugebauer, L. M. (2015). Developments 4.0 Prospects on future requirements and impacts on work and vocational education. *JOTED*, *3*, 117–133.

Grega, W., & Kornecki, A. J. (2015). Real-time cyber-physical Systems transatlantic engineering curricula framework. *Proceedings of the 2015 Federated Conference on Computer Science and Information Systems, FedCSIS 2015*, 755–762. 10.15439/2015F45

Grenčíková, A., Kordoš, M., & Berkovič, V. (2020). The Impact of Industry 4.0 on Jobs Creation within the Small and Medium-Sized Enterprises and Family Businesses in Slovakia. *Administrative Sciences 2020, 10*(3), 71. doi:10.3390/admsci10030071

Grimheden, M. E., & Törngren, M. (2014, October 12). Towards curricula for Cyber-Physical Systems. *2014 Workshop on Embedded and Cyber-Physical Systems Education, WESE 2014 - Proceedings*. 10.1145/2829957.2829965

Grzelczak, A., Kosacka, M., & Werner-Lewandowska, K. (2017). Employees competences for industry 4.0 in Poland–preliminary research results. *24th International Conference on Production Research, ICPR 2017*, 139–144. 10.12783/dtetr/icpr2017/17598

Gudanowska, A. E., Alonso, J. P., & Törmänen, A. (2018). What competencies are needed in the production industry? The case of the Podlaskie Region. *Engineering Management in Production and Services*, *10*(1), 65–74. doi:10.1515/emj-2018-0006

Guo, Q. (2015). Learning in a Mixed Reality System in the Context of Industrie 4.0. *Journal of Teacher Education*, *3*(2). Advance online publication. doi:10.48513/JOTED.V3I2.60

Hartmann, E. A., & Bovenschulte, M. (2013). Skills Needs Analysis for "Industry 4.0" Based on Roadmaps for Smart Systems. In *Using Technology Foresights for Identifying Future Skills Needs* (pp. 24–37). https://www.bmbf.de/pubRD/Umsetzungsempfehlungen_Industrie4_0.pdf

Hoberg, P., Krcmar, H., & Welz, B. (2017). *Skills for Digital Transformation*. Academic Press.

Imran, F., & Kantola, J. (2018). Review of Industry 4.0 in the Light of Sociotechnical System Theory and Competence-Based View: A Future Research Agenda for the Evolute Approach. *Advances in Intelligent Systems and Computing*, *783*, 118–128. doi:10.1007/978-3-319-94709-9_12

Industrial Internet Consortium. (2013). *Fact Sheet*. https://www.iiconsortium.org/docs/IIC_FACT_SHEET.pdf

Jaschke, S. (2014). Mobile learning applications for technical vocational and engineering education: The use of competence snippets in laboratory courses and industry 4.0. *Proceedings of 2014 International Conference on Interactive Collaborative Learning, ICL 2014*, 605–608. 10.1109/ICL.2014.7017840

Kagermann, H., Wahlster, W., Helbig, J., Hellinger, A., Stumpf, M. A. V., Treugut, L., Blasco, J., Galloway, H., & Findeklee, U. (2013). *Recommendations for implementing the strategic initiative Industrie 4.0: Final report of the Industrie 4.0*. http://alvarestech.com/temp/tcn/CyberPhysicalSystems-Industrial4-0.pdf

Kargas, A., Kiriakidis, M., & Zacharakis, E. (2020). Europe's Economic Crisis: Re - Clustering European Economies. *European Journal of Social Science Education and Research*, *7*(1), 41. doi:10.26417/ejser.v7i1.p41-50

Kargas, A., & Tsokos, A. (2020). Employer Branding Implementation and Human Resource Management in Greek Telecommunication Industry. *Administrative Sciences*, *10*(1), 17. doi:10.3390/admsci10010017

Kargas, A., & Varoutas, D. (2020). Industry 4.0 in Cultural Industry. A Review on Digital Visualization for VR and AR Applications. In C. M. Bolognesi & S. Cettina (Eds.), *Impact of Industry 4.0 on Architecture and Cultural Heritage* (pp. 1–19). IGI Global. doi:10.4018/978-1-7998-1234-0.ch001

Kergroach, S. (2017). Industry 4.0: New challenges and opportunities for the labour market. *Foresight and STI Governance*, *11*(4), 6–8. doi:10.17323/2500-2597.2017.4.6.8

Kiesel, M., & Wolpers, M. (2015). Educational challenges for employees in project-based Industry 4.0 scenarios. *ACM International Conference Proceeding Series*. 10.1145/2809563.2809602

Kortuem, G., Bandara, A. K., Smith, N., Richards, M., & Petre, M. (2013). Educating the Internet-of-Things Generation. *Computer*, *46*(02), 53–61. doi:10.1109/MC.2012.390

Kravcik, M., Wang, X., Ullrich, C., & Igel, C. (2018). Towards Competence Development for Industry 4.0. Lecture Notes in Computer Science, 10948, 442–446. doi:10.1007/978-3-319-93846-2_83

Laitsou, E., Kargas, A., & Varoutas, D. (2020). Digital Competitiveness in the European Union Era: The Greek Case. *Economies*, *8*(4), 85. doi:10.3390/economies8040085

Liboni, L. B., Cezarino, L. O., Jabbour, C. J. C., Oliveira, B. G., & Stefanelli, N. O. (2019). Smart industry and the pathways to HRM 4.0: Implications for SCM. *Supply Chain Management*, *24*(1), 124–146. doi:10.1108/SCM-03-2018-0150

Liszka, K., Klimkiewicz, K., & Malinowski, P. (2019). Polish foundry engineer with regard to changes carried by the industry 4.0. *Archives of Foundry Engineering*, *19*(1), 103–108. doi:10.24425/AFE.2019.127102

Lorenz, M., Russmann, M., Strack, R., Lasse Lueth, K., & Bolle, M. (2015). *Man and Machine in Industry 4.0: How Will Technology Transform the Industrial Workforce Through 2025?* Academic Press.

Mäenpää, H., Tarkoma, S., Varjonen, S., & Vihavainen, A. (2015). Blending problem- and project-based learning in internet of things education: Case greenhouse maintenance. *SIGCSE 2015 - Proceedings of the 46th ACM Technical Symposium on Computer Science Education,* 398–403. doi:10.1145/2676723.2677262

Maisiri, W., Darwish, H., & van Dyk, L. (2019). An investigation of industry 4.0 skills requirements. *South African Journal of Industrial Engineering*, *30*(3), 90–105. doi:10.7166/30-3-2230

Mavrikios, D., Georgoulias, K., & Chryssolouris, G. (2018). The Teaching Factory Paradigm: Developments and Outlook. *Procedia Manufacturing*, *23*, 1–6. doi:10.1016/j.promfg.2018.04.029

Perini, S., Arena, D., Kiritsis, D., & Taisch, M. (2017). An Ontology-Based Model for Training Evaluation and Skill Classification in an Industry 4.0 Environment. *IFIP Advances in Information and Communication Technology, AICT*, *513*(Part I), 314–321. doi:10.1007/978-3-319-66923-6_37

Petrelli, D. (2017). Industry 4.0: Is It Time for Interaction Design Craftsmanship? *The Design Journal*, *20*(sup1), 2735–2745. doi:10.1080/14606925.2017.1352785

Pinzone, M., Fantini, P., Perini, S., Garavaglia, S., Taisch, M., & Miragliotta, G. (2017). Jobs and Skills in Industry 4.0: An Exploratory Research. *IFIP Advances in Information and Communication Technology*, *513*, 282–288. doi:10.1007/978-3-319-66923-6_33

Prifti, L., Knigge, M., Kienegger, H., & Krcmar, H. (2017). A Competency Model for "Industrie 4.0" Employees. *13th International Conference on Wirtschaftsinformatik (WI)*, 44–60.

Sackey, S. M., & Bester, A. (2016). Industrial engineering curriculum in industry 4.0 in a South African context. *South African Journal of Industrial Engineering*, *27*(4), 101–114. doi:10.7166/27-4-1579

Schallock, B., Rybski, C., Jochem, R., & Kohl, H. (2018). Learning Factory for Industry 4.0 to provide future skills beyond technical training. *Procedia Manufacturing*, *23*, 27–32. doi:10.1016/j.promfg.2018.03.156

Schuh, G., Potente, T., Varandani, R., & Schmitz, T. (2014). Global Footprint Design based on genetic algorithms – An "Industry 4.0" perspective. *CIRP Annals*, *63*(1), 433–436. doi:10.1016/j.cirp.2014.03.121

Schumacher, A., Erol, S., & Sihn, W. (2016). A Maturity Model for Assessing Industry 4.0 Readiness and Maturity of Manufacturing Enterprises. *Procedia CIRP*, *52*, 161–166. doi:10.1016/j.procir.2016.07.040

Selamat, A., Taspir, S. H., Puteh, M., & Alias, R. A. (2017). Higher Education 4.0 Current Status and Readiness in Meeting the Fourth Industrial Revolution Challenges. *Redesigning Higher Education towards Industry, 1*, 23–24. https://pdfcoffee.com/higher-education-40-current-status-and-readiness-in-meeting-the-fourth-industrial-revolution-challenges-1-pdf-free.html

Shvetsova, O. A., & Kuzmina, A. D. (2018). Development of Engineering Personnel in the Era of the Fourth Industrial Revolution. *Proceedings of the 3rd International Conference Ergo-2018: Human Factors in Complex Technical Systems and Environments, Ergo 2018*, 45–48. 10.1109/ERGO.2018.8443927

SmitJ.KreutzerS.MöllerC.CarlbergM. (2016). *Industry 4.0*. https://op.europa.eu/en/publication-detail/-/publication/1b970736-9acb-11e6-868c-01aa75ed71a1

Stocker, A., Brandl, P., Michalczuk, R., & Rosenberger, M. (2014). Mensch-zentrierte IKT-Lösungen in einer Smart Factory. *Elektrotechnik Und Informationstechnik*, *131*(7), 207–211. doi:10.100700502-014-0215-z

Wahlster, W. (2013). *Industry 4.0: The Semantic Product Memory as a Basis for Cyber-Physical Production Systems*. Recent Trends in Artificial Intelligence and Cognitive Science.

Wang, C., Xu, H., & Mao, X. (2012). Construction of hardware curriculum group for transition from network to Internet of Things engineering major. *ICCSE 2012 - Proceedings of 2012 7th International Conference on Computer Science and Education*, 1575–1579. 10.1109/ICCSE.2012.6295364

World Economic Forum. (2016). *The future of jobs: employment, skills and workforce strategy for the Fourth Industrial Revolution*. World Economic Forum.

Xia, S. (2011). Training programs for excellent engineers with engineering of Internet of Thing. *ITME 2011 - Proceedings: 2011 IEEE International Symposium on IT in Medicine and Education, 1*, 610–615. 10.1109/ITiME.2011.6130912

Zinn, B. (2015). Conditional variables of 'Ausbildung 4.0' – Vocational education for the future. *JOTED, 3*, 1–9.

ADDITIONAL READING

Atiku, S. O. (Ed.). (2019). *Human capital formation for the fourth industrial revolution* (1st ed.). IGI Global.

Cantoni, F., & Mangia, G. (Eds.). (2019). *Human resource management and digitalization* (1st ed.). Routledge.

Cotet, G. B., Balgiu, B. A., & Zaleschi, V.-C. (2017). Assessment procedure for the soft skills requested by Industry 4.0. In *8th International Conference on Manufacturing Science and Education – MSE 2017 "Trends in New Industrial Revolution"* (pp. 1–8). 10.1051/matecconf/201712107005

Ejsmont, K. (2021). The Impact of Industry 4.0 on Employees—Insights from Australia. *Sustainability, 13*(6), 3095. doi:10.3390/su13063095

Fenton, A., Fletcher, G., & Griffiths, M. (Eds.). (2019). *Strategic digital transformation : a results-driven approach* (1st ed.). Routledge. doi:10.4324/9780429020469

Gebhardt, J., Flensburg, E.-U., & Neugebauer, L. M. (2015). Developments 4.0 Prospects on future requirements and impacts on work and vocational education. *JOTED, 3*, 117–133.

Poba-Nzaou, P., Galani, M., & Tchibozo, A. (2020). Transforming human resources management in the age of Industry 4.0: A matter of survival for HR professionals. *Strategic HR Review, 19*(6), 273–278. doi:10.1108/SHR-06-2020-0055

Prifti, L., Knigge, M., Kienegger, H., & Krcmar, H. (2017). A Competency Model for "Industrie 4.0" Employees. *13th International Conference on Wirtschaftsinformatik*, 44–60.

SmitJ.KreutzerS.MöllerC.CarlbergM. (2016). *Industry 4.0*. Retrieved from https://op.europa.eu/en/publication-detail/-/publication/1b970736-9acb-11e6-868c-01aa75ed71a1

KEY TERMS AND DEFINITIONS

Digital Transformation: The integration of digital technology into all areas of a business resulting in fundamental changes to how businesses operate and how they deliver value to customers. Digital transformation is not only about adopting and implementing technological solutions but more significantly about changing the "way" business is done, employees work, and customers gain value. Digital transformation is a new way of thinking and operating, which enriches the logic of both managers and employees.

European Skill/Competency Qualification and Occupation (ESCO): ESCO is the multilingual classification of European Skills, Competences, Qualifications and Occupations, launched by European Commission and currently run under DG Employment, Social Affairs and Inclusion, alongside with the consultation of various social stakeholders and by the European Centre for the Development of Vocational Training Cedefop. Its aim is to identify and categorize skills, competences, qualifications and occupations relevant for the EU labour market and education and training. ESCO is an important deliverable to support the Europe 2020 strategy and the New Skills Agenda for Europe.

Human Resource Transformation: Human resource transformation is the procedure of rethinking about which should be the values, skills, competencies, and principles required from employees. The whole procedure should be aligned with the overall business strategy and the willingness of top management for overall digital transformation. Under these circumstances it is required rechartering the HR function/department in the organization.

ICT-Based Jobs: The term often appears as ICT-based mobile work and refers to the advance use of information and communication technologies of various forms in order to achieve customized home office (teleworking is the most known form). Such an arrangement can be done in occasional or regular basis, partly or solely (refers to the hours of work provided from home). Jobs that can achieve such customizations, permitting and facilitating work arrangements carried out outside a person's 'main office', are called ICT-based jobs.

Industry 4.0: A "marriage" between the physical world/sciences with digital technologies. Digital technologies offer new ways of interconnection with "physical", effective data collection and wise systems capable to interpret the gathered data for a more holistic, informed decision making (action back to physical world).

APPENDIX 1

Box 1. Essential skills and competences – frequency 6-10

collect customer feedback on applications	6
legal requirements of ICT products	6
identify customer requirements	6
analyse business requirements	6
web programming	6
utilise computer-aided software engineering tools	6
provide ICT consulting advice	6
systems development life-cycle	7
replicate customer software issues	7
report test findings	7
address problems critically	8
provide software testing documentation	8
execute software tests	8
debug software	9
levels of software testing	9
interpret technical texts	9
create flowchart diagram	10
use software design patterns	10
use software libraries	10
integrated development environment software	10
ICT debugging tools	10

Box 2. Optional skills and competences – frequency 6-10

build business relationships	6
integrate system components	7
provide technical documentation	7
develop ICT test suite	7
utilise computer-aided software engineering tools	7
conduct ICT code review	7
use scripting programming	8
develop automated software tests	8
manage schedule of tasks	8
adapt to changes in technological development plans	8
develop creative ideas	8
debug software	8
design user interface	10
use concurrent programming	10
use functional programming	10
use automatic programming	10
use logic programming	10

Box 3. Optional Knowledge – frequency 6-10

systems development life-cycle	6
visual presentation techniques	7
unstructured data	7
software anomalies	9
tools for ICT test automation	9
ICT debugging tools	9
computer programming	10
KDevelop	10
Xcode	10
Eclipse (integrated development environment software)	10
object-oriented modelling	10
World Wide Web Consortium standards	10

Box 4. Essential skills and competences – frequency 11-15

tools for software configuration management	11
provide technical documentation	11
computer programming	11
develop software prototype	12
define technical requirements	13
analyse software specifications	14

Box 5. Optional skills and competences – frequency 11-15

use object-oriented programming	11

Box 6. Optional Knowledge – frequency 11-15

ICT security legislation	11
resource description framework query language	12
query languages	12
Salt (tools for software configuration management)	13
STAF	13
Puppet (tools for software configuration management)	13
Ansible	13
Apache Maven	13
Jenkins (tools for software configuration management)	13
Smalltalk (computer programming)	14
Erlang	14
CoffeeScript	14
XQuery	15
MDX	15
LDAP	15

APPENDIX 2

Table 4 Occupations - Essential skills and competences table – frequency 11-15

Row Labels	analyse software specifications	computer progra	define techni	develop sof	provide technica	tools for softwa	Grand Total
digital games developer	1	1		1		1	4
embedded system designer	1		1			1	3
embedded systems software developer	1	1		1	1	1	5
green ICT consultant			1				1
ICT application configurator	1	1		1	1	1	5
ICT application developer	1	1		1	1	1	5
ICT business analysis manager			1				1
ICT business analyst			1				1
ICT consultant	1		1				2
ICT intelligent systems designer			1				1
ICT research consultant				1	1		2
ICT system analyst	1		1				2
ICT system architect			1				1
ICT system developer	1	1		1	1	1	5
ICT system integration consultant			1				1
industrial mobile devices software developer	1	1		1	1	1	5
integration engineer					1		1
mobile application developer	1	1		1		1	4
numerical tool and process control programmer		1					1
software analyst			1	1			2
software architect	1		1		1	1	4
software developer	1	1	1	1	1	1	6
user experience analyst					1		1
user interface designer			1				1
user interface developer	1	1		1			3
web developer	1	1		1	1	1	5
Grand Total	**14**	**11**	**13**	**12**	**11**	**11**	**72**

Table 5 Occupations - Optional skills and competences table – frequency 11-15

Row Labels	use object-oriented programmi
digital games developer	1
embedded systems software developer	1
ICT application configurator	1
ICT application developer	1
ICT system architect	1
ICT system developer	1
industrial mobile devices software developer	1
mobile application developer	1
software developer	1
user interface developer	1
web developer	1
Grand Total	**11**

Table 6 Occupations - Optional Knowledge – frequency 11-15

Row Labels	Ansible	Apache Maven	CoffeeScript	Erlang	ICT security legisl	Jenkins (tools fo	LDAP	MDX	Puppet (tc	query lang	resource d	Salt (tools	Smalltalk	STAF	XQuery	Grand Tot
computer scientist							1	1		1	1				1	5
data analyst							1	1							1	3
data scientist							1	1							1	3
digital games developer	1	1				1			1			1		1		6
digital games tester							2	2		1	1				2	8
embedded system designer	1	1	1	1		1			1			1	1	1		9
embedded systems software developer	1	1			1	1			1			1		1		7
enterprise architect			1	1									1			3
ICT accessibility tester							1	1		1	1				1	5
ICT application configurator	1	1				1			1			1		1		6
ICT application developer	1	1			1	1			1			1		1		7
ICT auditor manager					1											1
ICT integration tester							1	1		1	1				1	5
ICT intelligent systems designer			1	1									1			3
ICT quality assurance manager					1											1
ICT research consultant							1	1		1	1				1	5
ICT system analyst			1	1			1	1		1	1		1		1	8
ICT system architect			1	1	1								1			4
ICT system developer	1	1			1	1			1			1		1		7
ICT system tester							1	1		1	1				1	5
ICT test analyst							1	1		1	1				1	5
ICT usability tester							1	1		1	1				1	5
industrial mobile devices software developer	1	1	1	1	1	1			1			1	1	1		10
integration engineer	1	1				1			1			1		1		6
mobile application developer	1	1	1	1	1	1			1			1	1	1		10
software analyst			1	1			1	1		1	1		1		1	8
software architect	1	1	1	1	1	1			1			1	1	1		10
software developer	1	1	1	1	1	1			1			1	1	1		10
software tester			1	1			1	1		1	1		1		1	8
user experience analyst							1	1		1	1				1	5
user interface designer			1	1									1			3
user interface developer	1	1	1	1		1			1			1	1	1		9
web developer	1	1	1	1	1	1			1			1	1	1		10
Grand Total	**13**	**13**	**14**	**14**	**11**	**13**	**15**	**15**	**13**	**12**	**12**	**13**	**14**	**13**	**15**	**200**

Chapter 2
Personalized Product Recommendation and User Satisfaction:
Theory and Application

Priyadarsini Patnaik
Birla Global University, India

ABSTRACT

A recommendation system is a significant part of artificial intelligence (AI) to help users' access information at any time and from anywhere. Online product recommender systems are widely used to recommend products based on consumers' preferences. The traditional recommendation algorithms of recommendation engines do not meet the needs of users in the AI environment when exposed to large amounts of data resulting in a low recommendation efficiency. To address this, a personalized recommendation system was introduced. These personalized recommendation systems (PRS) are an important component for ecommerce players in the Indian e-commerce aspects. Since personalized recommendations are becoming increasingly popular, this study examines information processing theory with respect to personalized recommendations and their impact on user satisfaction. Further, relationships between the variables were examined by conducting regression analysis and found a positive correlation exists between personalized product recommendation and user satisfaction.

DOI: 10.4018/978-1-7998-7793-6.ch002

Copyright © 2022, IGI Global. Copying or distributing in print or electronic forms without written permission of IGI Global is prohibited.

INTRODUCTION

A growing number of online recommendation systems now recognize that consumers' preferences on product attributes can support their shopping decisions better (Ghasemaghaei, Hassanein, & Benbasat, 2019). Online Product recommendation [hereinafter, it is called OPRs] on any shopping sites are the examples of suggestions made on the basis of user's interests, (G.Bathla 2017). A number of different techniques are used in these recommendation systems based on content, collaborative filtering, or trust-based recommendations. A collaborative filtering algorithm delivers personalized recommendations based on user activity, user's browsing history and information needs, to predict user's possible future behaviour, so as to provide the user with personalized recommendations,(Wu, H. 2021). Most recommendation systems use a collaborative filtering method because they do not need any previous knowledge about users or items; rather they make recommendations based on interactions between them, (Nassar, N.et.al, 2020). Based on the information about a customer's most recent purchase, frequency of purchase, and the value of past purchase, OPR predicts the likelihood of further or future purchasing Product recommendation engines in E-commerce websites recommend potentially interesting products to users, more quickly and efficiently.

Now days many companies are using Artificial Intelligence (AI) to deliver more personalized experiences to their customers to anticipate what they want or need. By using product recommendation engine, AI can predict potential customers who will buy the product. AI helps predict lead scoring through data analysis, perform content personalization, and improve the customer experience. Primarily AI sends highly customized and relevant suggestions to customers, taking into account their preferences, search history, personal preferences and spending patterns. So, eventually AI and its applications are adopted by the company and it will only continue to rise. Since the world becomes more digital, personalization creates unique experiences to keep users happy and engaged .Earlier traditional marketing focused on customer experience, functionality, and advertising for a highly targeted audience whereas today these are continuously improved with the use of Artificial Intelligence (AI).

The traditional recommendation algorithms, however, cannot provide users with accurate and fast recommendations and result low recommendation efficiency. So personalized recommendation were proposed to users. These personalised recommendations involve providing a specialized and customized products, services and information through the use of big data, (Subramanyan, 2014). Using this hyper-personalization, companies can create a customized online customer experience tailored to the needs of individual customers. Hyper-personalized recommendations which is driven by artificial intelligence (AI) can deliver more relevant content to its user which makes personalized marketing a step further. The advancement of technology allows customers to customize their environment based on their likes, interests, and beliefs. This concept can be used by companies to provide information based on customer needs. Marketers use hyper personalization to provide customers with personalized information. The key areas of hyper-personalization include social listening, data analysis, and content.

PURPOSE OF THE STUDY

Companies are using personalized product recommendation (PPRs) to deliver more personalized experiences to their customers to anticipate what they want or need and can predict potential customers who will buy the product. These predictions are derived using personal preferences, browsing history, spending patterns, customers' tastes, and recommend more relevant suggestions to their customers which make personalized marketing a step further. So, eventually PPRs are adopted by the company will only continue to rise and can make a compelling campaign more effective (Hirsh, Kang, and Bodenhausen, 2012). Hence, the persuasion process must be examined more closely, in e shopping to provide a comprehensive review of previous studies. The study is based on information processing theory and developed an integrated framework for helping customers make informed decisions when purchasing goods and services online. This proposed model is formulated that explains consumer satisfaction and the purchase process in the framework of affective and intellectual components of perceptions. Its uniqueness lies in an integration of persuasion as a separate factor, as persuaded customers don't always conclude a purchase after being persuaded. Lastly, it suggests how cognitive perceptions affect persuasion in two steps, looking first at how cognitive perceptions influence persuasion, then taking into account attitude as a moderating factor between persuasion and customer satisfaction. By identifying factors that can affect online shopping persuasion and how they impact each stage of the process, the study makes a positive contribution to the field. The study also considers how attitude play a role in concerning the persuasion process. The study provided an opportunity to expand knowledge on attitude .Identifying and examining the persuasion factors at each step will facilitate the refinement of personalized recommendations derived from the clarification of these research areas. The importance of customers' based on the relationship described above will be further emphasized by examining how persuasion plays a role in purchase intentions and satisfaction.

BACKGROUND

Personalization

Personalization means delivering messages tailored to the individual needs and anticipating their desires, which can improve customers' lives as well as increase engagement and loyalty. Offering tailored content to offer value on an individual basis has been a strategy online retailers use to attract and retain customers (Adobe, 2015). Personalization could lead to a reduction of almost 50% in acquisition costs, an increase of 15% in revenue, and an increase in marketing efficiency of up to 30% (Ariker et.al 2015).Providing customers with personalized information about a product or service can help convince them to purchase it (Ho & Bodoff, 2014; Pappas et.al.2016) in addition, it may result in persuasion. Customized messages are offered by online retailers through personalization. The effectiveness of customized marketing is much greater than that of generic mailings (Noar, Benac, & Harris, 2007) . In the context of personalization, online retailers are leveraging new technologies to offer digitally delivered offline experiences (Kohan, 2020), and use innovative solutions to offer their customers an abundance of information in order to refine their attention to personalized content that appears relevant to them (Grewal, et.al.2017) . An online shopping experience that is personalized is appealing to consumers (McKinsey, 2019a). Hence, customers are now receiving context-specific information relevant to their individual circumstances that reflects both historical data and current data as part of a new phenomenon that combines physical and digital dimensions, (Riegger, A. S et.al.2021)

Personalized Recommendation

A personalized recommendation service is used to maintain competitive advantage .There are several ecommerce companies that offer the service to their clients, such as Amazon, Google, and Netflix. Additionally, there is a debate over whether accurate recommendations or diverse recommendations have a greater influence on customer satisfaction and customers' satisfaction with personalized recommendation services is highly dependent on their accuracy. Customer satisfaction has increased significantly as a result of accurate recommendation (Kim, J., et al., 2021). Study demonstrated that as the accuracy of product recommendations increased, customer satisfaction increased. These results offer insight to providers. It is first important for providers to offer products that suit customer preferences to increase sales volume since accurate recommendations result in customer satisfaction. As the number of product recommendations increases, accuracy doesn't necessarily improve. This is why providers should provide sufficient product recommendations to customers.

The Role of Persuasion in Online Shopping

When people are encouraged to believe they will be successful in completing a task, like buying online, by using activities, strategies, or tactics, then they are persuaded into believing they will succeed. An activity, strategy, or tactic used to convince people that they will be successful in performing a particular task. So, persuasion is an activity to persuade activities, strategies or tactics used to convince people that they can successfully perform certain tasks, such as completing a purchase online, (Teeny, J. et.al. 2021). A person's attitude is neutral through persuasion and can change to another at a particular attitude or attitude (Petty, Fabrigar, and Wegener, 2003). So, customers are now receiving context-specific information relevant to their individual circumstances that reflects both historical data and current data as part of a new phenomenon that combines physical and digital dimensions, (Hamelin, N et.al.2020)

Advertisement is perhaps the most common form of persuasion in individuals' daily lives. In marketing research, theories of persuasion explain and predict customer behaviour effectively (Meyers-Levy & Malaviya, 1999). It is the primary goal of retailers to persuade customers to buy products and services, and, to accomplish this goal, they use a variety of strategies and tactics. Study previously examined the relationship between pricing tactics and Persuasive knowledge focused on price tactics as a compelling strategy (Kachersky, 2011; Pilai & Kumar, 2012). However a compelling strategy extends beyond price (MeyersLevy & Malaviya, 1999). In the context of online shopping, As well, retailers can make use of a variety of marketing strategies to engage customers, such as sending personalized messages based on customer creations. (Thompson & Malaviya, 2013). In spite of this, these tactics only increase persuasion if certain conditions are met (Thompson & Malaviya, 2013). Researchers have been exploring to have sought ways for customers to process persuasive messages through a variety of channels with the help of the information processing theory.

The emergence of technology enables eretailers to offer the effective methods of persuasion for their customers by offering personalized messages to the target customers. Hence, modern technology makes the process of personalizing messages to the specific audience making persuasion one of the most effective methods of communication today. It has been shown in a prodigious amount of research that individualization is achieved through persuasive content. The most reliable and impactful way of enhancing customization appeals is to present them as "persuasive", (Carpenter, 2012; Rothman, Desmarais, & Lenne, 2020).

The Role of Personalization in Persuasion

Personalization is the process of delivering more relevant content to customers according to their personal information, such as the items they have purchased. Past research has examined this process through the analysis of behaviour and intent to purchase in an attempt to perform a particular task by persuasive communication or motivating and convincing users to take action (Ha et.al. 2010; Pappas et al., 2016; Thongpapanl & Ashraf, 2011). Research says, persuasive strategies can influence attitudes and behaviours of customers by modifying how personalized services are provided. (Tam & Ho, 2005). An effective strategy for increasing the persuasive power of a proposition is to connect by content and source, (Tenny J et.al.2021)

It turns out that personality of an individual can influence consumer behaviour in terms of purchasing (Anaza, 2014) and that messages generated based on the particular customer's personality are more likely to be more effective and successful,(Hirsh et al., 2012). Bernkovsky et al. (2012). This might result in greater effectiveness for influencing user behaviour. Furthermore, customers prefer quality recommendations over quantity when persuasion mechanisms are used (Lee & Kwon, 2008). Therefore, online personalized shopping should emphasize factors that increase persuasion and increase purchase intentions, such as the quality of information and perceived benefits. Additionally, Yi et al. (2013) estimate that customers prefer to interact with familiar objects or parties, and that they favor detailed information, which indicates the purpose of offering more personalized services to provide more benefits and quality information to increase the effectiveness of persuasion, (Castiglioni et.al. 2020)

A persuasive message consists of four elements: its recipient, its message itself, its context and the source of the message from where the message is delivered, (McGuire, 1969). In this review, this study examined personalized matching, which focuses on one of the most common forms of matching: an alignment between the recipient's characteristics and one or more of the factors. Segmenting, customizing, targeting, and tailoring are also types of "matching to people" (Hawkins et al., 2008; Webb et al., 2013).

Information Processing Theory

Information Processing Theory is a cognitive theory containing information about the process of encoding information in memory. It describes how information is cognitively encoded in memory based on the processing of information. In this theory, the brain pays attention to a given time to explain information about how we learn new knowledge. The first thing we perceive is through all the sensory memories we see, hear, feel and taste. Since then, our short-term memory has been used to remember things in a short amount of time . By processing information rather than responding solely to stimuli, this theory suggests that we use information to function better as individuals. From this point of view, the mind behaves like a computer and is similar to it. Therefore, the brain acts like a biological computer that analyses data from the surrounding environment. Follows standard information processing models for mental development. The machine of mind contains a mechanism of attention to obtain information. To manipulate the information and make it available in the future (Psychology, Sixth Edition,) .As humans process information rather than only responding to stimuli, this theory proposes that information allows us to function better as individuals. The mind functions like a computer from this perspective, with analogies to how it works. Therefore, the brain functions like a biological computer which analyses data from its environment.

Consequently, persuasive campaigns may be more effective (Hirsh, Kang, & Bodenhausen, 2012). At the moment, however, most methods of persuasion described in research are not personalized. Although it is common practice in marketing practices to target an end goal to individuals, it is striking to see this on the Internet (Kaptein, Markopoulos, De Ruyter & Aarts, 2015). Users' attitudes and intentions can be changed by persuasive messages in online marketing (Chang, Yu, & Lu, 2015), and individual differences possess impact this is certainly considerable on their efficiency (Haddock et.al.2008). Persuasion, behavioural intentions, and choices could be affected by an individual's attitudes and evaluations, (Darley et.al.2010; Peck & Wiggins, 2006; See et.al.2008). Cognitive or affective components of a persuasive message may be used to increase its receptivity, depending on the individual's need related to cognition or emotion (Haddock et al., 2008). A marketing strategy that relies on interactive technology is one that aims to influence an individual's behaviour (Berkovsky et.al., 2012; Kaptein & Eckles, 2012). Fu et al. (2004) identified three key methods to persuade: rational arguments, persuasive appeals, and consultations.. Therefore, for businesses to succeed in persuading their customers, they should use an array of arguments, emotional appeals, and feedback that was gathered from and for customers.

Research Gap

Research in personalized online shopping examines various aspects of the cognitive phase including the factors that affect each stage and a variety of options, (Kaptein et al., 2015) Personalized interactive messages are appreciated by users, (Ho and Bodoff , 2014) and users relate to personalized messages that are interactive, (Tam and Ho 2006) .Also, these researchers have studied attention, cognitive processes, decision-making processes, and evaluation processes. Since, cognition, affect, and interactive personalization, should present in persuasive behaviour (Cesario, Higgins, & Scholer, 2008), affective responses (Pappas et al., 2016), as well as persuasion (Hsieh et.al.2014;Van et.al.2012) may also be affected by interactive and personalized messages. A persuasive message (e.g., irritation, anger) may cause negative affective reactions among customers (Holzwarth et al., 2006). Despite the importance of psychological factors (such as emotions) in retail and online shopping, the impact of these factors on purchase intentions, attitudes, satisfaction and behaviours remains poorly studied,(Pappas et.al. 2014). Also, in previous studies, in a personalized online shopping environment, Kansei and cognitive perception were not considered when developing a persuasive model for customers in order to explain their purchasing intentions and satisfaction. This study has conducted with an investigation of consumers' perception towards personalized recommender system and their satisfaction in the context of online purchases. Specifically, this study examines how PPR's quality influences consumer decision process. Therefore, a theoretical model developed in this study to define consumer satisfaction and purchasing intention.

Conceptual Framework and Proposed Research Model

Based on recommendations of the information processing theory, in the proposed model, the sequential presentation of an initial persuasive message followed by a series of cognitive activities. It follows initial exposure to a persuasive message in order to maximize its impact. McGuire (1968) analysed the attention effect, cognitive processing, and judgmental evaluation of the message, ultimately deciding whether it received acceptance or rejection. Previously, Tam and Ho (2005) examined the theory's application to web personalization and persuasion and found it to be a useful tool for conducting the theoretical propositions.

Assuming that online retailing influence persuasion based on the personalization strategies, the conceptual model proposes to influence persuasion. In order to reach the end user, the first component considers the communication method that will be used. The message should be communicated effectively so that it will engage the user's cognitive process and draw their attention. A personalized message's relevance will result in improved perceptions of the message in the context of eservices. Oinas-Kukkonen and Harjumaa (2009) refer to the content route as the quality of the communication. User evaluations of personalized messages relate them to a desired (outcome) performance and are the cornerstones of cognitive evaluation. A quality message and the persuasive effect have been shown to be positively correlated in existing studies on persuasion (Cesario et al., 2008; Petty & Cacioppo, 2012). The same is likely to be true for online personalization strategies (Oinas-Kukkonen & Harjumaa, 2009)

It has been proposed that information processing theory explains judgment changes as a result of rational cues. Even so, individuals rarely rely solely on rational reasoning to persuade them. The author reports that affective qualities, represented by discrete positive and negative emotions, influence how well a person can persuade (Griskevicius et al.2010; Petty et al., 2003).

Figure 1. Proposed Model

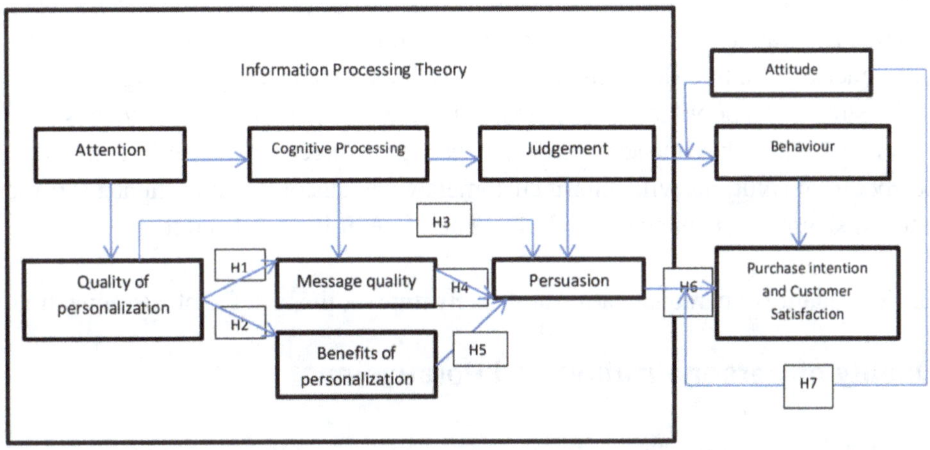

Quality of Personalization

This proposed model consists of several factors such as quality of personalization, message quality, benefits of personalization, persuasion, attitude and consumer satisfaction. Where all the variables are independent variable and customer satisfaction is the dependent variable. Attitude played as an influencing role in customer satisfaction. This model tried to establish how qualities of personalization, message quality and benefits of personalization persuade towards customer purchase intention and satisfaction.

Customers who receive special attention with the help of personalization, as they are provided with unique information that makes customers feel "closer" towards the services offered. Customers who use personalized services receive exclusive care; through the valuable information they receive, they feel more connected as it relates to the service offered (Kim & Ammeter, 2014). As a result, customers are more likely to perceive that they receive high quality information through personalized services, (Shang et.al.2005). Custom-made messages may affect the quality of a message greatly and a personalized message may have a great effect on its quality

(Hirsh et al., 2012). The improvement of perceived information quality is expected to occur when personalization and recommendation agents appear, instead of just simple information messages (Xu et.al.2013). Hence, it is postulated that:

H1: Personalization quality positively affects the quality of the message.

Personalization and Its Benefits

When developing persuasive messages, a customer's benefits must be determined and the best way to offer them should be communicated to them, (Lee et al., 2010). The benefits of online shopping, consisting of convenience, time savings, and cost savings make it a popular choice among customers. A personalized service is most effective when it takes into account customer interests, needs, (Xu et.al.2011). Hence, personalized solutions will benefit customers when customer convenience is taken into consideration, (Shang et al., 2005). Therefore, it is postulated that:

H2: The quality of personalization absolutely impacts the benefits of customization.

Quality of Personalization and Persuasion

As a result of personalization, retailers and consumers are likely to gain benefits from increased persuasion. Customers and retailers should benefit from personalized services as they will be persuaded by the increased efficiency of these services. Previous studies indicate that perceptions of relative advantage actually influence innovations adopted through the personalized services, (Chen, Gillenson, & Sherrell, 2002). By enhancing online shopping with specific techniques, retailers can increase customer satisfaction, increase product interest and increase purchase intent (Holzwarth et al., 2006). Information about retail options tailored to the needs or preferences of consumers makes their shopping experience more rewarding. In addition to providing contextualization value and satisfying customers' needs, personalized services are a great tool for retailers. Thus, the hypothesis can be postulated that:

H3: Quality of personalization positively influences persuasion.

Message Quality

In online shopping, information quality refers to the information on products and transactions; also it means the accuracy and completeness of the information (Yi & Gong, 2013). For potential purchasers, getting high-quality information is essential

(Miranda & Saunders, 2003). Information quality is one of the factors involved in customers' overall evaluation and usage of online services (Setia et.al, 2013). Therefore, it is hypothesized that:

H4: Quality of the message positively influences persuasion.

Benefits of Personalization

Research has shown that attitudes and intentions can be positively affected by perceptions of the benefits of using online services (Lee, 2009). Shopping online is a great way to obtain more value from it, which is one of the main reasons why customers prefer it (Forsythe et al., 2006). As a result of perceived benefits, customers will act differently as a result of these increases in value. The effectiveness of persuasion on individuals' online shopping behaviour can be determined by considering the perceived advantages of online shopping. Therefore, the below hypothesis can be proposed as:

H5: Benefits of personalization have a positive impact on persuasion

Persuasion

Persuasion is an activity to change the attitude toward something through some kind of communication. The theory of information processing states that each user will process information differently depending on their ability to think critically. Thus, attitudes and behaviours are likely to be affected by this information depending on the user's capacity to think critically. Hence, a user's ability to process a given argument may determine how the information is processed by them, so each individual's reactions to such information will vary according to that ability. As stated above, different influences will influence people in different ways and direct them towards a specific conclusion based on how they process information and think about it which will influence their attitudes, behaviours and purchase intentions, if the message is persuasive and involves an achievable goal. Persuasion has been studied in the past, however, with attention focused on its outcomes, not on persuasion itself (Ho & Bodoff, 2014; Lee et al., 2010; Thompson & Malaviya, 2013), therefore, the influence of persuasion needs to be investigated in more detail . The effectiveness of persuasion on individuals' online shopping behaviour can be determined by considering the perceived advantages of online shopping, (Holzwarth et al., 2006). Customers' attitudes toward products and the retailers are improved when specific persuasion agents are used.

Customer Satisfaction

Customer satisfaction is one of the most studied aspects of marketing. It affects both the retention of existing consumers and the introduction of new customers in the competitive climate of e-commerce also it is a key factor in determining whether or not a customer would stick with a product or service (Chung and Shin, 2010). Customer satisfaction is one of the crucial factor in an online environment, as it leads to improve customer retention and enhance growth for online businesses (Chen et al. 2012 ;Yiu et al. 2007) and helps in raising the number of repeat transactions and influence shoppers' purchasing decisions (Gupta and Kim, 2010). Online shoppers decide to make repeat purchases based on their satisfaction with the online environment, (Gupta and Kim, 2010). The customers who are satisfied intend to repurchasing in the future more often than the unsatisfied (Garcia et al. 2012)**..** So, web merchants should target customer satisfaction in the online shopping context. Hence, the hypothesis can be postulated as:

H6: Persuasion affects consumer satisfaction positively.

Attitude

"Attitude is a psychological tendency that is expressed by evaluating a particular entity with some degree of favour or disfavour" (Eagly & Chaiken, 1993, p. 4). Depending on the customer's purchase and service experiences, customer's attitude towards the retailer is characterized as either favouring or disfavouring the retailer. Essentially, customer's attitude is their psychological tendency, either in favour of the retailer or against it, based on their experiences with the business and how they purchase and use its products. The attitude of a customer is also a determinant of future behaviour (Innis & La Londe, 1994). Positive attitudes towards a company may increase the likelihood that a customer will maintain and expand a relationship with that enterprise. The behavioural intention of a person defines engagement in certain behaviours (Ajzen, 1991). Similarly, attitude refers to one's level of enthusiasm for participating in online buying. It is expected an individual with a positive attitude should be able to create an online purchase. Also, attitude defines one's willingness to engage in online purchasing, (Pavlou and Fygensen 2006 ; Chen et al. (2012) discovered that a happy attitude had a significant impact on internet purchases. Holzwarth, Janiszewski, & Neumann (2006) found that positive attitudes towards online retailers may positively influence their customers' attitudes towards them. Experience with a company/product/service shapes a customer's attitude. Whether a customer chooses to connect with a service provider by displaying favourable attitudes has been found to affect its likelihood to connect (Pomerantz, Chaiken, &

Tordesillas, 1995). Ajzen and Fishbein (1975) examined rational behaviour in order to discover the effect of purchase intent on real behaviour. Customers' high levels of satisfaction lead to their strong attitudes towards the online shopping also make them inclined to form relationships. (Ki & Hon, 2007) found that attitudes are a predictor of positive behavioural outcomes. Based on the findings of Szymanski and Henard (2001), a correlation exists between customer satisfaction (CS) and customer attitude (ATT). It found that attitudes are a consequence of satisfaction, according to Oliver's (1980) and LaBarbera and Mazursky (1983), study on Consumer satisfaction which examined an individual's memory and their effect by both indirect and direct cognitive effects of satisfaction. It follows that CS is positively correlated with ATT, based on the studies cited above. A higher degree of satisfaction with recommended products is another benefit of persuasion concepts in the recommendation process,(Felfernig A et.al.2008). As well, persuasion concepts can impact the recommendation process in different ways, resulting in a higher satisfaction rate with the products recommended. Thus, it is postulated that:

H7: Persuasion and consumer satisfaction are moderated by customers' attitudes.

RESEARCH METHODS

Primary and secondary data were collected to conduct the survey. The first step in this research was to critically examine the literature to date, as secondary data to investigate relationships between the variables. Primary data was collected by conducting online survey A web-based survey was distributed to Indian consumers who had experience with online shopping experiences .Content analysis was performed before survey and a survey instrument was used to collect data using a seven point Likert Scale. Sample test of questionnaire survey was done to collect the data for the study. Further, data analysed with the help of factor analysis and regression analysis and findings were presented.

Data Collection

In March and April of 2021, the survey was conducted. Profile samples used to reach customers who have previously experienced personalized online shopping. In the research instrument, participants are asked about their experiences with a personalized information service and online shopping. Answers were based on evaluations derived from participants' experiences with online shopping and personalized services . Data was collected by conducting an online questionnaire survey method. This survey excluded respondents who were unknown to online shopping with personalized services or recommendations.

Demographics

Demographic frequencies showed that there are 119 numbers of male respondents i.e. 59.5% of total sample and 81 numbers of female respondents were there i.e. 40.5% of the total samples for the survey. However, males showed a modestly higher response rate than females. The age group belongs to 15s to 20s was 17.5% of the total samples, 21s to 26s was 22.5% of the whole sample, 27s to 32s was 18% , 33s to 38s was 42%of the whole samples . The novice online buyers were 18.5% of the total sample, beginner were 18% of the total sample, competent online buyers were 30.5% of the total sample whereas expert buyers were 33% of the total sample. Similarly the education level of the sample respondents were graduation, post-graduation and other professional courses.44% of the sample were graduate, 38.5% of respondents were post graduate and professional courses enrolled respondents were 17.5% of the total population. The average monthly expenditure in online shopping which was less than INR 2000 was 22.5% of the full sample, INR 2000 to INR 4000 was 32.5% of the total sample, INR 4000 to INR 5000 was 23% of the total sample was more than INR 5000 was 22% the total sample.

Measures

A total of two parts comprised the questionnaire. In the first section, demographic questions were asked about the sample .Also, measures of various constructs from literature review were presented. Survey results were analysed using different scales to test the hypotheses. Table 2 represents the measures and their source of adoption. A7 point Likert scale from 1 (completely disagree) to 7 (completely agree) was anchored in this survey.

Data Analysis

Reliability

Reliability test was performed for the constructs by calculating Cronbach's alpha coefficient and all the value of CA were more than 0.70 which signifies the data is reliable.

Table 1. Demographic Profile of the Respondent

Category	Variable	Frequency	Percentage
Gender	Male	119	59.5
	Female	81	40.5
Age	15 -20	35	17.5
	21-26	45	22.5
	27-32	36	18
	33-38	84	42
Monthly Expenditure	2000 and below	45	22.5
	2001 -4000	65	32.5
	4001 -5000	46	23
	5001 and above	44	22
Qualification Enrolled	Graduate	88	44
	PG	77	38.5
	Professional course	35	17.5
User Experience(online buying)	Novice	37	18.5
	Beginner	36	18
	Competent	61	30.5
	Expert	66	33

Table 2. The Measurement of Research Variables

Variables	Items	Scale
Quality of personalization	2	Pappas et al. (2014)
Message quality	7	Kim and John (2008)
Benefits of personalization	5	Kim and John (2008)
Satisfaction	2	Bhattacherjee, A. 2001),
Persuasion	5	(Cesario et al. (2004)
Attitude	3	Yu et.al.(2005)

Table 3. Factor Loadings

Factor	Item Loadings	Cronbach's α
Message Quality		.930
MQ1	.751	
MQ2	.701	
MQ3	.874	
MQ4	.954	
MQ5	.765	
MQ6	.805	
MQ7	.809	
Benefits of Personalization		.914
BP1	.720	
BP2	.965	
BP3	.928	
BP4	.663	
BP5	.922	
Quality of Personalization		.935
QP1	.831	
QP2	.813	
Persuasion		.935
P1 P2 P3 P4 P5	.912 .804 .823 .936 .749	
Satisfaction		.813
S1 S2	.808 .749	
Attitude		.718
AT1 **AT2** **AT3**	**.540** **.725** **.760**	

Table 4. Model Summary

Model	R	R Square	Adjusted R Square	Std. Error of the Estimate
1	.682[a]	.466	.452	.6709
a. Predictors: (Constant), Attitude, Persuation, Benefits of personalization, Message quality, Quality of personalization				

Regression Analysis

Table 5. ANOVA[a]

Model		Sum of Squares	df	Mean Square	F	Sig.
1	Regression	76.137	5	15.227	33.832	.000[b]
	Residual	87.318	194	.450		
	Total	163.455	199			
a. Dependent Variable: Satisfaction						
b. Predictors: (Constant), Attitude, Persuasion, Benefits of personalization, Message quality, Quality of personalization						

Table 6. Coefficients

Model		Unstandardized Coefficients		Standardized Coefficients	t	Sig.
		B	Std. Error	Beta		
1	(Constant)	.412	.677		.608	.544
	Message quality	.117	.041	.172	2.867	.005
	Quality of personalization	-.012	.070	-.011	-.171	.864
	Benefits of personalization	.055	.045	.068	1.203	.230
	Persuasion	.764	.076	.593	10.056	.000
	Attitude	.037	.102	.020	.366	.715
a. Dependent Variable: Satisfaction						

Analysis of the regression equation shows the following results: R 2 =.466 which explains 46.6% of the total variation. F value was 33.832 which were significant at significance level. The above regression results indicate that message quality, quality of personalization, benefits of personalization, persuasion and attitude are positively related to satisfaction of users. This is evident from the positive signs of the estimated co-efficient of the correspondence variables. From the regression analysis (Table No.-6) and the above model summery (Table No.-7,8), Regression Equation of satisfaction of users with related to message quality, quality of personalization, benefits of personalization, persuasion and attitude can be denoted as:

(Satisfaction (S) = .412 + .115 Message quality+ .012 Quality of personalization + .055 Benefits of personalization + .764 Persuasion + .037 Attitude)

The significance of R square as tested by the F statistic indicated that the regression equation is significant hence all the hypothesis hold true.

DISCUSSION

Customer persuasion, message quality, and benefits associated with personalization are significantly enhanced in online shopping, demonstrating that persuasion is influenced by personalization .In online shopping, quality of personalization gains customers' loyalty and enhances their perception of message quality, indicating that qualitative personalization predicts persuasiveness and customized services are remarkably more effective in influencing customers. This study extends recent research suggesting that persuasion and personalization is correlated. From this study it is evidential that the advantages of personalization and the importance of quality of the message work together to persuade customers.. However, personalization has a greater influence on persuasion than does quality of message. According to emerging theories, the attention stage of online persuasion may be more important than ever in the context of online retailing, just as it has so substantially increased in importance. Persuasion also increases the likelihood of an online purchase. As persuasion is defined as the ability to persuade customers and influence those using personalized services, this was expected as this is one of the qualities a web site and online retailer must have. Therefore, getting targeted messages that increase the effectiveness of services and the persuasion of customers will eventually increase their intentions to buy online. Persuasion plays a significant role in users' behaviour, (Lee et al., 2010; Tam & Ho, 2005), and contributes to predict purchase intentions. Also, from the analysis, it is clear that customer satisfaction is dependent on message quality, benefits of personalization, persuasion of personalized recommendation towards customer and the attitude of the customer to use the recommended product.

LIMITATIONS

The limitations of this study are as follows:. A generalization of the findings in this study requires further research with other product domains. In this study, personalized recommendation was used to make recommendations. However, this cannot be certain that other methods, such as trust based recommendation systems and customer generated recommendations (those are based on product reviews) would produce the same results. In the future, it may be worthwhile to investigate the differences between these two recommendations in customer satisfaction.

SCOPE

Future research recommends investigating more detailed aspects of positive and negative attitudes and emotions towards customer satisfaction .It should also examine how different persuasion techniques can invoke or inhibit different types of emotions depending on what is desired by the persuader. Furthermore, future research would also be wise to examine other methods for capturing emotions and attitudes that might influence purchase intentions (Bagozzi et.al.2016), and by measuring customer satisfaction, it can provide a more detailed understanding of the way the customer feels during the persuasion process. Understanding how customers are feeling during persuasion provides deeper insights into how to best serve them. Research has shown that it is important to examine both positive and negative emotions since they are inextricably linked (Barclay & Kiefer, 2014; Pappas et al., 2014, 2016). To persuade customers' online retailers can identify customers' preference by recommending personalized recommendations and may deliver items to them which indeed can change the continuing business structure of merchants towards buyer. Accordingly products can be delivered to customers with having an option to return back (Agrawal et al. 2018; Gans et al. 2017) and the impact that is negative with item returns may be averted. So, marketers can utilize this personalized design to anticipate and forecast the customers demand.

FUTURE RESEARCH DIRECTION

In today's world, marketers are increasingly looking for ways to improve their performance by personalizing their messages and actions. Through the use of modern technology, data collection and analysis have become possible to create personalized marketing campaigns and offer various products and services to meet the needs of the individual. In this context, the diversity of recommendation is a requirement for e-commerce businesses to provide new products and services to their customers, (Kim, J et al. 2021). This process involves analysing the recommendations that were provided to them by an AI driven recommender system. It is also known that if the recommender system is accurate, the customer satisfaction level is high. However, if the same item is given repeatedly, the reliability of the system will decrease. Other studies suggest that the quality of the recommendation is not the only consideration when it comes to measuring its effectiveness, (Zhang, L. et al.2020). A diverse list of recommendations can also help a customer make a better decision. A good recommendation list should contain diverse items and should not be limited to certain items which ensures that the customer receives a better and more accurate recommendation, (Silveira, T.et al.2019)

The study focused on recommending items based on the user's browsing history and preference. The study revealed that the factors of recommendation accuracy and diversity are important factors that affect customer satisfaction. It also examined the effect that these recommendations had on the customer satisfaction. The results showed that applying a deep learning system for recommending products positively affects customer satisfaction. Further study can identify factors that can improve the customer satisfaction of recommender systems. The relationship needs to be analysed further between customer feedback and other evaluation metrics.

Since the survey was conducted using a convenience sampling method, the data collected were limited to a certain number of respondents. This means that the findings of the study can be used to draw new conclusions. In order to properly analyse the factors that influence the purchase decision and customer satisfaction. it is necessary to carry out follow-up studies that can expand the scope of the study. This method will be useful if the study is carried out on multiple ages.

CONCLUDING REMARKS

Artificial Intelligence in marketing is indicative of its adoption by most individuals and organizations. AI is already contributing an effective and improved user experience by offering personalized buying experiences to its customers and strengthens the customer retention and satisfaction. Whereas recommendation systems are an effective way to offer personalized service. In current recommendations systems, recommendation algorithms provide accurate recommendations. In order to establish a long-term solid relationship with consumers, a successful recommendation system should utilize a personalized recommendation algorithm. For recommended products, accuracy is essential. Customers are more likely to be satisfied with accurate recommendations when they are coupled with quality of message and their benefits. Personalized recommendation in persuasion pertains to a variety of persuasive matches, including the key psychological mechanisms underlying the impact of these matches, and the primary characteristics of the targets that make each match effective. To amplify a persuasive appeal, it is highly effective for it to be tailored to meet the needs of the consumer. In addition, most research on personalized recommendation shows that personalization makes customers more likely to buy; this study also summarized how personalization affects customer satisfaction. It's not just about customer satisfaction, but also about boosting sales with accurate recommendations. Withdrawing on theoretical foundation, this study adopted a conceptual framework of personalized recommendation and expanded upon how personalized recommendations are key determinants of consumer satisfaction and purchase intention. In light of the above insights, e-commerce platforms could rethink their recommendation algorithms to select more appropriate product. It is therefore recommended that online retailers focus on guiding and cultivating customer consumption by studying customer feedback behaviour through interactive interfaces which can further enhance customer satisfaction and increase sales.

REFERENCES

Adobe. (2015). *Four advantages of a planned approach to digital maturity*. Retrieved from Adobe Systems: Retrieved from https://landing. adobe.com/dam/downloads/whitepapers/192320.en.digital-marketing -survey-report.pdf

Agarwal, D. (2019). *Top 5 trends that will rule fashion retail in 2019*. Available at: www.indianretailer. com/article/whats-hot/trends/Top-5-trends-that-will-rule-fashion-retail-in-2019.a6270/

Agarwal, Vempati, & Borar. (2018). *Personalizing similar product recommendations in fashion e-commerce*. arXiv preprint arXiv:1806.11371.

Anaza, N. A. (2014). Personality antecedents of customer citizenship behaviours in online shopping situations. *Psychology and Marketing*, *31*, 251–263.

Angst, C. M., & Agarwal, R. (2009). Adoption of electronic health records in the presence of privacy concerns: The elaboration likelihood model and individual persuasion. *Management Information Systems Quarterly*, *33*(2), 339–370. doi:10.2307/20650295

Ariker, M., Heller, J., Diaz, A., & Perrey, J. (2015). How marketers can personalize at scale. *Harvard Business Review*. Retrieved from https://hbr.org/ 2015/11/how-marketers-can-personalize-at-scale

Aurier, P., & Guintcheva, G. (2014). Using affect–expectations theory to explain the direction of the impacts of experiential emotions on satisfaction. *Psychology and Marketing*, *31*(10), 900–913. doi:10.1002/mar.20742

Bagozzi, R. P., Belanche, D., Casaló, L. V., & Flavián, C. (2016). The role of anticipated emotions in purchase intentions. *Psychology and Marketing*, *33*(8), 629–645. doi:10.1002/mar.20905

Barclay, L. J., & Kiefer, T. (2014). Approach or avoid? Exploring overall justice and the differential effects of positive and negative emotions. *Journal of Management*, *40*(7), 1857–1898. doi:10.1177/0149206312441833

Bathla, G., Aggarwal, H., & Rani, R. (2020). A graph-based model to improve social trust and influence for social recommendation. *The Journal of Supercomputing*, *76*(6), 4057–4075. doi:10.100711227-017-2196-2

Beatty, S. E., & Elizabeth Ferrell, M. (1998). Impulse buying: Modeling its precursors. *Journal of Retailing*, *74*(2), 169–191. doi:10.1016/S0022-4359(99)80092-X

Berkovsky, S., Freyne, J., & Oinas-Kukkonen, H. (2012). Influencing individually: Fusing personalization and persuasion. *ACM Transactions on Interactive Intelligent Systems*, *2*(2), 9. doi:10.1145/2209310.2209312

Bhattacherjee, A., & Sanford, C. (2006). Influence processes for information technology acceptance: An elaboration likelihood model. *Management Information Systems Quarterly*, *30*(4), 805–825. doi:10.2307/25148755

Biernacki, P., & Waldorf, D. (1981). Snowball sampling: Problems and techniques of chain referral sampling. *Sociological Methods & Research*, *10*(2), 141–163. doi:10.1177/004912418101000205

Byrne, B. M. (2016). *Structural equation modeling with AMOS: Basic concepts, applications, and programming*. Routledge/Taylor & Francis. doi:10.4324/9781315757421

Castiglioni, M., Celli, A., Marchesi, A., & Gatti, N. (2020). Online Bayesian persuasion. *Advances in Neural Information Processing Systems*, 33.

Cesario, J., Grant, H., & Higgins, E. T. (2004). Regulatory fit and persuasion: Transfer from "feeling right.". *Journal of Personality and Social Psychology*, *86*(3), 388–404. doi:10.1037/0022-3514.86.3.388 PMID:15008644

Cesario, J., Higgins, E. T., & Scholer, A. A. (2008). Regulatory fit and persuasion: Basic principles and remaining questions. *Social and Personality Psychology Compass*, *2*(1), 444–463. doi:10.1111/j.1751-9004.2007.00055.x

Chang, E.-C., Lv, Y., Chou, T.-J., He, Q., & Song, Z. (2014). Now or later: Delay's effects on post-consumption emotions and consumer loyalty. *Journal of Business Research*, *67*(7), 1368–1375. doi:10.1016/j.jbusres.2013.08.016

Chang, Y.-T., Yu, H., & Lu, H.-P. (2015). Persuasive messages, popularity cohesion, and message diffusion in social media marketing. *Journal of Business Research*, *68*(4), 777–782. doi:10.1016/j.jbusres.2014.11.027

Chattopadhyay, S., Shankar, S., Gangadhar, R. B., & Kasinathan, K. (2018). Applications of artificial intelligence in assessment for learning in schools. In *Handbook of research on digital content, mobile learning, and technology integration models in teacher education* (pp. 185–206). IGI Global. doi:10.4018/978-1-5225-2953-8.ch010

Chen, L., Gillenson, M. L., & Sherrell, D. L. (2002). Enticing online consumers: An extended technology acceptance perspective. *Information & Management, 39*(8), 705–719. doi:10.1016/S0378-7206(01)00127-6

Chen, S.-H., & Lee, K.-P. (2008). The role of personality traits and perceived values in persuasion: An elaboration likelihood model perspective on online shopping. *Social Behaviour and Personality: An International Journal, 36*(10), 1379–1399. doi:10.2224bp.2008.36.10.1379

Choi, K., Yoo, D., Kim, G., & Suh, Y. (2012). A hybrid online-product recommendation system: Combining implicit rating-based collaborative filtering and sequential pattern analysis. *Electronic Commerce Research and Applications, 11*(4), 309–317. doi:10.1016/j.elerap.2012.02.004

Coviello, L., Sohn, Y., Kramer, A. D. I., Marlow, C., Franceschetti, M., Christakis, N. A., & Fowler, J. H. (2014). Detecting emotional contagion in massive social networks. *PLoS One, 9*(3), e90315. doi:10.1371/journal.pone.0090315 PMID:24621792

Cui, Z., Xu, X., Fei, X. U. E., Cai, X., Cao, Y., Zhang, W., & Chen, J. (2020). Personalized recommendation system based on collaborative filtering for IoT scenarios. *IEEE Transactions on Services Computing, 13*(4), 685–695. doi:10.1109/TSC.2020.2964552

Darley, W. K., Blankson, C., & Luethge, D. J. (2010). Toward an integrated framework for online consumer behaviour and decision making process: A review. *Psychology & Marketing, 27*, 94–116.

Davenport, T., Guha, A., Grewal, D., & Bressgott, T. (2020). How artificial intelligence will change the future of marketing. *Journal of the Academy of Marketing Science, 48*(1), 24–42. doi:10.100711747-019-00696-0

Davis, F. D. (1989, September). Perceived usefulness, perceived ease of use, and user acceptance of information technology. *Management Information Systems Quarterly, 13*(3), 319–340. doi:10.2307/249008

Deng, X., Doll, W. J., Hendrickson, A. R., & Scazzero, J. A. (2005). A multi-group analysis of structural invariance: An illustration using the technology acceptance model. *Information & Management, 42*(5), 745–759. doi:10.1016/j.im.2004.08.001

DeSteno, D., Petty, R. E., Rucker, D. D., Wegener, D. T., & Braverman, J. (2004). Discrete emotions and persuasion: The role of emotion-induced expectancies. *Journal of Personality and Social Psychology*, *86*(1), 43–56. doi:10.1037/0022-3514.86.1.43 PMID:14717627

Eurostat. (2012). *Population statistics for Mediterranean countries*. Retrieved from https://www.eea.europa.eu/data-and-maps/daviz/sds/population -statistics-for-mediterranean-countries-eurostat/@@view

Eurostat. (2014). *Digital single market-promoting e-commerce for individuals*. Retrieved from http://ec.europa.eu/eurostat/web/products-datasets/ -/isoc_bdek_smi

Felfernig, A., Gula, B., Leitner, G., Maier, M., Melcher, R., & Teppan, E. (2008). Persuasion in Knowledge-Based Recommendation. In H. Oinas-Kukkonen, P. Hasle, M. Harjumaa, K. Segerståhl, & P. Øhrstrøm (Eds.), Lecture Notes in Computer Science: Vol. 5033. *Persuasive Technology. PERSUASIVE 2008*. Springer. doi:10.1007/978-3-540-68504-3_7

Fornell, C., & Larcker, D. F. (1981). Structural equation models with unobservable variables and measurement error: Algebra and statistics. *JMR, Journal of Marketing Research*, *18*(3), 382–388. doi:10.1177/002224378101800313

Forsythe, S., Liu, C., Shannon, D., & Gardner, L. C. (2006). Development of a scale to measure the perceived benefits and risks of online shopping. *Journal of Interactive Marketing*, *20*(2), 55–75. doi:10.1002/dir.20061

Fu, P. P., Kennedy, J., Tata, J., Yukl, G., Bond, M. H., Peng, T.-K., & Koopman, P. (2004). The impact of societal cultural values and individual social beliefs on the perceived effectiveness of managerial influence strategies: A meso approach. *Journal of International Business Studies*, *35*(4), 284–305. doi:10.1057/palgrave.jibs.8400090

Gans, H. J. (2017). The participant-observer as a human being: Observations on the personal aspects of field work. In *Institutions and the Person* (pp. 300–138). Routledge. doi:10.4324/9780203788448-23

Ganu, G., Kakodkar, Y., & Marian, A. (2013). Improving the quality of predictions using textual information in online user reviews. *Information Systems*, *38*(1), 1–15. doi:10.1016/j.is.2012.03.001

Ghasemaghaei, M., Hassanein, K., & Benbasat, I. (2019). Assessing the design choices for online recommendation agents for older adults: Older does not always mean simpler information technology. *Management Information Systems Quarterly*, *43*(1), 329–346. doi:10.25300/MISQ/2019/13947

Grewal, D., Roggeveen, A. L., & Nordfält, J. (2017). The future of retailing. *Journal of Retailing, 93*(1), 1–6. doi:10.1016/j.jretai.2016.12.008

Griskevicius, V., Goldstein, N. J., Mortensen, C. R., Sundie, J. M., Cialdini, R. B., & Kenrick, D. T. (2009). Fear and loving in Las Vegas: Evolution, emotion, and persuasion. *JMR, Journal of Marketing Research, 46*(3), 384–395. doi:10.1509/jmkr.46.3.384 PMID:19727416

Griskevicius, V., Shiota, M. N., & Neufeld, S. L. (2010). Influence of different positive emotions on persuasion processing: A functional evolutionary approach. *Emotion (Washington, D.C.), 10*(2), 190–206. doi:10.1037/a0018421 PMID:20364895

Griskevicius, V., Shiota, M. N., & Nowlis, S. M. (2010). The many shades of rose-colored glasses: An evolutionary approach to the influence of different positive emotions. *The Journal of Consumer Research, 37*(2), 238–250. doi:10.1086/651442

Ha, H.-Y., Muthaly, S. K., & Akamavi, R. K. (2010). Alternative explanations of online repurchasing behavioral intentions: A comparison study of Korean and UK young customers. *European Journal of Marketing, 44*(6), 874–904. doi:10.1108/03090561011032757

Haddock, G., Maio, G. R., Arnold, K., & Huskinson, T. (2008). Should persuasion be affective or cognitive? The moderating effects of need for affect and need for cognition. *Personality and Social Psychology Bulletin, 34*(6), 769–778. doi:10.1177/0146167208314871 PMID:18344496

Hamelin, N., Thaichon, P., Abraham, C., Driver, N., Lipscombe, J., & Pillai, J. (2020). Storytelling, the scale of persuasion and retention: A neuromarketing approach. *Journal of Retailing and Consumer Services, 55*, 102099. doi:10.1016/j.jretconser.2020.102099

Hellenic Statistical Authority. (2015). *Survey on the use of information and communication technologies by households: 2015.* Retrieved from https://www.statistics.gr/documents/20181/41c9a392-34c6-4250-87e1-0c7858f813e4

Higgins, E. T. (2000). Making a good decision: Value from fit. *The American Psychologist, 55*(11), 1217–1230. doi:10.1037/0003-066X.55.11.1217 PMID:11280936

Higgins, E. T. (2005). Value from regulatory fit. *Current Directions in Psychological Science, 14*(4), 209–213. doi:10.1111/j.0963-7214.2005.00366.x

Higgins, E. T. (2006). Value from hedonic experience and engagement. *Psychological Review, 113*(3), 439–460. doi:10.1037/0033-295X.113.3.439 PMID:16802877

Hirsh, J. B., Kang, S. K., & Bodenhausen, G. V. (2012). Personalized persuasion: Tailoring persuasive appeals to recipients' personality traits. *Psychological Science*, *23*(6), 578–581. doi:10.1177/0956797611436349 PMID:22547658

Ho, S. Y., & Bodoff, D. (2014). The effects of web personalization on user attitude and behavior: An integration of the elaboration likelihood model and consumer search theory. *Management Information Systems Quarterly*, *38*(2), 497–520. doi:10.25300/MISQ/2014/38.2.08

Holzwarth, M., Janiszewski, C., & Neumann, M. M. (2006). The influence of avatars on online consumer shopping behaviour. *Journal of Marketing*, *70*(4), 19–36. doi:10.1509/jmkg.70.4.019

Hsieh, J.-K., Hsieh, Y.-C., Chiu, H.-C., & Yang, Y.-R. (2014). Customer response to web site atmospherics: Task-relevant cues, situational involvement and PAD. *Journal of Interactive Marketing*, *28*(3), 225–236. doi:10.1016/j.intmar.2014.03.001

Iacobucci, D., Posavac, S. S., Kardes, F. R., Schneider, M., & Popovich, D. (2015). Toward a more nuanced understanding of the statistical properties of a median split. *Journal of Consumer Psychology*, *25*(4), 652–665. doi:10.1016/j.jcps.2014.12.002

Jai, T.-M. C., Burns, L. D., & King, N. J. (2013). The effect of behavioral tracking practices on consumers' shopping evaluations and repurchase intention toward trusted online retailers. *Computers in Human Behavior*, *29*(3), 901–909. doi:10.1016/j.chb.2012.12.021

Kachersky, L. (2011). Reduce content or raise price? The impact of persuasion knowledge and unit price increase tactics on retailer and product brand attitudes. *Journal of Retailing*, *87*(4), 479–488. doi:10.1016/j.jretai.2011.08.001

Kalyanaraman, S., & Sundar, S. S. (2006). The psychological appeal of personalized content in web portals: Does customization affect attitudes and behaviour? *Journal of Communication*, *56*(1), 110–132. doi:10.1111/j.1460-2466.2006.00006.x

Kaptein, M., & Eckles, D. (2012). Heterogeneity in the effects of online persuasion. *Journal of Interactive Marketing*, *26*(3), 176–188. doi:10.1016/j.intmar.2012.02.002

Kaptein, M., Markopoulos, P., De Ruyter, B., & Aarts, E. (2015). Personalizing persuasive technologies: Explicit and implicit personalization using persuasion profiles. *International Journal of Human-Computer Studies*, *77*, 38–51. doi:10.1016/j.ijhcs.2015.01.004

Kim, D., & Ammeter, T. (2014). Predicting personal information system adoption using an integrated diffusion model. *Information & Management, 51*(4), 451–464. doi:10.1016/j.im.2014.02.011

Kim, D. H., & Sung, Y. (2013). Gucci versus Old Navy: Interplay of brand personality and regulatory focus in advertising persuasion. *Psychology and Marketing, 30*(12), 1076–1087. doi:10.1002/mar.20668

Kim, H., & John, D. R. (2008). Consumer response to brand extensions: Construal level as a moderator of the importance of perceived fit. *Journal of Consumer Psychology, 18*(2), 116–126. doi:10.1016/j.jcps.2008.01.006

Kim, J., Choi, I., & Li, Q. (2021). Customer Satisfaction of Recommender System: Examining Accuracy and Diversity in Several Types of Recommendation Approaches. *Sustainability, 13*(11), 6165. doi:10.3390u13116165

Kohan, S. E. (2020). Amazon's sharing of cutting-edge technology may change the way you shop for groceries. *Forbes*. Retrieved April 4, 2020 from https://www.forbes.com/sites/shelleykohan/2020/03/15/amazons-sharing-of-cutting-edge-technology-may-change-the-way-you-shop-for-groceries/

Koo, D.-M., & Ju, S.-H. (2010). The interactional effects of atmospherics and perceptual curiosity on emotions and online shopping intention. *Computers in Human Behavior, 26*(3), 377–388. doi:10.1016/j.chb.2009.11.009

Kuo, Y.-F., & Wu, C.-M. (2012). Satisfaction and post-purchase intentions with service recovery of online shopping websites: Perspectives on perceived justice and emotions. *International Journal of Information Management, 32*(2), 127–138. doi:10.1016/j.ijinfomgt.2011.09.001

Lee, A. Y., & Aaker, J. L. (2004). Bringing the frame into focus: The influence of regulatory fit on processing fluency and persuasion. *Journal of Personality and Social Psychology, 86*(2), 205–218. doi:10.1037/0022-3514.86.2.205 PMID:14769079

Lee, A. Y., Keller, P. A., & Sternthal, B. (2010). Value from regulatory construal fit: The persuasive impact of fit between consumer goals and message concreteness. *The Journal of Consumer Research, 36*(5), 735–747. doi:10.1086/605591

Lee, K. C., & Kwon, S. (2008). Online shopping recommendation mechanism and its influence on consumer decisions and behaviours: A causal map approach. *Expert Systems with Applications, 35*(4), 1567–1574. doi:10.1016/j.eswa.2007.08.109

Lee, M.-C. (2009). Factors influencing the adoption of internet banking: An integration of TAM and TPB with perceived risk and perceived benefit. *Electronic Commerce Research and Applications*, *8*(3), 130–141. doi:10.1016/j.elerap.2008.11.006

Loukis, E., Ferro, E., & Arvanitis, S. (2017). Digital technologies in the Mediterranean region [special section]. *Telematics and Informatics*, *34*(5), 694–809. doi:10.1016/j.tele.2016.12.008

MacKenzie, S. B., & Podsakoff, P. M. (2012). Common method bias in marketing: Causes, mechanisms, and procedural remedies. *Journal of Retailing*, *88*(4), 542–555. doi:10.1016/j.jretai.2012.08.001

MacKinnon, D. P., Lockwood, C. M., & Williams, J. (2004). *Confidence limits for the indirect effect: Distribution of the product and resampling methods*. Academic Press.

Maggon, M., & Chaudhry, H. (2018). Exploring relationships between customer satisfaction and customer attitude from customer relationship management viewpoint: An empirical study of leisure travellers. *FIIB Business Review*, *7*(1), 57–65. doi:10.1177/2319714518766118

Martín, S. S., Camarero, C., & José, R. S. (2011). Does involvement matter in online shopping satisfaction and trust? *Psychology & Marketing, 28*, 145– 167.

Matthijs, N., & Radlinski, F. (2011). Personalizing web search using long term browsing history. *Proceedings of the Fourth ACM International Conference on Web search and data mining*. 10.1145/1935826.1935840

McGuire, W. J. (1968). Personality and attitude change: An information processing theory. In A. G. Greenwald, T. C. Brock, & T. M. Ostrom (Eds.), *Psychological foundation of attitudes* (pp. 171–196). Academic Press. doi:10.1016/B978-1-4832-3071-9.50013-1

McKinsey. (2019 a). *A transformation in store*. McKinsey. Retrieved March 16, 2020 from https://www.mckinsey.com/business-functions/operations/our-insights/a-transformation in-store.

Meyers-Levy, J., & Malaviya, P. (1999). Consumers' processing of persuasive advertisements: An integrative framework of persuasion theories. *Journal of Marketing*, *63*, 45–60.

Miranda, S. M., & Saunders, C. S. (2003). The social construction of meaning: An alternative perspective on information sharing. *Information Systems Research*, *14*(1), 87–106. doi:10.1287/isre.14.1.87.14765

Mosteller, J., Donthu, N., & Eroglu, S. (2014). The fluent online shopping experience. *Journal of Business Research*, *67*(11), 2486–2493. doi:10.1016/j.jbusres.2014.03.009

Nassar, N., Jafar, A., & Rahhal, Y. (2020). A novel deep multi-criteria collaborative filtering model for recommendation system. *Knowledge-Based Systems*, *187*, 104811. doi:10.1016/j.knosys.2019.06.019

Noar, S. M., Benac, C. N., & Harris, M. S. (2007). Does tailoring matter? Metaanalytic review of tailored print health behavior change interventions. *Psychological Bulletin*, *133*(4), 673–693. doi:10.1037/0033-2909.133.4.673 PMID:17592961

O'brien, R. M. (2007). A caution regarding rules of thumb for variance inflation factors. *Quality & Quantity*, *41*(5), 673–690. doi:10.100711135-006-9018-6

Oinas-Kukkonen, H., & Harjumaa, M. (2009). Persuasive systems design: Key issues, process model, and system features. *Communications of the Association for Information Systems*, *24*, 28. doi:10.17705/1CAIS.02428

Pappas, I. O., Kourouthanassis, P. E., Giannakos, M. N., & Chrissikopoulos, V. (2014). Shiny happy people buying: The role of emotions on personalized e-shopping. *Electronic Markets*, *24*(3), 193–206. doi:10.100712525-014-0153-y

Pappas, I. O., Kourouthanassis, P. E., Giannakos, M. N., & Chrissikopoulos, V. (2016). Explaining online shopping behavior with fsQCA: The role of cognitive and affective perceptions. *Journal of Business Research*, *69*(2), 794–803. doi:10.1016/j.jbusres.2015.07.010

Pappas, I. O., Kourouthanassis, P. E., Giannakos, M. N., & Lekakos, G. (2017). The interplay of online shopping motivations and experiential factors on personalized e-commerce: A complexity theory approach. *Telematics and Informatics*, *34*(5), 730–742. doi:10.1016/j.tele.2016.08.021

Pateli, A. G. (2011). E-, M-business status in the Mediterranean region. *International Journal of E-Services and Mobile Applications*, *3*, 1–91.

Peck, J., & Wiggins, J. (2006). It just feels good: Customers' affective response to touch and its influence on persuasion. *Journal of Marketing*, *70*, 56–69.

Petty, R., & Cacioppo, J. (2012). *Communication and persuasion: Central and peripheral routes to attitude change*. Springer Science & Business Media.

Petty, R. E., Fabrigar, L. R., & Wegener, D. T. (2003). Emotional factors in attitudes and persuasion. In R. J. Davidson, K. R. Scherer, & H. H. Goldsmith (Eds.), *Handbook of affective sciences* (pp. 752–772). Series in affective science. Oxford University Press.

Pillai, K. G., & Kumar, V. (2012). Differential effects of value consciousness and coupon proneness on consumers' persuasion knowledge of pricing tactics. *Journal of Retailing*, *88*(1), 20–33. doi:10.1016/j.jretai.2011.03.002

Podsakoff, P. M., MacKenzie, S. B., Lee, J.-Y., & Podsakoff, N. P. (2003). Common method biases in behavioural research: A critical review of the literature and recommended remedies. *The Journal of Applied Psychology*, *88*(5), 879–903. doi:10.1037/0021-9010.88.5.879 PMID:14516251

Psychology. (2010). 6th ed.). Worth Publishers.

Putrevu, S. (2014). Effects of mood and elaboration on processing and evaluation of goal-framed appeals. *Psychology and Marketing*, *31*(2), 134–146. doi:10.1002/mar.20682

Riegger, A. S., Klein, J. F., Merfeld, K., & Henkel, S. (2021). Technology-enabled personalization in retail stores: Understanding drivers and barriers. *Journal of Business Research*, *123*, 140–155. doi:10.1016/j.jbusres.2020.09.039

Scherer, K. R., Shuman, V., Fontaine, J. R., & Soriano, C. (2013). The GRID meets the Wheel: Assessing emotional feeling via self-report. In J. R. J. Fontaine, K. R. Scherer, & C. Soriano (Eds.), *Components of Emotional Meaning: A Sourcebook* (pp. 281–298). Oxford University Press. doi:10.1093/acprof:oso/9780199592746.003.0019

See, Y. H. M., Petty, R. E., & Fabrigar, L. R. (2008). Affective and cognitive meta-bases of attitudes: Unique effects on information interest and persuasion. *Journal of Personality and Social Psychology*, *94*(6), 938–955. doi:10.1037/0022-3514.94.6.938 PMID:18505310

Setia, P., Venkatesh, V., & Joglekar, S. (2013). Leveraging digital technologies: How information quality leads to localized capabilities and customer service performance. *Management Information Systems Quarterly*, *37*(2), 565–590. doi:10.25300/MISQ/2013/37.2.11

Shang, R.-A., Chen, Y.-C., & Shen, L. (2005). Extrinsic versus intrinsic motivations for consumers to shop on-line. *Information & Management*, *42*(3), 401–413. doi:10.1016/j.im.2004.01.009

Silveira, T., Zhang, M., Lin, X., Liu, Y., & Ma, S. (2019). How good your recommender system is? A survey on evaluations in recommendation. *International Journal of Machine Learning and Cybernetics*, *10*(5), 813–831. doi:10.100713042-017-0762-9

Steinmann, S., Mau, G., & Schramm-Klein, H. (2015). Brand communication success in online consumption communities: An experimental analysis of the effects of communication style and brand pictorial representation. *Psychology and Marketing*, *32*(3), 356–371. doi:10.1002/mar.20784

Tam, K. Y., & Ho, S. Y. (2005). Web personalization as a persuasion strategy: An elaboration likelihood model perspective. *Information Systems Research*, *16*(3), 271–291. doi:10.1287/isre.1050.0058

Tam, K. Y., & Ho, S. Y. (2006). Understanding the impact of web personalization on user information processing and decision outcomes. *Management Information Systems Quarterly*, *30*(4), 865–890. doi:10.2307/25148757

Tandon, U., Kiran, R., & Sah, A. (2017). Analyzing customer satisfaction: Users perspective towards online shopping. *Nankai Business Review International*, *8*(3), 266–288. doi:10.1108/NBRI-04-2016-0012

Teeny, J. D., Siev, J. J., Briñol, P., & Petty, R. E. (2021). A review and conceptual framework for understanding personalized matching effects in persuasion. *Journal of Consumer Psychology*, *31*(2), 382–414. doi:10.1002/jcpy.1198

Thompson, D. V., & Hamilton, R. W. (2006). The effects of information processing mode on consumers' responses to comparative advertising. *The Journal of Consumer Research*, *32*(4), 530–540. doi:10.1086/500483

Thompson, D. V., & Malaviya, P. (2013). Consumer-generated ads: Does awareness of advertising co-creation help or hurt persuasion? *Journal of Marketing*, *77*(3), 33–47. doi:10.1509/jm.11.0403

Thongpapanl, N., & Ashraf, A. R. (2011). Enhancing online performance through website content and personalization. *Journal of Computer Information Systems*, *52*, 3–13.

Turk, T., Blažic, B. J., & Trkman, P. (2008). Factors and sustainable strategies ˇ fostering the adoption of broadband communications in an enlarged European Union. *Technological Forecasting and Social Change*, *75*(7), 933–951. doi:10.1016/j.techfore.2007.08.004

Van Noort, G., Voorveld, H. A., & Van Reijmersdal, E. A. (2012). Interactivity in brand web sites: Cognitive, affective, and behavioural responses explained by consumers' online flow experience. *Journal of Interactive Marketing*, *26*(4), 223–234. doi:10.1016/j.intmar.2011.11.002

Venkatesh, V., Morris, M. G., Davis, G. B., & Davis, F. D. (2003). User acceptance of information technology: Toward a unified view. *Management Information Systems Quarterly*, *27*(3), 425–478. doi:10.2307/30036540

Verhagen, T., & van Dolen, W. (2011). The influence of online store beliefs on consumer online impulse buying: A model and empirical application. *Information & Management*, *48*(8), 320–327. doi:10.1016/j.im.2011.08.001

Walsh, G., Shiu, E., Hassan, L. M., Michaelidou, N., & Beatty, S. E. (2011). Emotions, store-environmental cues, store-choice criteria, and marketing outcomes. *Journal of Business Research*, *64*(7), 737–744. doi:10.1016/j.jbusres.2010.07.008

Wang, Y. J., Minor, M. S., & Wei, J. (2011). Aesthetics and the online shopping environment: Understanding consumer responses. *Journal of Retailing*, *87*(1), 46–58. doi:10.1016/j.jretai.2010.09.002

Wu, H. (2021, February). Application of Collaborative Filtering Personalized Recommendation Algorithms to Website Navigation. *Journal of Physics: Conference Series*, *1813*(1), 012048. doi:10.1088/1742-6596/1813/1/012048

Xu, H., Luo, X. R., Carroll, J. M., & Rosson, M. B. (2011). The personalization privacy paradox: An exploratory study of decision making process for location-aware marketing. *Decision Support Systems*, *51*(1), 42–52. doi:10.1016/j.dss.2010.11.017

Xu, J. D., Benbasat, I., & Cenfetelli, R. T. (2013). Integrating service quality with system and information quality: An empirical test in the e-service context. *Management Information Systems Quarterly*, *37*(3), 777–794. doi:10.25300/MISQ/2013/37.3.05

Yi, Y., & Gong, T. (2013). Customer value co-creation behaviour: Scale development and validation. *Journal of Business Research*, *66*(9), 1279–1284. doi:10.1016/j.jbusres.2012.02.026

Zhang, L., Wei, Q., Zhang, L., Wang, B., & Ho, W. H. (2020). Diversity balancing for two-stage collaborative filtering in recommender systems. *Applied Sciences (Basel, Switzerland)*, *10*(4), 1257. doi:10.3390/app10041257

KEY TERMS AND DEFINITIONS

Artificial Intelligence: The field of artificial intelligence is concerned with creating smart machines that can perform various tasks autonomously.

Consumer's Attitude: A consumer's attitude describes (1) his or her beliefs about, (2) feelings about, and (3) intentions toward a particular object.

Consumer's Satisfaction: A consumer's satisfaction is linked to their various behavioural intentions and beliefs about an object. A satisfied customer is a measure of how happy they are with a company's products and services.

Hyper-Personalization: Hyper-personalization is the process of creating personalized experiences for individual customers. It uses data and AI to create customized experiences that are targeted to their individual needs.

Personalization: The goal of personalization is to tailor a business's interactions with customers based on information about them. By personalizing services, businesses can tailor electronic commerce interactions between them and their customers. Personalization is a wide concept that covers various aspects of marketing. It is mainly focused on the execution of personalized marketing strategies and methods to create various benefits for the customer. These include better products, better service, and more communication.

Personalized Recommendation: A personalized recommendation system uses user behaviour to determine which items a customer might want to buy or avoid purchasing. These are items that have been frequently viewed, considered, or purchased with the one the customer is currently considering. It uses the user's past purchase history to suggest products that are relevant to their current situation.

Persuasion: Persuasion is the process by which a person's actions or attitudes are influenced by others. It is the process of influencing a person's behaviour or attitudes.

Recommender System: A recommender system is a computer program that uses its recommendations to help users make informed buying decisions based on their preference, browsing history and their buying pattern. Online product recommendation (OPR) is a strategy that enables products to be dynamically populated with customer data such as browsing history and context. This strategy provides a personalized shopping experience.

Chapter 3
Sustainable Development: A New Frontier for SMEs

Daniele Giordino
https://orcid.org/0000-0001-5507-6270
University of Turin, Italy

Edoardo Crocco
University of Turin, Italy

ABSTRACT

Climate change, pollutants, sustainable development, and public health have become increasingly more relevant issues that continuously get addressed and discussed by governments and entities all over the globe. Through the adoption of policies and recyclable methods, they hope to encourage and aid the responsible consumption of natural resources so as to reduce the creation of waste. Furthermore, the generation of sustainable communities is encouraged so as to safeguard and protect the population's health against the risks associated with different types of pollutants. To support SMEs in the adoption of sustainable practices, this chapter aims to introduce, guide, and provide some useful tools that can then be utilized by readers and professionals operating within SMEs to maximize the effectiveness of their sustainability approaches and tools while also providing knowledge on how the implementation of sustainable practices could be integrated within their businesses.

DOI: 10.4018/978-1-7998-7793-6.ch003

Copyright © 2022, IGI Global. Copying or distributing in print or electronic forms without written permission of IGI Global is prohibited.

INTRODUCTION

Climate change, pollutants, sustainable development and public health have become increasingly more relevant issues which continuously get addressed and discussed by governments and entities all over the globe. Such entities and countries aim to establish sustainable development policies which discuss and dwell on the previously reported issues. Through the adoption of policies and recyclable methods they hope to encourage and aid the responsible consumption of natural resources so as to reduce the creation of waste. Furthermore, the generation of sustainable communities is encouraged so as to safeguard and protect the population's health against the risks associated with different types of pollutants. However, the proposed and adopted policies not only serve as guidelines to countries and public entities. They are also made available to ensure that businesses contribute and integrate such policies to promote the integration of environmental concerns and sustainable development practices within their business (European Commission, 2021).

However, there has been an increased focus amongst governments around the globe to promote further development and expand the adoption rate of environmental development and policies amongst small and medium enterprises (SMEs). SMEs are often responsible for the majority of the environmental impact of specific regions. For example, Hillary (2017) presented evidence which suggests that SMEs account for 70% circa of industrial pollution worldwide. Furthermore, Calogirou *et al* (2010) offered evidence which suggests that Small to Medium Sized Enterprises (SMEs) contribute up to 64% of the environmental impact of the European Union. SMEs have become driving forces of the economy. Consequently it would be blindsided not to address such entities and promote their involvement within the social and environmental issues. Some countries have recognized SMEs importance and have made an effort to implement and better represent SMEs and how their contribution could benefit the local communities as well as the environment (Pimenova and Van Der Vorst, 2004, Blundel *et al,* 2013).

Despite the aforementioned figures and the potential benefits associated with the implementation of sustainability management tools (Cantele & Zardini, 2020; Testa, Boiral & Iraldo, 2018) SMEs struggle to implement and integrate sustainability within their business. The tools and instruments discovered and proposed by the literature and professionals all over the globe are often unknown to small and medium enterprises' owners (Johnson & Schaltegger, 2015).

Consequently, to support SMEs in the adoption of sustainable practices, this chapter aims to introduce, guide and provide some useful tools which can then be utilized by readers and professionals operating within SMEs to maximize the effectiveness of their sustainability approaches while also providing knowledge on how the implementation of sustainable practices could be integrated within their businesses. To do so we aim to conduct a narrative literature review which addresses the following question: Which specific sustainability management tools have been proposed and observed by previous researchers within SMEs' context?

Furthermore, few recommendations will be made based on what peer reviewed articles have found to be beneficial to SMEs' sustainable development. Moreover, the role of disclosure and reporting will be analyzed to further understand how such elements and practices affect stakeholders perceptions, as well as, firms' competitive advantage. Finally, barriers to SMEs' adoption of sustainable practices will be discussed to provide insights into which factors are detrimental to the wider adoption of sustainable development of SMEs.

The paper is structured as follows. Firstly, we present and discuss Corporate Social Responsibility and Sustainability reporting as well as why SMEs should adopt sustainable management techniques. Secondly, we consider multiple tools utilised to implement and enhance the sustainability management within SMEs. The instruments and techniques discussed in this section of the chapter are withdrawn from previous field studies that have been published in peer reviewed journals and other forms of professional publications. Thirdly, we discuss some of the barriers to sustainability management implementation within SMEs' business processes that have been found to be materials by previous field studies. Finally, we discuss future research avenues and how the sustainability management implementation research field is evolving and developing.

Corporate Social Responsibility and Sustainability Reporting: A Matter of Perspectives

Over the years, we have witnessed a growing interest from businesses towards reporting and disclosure, as most realise that it should go beyond simple accountability. Corporate Social Responsibility (CSR) requires business to be responsible for social, environmental, and financial aspects of their daily operational life (Elkington, 1998). By the same token, demands on internal governance and performance excellence are inevitable (Huang, Pepper & Bowrey, 2014). This underlines a strict connection between performance and sustainability, on financially, socially and environmentally perspectives (Mintz, 2011). However, as few authors have pointed out, the field of sustainability is still rapidly evolving and there are aspects that are yet to be fully explored and understood. For instance, Assunção, Luca & Vasconcelos (2016) have pointed out the topic of financial performance and CSR is complex and requires further mapping, especially in relation to the financial implications of sustainability research. In other words, sustainability must be analyzed using the most acceptable financial measurement of the company's future performance by examining associations between the elements of sustainable reporting towards future share performance.

Sustainability reporting is becoming a global trend and an obligation in current times and this provides a challenge to managers (KPMG, 2011). The use of balanced scorecards has been increasingly utilised for the display and reporting of sustainability data. But why should organizations account for their economic, social, and environmental impacts to improve their sustainability performance? Many authors have explored the topic and have been providing various answers. Some motivations found in the literature are based upon a variety of theories. Hansen and Schaltegger (2016), for instance, elaborated a list of different approaches that could be used in regards to the topic of sustainability, highlighting how the perspective could be instrumental, social, political and even normative. They also highlighted the drivers behind the aforementioned approaches. Starting from the instrumental perspective, that sees organizations make use of sustainability performance in an effort to reach their operational and corporate goals (Hansen and Schaltegger, 2016). These goals can be totally upfront and standardized, for instance a set amount of profits to be achieved, an ideal market square or a new market segment to be conquered.

Alongside this approach, the strategic stakeholder theory goes beyond the concept of shareholder (Freeman, 1994, 2010; Freeman et al., 2004) and embraces a much larger perspective, considering the entire set of stakeholders surrounding the organization (Mitchell et al., 1997).

Similarly to the instrumental perspective, the principal agent theory highlights information asymmetries in regards to the relationship between an organization and its stakeholders (Hahn and Kühnen, 2013; Pratt and Zeckhauser, 1985; Ross, 1973; Spence, 1974). However, sustainability reporting (SR) can be used as an instrument to reduce those information asymmetries which is ideal for satisfying stakeholders' requests for information (Comyns and Figge, 2015; Hahn and Kühnen, 2013). That is why SR can become a control mechanism to match diverging interests between stakeholders and the management and consequently a valuable tool (Frias-Aceituno et al., 2013; Lee and Maxfield, 2015). The greater degree of trust between stakeholders and the organization can lead to long term performance benefits, but it is not an overnight effort as it requires constant adjustments and will to improve (Ferrero-Ferrero et al., 2018).

Overall, SR serves to create transparency in regards to the day to day operations of a company. This is particularly important for influential or strategically relevant stakeholder groups (Freeman, 2010; Hahn and Kühnen, 2013; Mitchell et al., 1997; Van der Laan Smith et al., 2005). In addition, organizations have to integrate stakeholders' expectations and values within the organizational control mechanisms to address them in a sufficient way (Durden, 2008; Garcia et al., 2016; Caliskan, 2014).

The strict interplay between SR and MCS is not purely formal, but it does have an effect on the day-to-day operational decisions. In fact, sustainability often translates into a series of Key Performance Indicators (KPI) that drastically change the way a company operates in order to achieve said goals (Hristov & Chirico, 2019). For instance, Cristea & Cristea (2021) have identified a number of KPIs related to packaging and they have highlighted the importance of environmental protection and customer satisfaction in their research. Previously, Adams & Frost (2008)

have also pointed out how organisations have been actively integrating the aforementioned topics into their strategic thinking and decision making processes, in an effort to become more aware and proactive overall.

Finally, the social perspective of SR somewhat ties with what has been said previously, as companies are willing to meet their stakeholders' expectations and contribute to society with their work. Social Sustainability explores said topic, which is growing in relevance despite still somewhat lagging behind the other major aspects of SR (Eizenberg & Jabareen, 2017). Although the topic of the social consequences to SR has been explored multiple times in the literature already (Gray, 2006), the correlation between SR and MCS is still a source of debate for authors. For instance, Hansen & Schaltegger (2016) highlighted the fact SR is not able to strictly increase a company's performance in itself, rather its true strength resides in the fact it allows for a quick reaction to society's expectations for the company.

Sustainability issues are becoming increasingly important in organizations as their disclosures to stakeholders are being addressed as moral duty, rather than standard bureaucracy. This is where normative stakeholder theory comes into play (Zakhem & Palmer, 2017), as opposed to the strategic perspective of stakeholder theory which focuses more on the ties between stakeholders expectations and competitive advantage for the company in question. This model can be perceived as an alternative to the aforementioned perspective, albeit the normative stakeholder theory appears to be much less relevant both in the literature and in the business world (Dawid et al., 2019). However, society has been increasingly putting more and more emphasis on the moral expectations they have from major companies. As such, companies and managers alike feel like they have ethical obligations towards society and its individual members (Kim et al., 2019).

We wrap up this theoretical excursus by highlighting the strict correlation between MCS and SR. Sustainability and strategy go hand in hand, in a way that really underlines the importance of each topic and how they are interconnected with one another (Bui & De Villiers, 2017).

Given the increasing importance of SMEs in the world's economy, however, the proverbial ball is now in their court as much as it is in the larger companies' one. What can they do to adopt a more sustainable approach to their daily activities and how can this strategic decision impact their performance? We will attempt to find answers in the next paragraph.

Why Should SMEs Adopt Sustainable Management?

It has been found that SMEs' approach CSR in a way that focuses on the ethical aspects of it rather than the economic aspects (Jamali *et al*, 2009). SMEs often do not attempt to communicate how they take action when it comes to their sustainable practices due to their low level of visibility and due to the fact that they often perceive their environmental impact to be limited or negligible (El Baz *et al*, 2016). However, Agan *et al* (2013) has highlighted how environmental management tools have a positive effect on performance. Furthermore, they have shown evidence which suggests that cost savings and increased competitiveness can be obtained through the adoption of environmental practices (Bagur-Femenias *et al*, 2013).

It has been discovered that sustainable management can have a positive impact on the SMEs' financial and social performance (Kopnina & Blewitt, 2018). By doing so, companies have the opportunity to strengthen their brand reputation as well as their ability to generate profit (Sen *et al*, 2006). SMEs often adopt sustainable management as a way to gather society's favour since they have the opportunity to show how they have reduced their environmental impact (Franco and Rodrigues, 2019). Furthermore, such practices permit an improved and more sustainable development of the economic and social aspects of the area in which these SMEs operate (Gomes *et al*, 2015).

Considering the aforementioned motives, the necessary question becomes: Which tools can be utilised by SMEs to foster their sustainability practices? In the following portions of the chapter we will try to further explore some of the tools that have been found to nurture sustainability practices.

Social Benchmarking

The growth of global competition has fuelled the need for companies to analyse competitors' strengths and achievements. By doing so, firms hope to utilise such analysis to promote their own development and competitiveness. Hence why, benchmarking has become one of the most important instruments in the analysis and promotion of different activities of corporations (Klychova *et al*, 2017). Benchmarking can be defined as a tool in which the external and internal environment in which the company operates are analysed and utilised by a firm which objective is to learn and develop through the study of the "best examples" (Camp, 1989; Carpinetti & De Melo, 2002; Klychova *et al*, 2017). The main classes of benchmarking found in the literature are as follows (Camp, 1989):

- Internal benchmarking which compares the performances of different departments, units or business units within one organization.

- Functional benchmarking which aims to compare a business function between multiple organizations which operate in the same industry.
- Competitive benchmarking. Its scope is to compare the company's performance with its direct product or service rivals.
- Generic benchmarking which emulates what functional benchmarking does. However instead of assessing corporations within the same industry, it evaluates the best firms disregarding the sector in which they operate.

The procedure utilized so to conduct a benchmark is well detailed and described in the economic literature and consists of four different stages: The first stage is considered to be a preparatory stage in which the company forms a team which task is to determine the object of benchmarking as well as establish the relevance and importance of the objectives of the company. In this stage problems and areas of interest are established (Klychova *et al*, 2017). In the second stage the company needs to collect data while also examining said data so as to have a greater understanding of the activities, works, and products which are under scrutiny. In the third stage deviances need to be identified so that there is the opportunity to create and implement recommendations based on the previous data analysis. Finally, in the fourth and last stage the company has to adapt its processes. To do so the creation and implementation of a program is developed.

It is important to note that during a benchmarking process, the aim is to establish optimal parameters of activities which in most cases belong to multiple firms and actors. There is no selection of a single firm which is considered to be the "best" within that specific sector, production etc.

The use of benchmarking can be applied to evaluate the best practices related to the social and environmental aspects of firms. However, Johnson (2015) reported that social benchmarking had an awareness rate of 7,56% and an adoption rate of 2,33% while ecological benchmarking had an awareness rate of 9,30% and an adoption rate of 1,16% amongst German SMEs. These results suggest how this tool has been under-utilized in the past.

Through the application of social and environmental benchmarking companies will have the possibility to set the gap between the leaders and their own firm creating a standard for comparison. By doing so it would be possible to improve their own operation, resource management, actions etc. Therefore, benchmarking can be utilized as a test of excellence which permits the establishment of socio and environmental indicators through which a firm can set solutions and associated changing approaches to achieve leading success (Klychova *et al*, 2017).

Balanced Scorecard in Sustainability Reporting

The concept of the balanced scorecard was developed in the early 1990s as a new performance approach that focuses on corporate strategy in four perspectives (Kaplan and Norton, 1992). The four perspectives are financial, customer, learning and growth and internal business processes. In each perspective, key performance indicators (KPIs) are selected in a way that relates to the organisation's strategic vision. Kaplan & Norton (1992) suggest the important role of KPIs for managers and companies, as they allow for a constant, reliable, real time perspective on the company's progress at any given point in time. The Balanced Scorecard, if combined with sustainability management logics could potentially open up further opportunities and managerial perspectives, while at the same time integrating the entire system into one single, specific tool.

Figge et al. (2002) demonstrate how the balanced scorecard with associated perspectives and sustainability with associated aspects have a common grounding, in that they are both financial and non-financial KPIs. Whilst practices that are beneficial for society and the environment may appear to negatively impact corporate profitability, the use of a balanced scorecard can result in a clear picture of the relationship among sustainable practices, corporate strategies and profitability (Butler et al., 2011). One of the ways of integrating sustainability aspects into the balanced scorecard is to include the various sustainability aspects under the four existing perspectives, like traditional strategic aspects would usually be incorporated (Figge et al., 2002). In this way the relative economic, environmental and social sustainability aspects are then mapped onto the existing four perspectives. A second method described by Figge et al. (2002) and Butler et al. (2011) is to introduce an additional fifth, non-market perspective for integrating environmental and social strategies into an organisation.

The study by Eklund (2020) reveals multi-disciplinary overlooked research paths on the topic. For instance, in the area of social sciences, the ethical and normative perspective of the Sustainability Balanced Scorecard (SBSC), the cultural and sociological impacts on SBSC, internal actors, psychological and behavioral aspects of SBSC can be investigated from the assumptions of normative theory, business ethics and virtue ethics theory, accountability, legitimacy, socio-cultural, and psychology theories, respectively. Moreover, the economic and socio-political aspects of SBSC, such as the implementation of SBSC in the public sector and its impact on public sector reforms and economy in developing and developed countries, can be researched further in line with economic and socio-political theories. In the discipline of business and management, theory-driven and mixed-method studies can be performed in the areas of institutional entrepreneurship, corporate governance structures, executive compensation, management and employee motivation and synergy, community-driven success, organizational culture, and value creation.

Jassem et al. (2021) provide a comprehensive review of the current state of the art of sustainability reporting and Balanced Scorecard science. Their findings indicate a lack of consensus on establishing a clear linkage on the relationship between SBSC architecture and environmental performance outcomes. As a result, a holistic conceptual framework where SBSC knowledge acts as a mediator and presence of experts as a moderator may be able to provide a more consistent relationship between SBSC architecture and environmental performance outcomes. The goal of their research is to propose a model for future research regarding the link between SBSC and environmental performance outcomes with expert managers acting as moderators and SBSC knowledge acting as a mediator.

Life Cycle Assessment

The Life cycle assessment (LCA) has been defined as an environmental management tool which enables users to identify and quantify the environmental impact that a specific product, process, or activity might have throughout its entire life cycle (Dewulf & Van Langenhove, 2006). This management tool has been used in some industrial sectors for quite a while. However, after the legislative acts of EU Eco-Management and Audit Schemes, ISO 14000 Environmental Management Systems and the EC Directive on Integrated Pollution Prevention and Control the diffusion of the LCA tool through the adoption of life cycle thinking within various companies has drastically increased (Dewulf & Van Langenhove, 2006).

The LCA helps evaluate the inputs, outputs, and environmental impacts that a specific product, process or activity might have during its life cycle. According to ISO 14040, the process necessary to evaluate a product LCA should follow the four phases listed below (Dewulf & Van Langenhove, 2006):

1. Goal and Scope Definition: To conduct an LCA it is necessary to firstly establish who is going to be the final user of this methodology outcome. LAC is often used in manufacturing processes so that the company has the opportunity to apply it internally to reduce the environmental impacts of that specific product. However, LCA could also be a useful tool for the external promotion of the company's environmental practices. Consequently, the LCA could be targeted at customers or other external users for marketing purposes. During this first step it is necessary for the company to review and analyse the quality of data by checking the consistency, completeness, representativeness, and reproducibility of said data. Finally, this phase needs to address assumptions and limitations of the LCA study.

2. Inventory Analysis: The second phase involves the analysis of environmental liabilities which could cause potential arm to the air and liquid effluents. Additionally, during this phase it is necessary for the company to address the solid discharges that the manufacturing of said product might cause. To do so the company should utilise the life cycle inventory (LCI) which analyses all of the previously listed factors. During this process, environmental burdens are identified and quantified. If the process under study produces more than one functional output, then it is necessary for the company to allocate the environmental burdens among all said outputs. The allocation of an appropriate method is crucial since it will normally influence the results of the LCA.
3. Impact Assessment: The main purpose of this third phase is to translate the environmental burdens previously identified in the LCI into potential environmental impacts. To do so, it is necessary to follow these three steps: firstly, selection of impact categories, category indicators and LCIA models, secondly, classification and thirdly, characterization (Dewulf & Van Langenhove, 2006).
4. Interpretation: The objective of the final phase is to analyse the results previously obtained and provide evidence on the limitations and recommendations of the previous findings. The analysis carried out in the previous phases enabled the identification of the most important issues allowing the company to target the areas which require higher levels of improvement or innovation. During the fourth phase it is possible to carry out a sensitivity analysis which might help identify how the data gaps might affect the final results of the study. Basically, the sensitivity analysis indicates the level of reliability of the final results.

The findings of this analysis will then be reported in accordance with the use of the study.

Despite the benefits of LCA, there are several issues which prevent the adoption of said model such as cultural, practical, and methodological barriers (Almeida, Alvarenga & Sartor, 2019). Firstly, there is the need for greater diffusion of the information in relation to LCA and its use within industries (Almeida, Alvarenga & Sartor, 2019). The lack of awareness and knowledge which surrounds LCA opposes one of the greatest obstacles to its diffusion (Almeida, Alvarenga & Sartor, 2019). Additionally, researchers have reported how LCA fails to take into account the possible trade-offs between environmental protection and the social and economic aspects of the production life cycle (Dreyer, Hauschild & Schierbeck, 2006). Another fundamental issue related to LCA is the fact that it is a local technique that needs to be constantly adapted and updated (Reap *et al*, 2008a). For example, a change in the technology employed does affect many environmental stressors which need to be taken into account when completing such a model. Other factors that might limit the applicability of the LCA model are: physical flows, locations, facilities and production lines (Reap *et al*, 2008a). Additionally, the LCA fails to consider changes in land usage (Reap *et al*, 2008b). Some land use can be included in some categories while other aspects might require new categories which need to be implemented within the LCA model. Some infrastructures utilised in the production of a specific item, such as mines, farms and factories have the potential to reduce biodiversity and soil quality (Canals *et al*,2006). Not only, such structures might drastically change the hydrological patterns resulting in climate changes (Foley *et al*, 2005; Turner *et al*, 2001).

Eco-Mapping

Eco- mapping is a visual toolbox which allows employees to get involved in environmental practices. Furthermore, it allows the companies which adopt it to set a stronger foundation to the implementation of ISO 14001 (Korojiva & Voronova, 2007). Eco-mapping is an instrument that allows SMEs to consider their day-to-day activities by gathering useful information which require an immediate environmental response. Most of the details provided by the eco-map are location based and that allows the company which adopts such a tool to have an on-site environmental review. Eco-mapping can be considered an action-based tool; however, it does also expand the company's awareness in relation to how some activities negatively affect environmental practices (Korojiva & Voronova, 2007).

Eco-mapping is considered to be fit for SMEs since it is an inexpensive system that requires little time and resources, however it presents a clear picture of the company's environmental situation (Korojiva & Voronova, 2007). Additionally, eco-mapping assists SMEs in understanding environmental problems related to different activities (Korojiva & Voronova, 2007). Multiple copies of this plan are made for the various areas of the company's operations such as: energy map, risks map, water map, material and resource flow map (Burke & Gaughran; 2006). Eco-mapping further encourages the participation of staff since it is possible to have time allocated to mini audits which allow employees to express their opinions on how the current efforts might impact the environmental sustainability implementation (Burke & Gaughran, 2006).

Due to the visual form, Eco-map helps have a fast and adequate analysis of the environmental problem observed. It includes specific symbols which help visualize the problem. However, part of the interest that lies within eco-mapping is related to the fact that it is a participatory learning process. Consequently, it gives the opportunity to immediately assess and take positive actions which are drivers of concrete results (Korojiva & Voronova, 2007). Furthermore, this toolbox permits

SMEs to review how efficiently their business is utilizing their resources (Korojiva & Voronova, 2007).

Eco mapping is not a well known tool as shown by Matthew P. Johnson (2015). In his study he discovered how, out of the 36 environmental management tools discussed, eco-mapping was in the 36th place for awareness and level of implementation. However, it has been proved to be a reliable and effective tool which has been applied to multiple realities located in Russia, Hungary, UK, France, Belgium, Italy, Estonia and Canada (Korojiva & Voronova, 2007).

EPM-Kompas Software

It is extremely important for a company to analyse the performance and results achieved through the usage of its management system. Consequently, it is deemed to be important for a company to analyse and identify the actual results of their environmental management. The concept of environmental performance measurement (EPM) permits the assessment as well as the recording of the company's environmental results. EPM-Kompas is an instrument which assists SMEs in the environmental performance measurement by attempting to solve the difficulties related to the strategic environment information, management, and decision-making processes in SMEs (Günther& Kaulich, 2005).

The tool fosters strategic actions through the analysis of environmental, as well as company's information. It is necessary for the firm to consider the weaknesses and strengths of the company while also identifying the threats and opportunities of the environment in which the SME operates. Furthermore, the EPM-Kompas must set the objectives while also improving the strategy resulting in a model which needs to be of a timely manner.

The main idea behind the EPM-Kompas is to control the corporate environmental performance while also integrating it with the SME's decision-making process. However, it is important to acknowledge that such an instrument does also support the analysis of the firm and process information, investment appraisal and ecological breakdown of efficiency as well as identify which performance drivers affect SMEs' environmental performance (Günther& Kaulich, 2005).

The EPM-Kompas instrument supports strategic thinking in SMEs when considering the environmental management and environmental performance of that company (Günther& Kaulich, 2005) and it does that by: reducing the complexity of significant environmental aspects, identifying threats and opportunities through the analysis of current environmental topics, by providing SMEs with key environmental factors on which they need to focus on effective measures, supporting the data collection and structuring as well as supporting the decision making process through the analysis of quantitative environmental assessments (Günther& Kaulich, 2005).

Barriers to SMEs' Adoption of Sustainable Practices

The current literature has identified three main factors which act as barriers to SMEs adoption of sustainable practices. Several studies show how SMEs usually have a lack of resources and time which they can then allocate to the development of environmental policies (Côté *et al*, 2006; Halila, 2007). Moreover, the limited resources available within SMEs equate to a lower degree of training that can be utilised so to form expertise amongst employees. In order to implement sustainable practices, SMEs necessitate specific and technical skills (Aragon-Correa *et al*, 2008; Christmann, 2000; Hart, 1995). Furthermore, managers also suffer from this deficiency of resources since they often lack the access to informational tools about environmental innovation (Biondi, Frey & Iraldo, 2000). The skills and information necessary to successfully manage sustainability issues are onerous to acquire and difficult to develop (Boiral *et al*, 2019).

Secondly, the lack of time and resources further affects the ability of SMEs to adopt sustainability practices since their employees are usually responsible for multiple activities and business functions (Brunninge *et al*, 2007; Hewitt-Dundas, 2006; Smith *et al*, 2007). Consequently, it becomes difficult to add new tasks to the already busy work schedule of SMEs' employees (Johnson & Schaltegger, 2015). Additionally, this is particularly difficult since sustainability development is perceived to be a less urgent issue in comparison to the organization's core operations and critical priorities (Biondi *et al*, 2000; Journeault, Perron & Vallières 2021). However, it has been reported by previous research that the tendency to focus on operational and core issues within a business is damaging to the strategic planning of the company (Temtime, 2002). Moreover,, SMEs have limited financial resources and that equates to an increased difficulty when it comes to investments whose aim is to acquire sustainable tools, equipment and practices (Brammer *et al*, 2012). SMEs often lack the working capital and funds to access sustainable technologies which may often be profitable to the business (Journeault, Perron & Vallières 2021). Another aspect associated with this element is the lack of awareness on which tools and instruments exist for SMEs to implement and adopt sustainability practices. Due to their time constraints, managers and professionals are often unaware of the tools available (Johnson & Schaltegger, 2015).

Thirdly, managers are often unaware of the social and environmental impacts that SMEs have (Brammer *et al*, 2012; Johnson and Schaltegger, 2015). Consequently, they do not feel the need to prioritize such practices since they think that there would be no need to engage in such social and environmental improvements (Parker *et al*, 2009).

Moreover, managers are often misinformed about the costs and benefits associated with sustainable practices. SMEs often lack the tools and information which are necessary to effectively evaluate how such costs and benefits would impact the firm (Friedman and Miles, 2002). In fact, many SMEs' managers are often misinformed and perceive sustainability management as a costly investment for their firms (Hilary, 2004; Revell & Rutherford, 2003).

Therefore, managers often want to make sure that the adoption of sustainable development practices will be beneficial and profitable to their businesses. Although, the points previously presented became a main obstacle to the adoption of social and environmental practices.

In conclusion, the three main barriers to the adoption of sustainability within SMEs that have been identified by the literature are: the lack of awareness of the impact of sustainability, lack of skills and lack of time and resources (Journeault, Perron & Vallières 2021).

FUTURE RESEARCH DIRECTIONS

Discuss future and emerging trends. Provide insight about the future of the book's theme from the perspective of the chapter focus. Viability of a paradigm, model, implementation issues of proposed programs, etc., may be included in this section. If appropriate, suggest future research opportunities within the domain of the topic.

Some of the emerging trends that we have been able to identify are:

- industry 4.0 and the advent of digital technologies in the implementation of sustainability management tools within SMEs context
- Covid-19 and its impact on the sustainability adoption within SMEs' processes

Consequently, future studies might want to focus on the exploration of how the use of technology aids the development of sustainable management (Nagalakshmi & Kumar, 2020) as well as, how the covid-19 pandemic has impacted SMEs and their efforts to implement sustainable management tools (Kumar *et al*, 2020; Patma *et al* 2021). Furthermore, it might be necessary to conduct further research to investigate how governments of different countries can assist and act as a support to SMEs sustainability implementation (Pu *et al*, 2021). Due to the very specific nature of government regulations and incentives, it is necessary to explore and assess a multitude of different realities to garner a more comprehensive understanding of the correlation existing between government and their mediating role.

Moreover, future research could help determine whether the aforementioned tools are sufficient for SMEs sustainability management or, if it is necessary to address and discuss further elements developed by professionals and academics all over the globe.

Researchers and future journals' call for paper might need to spend additional efforts in an attempt to better understand the long term benefits that sustainability management tools create for small and medium enterprises especially in relation to the perceived benefits of local programs and partnerships.

CONCLUSION

Based upon the information we have gathered and highlighted throughout this review, the following takeaways can be listed as follows.

Overall, SR heavy approaches do not lead to, nor do they require massive organizational overhauls in order to be achieved. In fact, while SBSC can be considered a useful tool for managers and organizations looking for ways to constantly improve and keep track of their progress, it cannot be implemented as a lone, independent strategy tool. In fact, SBSC should be considered as an effective supplementary tool meant to enforce and strengthen the sustainability vision and strategy of a company, but it has to be integrated with the rest of MCS tools in order to achieve the maximum degree possible of effectiveness.

Furthermore, we have discussed at length the role of disclosure and reporting, focusing on how it can be used as a means to gain a competitive advantage over competitors while winning the stakeholders' appreciation, rather than simply relegating it to a marginal, accountability based role. Out of all the perspectives we have listed, it's evident that the social connotations of disclosure and reporting are drastically increasing in relevance, both within the literature and the business world.

However, despite the importance of the elements that we have listed and explored in detail, SMEs are still lagging behind when it comes to SR. The most noticeable takeaway from our review is the interplay between the importance of the social aspects of SR and the fact that the impact on society is being perceived by SMEs owners as marginal and not worth pursuing. The mismatch between what's being perceived by SMEs and what has been explored in the literature could provide prompts for future research on the topic. What's missing here is the cultural aspect of sustainability and how SMEs should be "educated" and made aware of the actual impact they have in today's economies, especially in Europe.

This ties to another important contribution that our review provides to readers and managers alike. SR is a delicate topic, which requires not only time and resources, but also a consistent knowledge of how to successfully implement it. Future research trends could explore and bridge the knowledge gap within the SME world. Making SR accessible to SMEs, while simplifying and lowering the amount of skill required in order to implement said logics in the company's MCS which could be a key topic worthy of further research and thought. Moreover, this chapter highlights how little to no knowledge SMEs have when it comes to the sustainability management tools available to them. Part of the tools discussed are considered to be easily accessible to SMEs. For example, the implementation of Eco-mapping has shown how little to no resources are required for its successful implementation. This demonstrates how often the lack of awareness prevents managers and owners from exploring multiple sustainability tools.

Consequently, we believe that the current body of work does summarize and condense previous research findings and discoveries making it more accessible and digestible for SMEs looking to dabble within sustainability for their first time.

REFERENCES

Adams, C. A., & Frost, G. R. (2008). Integrating sustainability reporting into management practices. *Accounting Forum*, *32*(4), 288–302. doi:10.1016/j.accfor.2008.05.002

Agan, Y., Acar, M. F., & Borodin, A. (2013). Drivers of environmental processes and their impact on performance: A study of Turkish SMEs. *Journal of Cleaner Production*, *51*, 23–33. doi:10.1016/j.jclepro.2012.12.043

Almeida, A. R., Alvarenga, R. A., Sartor, L. B., & Simioni, F. J. (2019). Mitigating environmental impacts using life cycle assessment in Brazilian companies: A stakeholders' perspective. *Journal of Environmental Management*, *236*, 291–300. doi:10.1016/j.jenvman.2019.01.094 PMID:30738299

Aragón-Correa, J. A., Hurtado-Torres, N., Sharma, S., & García-Morales, V. J. (2008). Environmental strategy and performance in small firms: A resource-based perspective. *Journal of Environmental Management*, *86*(1), 88–103. doi:10.1016/j.jenvman.2006.11.022 PMID:17239519

Assunção, R. R., Luca, M. M. M., & de Vasconcelos, A. C. (2016). Complexity and corporate governance: An analysis of companies listed on the BM & FBOVESPA. *Revista Contabilidade & Finanças*, *28*(July), 213–228. doi:10.1590/1808-057x201702660

Benchmarking: The search for industry best practices that lead to superior performance. (1989). *Choice Reviews Online, 27*(4), 27-2173-27-2173. doi:10.5860/CHOICE.27-2173

Beschorner, T. (2013). Creating Shared Value: The One-Trick Pony Approach. *Business Ethics Journal Review, 1*(17), 106–112. doi:10.12747/bejr2013.01.17

Biondi, V., Frey, M., & Iraldo, F. (2000). Environmental management systems and SMEs. *Greener Management International, 2000*(29), 55–69. doi:10.9774/GLEAF.3062.2000.sp.00007

Blundel, R., Monaghan, A., & Thomas, C. (2013). SMEs and environmental responsibility: A policy perspective. *Business Ethics (Oxford, England), 22*(3), 246–262. doi:10.1111/beer.12020

Boiral, O., Ebrahimi, M., Kuyken, K., & Talbot, D. (2017). Greening remote SMEs: The case of small regional airports. *Journal of Business Ethics, 154*(3), 813–827. doi:10.100710551-017-3447-0

Brammer, S., Hoejmose, S., & Marchant, K. (2011). Environmental management in SMEs in the UK: Practices, pressures and perceived benefits. *Business Strategy and the Environment, 21*(7), 423–434. doi:10.1002/bse.717

Brammer, S., Jackson, G., & Matten, D. (2012). Corporate social responsibility and institutional theory: New perspectives on private governance. *Socio-economic Review, 10*(1), 3–28. doi:10.1093er/mwr030

Branco, M. C., & Rodrigues, L. L. (2006). Corporate social responsibility and resource-based perspectives. *Journal of Business Ethics, 69*(2), 111–132. doi:10.100710551-006-9071-z

Brunninge, O., Nordqvist, M., & Wiklund, J. (2007). Corporate governance and strategic change in SMEs: The effects of ownership, board composition and top management teams. *Small Business Economics, 29*(3), 295–308. doi:10.100711187-006-9021-2

Bui, B., & De Villiers, C. (2017). Management control systems to support sustainability and integrated reporting. In *Sustainability Accounting and Integrated Reporting* (pp. 121–148). Routledge. doi:10.4324/9781315108032-11

Burke, S., & Gaughran, W. F. (2006). Intelligent environmental management for SMEs in manufacturing. *Robotics and Computer-integrated Manufacturing, 22*(5–6), 566–575. doi:10.1016/j.rcim.2005.11.008

Butler, J. B., Henderson, S. C., & Raiborn, C. (2011, Winter). Sustainability and the Balanced Scorecard: Integrating Green Measures into Business Reporting. *Management Accounting Quarterly*, *12*(2), 1–10.

Calogirou, C., Sørensen, S. Y., Bjørn Larsen, P., & Alexopoulou, S. (2010). *SMEs and the Environment in the European Union PLANET SA and Danish Technological Institute for European Commission, DG Enterprise and Industry, Brussels*. Available at: https://op.europa.eu/en/publication-detail/-/publication/aa507ab8-1a2a-4bf1-86de-5a60d14a3977

Cantele, S., & Zardini, A. (2020). What drives small and medium enterprises towards sustainability? Role of interactions between pressures, barriers, and benefits. *Corporate Social Responsibility and Environmental Management*, *27*(1), 126–136. doi:10.1002/csr.1778

Carpinetti, L. C., & De Melo, A. M. (2002). What to benchmark? *Benchmarking*, *9*(3), 244–255. doi:10.1108/14635770210429009

Christmann, P. (2000). Effects of "Best practices" Of environmental management on cost advantage: The role of complementary assets. *Academy of Management Journal*, *43*(4), 663–680. doi:10.2307/1556360

Côté, R., Booth, A., & Louis, B. (2006). Eco-efficiency and SMEs in Nova Scotia, Canada. *Journal of Cleaner Production*, *14*(6-7), 542–550. doi:10.1016/j.jclepro.2005.07.004

Cristea, C., & Cristea, M. (2021). KPIs for Operational Performance Assessment in Flexible Packaging Industry. *Sustainability*, *13*(6), 3498. doi:10.3390u13063498

Dawid, G., Magdalena, K., & Karolina, K. (2019). CSR Practices in Polish and Spanish Stock Listed Companies: A Comparative Analysis. *Sustainability*, *11*(4), 1054. doi:10.3390u11041054

Dewulf, J., & Van Langenhove, H. (Eds.). (2006). *Renewables-based technology: sustainability assessment*. John Wiley & Sons. doi:10.1002/0470022442

Dreyer, L., Hauschild, M., & Schierbeck, J. (2006). A framework for social life cycle impact assessment (10 pp). *The International Journal of Life Cycle Assessment*, *11*(2), 88–97. doi:10.1065/lca2005.08.223

Du, S., Yu, K., Bhattacharya, C. B., & Sen, S. (2017). The Business Case for Sustainability Reporting: Evidence from Stock Market Reactions. *Journal of Public Policy & Marketing*, *36*(2), 312–330. doi:10.1509/jppm.16.112

Eizenberg, E., & Jabareen, Y. (2017). Social Sustainability: A New Conceptual Framework. *Sustainability*, *9*(1), 68. doi:10.3390u9010068

Eklund, M. A. (2020). Future Prospects in Balanced Scorecard Research: Sustainability Perspective. *Indonesian Journal of Sustainability Accounting and Management*, *4*(2), 192. doi:10.28992/ijsam.v4i2.263

El Baz, J., Laguir, I., Marais, M., & Staglianò, R. (2014). Influence of national institutions on the corporate social responsibility practices of small- and medium-sized enterprises in the food-processing industry: Differences between France and Morocco. *Journal of Business Ethics*, *134*(1), 117–133. doi:10.100710551-014-2417-z

Elkington, J. (1994). Towards the sustainable corporation: win– win–win business strategies for sustainable development. *California Management Review*, *36*(2), 90 – 100. doi:10.2307/41165746

environmental practices a strategical decision for small service companies? Management Decision, 51(1), 41–62. doi:10.1108/00251741311291300

European Commission. (2021). *A European Green Deal*. Available at: https://ec.europa.eu/info/strategy/priorities-2019-2024/european-green-deal_en

Ferrero-Ferrero, I., Fernández-Izquierdo, M. Á., Muñoz-Torres, M. J., & Bellés-Colomer, L. (2018). Stakeholder engagement in sustainability reporting in higher education. *International Journal of Sustainability in Higher Education*, *19*(2), 313–336. doi:10.1108/IJSHE-06-2016-0116

Figge, F., Hahn, T., Schaltegger, S., & Wagner, M. (2002). The sustainability balanced scorecard - linking sustainability management to business strategy. *Business Strategy and the Environment*, *11*(5), 269–284. doi:10.1002/bse.339

Foley, J. A., DeFries, R., Asner, G. P., Barford, C., Bonan, G., Carpenter, S. R., Chapin, F. S., Coe, M. T., Daily, G. C., Gibbs, H. K., Helkowski, J. H., Holloway, T., Howard, E. A., Kucharik, C. J., Monfreda, C., Patz, J. A., Prentice, I. C., Ramankutty, N., & Snyder, P. K. (2005). Global Consequences of Land Use. *Science*, *309*(5734), 570–574. doi:10.1126cience.1111772 PMID:16040698

Franco, M., & Rodrigues, M. (2019). Sustainable practices in SMEs: Reducing the ecological footprint. *The Journal of Business Strategy*, *42*(2), 137–142. doi:10.1108/JBS-07-2019-0136

Freeman, R. E. (1994). The politics of stakeholder theory: Some future directions. *Business Ethics Quarterly*, *4*(4), 409–421. doi:10.2307/3857340

Freeman, R. E. (2010). *Strategic Management*. Cambridge University Press. doi:10.1017/CBO9781139192675

Freeman, R. E., Wicks, A. C., & Parmar, B. (2004). Stakeholder theory and "The corporate objective revisited". *Organization Science*, *15*(3), 364–369. doi:10.1287/orsc.1040.0066

Friedman, A. L., & Miles, S. (2002). SMEs and the environment: Evaluating dissemination routes and handholding levels. *Business Strategy and the Environment*, *11*(5), 324–341. doi:10.1002/bse.335

Gomes, C. M., Kneipp, J. M., Kruglianskas, I., Rosa, L. A., & Bichueti, R. S. (2015). Management for sustainability: An analysis of the key practices according to the business size. *Ecological Indicators*, *52*, 116–127. doi:10.1016/j.ecolind.2014.11.012

Gray, R. (2006). Social, environmental and sustainability reporting and organisational value creation? *Accounting, Auditing & Accountability Journal*, *19*(6), 793–819. doi:10.1108/09513570610709872

Günther, E., & Kaulich, S. (2005). The EPM-KOMPAS: An instrument to control the environmental performance in small and medium-sized enterprises (SMEs). *Business Strategy and the Environment*, *14*(6), 361–371. doi:10.1002/bse.437

Hahn, R., & Kühnen, M. (2013). Determinants of sustainability reporting: A review of results, trends, theory, and opportunities in an expanding field of research. *Journal of Cleaner Production*, *59*, 5–21. doi:10.1016/j.jclepro.2013.07.005

Halila, F. (2007). Networks as a means of supporting the adoption of organizational innovations in SMEs: The case of environmental management systems (EMSs) based on ISO 14001. *Corporate Social Responsibility and Environmental Management*, *14*(3), 167–181. doi:10.1002/csr.127

Hansen, E. G., & Schaltegger, S. (2014). The Sustainability Balanced Scorecard: A Systematic Review of Architectures. *Journal of Business Ethics*, *133*(2), 193–221. doi:10.100710551-014-2340-3

Hansen, E. G., & Schaltegger, S. (2016). Sustainability Balanced Scorecards and their Architectures: Irrelevant or Misunderstood? *Journal of Business Ethics*, *150*(4), 937–952. doi:10.100710551-017-3531-5

Hart, S. L. (1995). A natural-resource-Based view of the firm. *Academy of Management Review*, *20*(4), 986–1014. doi:10.5465/amr.1995.9512280033

Hewitt-Dundas, N. (2006). Resource and capability constraints to innovation in small and large plants. *Small Business Economics, 26*(3), 257–277. doi:10.100711187-005-2140-3

Hillary, R. (2004). Environmental management systems and the smaller enterprise. *Journal of Cleaner Production, 12*(6), 561–569. doi:10.1016/j.jclepro.2003.08.006

Hillary, R. (Ed.). (2017). *Small and Medium-Sized Enterprises and the Environment*. Routledge. doi:10.4324/9781351282840

Hristov, I., & Chirico, A. (2019). The Role of Sustainability Key Performance Indicators (KPIs) in Implementing Sustainable Strategies. *Sustainability, 11*(20), 5742. doi:10.3390u11205742

Hsu, C., Hu, A. H., Chiou, C., & Chen, T. (2011). Using the FDM and ANP to construct a sustainability balanced scorecard for the semiconductor industry. *Expert Systems with Applications, 38*(10), 12891–12899. doi:10.1016/j.eswa.2011.04.082

Huang, T., Pepper, M., & Bowrey, G. (2014). Implementing a sustainability balanced scorecard to contribute to the process of organisational legitimacy assessment. Australasian Accounting. *Business and Finance Journal, 8*(2), 15–34. doi:10.14453/aabfj.v8i2.3

Hudson Smith, M., & Smith, D. (2007). Implementing strategically aligned performance measurement in small firms. *International Journal of Production Economics, 106*(2), 393–408. doi:10.1016/j.ijpe.2006.07.011

Jamali, D., Zanhour, M., & Keshishian, T. (2008). Peculiar strengths and relational attributes of SMEs in the context of CSR. *Journal of Business Ethics, 87*(3), 355–377. doi:10.100710551-008-9925-7

Jassem, S., Zakaria, Z., & Che Azmi, A. (2021). Sustainability balanced scorecard architecture and environmental performance outcomes: a systematic review. *International Journal of Productivity and Performance Management*. doi:10.1108/IJPPM-12-2019-0582

Johnson, M. P. (2015). Sustainability management and small and medium-sized enterprises: Managers' awareness and implementation of innovative tools. *Corporate Social Responsibility and Environmental Management, 22*(5), 271–285. doi:10.1002/csr.1343

Johnson, M. P., & Schaltegger, S. (2015). Two decades of sustainability management tools for SMEs: How far have we come? *Journal of Small Business Management, 54*(2), 481–505. doi:10.1111/jsbm.12154

Journeault, M., Perron, A., & Vallières, L. (2021). The collaborative roles of stakeholders in supporting the adoption of sustainability in SMEs. *Journal of Environmental Management*, *287*, 112349. doi:10.1016/j.jenvman.2021.112349 PMID:33735683

Kaplan, R., & Norton, D. (1992). The Balanced Scorecard – measures that drive performance. *Harvard Business Review*, 71–79. PMID:10119714

Kim, J., Kim, H., & Kwon, H. (2019). Corporate Social Responsibility Activity Combinations for Sustainability: A Fuzzy Set Analysis of Korean Firms. *Sustainability*, *11*(24), 7078. doi:10.3390u11247078

Klychova, G. S., Ziganshin, B. G., Zakirova, A. R., Valieva, G. R., & Klychova, A. S. (2017). Benchmarking as an efficient tool of social audit development. *Journal of Engineering and Applied Sciences (Asian Research Publishing Network)*, *12*(19), 4958. doi:10.36478/jeasci.2017.4958.4965

KopninaH.BlewittJ. (2018). *Sustainable business*. doi:10.4324/9781315110172

Koroljova, A., & Voronova, V. (2007). Eco-mapping as a basis for environmental management systems integration at small and medium enterprises. *Management of Environmental Quality*, *18*(5), 542–555. doi:10.1108/14777830710778300

KPMG International Cooperative (KPMG). (2011). Integrated Reporting. *Performance insight through Better Business Reporting – Issue 1*. Available from: http://www.kpmg.com/Global/en/IssuesAndInsights/ArticlesPublications/Documents/road- to-integrated-reporting.pdf

Kumar, M., Syed, D., Ali, A., & Pandey, D. (2020). *How adoption of online resources can help indian smes in improving performance during covid-19 pandemic*. Test Engineering and Management Journal.

Marín, L., & de Maya, S. R. (2013). The role of affiliation, attractiveness and personal connection in consumer-company identification. *European Journal of Marketing*, *47*(3), 655–673. doi:10.1108/03090561311297526

McWilliams, A., & Siegel, D. S. (2011). Creating and capturing value: Strategic corporate social responsibility, resource-based theory, and sustainable competitive advantage. *Journal of Management*, *37*(5), 1480–1495. doi:10.1177/0149206310385696

Milà i Canals, L., Bauer, C., Depestele, J., Dubreuil, A., Freiermuth Knuchel, R., Gaillard, G., Michelsen, O., Müller-Wenk, R., & Rydgren, B. (2006). Key elements in a framework for land use impact assessment within LCA (11 pp). *The International Journal of Life Cycle Assessment*, *12*(1), 5–15. doi:10.1065/lca2006.05.250

Mintz, S. M. (2011). Triple Bottom Line Reporting for CPAs. *The CPA Journal, 81*(12), 26–33.

Na, H. J., Lee, K. C., Choi, S. U., & Kim, S. T. (2020). Exploring CEO Messages in Sustainability Management Reports: Applying Sentiment Mining and Sustainability Balanced Scorecard Methods. *Sustainability*, *12*(2), 590. doi:10.3390u12020590

Nagalakshmi, M., & Kumar, M. (2020). Key Tool of Sustainable Management during COVID-19: WFH and Technology. *PIMT Journal of Research, 12*(4).

Parker, C. M., Redmond, J., & Simpson, M. (2009). A review of interventions to encourage SMEs to make environmental improvements. *Environment and Planning. C, Government & Policy*, *27*(2), 279–301. doi:10.1068/c0859b

Patma, T. S., Wardana, L. W., Wibowo, A., Narmaditya, B. S., & Akbarina, F. (2021). The impact of social media marketing for Indonesian SMEs sustainability: Lesson from Covid-19 pandemic. *Cogent Business & Management*, *8*(1), 1953679. doi:10.1080/23311975.2021.1953679

Pimenova, P., & Van der Vorst, R. (2004). The role of support programmes and policies in improving SMEs environmental performance in developed and transition economies. *Journal of Cleaner Production*, *12*(6), 549–559. doi:10.1016/j.jclepro.2003.07.001

Pu, G., Qamruzzaman, M., Mehta, A. M., Naqvi, F. N., & Karim, S. (2021). Innovative Finance, Technological Adaptation and SMEs Sustainability: The Mediating Role of Government Support during COVID-19 Pandemic. *Sustainability*, *13*(16), 9218. doi:10.3390u13169218

Reap, J., Roman, F., Duncan, S., & Bras, B. (2008). A survey of unresolved problems in life cycle assessment. *The International Journal of Life Cycle Assessment, 13*(5), 374–388. doi:10.100711367-008-0009-9

Revell, A., & Rutherfoord, R. (2003). UK environmental policy and the small firm: Broadening the focus. *Business Strategy and the Environment*, *12*(1), 26–35. doi:10.1002/bse.347

Schaltegger, S., & Wagner, M. (2006). Managing Sustainability Performance Measurement and Reporting in an Integrated Manner. Sustainability Accounting as the Link between the Sustainability Balanced Scorecard and Sustainability Reporting. *Sustainability Accounting and Reporting*, 681–697. doi:10.1007/978-1-4020-4974-3_30

Sen, S. (2006). The role of corporate social responsibility in strengthening multiple stakeholder relationships: A Field experiment. *Journal of the Academy of Marketing Science*, *34*(2), 158–166. doi:10.1177/0092070305284978

Sen, S., & Cowley, J. (2013). The Relevance of Stakeholder Theory and Social Capital Theory in the Context of CSR in SMEs: An Australian Perspective. *Journal of Business Ethics*, *118*(2), 413–427. doi:10.100710551-012-1598-6

Temtime, Z. T., & Solomon, G. H. (2002). Total quality management and the planning behavior of SMEs in developing economies. *The TQM Magazine*, *14*(3), 181–191. doi:10.1108/09544780210425900

Testa, F., Boiral, O., & Iraldo, F. (2018). Internalization of environmental practices and institutional complexity: Can stakeholders pressures encourage greenwashing? *Journal of Business Ethics*, *147*(2), 287–307. doi:10.100710551-015-2960-2

Turner, M. G., Gardner, R. H., & O'Neill, R. V. (2001). *Landscape ecology in theory and practice: Pattern and process*. Springer Science & Business Media.

Zakhem, A., & Palmer, D. E. (2017). Normative Stakeholder Theory. In Stakeholder Management (pp. 49–73). Emerald Publishing Limited. doi:10.1108/S2514-175920170000003

ADDITIONAL READING

Ali, K., & Johl, S. K. (2021, June). Impact of total quality management on SMEs sustainable performance in the context of industry 4.0. In *International Conference on Emerging Technologies and Intelligent Systems* (pp. 608-620). Springer.

Biryukov, E., Elina, O., Lyandau, Y., & Mrochkovskiy, N. (2021). Russian SMEs in achieving sustainable development goals. In *E3S Web of Conferences* (Vol. 258). EDP Sciences. doi:10.1051/e3sconf/202125806021

Dressler, M. (2021). Motivating sustainable entrepreneurship: The deployment of a visual navigation tool. *World Review of Entrepreneurship, Management and Sustainable Development*, *17*(1), 77–102. doi:10.1504/WREMSD.2021.112095

Ferber Pineyrua, D. G., Redondo, A., Pascual, J. A., & Gento, Á. M. (2021). Knowledge Management and Sustainable Balanced Scorecard: Practical Application to a Service SME. *Sustainability*, *13*(13), 7118. doi:10.3390u13137118

Jiménez, E., de la Cuesta-González, M., & Boronat-Navarro, M. (2021). How Small and Medium-Sized Enterprises Can Uptake the Sustainable Development Goals through a Cluster Management Organization: A Case Study. *Sustainability, 13*(11), 5939. doi:10.3390u13115939

Nassar, N., & Tvaronaviciene, M. (2021). A systematic theoretical review on sustainable management for green competitiveness. *Insights into Regional Development, 3*(2), 267–281. doi:10.9770/IRD.2021.3.2(7)

Pînzaru, F., Wereda, W., Moldoveanu, I., & Ciuciuc, V. E. (2021). Sustainable Management of IT Enterprises. In *Business Revolution in a Digital Era* (pp. 101–113). Springer. doi:10.1007/978-3-030-59972-0_8

Sinyuk, T., Panfilova, E., & Pogosyan, R. (2021). Digital transformation of SME business models as a factor of sustainable socio-economic development. In *E3S Web of Conferences* (Vol. 295, p. 01028). EDP Sciences. doi:10.1051/e3sconf/202129501028

Talbot, D., Raineri, N., & Daou, A. (2021). Implementation of sustainability management tools: The contribution of awareness, external pressures, and stakeholder consultation. *Corporate Social Responsibility and Environmental Management, 28*(1), 71–81. doi:10.1002/csr.2033

Vandenbrande, W. W. (2021). Quality for a sustainable future. *Total Quality Management & Business Excellence, 32*(5-6), 467–475. doi:10.1080/14783363.2019.1588724

KEY TERMS AND DEFINITIONS

Corporate Social Responsibility: The combination of norms and practices which businesses can adopt to be socially accountable and become conscious of the impact that they are having on all elements of society such as social, environmental, and economic aspects.

Environmental Impact: Any change to the environment resulting from human activities.

Environmental Performance: Indicators whose aim is to report the efficiency in resource utilization, waste and emission of different businesses or business's processes.

Small and Medium Enterprises: Businesses with fewer than 250 employees and a turnover that's lower than 50 million euro.

Sustainability: The avoidance of the depletion of natural resources without compromising the ability of future generations to utilize said resources to fulfill their own needs.

Sustainability Issues: The instances which prevent businesses from having processes which safeguard the territory causing environmental damages and depletion such as soil erosion, water management, reduced soil quality, and air and water pollution.

Sustainability Reporting: It is the key instrument for companies to communicate their sustainability performances and how their activities impact the environment and many other aspects of society.

Sustainable Development: The economic development that is conducted and structured in a way that does not deteriorate nor deplete the natural environment and natural resources.

Sustainable Management: The application of business processes whose aim is to not deteriorate nor deplete the natural resources and environment.

Sustainable Practices: The processes employed by entities to maintain the qualities of the natural resources utilised during its business processes.

Chapter 4
Digital Transformation Journey of HR:
The Effect of Big Data and Artificial Intelligence in HR Strategies and Roles

Tuğba Karaboğa
Yıldız Technical University, Turkey

Hasan Aykut Karaboğa
Amasya University, Turkey

Dogan Basar
Central Bank of the Republic of Turkey, Turkey

Songul Zehir
Duzce University, Turkey

ABSTRACT

Big data and artificial intelligence (AI) technologies have changed how we live, how we work, and how we organize businesses. Thus, it is no surprise that it is also changing how we manage human resources (HR). For HR leaders, digital transformation is a very hot topic, having the potential to create high value for businesses. First, HR can transform all functions, processes, and systems by leveraging digital platforms and applications. Second, HR can lead business digitalization, enabling a compelling employee experience where a digital culture, a digital workplace, and digital management are welcomed. To provide a more pragmatic perspective, this chapter discusses digitalization of HR with big data and artificial intelligence (AI) technologies and identifies key digital HR strategies and roles needed to sustain the digital transformation. Also, this chapter presents the advantages of digital HR and the basic pitfalls HR faces in the digital transformation of HR.

DOI: 10.4018/978-1-7998-7793-6.ch004

Copyright © 2022, IGI Global. Copying or distributing in print or electronic forms without written permission of IGI Global is prohibited.

INTRODUCTION

The digitization and datafication of the work environment are responsible for high uncertainty, complexity and ambiguity for companies. To deal with the challenges, businesses have been focusing on digital work designs with higher flexibility, speed and agility (Richter et al., 2018; Vom Brocke et al., 2018). Digital technologies are important to achieve business goals and create value by means of innovative digital products and services. Artificial intelligence (AI), the idea that machines can think and act like humans, is used by businesses to augment human work. Recent technological advances in big data and AI systems have increased human-machine interactions and have created computer-cantered cooperative work environments. For example, the internet of things (IoT) generates big data from various sensors around us as an input for AI by increasing the level of connectedness among computers and shareholders (Saarikko, Westergen & Blomquist, 2017; Krotov, 2017). Furthermore, intelligent assistants simplify daily tasks and virtual work groups exceed the physical boundaries of organizations. In this new world of organizations, intelligent robots have already adopted employee tasks, and data-driven managerial approaches have enhanced transparency and trustworthiness in the workplace (Wisskirchen et al., 2017).

Big data is separated from other data sets with its huge volume, high variety and velocity (Beyer & Laney, 2012). Big data analytics is a term used to describe advanced analytical techniques applied to big data to gain value from complex and unstructured data sets (Russom, 2011; Intel, 2012). AI techniques are closely related to big data analytics and have contributed significantly to big data analytics that resulting better data processing and better future forecasts (O'Leary, 2013). Many researchers and professionals believe that big data and AI applications have potential to transform traditional management and business processes. With the help of technological advances in big data and AI organizations change business processes, corporate structure and ecosystem (Brown et al., 2011); increase business value with the help of new organizational capabilities (Davenport et al., 2012); enhance machine learning, automation and human-machine interaction (Jarrahi, 2018); supporting human decision making with algorithms (McAfee et al., 2012) and innovate new business models (Brown et al., 2011).

Digital transformation is not only about upgrading technology. It is about fully adapting structures, processes, strategies, cultures and leadership toward a digital revolution. Digital transformation should be a part of organizational design by creating data-driven, collaborative and reactive structures. This is why HR has a critical role. According to a 2018 Deloitte Human Capital Survey, 72% of respondents saw the adoption of automation, robotics, and AI technologies as important. However, only

31% felt ready to utilize them. The lack of well-established digital strategies and collaboration tools reduces the courage of companies to implement the transformation.

From the HR perspective, leaders need stronger analytical capabilities to build upon HR's strategic role in the organization. There are large amounts of HR related data that can be retrieved from inside or outside a business. However, the largeness of data alone is not sufficient to create value. The important point is to make data "smarter" (George et al., 2014), by enabling big data analytics and AI systems to help leaders obtain the right information and make predictions. At this point big data analytics and AI systems help HR leaders to obtain new information from data and make predictions about HR issues by analyzing existing data. The main aim of this chapter is to show how to utilize big data analytics and AI systems in HR applications to emphasize the strategic value of HR in the organizations. Intelligent systems think and act like human beings, and most HR tasks are being realized by automated systems and machine-learning algorithms. For example, IBM is a giant technology company that carries out experiments to drive new digital HR solutions. IBM Watson Talent is an AI-based HR solution package that uses cognitive technology as an assistant to recruitment, career management, training and performance management. In addition to Watson, FirstJob's Mya (a chatbot) has been used to answer candidate questions during recruitment. Wade and Wendy is another chatbot service used for recruitment and career planning (Volini et al., 2017, pp. 90–91). These kinds of data-driven, intelligent HR systems create a more trustworthy HR function by eliminating individual judgements and biases in HR tasks.

The rest of the chapter is organized as follows. Chapter starts with big data analytics and its usage in HR. Big data, data analytics and HR analytics are defined and their contribution to HR is discussed. Second, AI and HR intelligence relation is emphasized and the contributions of HR intelligence and HR analytics on HR functions are discussed. How should HR strategies, HR roles, skills and capabilities be shaped in the context of digital transformation? Third, advantages and potential risks of data-driven HR applications are pointed out. What are the advantages provided to HR by means of analytical tools and intelligent HR systems and what are the barriers that prevent HR professionals from using big data in an efficient way? Fourth, future of HR and HR workplaces are discussed. What are the future expectations of digital technology utilization in HR and what can be new roles and responsibilities of HR? Finally, future directions for researchers and professionals related to HR analytics and intelligent HR systems are given to forward this study in a productive way.

BIG DATA AND AI REVOLUTION IN HR

Big data is defined as "data that exceeds the processing capacity of conventional database systems" (Dumbill, 2013, p. 1). It stands apart from standard data sets with its huge volume, high variety and tremendous velocity (Beyer & Laney, 2012). From an HR perspective, huge volumes of data are collected from different sources in various formats at high speeds. IoT-based big data analytics generate huge amounts of data from connected sensors and machines, transferring them to the businesses for use in decision making (Lee & Lee, 2015). This complex and transparent data create value for the business as a result of advanced analytical applications. It is obvious that large volumes of data alone are not strategic resources. The strategic value of big data comes from analyzing information and interpreting results accurately. In recent studies, the focus of big data has shifted from data size to data smartness. This reflects the extent to which data provides insights about the prediction of behaviors and outcomes in/for a company (George et al., 2014). In this context, big data analytics and AI-based systems and software have become important for companies that need to understand hidden information in big data sets. With the help of big data analytical techniques, terabytes, petabytes and exabytes of small-valued big data can be processed into high-valued small pieces of usable information while creating a meaningful comprehensive picture for HR and operations.

HR Analytics and Evidence-Based HR Operations

Analytics provides HR a chance to show actual value with contributions to the overall business using HR metrics. Workforce analytics is used to enable better evidence-based decisions on the human side of organizations and enhance individual and organizational performance (McIver, Lengnick–Hall & Lengnick–Hall, 2018; Bassi, 2011). To support organizational performance, HR analytics should transcend functional HR barriers. HR must take an "outside-in" approach by integrating the end-to-end business analytics, which will help HR realize its strategic role (Rasmussen & Ulrich, 2015).

HR has recently retreated from purely administrative processes and has become more solution oriented, using empirical and analytical evidence from HR analytical tools (Boudreau & Rice, 2015). Data-driven HR applications have created a more quantitative HR function. Evidence-based decision making has increased the levels of trust afforded to HR departments and has provided valuable contributions to overall business performance. Rasmussen and Ulrich (2015) investigated two HR analytics cases of an offshore drilling company, showing that the use of analytics led to a significant improvement in business performance. In one case, HR analytics was used to show the relationship between leadership quality and crew turnover.

Both are associated with crew competence, safety performance and maintenance efficiency. In the second case, HR analytics was used to fill lead specialist positions caused by an industry-wide talent shortage. In another study, Falletta (2014) investigated 220 high-performing organizations, finding that data and information usage shifted dramatically as companies built strategic capabilities and competitive advantages around advanced HR analytics. As it is understood, HR analytics can support business performance by improving retention, understanding satisfaction and motivation factors, filling talent gaps by training from inside and improving strategic capabilities and competitive advantage.

AI: New Driving Force of the HR Revolution

In 1988, Holloway and Hand (p. 70) stated that "AI is no longer an academic term, but a reality. And in some companies, it seems that the AI system has replaced the human as the business and ethical decision maker". Whereas this sounds like old news, its importance has not diminished.

AI technology is found in every area of life. Facebook uses it for face recognition. Virtual assistants, such as Siri and Alexa, use it for voice interaction. Google search engines, video games, self-driving cars, customer-service chatbots, fraud detection tools and smart-home automation capabilities use it for various essential tasks. It is obvious that all industries have been affected in some way by big data, AI and robotics. Companies from all sectors want to digitize their operations and their business model in some way.

Intelligent HR applications support communication between people and machines. These systems think and act like human beings and require huge data-storage capacities. They emulate human logic and analysis (Huang et al., 2004). AI systems can support HR with its complex and ambiguous business environments and can help expand their traditional administrative roles to more creative and innovative endeavors. According to Volini et al., (2016, p. 77), "HR's role is expanding beyond its traditional focus on talent management, process and transactions. HR is becoming an innovative consultant with a broader responsibility to design, simplify and improve the entire employee and candidate experience". Therefore, it is time for HR to change its mind set to become more data driven and AI oriented.

Smart HR management (HRM) is a concept that emerged from the rise of AI-based HR technologies (Hecklau et al., 2016). Many high-performing international companies have already adopted AI technologies for their HR applications. HR analytics and AI-based systems are used in a wide range of HR functions, and vendors worldwide offer different solutions, from recruiting to workforce planning, compensation, retention and performance management (Manuti & Palma, 2018). For example, Pymetrics, HireVue, Entelo and Textio provide AI-based recruitment solutions; Degreed, EdCast and Filtered provide AI-based solutions for employee development and learning; BetterWorks, Zugata and Humanyze provide AI-based solutions for performance management and VirginPulse, CultureAmp and TinyPulse provide AI-based solutions for employee engagement and feedback (Bersin, 2018). AI-based systems increase the objectiveness of HR functions and prevent the wastage of time and money. However, digitization alone is not sufficient for transformation. Digital transformation across the whole organization requires a strong HR contribution and support structure. Only HR has the ability to create a digital ecosystem by adapting people, culture, strategy, technology, leadership and processes. The rest of the paper emphasizes the importance of HR in the digital transformation of business by redefining digital HR strategies and roles.

DIGITAL HR STRATEGIES AND ROLES

The usage of smart HR applications for different HR functions has forced HR professionals to think about new HR strategies, new HR roles, and new HR skills and capabilities in the context of digital technologies. In order to collaborate with machines and systems, employees will need higher analytical skills and capabilities because new roles and jobs will be created as a result of big data, AI and robotics technologies (Frank, 2018; Codorniou, 2018; White, 2018). One of the research, Accenture survey with 1,770 managers from 14 countries, indicates that in the near future successful managers will leave administrative tasks to intelligent systems and robots, behave intelligent machines as colleagues depending on their data-driven simulations and decisions as their assistant or adviser, focus on judgment oriented skills, design thinking and network skills which are the top skills required to succeed in the near future such as digital and technological skills, creative thinking and experimentation, data analysis, strategy creation, collaboration, social networking, people development and coaching (Kolbjørnsrud, Amico & Thomas, 2016). In this context, one of the main roles of HR function should be helping AI transformation in the entire business by understanding and supporting employees for the development of new employee skills and capabilities which are necessary for successful AI transformation. The other important point should be strategy creation. The use of big data and intelligent systems created a very dynamic business environment and forced companies to become flexible and adaptable to rapidly changing conditions. Therefore HR professionals should think about how to support flexible digital business strategies with digital HR strategies.

Digital HR strategies

Big data and intelligent systems have spawned dynamic new business environments and have forced companies to become more flexible and adaptable. HR professionals are thinking about how to support this digital transformation with strategy. Digital HR strategies facilitate transformation of business and HR operations, and they help design the future organizations and identify digital employee capabilities which will decide job retention and job losses in the future.

Figure 1. Focus of digital HR strategies (created by authors)

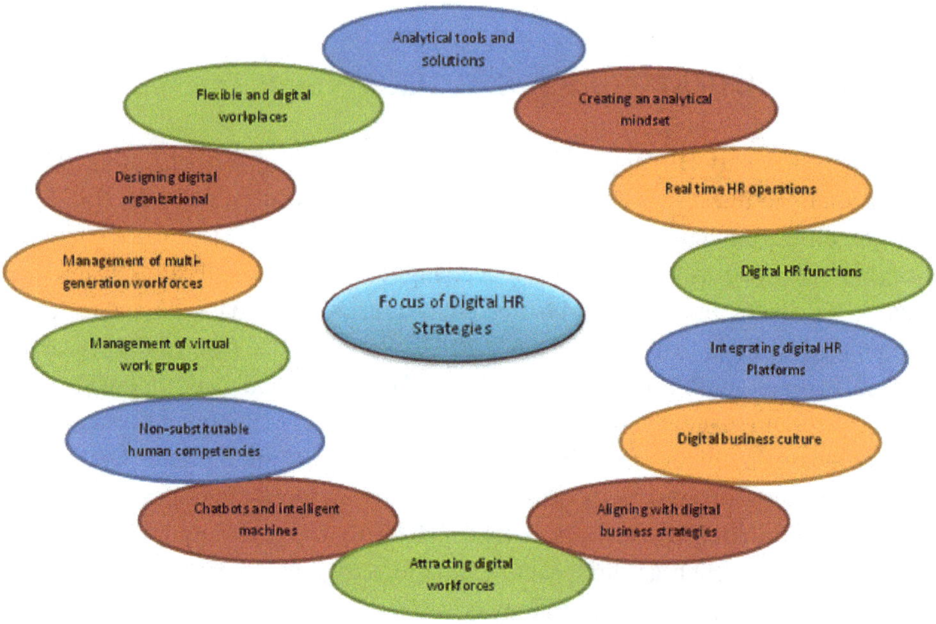

According to Stephan et al., (2016), for an effective digital transformation one of the strategic roles of HR is to "help business leaders and employees shift to a digital mind-set, a digital way of managing, organizing, and leading change" (p.97). In today's digital era, HR has a bigger role in organizations in helping them "to be digital not just do digital" (Volini et al., 2017:87). In order to achieve this role HR should focus on change in three areas: "digital workforce, digital workplace and digital HR" (Volini et al., 2017:87). For digital workforce, HR professionals support employees in achieving new capabilities and skills. In the digital world, digital workforce need general competencies such as future orientation, digital fluency, strategic thinking, system understanding, big data knowledge, social media skills, analytical skills, interpersonal skills, communication ability both in virtual and real world, multi-tasking, life-long learning, working ability with multigenerational workforce and cross-cultural competency (Thite, 2019). For digital workplaces, organizations need a new structure which is more suitable for innovation, creativity, change management and technology adaptation and this new structure is characterized by flatter design, less rules, flexibility, decentralization, collaboration and team work (Daft, 2015; Shamim et al., 2016).

As a strategic partner, HR professionals should view their operations with a business lens and focus on numbers and analytics to connect their contribution to outcomes. One of today's most important business challenges is the digital transformation of organizations. HR is in a position to generate business value by leading the way. Thus, the main focus of digital HR should be aligning strategies with digital business outcomes. However, effective digital transformation requires digital organizational structures and workplaces, characterized by a flatter design, fewer rules, flexibility, decentralization, collaboration and teamwork (Shamim et al., 2016). Digital structures enable non-hierarchical work environments and facilitate the use of common platforms, virtual teams and networks. Digital workplaces are characterized by a series of digital connections among people, tools, the business and employees. Digital workplaces and digital structures show that work does not need to be a physical place to go. It can be independent of time and location. Digital workplaces can integrate all software systems on one platform (e.g. cloud) to simplify multiple workflows, increase efficiency and productivity, support innovative culture, creativity, technology adaptation and enhance employee engagement and satisfaction.

According to Stephan et al., (2016), to achieve an effective digital transformation, HR must assume the strategic role of "helping business leaders and employees shift to a digital mindset, a digital way of managing, organizing, and leading change" (p. 97). A joint digital mindset among top management and organizational culture is definitely required to attract and retain a highly talented digital workforce. Digital culture offers new ways to achieve digital goals and objectives. A well-established digital culture is customer-centric and values collaboration, teamwork, speed, information sharing, delegation, communication, transparency, risk-taking and innovation. Without a digitally skilled staff and a change in the way employees work and behave, technological initiatives inevitably fail. Digital skills and competencies are crucial. The Boston Consulting Group expects a severe digital talent shortfall worldwide by 2020, and a Gartner study stated that 30% of all tech jobs will be unfilled because of shortfalls (Strack et al., 2017). Even today, digitally skilled employees are highly sought by large companies. Businesses can respond to this challenge in two ways. One way is to attract and retain outside talent. Second way is supporting current talent in achieving new and relevant digital capabilities and skills. Another people-related HR issue is the management of virtual work groups.

Virtual workers use digital devices to work, communicate and collaborate from anywhere at any time. The integration of a virtual workforce in a physical business environment is crucial for HR and businesses.

Digitization has already transformed HR operations. Big data and AI technologies support data-driven decision making and real-time HR operations. As a pioneer of change, HR departments have transformed their functions using digital technologies. HR analytics and intelligent HR systems are used in a wide range of functions, such as recruiting, workforce planning, compensation, retention and performance management. Chatbots and intelligent machines have become important assistants for HR professionals. Routine and repetitive tasks are being accomplished by automated systems and machines without human interaction. For example, Brilliant U, an online learning, training and development tool created by GE, aims to enhance the workforce by sharing knowledge throughout the organization. Embark is a pre-boarding application developed by Royal Bank of Canada to help new employees learn about their jobs, company culture and workplace (Volini et al., 2017, pp. 90–91). Thanks to digital technologies, HR's administrative roles are reduced and their creativity is less restricted. Innovation and technology-oriented roles become more important. In the coming years, the speed of HR adaptation to changing technologies, human-machine interaction and integrated HR platforms will become major trends. Today, high performing international companies like IBM, Google, Microsoft and GE use intelligent digital platforms to increase operation speed, efficiency and transparency.

Digital HR roles

A crucial aspect of the digital HR revolution involves the HR roles. Traditional HR roles will not be sufficient, and new roles will be needed to cope with the challenges. In 1998, Ulrich proposed key HR roles to emphasize its strategic nature: administrative expert, employee champion, change agent and strategic business partner. Later, in 2013, Ulrich and his colleagues arranged roles again by adding innovator/integrator and technology proponent. In their final study (Ulrich et al., 2017, pp. 37–38), HR roles were categorized into three dimensions with nine competencies. Core competencies included strategic positioner, credible activist and paradox navigator; organization enablers included culture and change champion, human capital curator and total reward steward; delivery enablers included technology and media integrator, analytics designer and interpreter and compliance manager. It is clear from Ulrich's studies from 1998 to 2017, administrative roles lost importance to pioneers roles of innovation, analytics, technology, organizational change and transformation. Role changes should occur simultaneously with development and progress of technological advances. The effect of technology on HR roles is an attractive topic and a few recent studies have focused on it. According to Volini et al., (2016, pp. 79–80) HR is moving from service provider to valued talent, design and employee-experience consultants. Jesuthasan (2017, p. 61) defined the new role of HR as "steward of the work and enabler of digital engagement". Depending on the effects of digitization in workplaces, workforces and operations, we classify digital HR roles into six dimensions: digital enabler, digital integrator, digital designer, digital talent advocate, digital engagement and digital innovation agent.

Digital enabler: According to the 2018 World Economic Forum Report, AI, data analytics and automation were touted to enhance the strategic importance of HR in business transformations by impacting culture and business processes. Intelligent systems, processes and machines are the core of digital transformation. However, it is not enough to have these technologies alone. HR has two key enabler tasks in this digital adaptation process: transforming HR operations and transforming workplaces, organizational culture and digital way of doing work. HR professionals take part in digital technologies across the organization to create a digital workplace and ensure that their implementation combines all the areas in the business holistically.

Digital integrator: HR has closer relationships with different business functions and internal customer segments. HR professionals can respond to employees and managers at all levels during the digital transformation. Some employees see this transformation as a threat: "the machines will make us unemployed", "we won't be able to adjust ourselves to digital technologies", or "all of us will suffer from this change". According to Ingrid Jenkins, Microsoft Australia HR director, during a digital transformation, HR has a leading integrator role and must foster communication between managers and employees. Communicating digital transformation effectively at all levels and highlighting positive implications of changes are fundamental components for success (Donaldson, 2016)

Digital designer: Easy-to-access online applications and integrated platforms are highly demanded by today's employees and business leaders. However, digital innovations and newly emerging jobs are not applicable in traditional organizational structures. Therefore, digital HR is expected to make radical changes to organizational structures and job designs, making them more compatible with digital work necessities. For example, Mercedes redesigned its traditional rigid manufacturing processes around human–machine collaborations, putting humans in control with less manual labor and more robot tasks. When AT&T switched from landline telephone services to mobile networks, they redesigned their organizational structure, and 100, 000 employees were retained for new positions. They created nearly 2000 job titles covering similar skills and capabilities. As a result, the company becomes flatter and more flexible by avoiding rigid job titles (Wilson & Daugherty, 2018).

Digital talent advocate: Digital talent shortage is a major challenge of today's digital era. According to a recent report by Capgemini and LinkedIn (2017), attracting, developing and retaining highly qualified digital talent will be an important job for HR to handle in the coming years. Many global organizations will be affected by shortages, which will cause loss of competitive advantage and failures in the digital transformation of companies. Therefore, HR workers should create strategies to define required talent skills to make their workplace attractive to potential digital employees. Furthermore, they should always be actively seeking digital talent on different platforms, such as LinkedIn, Glassdoor and other social media tools.

Digital engagement: Employee engagement is related to employee commitment and motivation. Higher levels of engagement create higher productivity and performance outcomes. For employees, tech-driven experience design is valuable. HR helps the business use digital technologies such as social media, analytics and other digital communication tools to enhance sustainable digital engagement (Jesuthasan, 2017). For example, IBM's Checkpoint provides rapid feedback to increase engagement and to align employees around business objectives (Volini et al., 2017, pp. 90–91).

Digital innovation agent: Digital technologies are rapidly evolving, and digital transformation requires continuous renewal and refocusing in line with technological developments. HR professionals foster digital innovation in various ways. They give priority to hiring creative and innovative people who can think outside the box. Different viewpoints, new ideas, new concepts, continuous learning and new ways of doing business are more valuable now. Reward and compensation strategies can be rebuilt to push and encourage innovative behaviors. Furthermore, HR will build a culture of innovation which will be the cornerstone of digital workplaces in the future.

BENEFITS AND POTENTIAL RISKS OF DIGITAL HRM APPLICATIONS

Intelligent systems and machines support HR decisions and operations by analyzing data sources from inside and outside the organization. For example, social media sites have become an important tool for HR workers to understand employee preferences and thoughts (Kaplan & Haenlein, 2010). Digital cues embedded in social media sites can also be used in personnel selection, analyzing training needs, motivating employees, increasing loyalty levels and preparing rewards and benefits. Data analytics are useful for simplifying complex HR problems into simple answerable questions. Analytical formulations of HR problems are reliable and bias free when compared to subjective solutions depending on human judgements. Therefore, analytical tools and AI applications increase efficiency, speed, reliability and productivity of HR operations. Intelligent HR systems support HR people in choosing the right employees for the right positions while saving money and time. For example, Unilever, a leading international consumer-goods company, uses human and AI capabilities together to create an individualized hiring process. Gamification is used by Unilever to understand candidate suitability for specific positions. In the following phase, applicants' answers to position-specific questions are video-recorded, and their responses, body language and tones are analyzed by AI systems. In the final round, the best candidates identified by AI systems are invited to face-to-face interviews (Wilson & Daugherty, 2018).

Big data and AI, however, have some difficulties in usage. The most important challenges are related to data quality, data privacy, data security and the shortage of qualified talent (Lee, 2017). Other pitfalls are related to choosing the right implementation approach and eliminating biases. Even if one has right data sets, results are likely to be wrong because of using wrong analytical tools. Additionally, algorithms and codes are written by humans. Even small mistakes or biases can create very large decision errors. Furthermore, AI systems can institutionalize unconscious corporate biases in a company, because the systems learn from historical corporate data sets and update accordingly. Recently, Amazon stopped using AI-based recruitment software, because the recruitment engine consistently downgraded women candidates. Amazon's machine learning based recruitment tool learned the unconscious gender biases of the company. Amazon machine learning specialists reset the system to create gender neutral results but they could not guarantee the discrimination would not return. Therefore, they stopped using the engine (Dastin, 2018). Privacy and security are other concerns. Social media accounts, personal information in curriculum vitae, wages, previous work experiments, and other information can be followed. For ethical purposes, HR should maintain privacy of personal data, transparency about how personal data is processed and the informed consent of individuals (Lengnick–Hall, Neely & Stone, 2018, pp. 1–30).

Powerful AI technologies use company data sets and take data-driven operations steps further. In complex tasks, superior computational and analytical capabilities provide effective solutions and create new opportunities for human decision makers by reducing complexity of problems (Jarrahi, 2018; Kaplan & Haenlein, 2018). AI can increase employee productivity and efficiency by augmenting complex job tasks. AI technologies promise to be more powerful with higher speeds without computational mistake. Errors will be reduced, personal bias and judgements in HR decisions will diminish. Customization by AI increases employee engagement, digital assistants make work easier and digital platforms enable working from anywhere at any time. With these significant benefits, companies retain doubts about implementation. It is expensive and there are limited successfully proven applications worldwide. Additionally, digital talent shortages, lack of human intervention and high unemployment expectations of workers are barriers that slow the acceptance of these technologies. Robot workers are another concern. Time-consuming and routine HR activities could be realized by bots in a more systematic and orderly manner, but employees have legitimate concerns about human-machine interactions. HR should focus on integrating people and machines to work together in an efficient way by maintaining human employees' well-being (Lengnick–Hall, Neely & Stone, 2018, pp. 1–30).

Figure 2 summarizes the advantages and disadvantages of digitalization in HR

Figure 2. Major benefits and challenges of smart/digital HR technologies (created by authors)

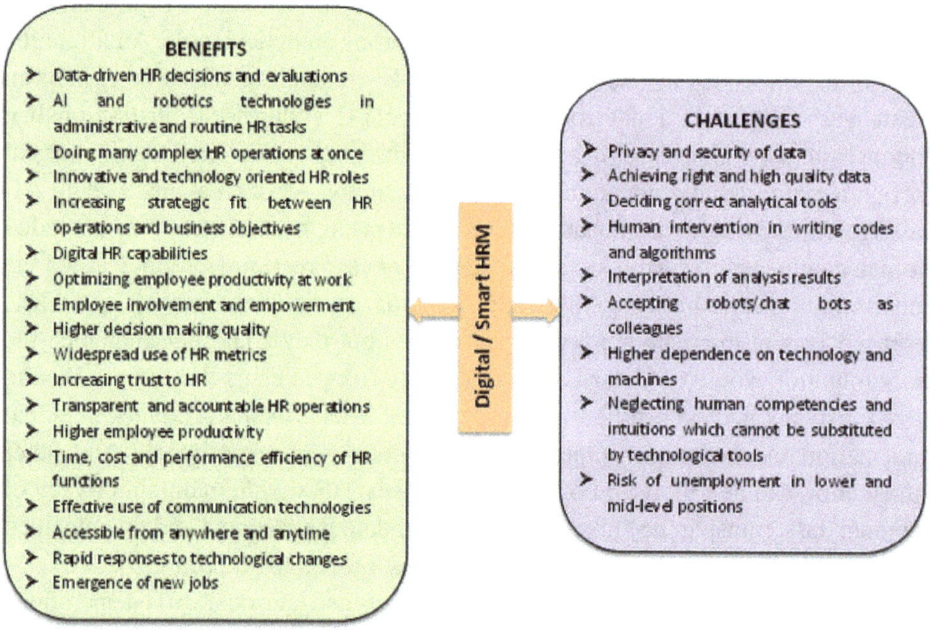

FUTURE RESEARCH DIRECTIONS

There are different views on how AI technologies and robotics will affect future business environment and employment. On one side, some business people and researchers (such as Stephen Hawking and Bill Gates) believe that AI technologies and robotics will replace human labor by machines and automated systems and as a result many jobs will be eliminated, inequality between wealthy and poor will increase and the power of capitalist system will continue to rise (Bort, 2014; Lynch,

2015; Brougham & Haar, 2018). This is the worst case. On the other hand, some people accept the rise of digital workplaces with AI technologies and they believe that automated processes and human machine interaction will help businesses and people to realize some tasks which are not possible by human intelligence. So, they believe human labor will not be replaced by machines and some kinds of automated software systems. Intelligent machines and robots will simplify jobs and improve productivity and safety (Frank, 2018; Codorniou, 2018; White, 2018).

In the organizations, HR has a great role for the sustainable digital transformation. Jesuthasan (2017:61) defines the new role of HR as "steward of the work and enabler of digital engagement". According to this new role as a strategic partner, HR helps organization to adapt the new ways of working and enables digital engagement by helping business to adapt latest digital technologies. Also, to achieve this new role HR should be a "trusted advisor" (Jesuthasan 2017:65) in realizing organizational transformation in adapting new digital technologies.

Smarter HR departments utilize AI based HR technologies strategically to reduce administrative tasks. Major benefits of smart HRM are lean HR functions, faster and efficient HR operations; major challenges of smart HRM are finding right technological tools and changing existing traditional culture and managing expectations of multi-generation employees (Sivathanu & Pillai, 2018). In this context, managing digital transformation in the whole organization and empowering employees with new skills to adapt changing technologies, digital strategies, structures and culture in the workplaces, will be new roles of HR people in the future.

HR transformation in the context of big data and AI technologies is a new subject and it is open to experimental or qualitative investigations from different perspectives in the future. Some of the future research areas in HR transformation are given for the followers in the rest of the paper. Firstly, the amount of data increasing rapidly but existing analytical tools and systems are not sufficient enough to analyze all data. Therefore, data selection in HR analytics will be one of the critical decisions in the future. Selecting right data provide highest value for the solution of business problems and HR efficiency. Following researchers can study data selection and data integration from different sources of data for HR analytics and intelligent HR systems. Also, selection of appropriate data analysis methods is another concern for data-driven HR. HR analysts should have high levels of analytical capability and statistical knowledge and should use various statistical and analytical programs which are necessary to analyze big data sets. Future researches can focus on statistical programs, analytical tools and AI systems which are required in HR functions to create intelligent, data-driven and rapid HR solutions. Another important point is HR metrics which are the most important display of data-driven HR decisions. HR metrics are generally used to evaluate the success of HR applications and to show the contribution of HR initiatives to whole business performance. In the future, with the expansion of the usage of intelligent HR systems and big data applications in HR, existing HR metrics cannot be sufficient. Enterprises and researchers can think about what kinds of new HR metrics can be developed in future to evaluate HR performance in accordance with AI technologies.

AI technologies have forced companies to make radical changes and HR department has a great importance in this change and transformation. Changing mindset of employees, redesigning organizational structure, strategy and culture, empowering employees with new skills and capabilities are main responsibilities of HR in the overall AI transformation. In order to manage this transformation successfully, HR has to change its way of doing business. While administrative roles of HR are losing importance, pioneers roles in strategy making, design and creative thinking, change management, technology advocate, catalyst/facilitator roles become important. Following studies can deeply investigate AI based HR roles and competencies. The other important about HR revolution with AI technologies is related to job redesign. Developments in smart HR technologies are expected to create technology-driven unemployment especially in low and medium skilled routine and repetitive jobs and the coming generation will be employed in jobs which do not exist even today but will emerge in the near future depending on AI technologies (PwC, 2015). Also, the collaboration between robot workers and human workers will change workloads and productivity of human employees. Future researchers can investigate redesign of jobs in this direction. What will be potential jobs of coming years, how can companies satisfy employees in their relationships with robot colleagues. Throughout the study findings of quantitative and qualitative studies are used. It is observed that there is not any sufficient empirical study to show the relationship between data-driven HR or AI based HR – HR performance and overall firm performance. Future studies should focus on how intelligent HR systems and HR analytics support HR performance and business performance.

CONCLUSION

Digitalization of workplaces has recently revealed a more important role of HR in organizational architecture, work design, culture creation and people management. In this chapter, practical information is given for both researchers and leaders about how big data and AI technologies transformed HR operations. In addition, the new ways of working, new HR roles and strategies and potential advantages and challenges of digital transformation in HR are discussed.

HR implementations combine all functions, employees, processes and leaders in a business. Therefore, HR has a big impact on a company's workforce and operations. Today, companies and progressive business leaders consider HR to be a consultant for creating a digital ecosystem to achieve business goals and objectives. In this regard, well-established digital strategies built around HR and business operations, workforces, workplaces and culture will be essential during the digital transformation. Creating digital cultures, structures, workplaces and empowered staff are key HR strategies. Managing virtual workforce, integrated platforms and human-machine collaboration are also crucial. Coordinating digitalization of workplaces and workforces has also led to the formation of new digital HR roles. New operating models, cognitive technologies and changing employee expectations call for new skills and capabilities. HR becomes the enabler of digital transformation of businesses, integrator among managers, employees and machines, advocate of digital talents, innovation agent and designer of digital workplaces and employee experience.

While digitalization continues at a dizzying speed, the concerns about the future of jobs and employment also increase. According to the World Economic Forum's 2018 Future of Jobs report, major impacts of AI in the global labor market were related to digital skill gaps and talent shortages. They were also related to increasing robotization and human-machine interaction, changing employment types and emergence of new jobs which are expected to offset decline in standardized-routine jobs. The report stated that human-robot interaction was a driving force of future job transformations. In the future, employees will be expected to work with robots and intelligent machines. The full adoption of human tasks by machines and robots is not feasible today. However, in the coming years, it is obvious that the shares of machines in completing job tasks will increase. Furthermore, human employment types will change, and new jobs will emerge. These new job profiles will require digital skills and capabilities, including creativity, originality, critical thinking, initiative, persuasion and negotiation. Therefore, HR leaders should be prepared for the questions of human-machine collaboration, digital talent skills and transforming jobs task while mapping digital transformation of HR functions and business operations.

REFERENCES

Bassi, L. (2011). Raging debates in HR analytics. *People and Strategy*, *34*(2), 14.

Bersin, J. (2018, June 18). AI In HR: A Real Killer App. *Forbes*. Available at https://www.forbes.com/sites/joshbersin/2018/06/18/ai-in-hr-a-real-killer-app/#4546756948f1

Beyer, M. A., & Laney, D. (2012). *The importance of 'big data': a definition*. Gartner.

Bort, J. (2014). *Bill Gates: People don't realise how many jobs will soon be lost to computers*. Retrieved October 10, 2018, from http://www.thejournal.ie/bill-gates-software-automatic-jobs-loss-bots-1363435-Mar2014/

Boudreau, J., & Rice, S. (2015). Bright, Shiny Objects and the Future of HR How Juniper Networks tests and integrates the most valuable new approaches. *Harvard Business Review*, *93*(7-8), 72–78.

Brougham, D., & Haar, J. (2018). Smart Technology, Artificial Intelligence, Robotics, and Algorithms (STARA): Employees' perceptions of our future workplace. *Journal of Management & Organization*, *24*(2), 239–257. doi:10.1017/jmo.2016.55

Brown, B., Chui, M., & Manyika, J. (2011). Are you ready for the era of 'big data'. *The McKinsey Quarterly*, *4*(1), 24–35.

Capgemini Research Institute and LinkedIn. (2017). *The Digital Talent Gap: Are Companies Doing Enough?* Available at https://www.capgemini.com/wp-content/uploads/2017/10/Digital-Talent-Gap-Report_Digital.pdf

Codorniou, J. (2018). *6 Trends Shaping a Future for People in the Workplace*. Available at https://www.entrepreneur.com/article/309804

Daft, R. L. (2015). *Organization theory and design*. Cengage Learning.

Dastin, J. (2018, October 10). Amazon scraps secret AI recruiting tool that showed bias against women. *Reuters*. Available at https://www.reuters.com/article/us-amazon-com-jobs-automation-insight/amazon-scraps-secret-airecruiting-tool-that-showed-bias-against-women-idUSKCN1MK08G

Davenport, T. H., Barth, P., & Bean, R. (2012). How'big data'is different. *MIT Sloan Management Review*.

Deloitte. (2018). *The rise of the social enterprise. 2018 Deloitte global human capital trends*. Available at: www2.deloitte.com/content/dam/Deloitte/at/Documents/human-capital/at2018-deloitte-human-capital-trends.pdf

Donaldson, C. (2016, December 5). How Microsoft is driving digital HR transformation. *Inside HR*. Available at https://www.insidehr.com.au/microsoft-driving-digital-hr-transformation/

Dumbill, E. (2013). *Making sense of big data*. Academic Press.

Falletta, S. (2014). In search of HR intelligence: Evidence-based HR analytics practices in high performing companies. *People and Strategy*, *36*(4), 28.

Frank, A. (2018). *How Artificial Intelligence Will Impact the Future of Work.* Available at https://www.cmswire.com/digital-workplace/how-artificial-intelligence-will-impact-the-future-of-work/

George, G., Haas, M., & Pentland, A. (2014). 'Big data and management'. *Academy of Management Journal*, *57*(2), 321–326. doi:10.5465/amj.2014.4002

Hecklau, F., Galeitzke, M., Flachs, S., & Kohl, H. (2016). Holistic approach for human resource management in Industry 4.0. *Procedia CIRP*, *54*, 1–6. doi:10.1016/j.procir.2016.05.102

Holloway, C., & Hand, H. H. (1988). Who's running the store, anyway? Artificial intelligence!!! *Business Horizons*, *31*(2), 70–76. doi:10.1016/0007-6813(88)90084-5

Huang, L. C., Huang, K. S., Huang, H. P., & Jaw, B. S. (2004, June). Applying fuzzy neural network in human resource selection system. In *Fuzzy Information, 2004. Processing NAFIPS'04. IEEE Annual Meeting of the* (Vol. 1, pp. 169-174). IEEE.

Huselid, M., & Minbaeva, D. (2018) *Big Data and Human Resource Management.* Academic Press.

Intel I. T. Center. (2012). *Big Data analytics. Intel's IT manager survey on how organizations are using big data.* Author.

Jarrahi, M. H. (2018). Artificial intelligence and the future of work: Human-AI symbiosis in organizational decision making. *Business Horizons*, *61*(4), 577–586. doi:10.1016/j.bushor.2018.03.007

Jesuthasan, R. (2017). HR's new role: Rethinking and enabling digital engagement. *Strategic HR Review*, *16*(2), 60–65. doi:10.1108/SHR-01-2017-0009

Kaplan, A., & Haenlein, M. (2018). Siri, Siri, in my hand: Who's the fairest in the land? On the interpretations, illustrations, and implications of artificial intelligence. *Business Horizons*.

Kaplan, A. M., & Haenlein, M. (2010). Users of the world, unite! The challenges and opportunities of Social Media. *Business Horizons*, *53*(1), 59–68. doi:10.1016/j.bushor.2009.09.003

Kolbjørnsrud, V., Amico, R., & Thomas, R. J. (2016). How artificial intelligence will redefine management. *Harvard Business Review*, 2.

Krotov, V. (2017). The Internet of Things and new business opportunities. *Business Horizons*, *60*(6), 831–841. doi:10.1016/j.bushor.2017.07.009

Lee, I. (2017). Big data: Dimensions, evolution, impacts, and challenges. *Business Horizons*, *60*(3), 293–303. doi:10.1016/j.bushor.2017.01.004

Lee, I., & Lee, K. (2015). The Internet of Things (IoT): Applications, investments, and challenges for enterprises. *Business Horizons*, *58*(4), 431–440. doi:10.1016/j.bushor.2015.03.008

Lengnick-Hall, M. L., Neely, A. R., & Stone, C. B. (2018). Human Resource Management in the Digital Age: Big Data, HR Analytics and Artificial Intelligence. In P. N. Melo & C. Machado (Eds.), *Managaement and Technological Challenges in the Digital Age* (pp. 1–30). CRC Press. doi:10.1201/9781351238922-1

Lynch, C. (2015). *Stephen Hawking on the Future of Capitalism and Inequality*. Available at https://www.counterpunch.org/2015/10/15/stephen-hawkings-on-the-tuture-of-capitalism-and-inequality/

Manuti, A., & de Palma, P. D. (2018). The Cognitive Technology Revolution: A New Role of HR Practices? In Digital HR (pp. 39-53). Palgrave Macmillan. doi:10.1007/978-3-319-60210-3_3

McAfee, A., Brynjolfsson, E., Davenport, T. H., Patil, D. J., & Barton, D. (2012). Big data: The management revolution. *Harvard Business Review*, *90*(10), 60–68. PMID:23074865

Mclver, D., Lengnick-Hall, M. L., & Lengnick-Hall, C. A. (2018). A strategic approach to workforce analytics: Integrating science and agility. *Business Horizons*, *61*(3), 397–407. doi:10.1016/j.bushor.2018.01.005

O'Leary, D. E. (2013). Artificial intelligence and big data. *IEEE Intelligent Systems*, *28*(2), 96–99. doi:10.1109/MIS.2013.39

PwC. (2015). *Workforce of the future: The competing forces shaping 2030*. Available at https://www.pwc.com/gx/en/services/people-organisation/workforce-of-the-future/workforce-of-the-future-the-competing-forces-shaping-2030-pwc.pdf

Rasmussen, T., & Ulrich, D. (2015). Learning from practice: How HR analytics avoids being a management fad. *Organizational Dynamics*, *44*(3), 236–242. doi:10.1016/j.orgdyn.2015.05.008

Richter, A., Heinrich, P., Stocker, A., & Schwabe, G. (2018). Digital work design. *Business & Information Systems Engineering*, *60*(3), 259–264. doi:10.100712599-018-0534-4

Russom, P. (2011). Big data analytics. *TDWI Best Practices Report*, *19*, 40.

Saarikko, T., Westergren, U. H., & Blomquist, T. (2017). The Internet of Things: Are you ready for what's coming? *Business Horizons*, *60*(5), 667–676. doi:10.1016/j.bushor.2017.05.010

Shamim, S., Cang, S., Yu, H., & Li, Y. (2016, July). Management approaches for Industry 4.0: A human resource management perspective. In *Evolutionary Computation (CEC), 2016 IEEE Congress on* (pp. 5309-5316). IEEE.

Sivathanu, B., & Pillai, R. (2018). Smart HR 4.0–how industry 4.0 is disrupting HR. *Human Resource Management International Digest*, *26*(4), 7–11. doi:10.1108/HRMID-04-2018-0059

Stephan, M., Uzawa, S., Volini, E., Walsh, B., & Yoshida, R. (2016). Digital HR: Revolution, not evolution. In B. Pelster & J. Schwartz (Eds.), Global Human Capital Trends 2016 - The new organization: Different by design (pp. 97–103). Academic Press.

Strack, R., Dyrchs, S., Kotsis, A., & Mingardon, S. (2017). *How to Gain and Develop Digital Talent and Skills.* Boston Consulting Group. Available at https://image-src.bcg.com/Images/BCG-How-to-Gain-and-Develop-Digital-Talent-and-Skills-July-2017_tcm9-165367.pdf

Thite, M. (Ed.). (2019). *E-HRM: Digital Approaches, Directions & Applications.* Routledge.

Ulrich, D. (1998). A new mandate for human resources. *Harvard Business Review*, *76*, 124–135. PMID:10176915

Ulrich, D., Kryscynski, D., Ulrich, M., & Brockbank, W. (2017). Competencies for HR Professionals Who Deliver Outcomes. *Employment Relations Today*, *44*(2), 37–44. doi:10.1002/ert.21623

Ulrich, D., Younger, J., Brockbank, W., & Ulrich, M. D. (2013). The state of the HR profession. *Human Resource Management*, *52*(3), 457–471. doi:10.1002/hrm.21536

Volini, E., Mazor, A., Schaefer, F., Tsuchida, A., & Walsh, B. (2016). Global human capital trends 2016: HR growing momentum toward a new mandate. Deloitte University Press.

Volini, E., Occean, P., Stephan, M., & Walsh, B. (2017). Digital HR: Platforms, people, and work. In G. Lahiri & D. Singh (Eds.), Global Human Capital Trends 2017: Rewriting the Rules for the Digital Age (pp. 87–93). Academic Press.

Vom Brocke, J., Maaß, W., Buxmann, P., Maedche, A., Leimeister, J. M., & Pecht, G. (2018). Future Work and Enterprise Systems. *Business & Information Systems Engineering*, 1–10.

White, S. K. (2018). *AI's impact on the future of work.* Available at https://www.cio.com/article/3285705/artificial-intelligence/ais-impact-on-the-future-of-work.html

Wilson, H. J., & Daugherty, P. R. (2018). Collaborative intelligence: Humans and AI are joining forces. *Harvard Business Review.*

Wisskirchen, G., Biacabe, B. T., Bormann, U., Muntz, A., Niehaus, G., Soler, G. J., & von Brauchitsch, B. (2017). *Artificial intelligence and robotics and their impact on the workplace.* International Bar Association Global Employment Institute, April 2017 Report.

World Economic Forum. (2018). *The future of jobs report.* Available at https://www3.weforum.org/docs/WEF_Future_of_Jobs_2018.pdf

ADDITIONAL READING

Al Haziazi, M., Muthuraman, S., Al Yahyaei, N., & Al Balusi, A. (2021, March). Influence of HR Digital Transformation in the Cognitive Technology Era of the Sultanate of Oman. In *2021 7th International Conference on Information Management (ICIM)* (pp. 123-127). IEEE. 10.1109/ICIM52229.2021.9417155

Bennett, E. E., & McWhorter, R. R. (2021). Virtual HRD's role in crisis and the post Covid-19 professional lifeworld: Accelerating skills for digital transformation. *Advances in Developing Human Resources*, *23*(1), 5–25. doi:10.1177/1523422320973288

Dahlbom, P., Siikanen, N., Sajasalo, P., & Jarvenpää, M. (2019). Big data and HR analytics in the digital era. *Baltic Journal of Management*, *15*(1), 120–138. doi:10.1108/BJM-11-2018-0393

DiRomualdo, A., El-Khoury, D., & Girimonte, F. (2018). HR in the digital age: How digital technology will change HR's organization structure, processes and roles. *Strategic HR Review*, *17*(5), 234–242. doi:10.1108/SHR-08-2018-0074

Fenech, R., Baguant, P., & Ivanov, D. (2019). The changing role of human resource management in an era of digital transformation. *Journal of Management Information and Decision Sciences*, *22*(2), 1–10.

Minbaeva, D. (2020). Disrupted HR? *Human Resource Management Review.*

Mitrofanova, E. A., Konovalova, V. G., & Mitrofanova, A. E. (2018). Opportunities, problems and limitations of digital transformation of HR management. In The European Proceedings of Social & Behavioural Sciences EpSBS (pp. 1717-1727). Academic Press.

Wessel, L., Baiyere, A., Ologeanu-Taddei, R., Cha, J., & Blegind-Jensen, T. (2021). Unpacking the difference between digital transformation and IT-enabled organizational transformation. *Journal of the Association for Information Systems*, *22*(1), 102–129. doi:10.17705/1jais.00655

KEY TERMS AND DEFINITIONS

Artificial Intelligence: They are systems that recursively process and improve the collected data by mimicking the way people think and behave to perform certain tasks.

Automation: It is the process of doing things by means of automatic vehicles without human effort and intervention.

Big Data: It is a mass of data that is constantly flowing through various channels at a great speed and in a wide variety of structures and is difficult to process with traditional database systems.

Digital HRM: It is the automation of HR processes and systems in accordance with the digital transformation trend and making them data driven.

Digital Transformation: It is meeting the needs of individuals, societies, and industries by utilizing digital technologies and accordingly shaping new business models, finding new ways of doing business, creating new digital strategies and cultures.

Digitalization: It is the transfer, storage and processing of data or resources in a way that can be understood by computers.

HR Analytics: It is the collection, processing, and analysis of HR data with various data analytics methods to enhance data-driven decision making.

Chapter 5
Digital Transformation in Ship Operations and Management:
Digital Twin Technology Applications

Murat Selçuk Solmaz
https://orcid.org/0000-0002-8528-2865
Piri Reis University, Turkey

Cihat Aşan
https://orcid.org/0000-0003-3674-6616
Piri Reis University, Turkey

Aydın Şıhmantepe
Piri Reis University, Turkey

ABSTRACT

Many businesses around the world have begun to take advantage of digital technology in recent years. Making use of digital technology enables one to do things in less time, need fewer employees, reduce costs, use information and resources effectively, produce the most products with the least resources, and consequently, increase the profitability of the enterprises. The shipping sector is one of the building blocks of the maritime industry. It aims to increase its profitability by digitizing in today's increasingly competitive conditions. In recent years, digital twin (DT) technology has been used extensively for the digitalization of the sector. This chapter introduces the current and potential uses of DT technology in ship operations and management and gives an idea about how DT technology will create an opportunity to develop the shipping sector.

DOI: 10.4018/978-1-7998-7793-6.ch005

Copyright © 2022, IGI Global. Copying or distributing in print or electronic forms without written permission of IGI Global is prohibited.

INTRODUCTION

Organizations operating in a classial structure lose time, money, and therefore their competitive power day by day, compared to organizations that use digital technology available today. This is because works on paper require more time and manpower. Today, there is almost no institution left that is still working on paper, however using computers in an organization does not necessarily mean that digital transformation is fully realized. Digital transformation also defines an organizational transformation. Using digital systems is only a means of full scale transformation. Digital transformation can be defined as organizational transformation in the digital age, where people's purchasing preferences are shaped by developments in information technologies (Tanniru, Xi, & Sandhu, 2020). Digital transformation strategies have four basic dimensions: the use of technologies, changes in value creation, structural changes, and financial aspects (Matt, Hess, & Benlian, 2015). Although digital transformation is a difficult and time-consuming process, it still helps organizations to achieve more profit by ensuring sustainability and competitiveness. However, current efforts to realize digital transformation do not yet have clear standards and they may require different processes for individual institution. Despite the difficulties in the transformation period, due to the magnitude of the benefits to be achieved, today all organizations in the world are trying to achieve digital transformation. With the encouragement of increasing competition in recent years, digital transformation efforts in the maritime industry have also gained momentum. DT technology, as an integral part of this transformation, has become a step ahead and found a wider place in maritime industry.

Ship operations and management, which covers all maritime trade, is a sub-field under the maritime industry. The maritime industry includes shipbuilding, marine resources and marine fisheries, marine tourism, and ship operations and management (Stopford, 2009). In this chapter, the "Ship operations and management" sub-field of the maritime industry has been focused on, studies conducted with digital twin technology have been examined and future projections have been made.

The concept of DT refers to a copy of a real object in a virtual environment. The twin-generated object can be a simple device or a complex system. Talking about the twin of an object is possible by transferring all its information to its twin. For this reason, the created twin needs to be constantly updated with current data. This is the most evident difference between the DT and the simulation. While there is no information transfer from the real object in simulation technology, there is a continuous data flow from the real object to the twin in the DT technology. On the other hand simulations use assumptions whereas DT uses real data to perform their functions. A DT is an integrated multi-physics, multi-scale, and probabilistic simulation of a complex object. It consists of a physical object, a virtual object, and the data that connects them. It functions to realize the convergence of physical object and virtual object and by doing so it reflects the actual life of its corresponding twin - the original object. It also uses the best physical models and sensor updates to ensure efficiency and sustainability in design, production, and service periods that constitute the life cycle of a product (Tao et al., 2018). Today DT technology is used in many sectors such as aviation, space, automotive, energy, healthcare, and maritime industry.

The maritime industry has started to benefit from DT technology in recent years within the scope of digital transformation. Especially in the ship operations and management sub-group of the maritime industry, many pilot projects are carried out on ship and port operation/management. Thus, it is aimed to establish a sustainable, competitive, and profitable system by finding the most optimal solutions in the complex environment of maritime transportation and port management. Thus, the research question in this study is, "could DT technology be useful for digital transformation in ship operations and management?" Hence the study examines applications conducted with DT technology in ship operations and management. The aim of the section is to introduce the potential uses of DT technology in ship operations and management within digital transformation and to provide insight into how DT technology can create opportunities to solve current and potential problems in the sector.

BACKGROUND

Digital Transformation

Digital transformation is an inevitable end for all organizations around the world today. Because it has become impossible for organizations that cannot achieve digital transformation to survive in a highly competitive environment. Digital transformation reduces costs by ensuring the economical use of resources. Production of goods or services is done in a shorter time. Access to information is very fast and therefore problems are solved faster. Therefore, the profitability of organizations increases more. Digital transformation is to use digital capabilities to maximize the performance of traditional business (Weill & Woerner, 2018). Transformation means a fundamental change in an organization because it causes major changes in the organization's strategy, structure, and power distribution (Berghaus & Back, 2016). Digital transformation aims to benefit from information technologies in order to achieve these fundamental changes in the organization. Information technology is the technology that involves the development, use, and maintenance of computer hardware and software systems for data processing and distribution (Al Amoush & Sandhu, 2020).

Nowadays, fast access to goods and services for customers is one of the most important criteria for choosing the market they will shop, and businesses, being aware of this, attach importance to providing fast service to their customers (Tanniru, Xi, & Sandhu, 2020). Digital transformation provides many advantages in business. For example, information storage, processing, and access to information are very fast. In this way, company managers can make very fast decisions. With automation, e-commerce, digital signature, ease of payment, goods, and services can be traded very quickly. All these operations can be done remotely. Businesses may not need to work in large buildings. With these advantages, the business can increase its profitability. With the COVID-19 pandemic that affects the whole world these days, it has been confirmed once again that digital transformation is inevitable for organizations. Many companies directed their employees to work remotely, and those who have kept up with the digital age have had no trouble doing so and have been able to run their entire business as smoothly as if they were at the workplace. Those who lagged behind in this regard either suffered enormous losses or had to go bankrupt. For this reason, organizations have had to accelerate digital transformation.

Digital transformation for businesses is a difficult and lengthy process. It requires carefully planned and patiently administered work. In the initial period of the transformation process, the costs of the enterprise may increase. While the classic functioning of the business is maintained, efforts for transition to digitalization can be very tiring. Employees will need to maintain their daily work and at the same time do additional work for transformation. In short, the transition process can be very painful, both financially and morally. However, it is clear that the results, benefits, and solutions to be achieved with the completion of the transition process will make you forget this troubled process.

Mamede (2009) proposed a new methodology to support the full application lifecycle of digital businesses in small and medium-sized enterprises. Li (2020) examined digital transformation in creative industries and revealed that digital transformation can offer a much wider business model for companies. Tanniru, Xi, and Sandhu (2020) worked on leadership in digital transformation in the healthcare industry and stated that the four principles they identified could be used as a guide for transformation in this industry. Al Amoush and Sandhu (2020) examined how digital transformation affects the teaching techniques of students in higher education. Basole (2016) argued that digital transformation can be accelerated with programming interfaces that use technological factors such as mobile, social, analytics, and cloud. Gölzer and Fritzsche (2017) stated that digital transformation in industrial operations management can be achieved with components such as Big Data and the Internet of Things (IOT) within the scope of Industry 4.0. Von Leipzig et al. (2017) stated that digitalization shapes Industry 4.0, making business models even more effective. Heilig et al. (2017) analyzed the maritime logistics environment related to digital transformation in ports and argued that digital transformation can transform all aspects of the organization. Fletcher and Griffiths (2020) in their study of times when world economies are in lockdown, such as the pandemic, suggested that businesses improve their digital maturity to make them less vulnerable in such situations. Chanias et al. (2019) studied on the strategy required for a business that works with traditional methods to achieve digital transformation and suggested that the digital transformation strategy is not a finite process, but a dynamic process that includes repetition between learning and doing. Vial (2019) conducted a literature review on digital transformation and tried to determine the framework of digital transformation inductively. Singh and Hess (2017), in their study on Chief Digital Officers (CDOs), which manages the digital transformation efforts of companies, identified how CDOs fulfill their duties, their skills and competencies, and the main factors for their employment. Hess et al. (2016) has proposed a guide for companies involved in digital transformation efforts to create a digital transformation strategy by introducing digital transformation opportunities and risks. Mergel et al. (2019) conducted an empirically-based definition of digital transformation based on expert interviews and drew a conceptual framework for digital transformation in the public sector. Digital twin technology, which is one of the information technologies used to provide digital transformation, has started to be widely used in the maritime industry as in many areas in the world. In particular, ship operations and management that is a sub-field under the maritime industry has been focused on this subfield, as it is used more widely.

Ship Operations and Management

The maritime industry involves a variety of sub-areas. Main areas are associated with ship construction, marine resources, and marine fisheries. Tourism and ship operations and management form other important areas of the maritime industry (Stopford, 2009). As in all other industry branches, different aspects of the maritime industry require explicit knowledge base, training, and experience to handle the inherent necessities of that area.

Ship construction, as one of the major divisions of the maritime industry, involves all activities concerning designing and building of marine vessels. Shipbuilding is the area of naval architects and all the construction activities are performed in shipyards. Vessels may be built either for commercial or military purposes. One other important output of shipyards is the equipment for using the offshore energy industry. Within the maritime industry, another function of shipyards that produces economic revenue is the scrapping of the marine vessels for recycling purposes. (Kavussanos & Visvikis, 2016)

The marine resources aspect of the marine industry mostly concerns the extraction of carbon-based resources from the sea bed. Those activities involve drilling and building off-shore platforms that require enormous investments. While extraction of gas and oil are the major exercises, contemporary efforts include clean energy production such as building wind turbines. Investments to make use of sea minerals have also become an interest of recent marine resource value. (World Ocean Review, 2014)

Marine fisheries as an important sub-group of the marine industry includes commercial fishing activities, building and sustaining aquaculture facilities, and also the processing of seafood produced. (Stopford, 2009). Fishing activities are performed onboard a variety of vessels designed for the purpose. The whole activity also requires the fishing vessels to deliver their harvest to port facilities where it will be handed over to consumers and also the sea processing facilities. On the other hand, aquaculture is another option for commercial fishing. It involves the farming of marine species mostly in tanks or sub-sea cages along the coastline. Both harvests from fishing and fish farming will finally be delivered to seafood processing facilities to be prepared as final products for consumers.

Marine centered tourism provides twofold economic benefits. From entertainment and service aspects, marine tourism includes a variety of activities that range from yacht chartering to individual sports like scuba diving and windsurfing. Revenue covers the people engaged in those activities as business runners and trainers (Orams, 1999). Within this sub-group, services such as insurance, banking, legal services, shipbroking, and publishing are also included as economic benefit producing elements. (Stopford 2009)

The ship operations and management section of the marine industry holds a significant place in marine activities and is directly associated with the operation of vessels. This includes merchant shipping, ports, cruise vessels, and operations as well as naval shipping. Although naval vessels are not directly engaged in the commercial domain, still they contribute to preserving, protecting, and keeping the safety of international waterways for trade (Stopford 2009). Cruise operations involve ferries and ocean liners for the transportation of people as well as recreational voyages around the globe (Stopford, 2009). One other area to mention under ship operations and management is port business. Ports are commercial facilities where maritime business mostly takes place. For merchant ships, ports are places where vessels have access to land-based facilities to load, or unload their cargo. Ports also function as temporary terminals where the goods are stored in warehouses and depots for further processes. For incoming cargo, ports are the starting point of inland transportation, whereas for outgoing goods they are the loading points for sea-based transportation. (Stopford, 2009; Lee & Song, 2010).

When considered as a whole, merchant shipping covers the largest sub-area of the marine industry reaching one-third of the total turnover (Stopford, 2009). Today nearly 90% of world trade is carried out seaborne (United Nations Conference on Trade and Development [UNCTAD], 2017). As shipping companies provide the services for transporting goods, it is hard to generalize all the services given by those companies. This is due to a variety of reasons such as diversity of cargo types, services requested by the customers, and port facilities in hand at the destinations. In order to overcome this difficulty, liner, bulk, and specialized cargo services are established (Stopford, 2009). However, though these three services require different types of technical operations, the basic aim remains the same; loading, transporting and unloading the cargo safely and in the allocated time. For this reason, the safety of the ships, cargo and the people engaged must be observed at all times. There are of course rules and regulations at national and international levels to contribute to the safety of those operations. However minimum standards set by authorities should be reinforced by additional measures to render those efforts more resilient and fail-safe. Making backup plans, having alternative routes, or simulating possible defects and errors in advance may be a good starting point. An innovative way for achieving this goal and assuring safe operation is creating a DT of the relevant systems. Within ship operations and management, the DT approach may be incorporated in various applications and procedures. Creating a DT requires a seamless connection between the physical model and the virtual model of it. Moreover, this connection must provide real-time data through sensors.

DT Technology

Constantly updated needs and demands of consumers played a leading role in the changes of qualitative and quantitative structures of products. In this context, the production methods of these products have also developed continuously. Modern industrial development has lasted for several hundred years and three major industrial revolutions have emerged. Now, the fourth one, called Industry 4.0, has become the very reality of recent times.-Since the first, subsequent revolutions have created radical changes in production, from water and steam-electric machines to electronic and digital automated production. Manufacturing processes become increasingly complex, automated, and sustainable (Kagermann, H., W. Wahlster, and J. Helbig, 2013).

On the other hand, the continuous development of information and communication technologies also continued to offer great potential to manufacturing companies to meet their needs. The improvements in information and communication technologies

(ICTs) have greatly encouraged manufacturing growth (Liu, Fang, Dong, & Xu, 2020). Digital technologies such as; cloud computing, big data, the IOT, artificial intelligence, wireless sensor networks are evolving rapidly, and providing big opportunities for industry (Syafrudin, Alfian, Fitriyani, & Rhee, 2018). In addition to this, digitalization keeps continuing for smart factories producing smart products. The price decline in miniature products facilitates the aggregate of communication, information, and sensor technologies into even the weensiest products. Besides, to comprehend their environment, products come in possession of sense in their state. Pair up the capability to process and sharing this data paves the way for the creation of DTs (Haag & Anderl, 2018).

Through sensor technology, collecting and processing data, and transfer them between physical space and virtual space, which is characterized by DT, via communication technology represents the interests of the academic and industrial community in recent years. This physical and virtual data can be merged employing DTs throughout a product lifecycle, which prompts a tremendous volume of information that can be handled by cutting edge analytics (Tao, Zhang, Liu, & Nee, 2019). At that point, the analysis outcomes can be utilized to improve the fertileness of product in the physical space. DTs empower producers to make more delicate forecasts, reasonable choices, what's more, deliberative plans (Qi & Tao, 2018).

Although the definition of a DT and its conditions are not yet profoundly established and lacks of cognitive frame, there are several visions which firstly Grieves brought up into a presentation to the industry at the University of Michigan in 2002 and defined it as; "a concept for a virtual equivalent of a dynamic digital representation of a real system" (Grieves, 2014). Consecutive definition of DT in National Aeronautics and Space Administration (NASA) roadmaps can be found as; imaginary equipollent of satellites which were not accessible for reconnoiter and field survey (Shafto, Conroy, Doyle & Glaessgen, Kemp, LeMoigne, Wang, 2010). Within different aspect, DT is a truthful model of the present condition of the process in communication with their environment in reality (Rosen, Von Wichert, Lo, & Bettenhausen, 2015).

Besides the origin aspect, there are also other approaches to the term DT in the industry. Profound investigations by some manufacturers on creating a connection between the digital representation and the physical product enhancing production pliancy. On the other hand, while some part of manufacturers is focusing on using DT to enhance product design; others are dealing with DT to survey the product all along its life cycle developing quality in manufacturing (Schleich, Anwer, Mathieu, & Wartzack, 2017). Nowadays all data of product or manufacturing systems concerning operation, status, process, etc., bring out its own digital shadow. Based on Stark, Kind, & Neumeyer, (2017), DT is composed of a Digital Master model of an item, its singular Digital Shadow and a smart connection (algorithm, simulation model, correlation, etc.).

Simulations and data outputs of the DT provides the realization of new products or processes with low effort (Rosen, Boschert, & Sohr, 2018). In particular, the coalescence of engineering or simulation models and survey data is crucial. On the other hand, the initial impression of doable benefits has been already gained from particular realizations of DTs. As a further vision, Rosen et al. (2018) stated that: "In future, endeavors must be diverted to integrate product lifecycle management systems, cloud solutions, and further data artifacts as well as devices". The configuration of models and data with their official standards, additionally their notional annotations stay as further challenges.

RESEARCH METHODOLOGY

As the research question of the study, "could DT technology be useful for digital transformation in ship operations and management?" has been determined. A qualitative research method was used in the research. In this context, firstly the studies about DT in shipping industry have been examined through literature review and data have been collected. This data has been categorized under the subgroups of ship and port applications. The categorized information has been compared with the problems experienced in the sector today. Then, DT technology can find a solution to what kind of problems in ship operations and management in the future, and thus how DT technology can contribute to digital transformation has been evaluated.

DT TECHNOLOGY APPLICATIONS IN SHIP OPERATIONS AND MANAGEMENT

Although maritime transportation plays a dominant role in global transport, the excess of conclusion-oriented variables necessitates the cost-effective execution of each step of the process. In this context, it is crucial to foresee the effect of variables on the conclusion and to plan measures within the framework of risk analysis. DT applications in the maritime industry emerge as a very important factor in the cost-effective execution of processes. DT technology within the maritime industry is the real-time monitoring of the behavior patterns of any physical actor, affecting the process, in its operating environment on the virtual model via information flow provided by the sensors, and the reflection of the obtained results into the production phase within the life cycle. Comparing the manufacturing domain to the maritime domain, it can be deduced that more detailed guidance for the conceptual development and implementation of DT has been offered by the manufacturing domain. However, the maritime domain has produced valuable design patterns for DT solutions (Taylor et al., 2019). When the DT applications in the ship operations and management sub-field are examined, a wide range of products from specific asset modeling to process management is encountered.

Ship Applications

In parallel to the development of the sensors as well as improvements in the communication technology, obtaining data via sensors and relaying the gathered data to the desired location have become respectively easier. Lin et al. (2019) made a thorough investigation of the references of current DT applications to exhibit a variety of approaches to the subject. As data acquisition and transmission technology broadened their capabilities, DT applications have also expanded its scope accordingly. However especially when the seagoing part of the maritime industry is concerned, there still seems to exist some restrictions and difficulties to overcome. The first difficulty arises from the complexity of the data that ships need to process together with the environment involved for operation. As ships are capable of conducting extended and independent operations at sea, by their nature they must run like a floating city. Hence they have to manage and control a number of sub-systems such as air conditioning, water and sewage systems, long-range and local communication climate, and energy distribution. Safe operation of the ship will also require monitoring and controlling power production, fire and safety systems, as well as propulsion and navigation systems. As all those systems are not provided by a single manufacturer, integrating the data produced and the ownership of the produced data will be problematic. Moreover, as the connectivity of ships at sea will not have the same facilities as land-based stations, data transfer may pose additional difficulties. Rodseth & Berre (2018) after pinpointing the difficulties involved, propose a concept similar to "Industrial Data Space" (IDS) which has been developed to overcome similar problems for the land-based industry which they call "Maritime Data Space" (MDS). These facts may be translated into an understanding that DT applications for operations at sea part of the marine industry still has a way to go to come up with robust and reliable applications.

Perabo et al. (2020) created a sophisticated ship AC power and propulsion model which consists of DT modelling and co-simulation. In this work, local and upper-level controllers of ships power and propulsion system have been modelled as Functional Mock-up Units (FMUs) as well as the AC system in Open Simulation Platform (OSP) for co-simulation. By utilizing the DT model which has got different FMUs and OSP for having data from the operation environment, a test scenario is performed to demonstrate the straight running of power and impulsion system. As a conclusion, the authors stated that co-simulation, under the favor of digital model, is convenient to assay the ships power system stability and they also emphasized that all sub-assets such as switchboards, controllers, electronic appliances, etc., can be applied into the system. Additionally, it has been foreseen that different static and dynamic FMUs such as current, wave, hull, crane, etc., from different domains can be implemented into the OSP for making possible to a comprehensive simulation of a ship.

Another view is that the DT concept will remain a high priority on the agenda. This opinion is justified by taking into consideration the studies on models that involve vessel machinery systems' operating parameters to generate valuable insights. This view also suggests that it will not take too long to become a further step in cloud-based DT solutions. As far as real implementation of DT technology in Maritime domain is concerned, DNV GL appears under the name of COSSMOS (COmplex Ship Systems Modelling and Simulation). The company created virtual engine rooms named COSSMOS, which has got integration to ship machinery systems and information flow from it. COSSMOS models are effectually connected to ship's running parameters and create substantial data. Worldwide, DNV GL runs more than 60 ships within COSSMOS-based implementations and accumulating tangible experience. Another example in DNV GL, DT implementation falls into the Marine Cybernetics Advisory team. They created a Hardware-In-the- Loop (HIL) simulator which is the virtual model and simulates actual ship's propulsion systems, electronic devices and multifarious equipment as a DT. This simulator has been interconnected to more than 150 vessel's control systems, and it is asserted that technology can be implemented to any type of vessel. Besides of control systems, the company has developed a link between the ship's hull and DT to monitor the operating environment and stress condition of the ship's structure. This output lets the managers to foresee unexpected circumstances and may restrict the ship's operation for certain cases. (Smogeli, 2017)

In global maritime merchant fleet frame, automation and electric propulsion systems are new directions for cost-effectiveness. From this point of view, state monitoring and information flow are becoming more crucial. Bjørum (2019)'s study on the possibility of utilizing a DT of RV Gunnerus, Norwegian University of Science and Technology research vessel Permanent Magnet Azimuth (PM-AZ) thrusters, is another example for DT application in the maritime domain. The study focuses on state monitoring by using Permanent Magnet Synchronous Motors (PMSM) and failure detection techniques. The initial approach for power monitoring was a signal-based and model-based combination. However, due to insufficient and low-quality stream of sensor data from RV Gunnerus, a thermal modelling approach incorporated with a statistical fault detection algorithm was used as a foundation of the study. To simulate the thermal behavior of a PMSM, Lumped Parameter Thermal Network has been conducted which simulates the temperature in armature copper windings, the stator core, the rotor core and the permanent magnets. Based on the output of the research, eccentricity-related faults, bearing faults, stator faults and broken rotor bars are the key elements concerning failure detection and maintenance. Although non-invasive Motor Current Signature Analysis (MCSA) is the most appropriate way and the cost-effectiveness of data driven-methods on the foundation of artificial intelligence is crucial for the next step on state monitoring, without convenient sensor-data infrastructure, condition screening by a combination of model-based and data-driven is a beneficial tool for failure detection and lifelong prediction of electrical machinery. (Bjørum, 2019)

In recent years, environmental problems at the global scale (Gazioğlu, 2018) that may arise as a result of environmental pollution and climate changes have caused the studies on energy efficiency applications on ships to gain importance. Through these applications, it is aimed to reduce the fuel consumed by the ship, to reduce the emissions emitted by the ship and to achieve a sustainable environment as a result. In this context, Rolls-Royce Marine developed an Energy Management System for ships. The system records the data collected from the ships on a portal on land. These data are information about the vessel's performance. Later, this information is arranged and sent to the ship and the seafarers can see this information, helping to use energy efficiently. Since the system provides near real-time information flow, it enables instant decisions and corrective actions. As a result, the system saves energy and reduces costs (Taylor et al., 2019).

Marine fouling, as it affects both fuel consumption and dry-docking periods, hence costs, is one of the areas that DT applications may provide a step ahead. In a recent study, Coraddu et al., (2019) showed that a more precise and consistent prediction of the loss of performance can be achieved ahead of time by processing the data provided by the sensors mounted on ships. To predict the loss of speed due to fouling on the hulls and propellers of the ships, the authors created a data-driven model-based DT of the physical ship, where a lot of data is collected by many sensors installed in its structure. They also put to use the same model to predict the loss of speed and its deviation. In their work, they have shown that the average deviation of the speed loss times can be used to estimate the impact of marine fouling to the ship performance and this can be exploited to create a more efficient hull and propeller cleaning schedule. In their study, it has been emphasized that information flow between the DT and physical ship should be set up for initial phase which marine fouling has not existed and there should be ample range of time to observe ships behavior under different conditions.

The role of maritime transport in the transportation of goods globally will increase with the introduction of autonomous ships. Situational awareness (SA) systems and autonomous navigation systems (ANS) play a key role in autonomous ships, which are expected to provide great advantages in terms of reducing ship operating costs and environmental factors. Based on the study of Pedersen et al. (2020); in addition to real-life monitoring, the simulation-based testing system is also needed for assurance of the safe ANS deployment process. They provided a test system utilizing the combination of real-life monitoring and simulation-based testing with the light of DNV GL DT application perspective via focusing on creating scenario tests, function tests and their evaluation algorithm.

If one looks at the latest developments regarding the digital twin, two attempts appear to be remarkable. Furuno Hellas company created a virtual replica of the ship's bridge navigation and communication equipment using DT technology. The system named HermAce uploads the information coming from the equipment to its digital twin, enabling remote and real-time identification, diagnosis and resolution of problems. HermAce has been awarded the Digital Twin Ready certification of Lloyd's Register. Mitsui O.S.K. Lines (MOL) signed a contract with the National Institute of Maritime, Port and Aviation Technology (MPAT) and the National Maritime Research Institute (NMRI) to develop a digital twin model of the two-stroke main diesel engine using operational data collected from ships operated by MOL. (Mishra, 2020)

When the DT applications on the ships are examined, it is seen that the applications are aimed at providing more optimized use of the existing ships. However, it is clear that the ultimate goal is to create the infrastructure of autonomous ships.

Port Applications

Digital transformation has begun to take its place in maritime transportation as in all sectors. Studies on autonomous ships, in particular, continue without slowing down. Of course, some arrangements need to be made in ports that will serve autonomous ships. Digital information of the port is needed in order for autonomous ships to navigate safely in port entry and departure. In a sense, first of all, the port should have a digital map and dynamic information such as meteorological and oceanographic conditions, port ship traffic status should be added to this digital map. Thus, a DT of the port must be created and all the information covered by the DT must be transferred to the autonomous ships arriving or leaving the port. Today, the leading ports of the port industry have started to work on this issue. One of the best examples in this regard is the Port of Rotterdam, one of Europe's largest ports.

Port of Rotterdam port authority has started to work together with IT partners IBM, Cisco, Esri and Axians on digitalization of the port and use IOT technology. Port management aims to create a DT of the port by using all real-time information about the port from IOT sensors and display this information in a virtual environment. (Port of Rotterdam, 2019) Thus, ships arriving at the port and preparing to leave the port will be able to follow the meteorological and oceanographic status of the port and all other data on the DT of the port. Aware that autonomous ships will dominate maritime transportation in the future, preparations have started for autonomous ships to receive services from the port. In this context, work is underway to create the DT of the port. In order to create a DT of the port, work has been started on the creation of a digital map of the port. An autonomous boat named Floating Lab with two stereo cameras and six 360° cameras is used for this task. This boat records images of the port and creates a digital map of the port with these images. (Port of Rotterdam, 2018)

Ports are not only a platform for cargo transportation but also a part of the logistics system. The basis of logistics is based on the integration and optimization of different processes and functions to reduce costs. Ports are considered as logistics centers where all movements in the logistics chain are optimized. (Institute of Chartered Shipbrokers [ICS], 2007) Ports have a complex structure related to both ships and cargo. The important thing is to find the most optimal solutions in this complex structure and increase the efficiency of the port (Solmaz, & Koray, 2020). Complex systems are systems that exist in a dynamic environment, consisting of many heterogeneous components with a high degree of interconnections, relationships and dependencies (Selin, & Santos, 2018). Port efficiency, on the other hand, is based on balancing the demand for the port with the service supply provided by the port and a flexible integration within the entire transport system. The port's historical, ongoing, and predicted future trade can be blended with digital twin technology and used for strategic planning of the port. With the projections to be achieved in this way, strategic decisions such as how many berths are required for the ships in the port to meet the punctuality aim in the following periods and how much port yard area is required for the needs of all customers in shipping services can be easily made. At the same time, the optimization of port operations can be achieved with the digital twin technology fed from multiple data streams of real-time data and historical databases. (Lind et al., 2020)

Within the scope of the DT project, the Rotterdam port has started to digitalize its logistics activities. In order to turn containers into smart containers, the Rotterdam port has launched a project called Container 42 with the cooperation of IBM, Cisco, and Esri companies. In the project, a container equipped with sensors that can record information such as vibrations, inclination, location, noise, air pollution, humidity, and the temperature was left for circulation around the world for two years. The aim of this project is to identify the difficulties encountered during transportation and logistics with the data collected and to contribute to the development of a digital representation of the physical port area called the DT. With the completion of this project, the digitalization of port services and safer, faster, and more reliable transport of cargo will be achieved. It will enable autonomous transportation as the ultimate goal. (Port of Rotterdam, 2019; Weare42, n.d.) The data streams generated by smart containers are an invaluable resource for the digital twin created for ship operations and management optimization. Digital twin systems fed by these data will provide new solutions in port and terminal optimization, situational awareness, and optimization of supply chain operations. Containers are managed by many different carriers, especially in an end-to-end supply chain. A digital twin for supply chain optimization will provide opportunities for all actors in the system to optimize the choice of shipping mode and route of containers. It will also create an infrastructure to optimize the flow of empty containers. (Lind et al., 2020)

Like the work of Rotterdam port, creating a DT of Singapore port has been initiated with a project of the Center of Excellence in Modeling and Simulation of Next Generation Ports (C4NGP. The aim of the project is to test operational efficiency. In addition, through DT simulation, it will be possible to create test scenarios for possible interruptions in operations, including natural disasters and extreme weather conditions (Port Technology, 2018). Hamburg port has digitized 95 percent of its logistics processes so far within the scope of digital transformation and includes all transportation modes in the port with its automatic data collection and analysis system. With the DT technology, all these data collected are visualized on a single platform. In addition, with the project named 5G MoNarch, the port processes of the DT project are regulated. With the 5G technology integrated into the DT models, Hamburg Port provides intelligent control over all platforms in the port. (Piernext, 2020) The Port of Barcelona has monitored port operations for years and recorded the information obtained on a digital copy of the port. When needed, it can display this information on a two-dimensional map of the port. However, these data cannot be monitored in real-time. In order to fill this gap, the Barcelona port is working on creating the DT of the port. For this purpose, the Barcelona port is working on the three-dimensional representation of the port, 5G communication, and Wi-Fi, artificial intelligence, video image analysis, improvement of data flow. When the project is completed, its data can be represented in real-time on a DT model. This will help managers to make real-time decisions, increase port efficiency, increase the safety of port employees, increase transparency for port customers, and create an environment that provides more predictability in ship loading/unloading operations. (Piernext, 2020)

SOLUTIONS AND RECOMMENDATIONS

Every business working within the ship operations and management section of the Maritime industry, which includes ship and port operations, tries to optimize their activities and increase profits in order to survive in the fierce competition environment of today's trade. In order to achieve this optimization, the complex structure of maritime transportation and the large number of variables it contains requires information technologies that can achieve complex solutions. When the literature is reviewed, it is seen that the DT technology within the scope of ship operations and management is rising among the information technologies used and the digital twin applications are generally divided into two main areas as applications in ships and ports.

When the applications of DT in merchant ships are examined; due to the complex structure of the marine environment, complex systems of ships, the difficulty of data integration due to the different manufacturers of these systems, difficulties in transferring information from sea to land, it is seen that digital twin applications on ships are still at the beginning level and there are many virgin areas to find solid and reliable applications in this regard. However, considering the applications made so far regarding ships, it is seen that the following issues are most remarkable.

Within the scope of testing the propulsion systems of ships, which are difficult to do in real life and cause loss of time and money, the power and propulsion systems of the ships can be modeled with DT technology and thus the stability of the power transmission systems of the ships can be easily tested, and the information that is continuously fed from the ship engine systems to the digital twin. It is evaluated that unexpected situations can be detected in advance. It is also evaluated that other systems on the ships can be monitored with DT technology and the failure can be predicted in advance. Studies show that DT technology has been used mainly in ship main and auxiliary engine systems at the beginning. However, it has now begun to be used in all systems and devices of the ship, including bridge navigation and communication devices. Thus, all systems and devices of the ship can be remotely controlled, and any malfunction can be rectified.

Today, the efficient use of energy, the least pollution of the environment, and the establishment of a sustainable system are the most important issues in the maritime sector as in all sectors. The issues of energy efficiency in ships and the reduction of emissions from ships are among the issues promoted by the International Maritime Organization. With DT technology, the energy used by the ship and its emissions can be easily followed by both the company and the ship's crew. The goals to be achieved in this regard can be followed. It can provide instant decisions and corrective actions for deviations from targets.

Sea creatures adhering to the hulls and propellers of ships reduce the speed of the ship and docking intervals and increase fuel consumption and costs. It is considered that DT technology can be used to estimate the speed loss of the ship and the effect of this speed loss on ship performance and to create an efficient hull/propeller cleaning program.

It is clear that DT technology, which is currently encountered in individual pilot applications on ships, will be an indispensable technology for the foundation of autonomous ships by forming parts of the whole in the future. Because autonomous ships will be controlled remotely by humans owing to DT technology, faults and problems during a voyage can be solved remotely and necessary tests can be performed. When autonomous ships approach a port equipped with DT technology, they will be able exchange necessary information automatically and dock their berths by making their own maneuvers.

In summary, the benefits of DT technology on ships can be listed as follows: Remote control of the systems and devices on the ship, remote monitoring of the operating values it produces, determination of the probability of failure in advance, optimum planning of maintenance periods, keeping all records regularly in a historical process, being able to make tests on its twin. In addition, by ensuring that all systems and devices on the ship consume less energy, running costs will be reduced, energy efficiency will be achieved, and environmental protection will be maintained. As a result, the economic life of the ship can be extended and more optimal ships can be built with the information to be obtained over the years.

When the DT applications in ports are examined, it is seen that many projects have been conducted on the integration of the port with autonomous ships. In this context, first of all, work is being done on the creation of a digital and real-time map of the port. Dynamic information such as meteorological and oceanographic conditions, port and ship traffic should be displayed on the map instantly. This real-time map information should be passed on to all ships using the port. Today, this information can be used in the entrance and exit of classical manned merchant ships, but the ultimate goal is to enable autonomous ships to enter and exit the port by themselves in the near future. Of course, the work within the scope of autonomous ships and port practices should be compatible. Due to the global nature of maritime transport, it is inevitable to work towards standardization in digitalization projects related to autonomous ships and ports.

Another important part of DT applications in ports is the digitization of the logistics activities of ports. The basis of logistics is to provide integration and optimization of different processes and functions to increase customer satisfaction and reduce costs. By digitizing the logistics activities of ports, which are part of the logistics system, optimization of port and terminal activities, situational awareness within the port, optimization of the shipping mode and route selection of full containers within the scope of optimization of supply chain operations, as well as optimizing the flow of empty containers can be achieved. As a result, safer, faster, more reliable, and less costly cargo transportation will be obtained. In addition, the past, present, and future trade of the port can be blended with digital twin technology and this information can be used for strategic planning of the port. Thanks to good planning, the efficiency of the port can be increased. With the real-time processed information, it enables managers to make real-time and more accurate decisions, provides transparency for port customers, creates an environment that provides more predictability in ship loading/unloading operations, creates a safer environment for port employees, optimizes the maintenance plans of the systems and vehicles used in the port. With the simulation capability of DT technology, it will be possible to create test scenarios for possible disruptions in operations, including natural disasters and extreme weather conditions. With the widespread use of 5G technology, intelligent control will be provided on all platforms in the port.

FUTURE RESEARCH DIRECTIONS

As a result of this study, it is evaluated that DT technology could be useful for digital transformation in ship operations and management. However, this study is an overview study covering two subheadings within the scope of ship operations and management. DT technology is a new technology that is being used in maritime transportation. However, the study has shown that the potential capabilities of DT technology are already at a level that can solve many problems in the shipping sector. In the upcoming period, detailed and technical studies can be conducted on how to benefit from DT technology in order to achieve digital transformation in areas under each sub-heading within the scope of ship operations and management.

CONCLUSION

Digital transformation, which aims to provide organizational change by using digital technologies to increase performance in businesses, has started to be preferred by many sectors. With digital technology, jobs are to be done in a shorter time, fewer employees are needed, costs are reduced, information and resources are used effectively, the most products are produced with the least resources, and therefore the profitability of businesses increases. Ship operations and management is one of the building blocks of the maritime industry, which aims to increase its profitability by digitizing it in today's increasingly competitive conditions. In recent years, DT technology has been used for digitalization in ship operations and management. When studies on DT technology in ship operations and management are examined, it becomes evident that this technology can offer optimum solutions in ships and ports. The study concludes by stating that DT technology can help ship operations to attain more profit with less workload and promote achieving full-scale digital transformation in the maritime sector.

REFERENCES

Al Amoush, A. B., & Sandhu, K. (2020). Digital Transformation of Learning Management Systems at Universities: Case Analysis for Student Perspectives. *Digital Transformation and Innovative Services for Business and Learning,* 41-61. https://doi.org/ doi:10.4018/978-1-7998-5175-2.ch003

Basole, R. C. (2016). Accelerating digital transformation: Visual insights from the API ecosystem. *IT Professional, 18*, 20–25.

Berghaus, S., & Back, A. (2016). Stages in Digital Business Transformation: Results of an Empirical Maturity Study. *MCIS 2016 Proceedings. 22*. Retrieved from http://aisel.aisnet.org/mcis2016/22

Bjørum, L. O. (2019). *Development of a Digital Twin for Condition Monitoring, Focusing on Electrical Propulsion Systems for Marine Application.* Norwegian University of Science and Technology.

Chanias, S., Myers, M. D., & Hess, T. (2019). Digital transformation strategy making in pre-digital organizations: The case of a financial services provider. *The Journal of Strategic Information Systems, 28*(1), 17–33. doi:10.1016/j.jsis.2018.11.003

Coraddu, A., Oneto, L., Baldi, F., Cipollini, F., Atlar, M., & Savio, S. (2019). Data-driven ship digital twin for estimating the speed loss caused by the marine fouling. *Ocean Engineering, 186*(March), 106063. doi:10.1016/j.oceaneng.2019.05.045

Fletcher, G., & Griffiths, M. (2020). Digital transformation during a lockdown. *International Journal of Information Management, 102185*(June). doi:10.1016/j.ijinfomgt.2020.102185

Gazioğlu, C. (2018). Biodiversity, coastal protection, promotion and applicability investigation of the ocean health index for Turkish seas. *International Journal of Environment and Geoinformatics, 5*(3), 353–367. doi:10.30897/ijegeo.484067

Gölzer, P., & Fritzsche, A. (2017). Data-driven operations management: Organisational implications of the digital transformation in industrial practice. *Production Planning and Control, 28*(16), 1332–1343. doi:10.1080/09537287.2017.1375148

Grieves, M. (2014). *Digital Twin: Manufacturing Excellence through Virtual Factory Replication.* Academic Press.

Haag, S., & Anderl, R. (2018). Digital twin – Proof of concept. *Manufacturing Letters, 15*, 64–66. doi:10.1016/j.mfglet.2018.02.006

Heilig, L., Lalla-Ruiz, E., & Voß, S. (2017). Digital transformation in maritime ports: Analysis and a game theoretic framework. *NETNOMICS: Economic Research and Electronic Networking, 18*(2–3), 227–254. doi:10.100711066-017-9122-x

Hess, T., Benlian, A., Matt, C., & Wiesböck, F. (2016). Options for formulating a digital transformation strategy. *MIS Quarterly Executive, 15*(2), 123–139. doi:10.4324/9780429286797-7

Institute of Chartered Shipbrokers (ICS). (2007). *Port and Terminal Management.* London, UK: Witherbys Publishing Limited.

Kagermann, Wahlster, & Helbig. (2013). *Recommendations for implementing the strategic initiative Industrie 4.0: Final report of the Industrie 4.0 Working Group.* Acatech. https://doi.org/ doi:10.13140/RG.2.2.14480.20485

Kavussanos, M. G., & Visvikis, I. D. (2016). *The international handbook of shipping finance: Theory and practice.* Palgrave Macmillan.

Lee, E.-S., & Song, D.-W. (2010). Knowledge management for maritime logistics value: Discussing conceptual issues. *Maritime Policy & Management, 37*(6), 563–583. doi:10.1080/03088839.2010.514959

Li, F. (2020). The digital transformation of business models in the creative industries: A holistic framework and emerging trends. *Technovation, 92–93*(January), 102012. https://doi.org/ doi:10.1016/j.technovation.2017.12.004

Lin, K. Y. H., Zheng, P., & Chen, C. H. (2019). A state-of-the-art survey of Digital Twin: Techniques, engineering product lifecycle management and business innovation perspectives. *Journal of Intelligent Manufacturing, 31*, 1313–1337. doi:10.100710845-019-01512-w

Lind, M., Becha, H., Watson, R. T., Kouwenhoven, N., Zuesongdham, P., & Baldauf, U. (2020). Digital twins for the maritime sector. *Smart Maritime Network*, (August). Advance online publication. doi:10.13140/RG.2.2.27690.24006

Liu, M., Fang, S., Dong, H., & Xu, C. (2020). Review of digital twin about concepts, technologies, and industrial applications. *Journal of Manufacturing Systems*, (October), 1–16. https://doi.org/ doi:10.1016/j.jmsy.2020.06.017

Mamede, H. (2009). MICEP-A methodology for digital business in SME. *Revista de Ciências da Computação, 4*. https://www.researchgate.net/publication/228758013_MICEP-A_methodology_for_digital_business_in_SME

Matt, C., Hess, T., & Benlian, A. (2015). Digital Transformation Strategies. *Business & Information Systems Engineering, 57*(5), 339–343. doi:10.100712599-015-0401-5

Mergel, I., Edelmann, N., & Haug, N. (2019). Defining digital transformation: Results from expert interviews. *Government Information Quarterly*, *36*(4), 101385. doi:10.1016/j.giq.2019.06.002

Mishra, B. (2020). *Applying Digital Twin in Shipping and Maritime*. Sea News. Retrieved from https://seanews.co.uk/features/applying-digital-twin-in-shipping-and-maritime/

Orams, M. (1998). *Marine Tourism: Development, Impacts and Management*. Routledge.

Pedersen, T. A., Glomsrud, J. A., Ruud, E. L., Simonsen, A., Sandrib, J., & Eriksen, B. O. H. (2020). Towards simulation-based verification of autonomous navigation systems. *Safety Science, 129*(December), 104799. https://doi.org/ doi:10.1016/j.ssci.2020.104799

Perabo, F., Park, D., Zadeh, M. K., Smogeli, O., & Jamt, L. (2020). Digital Twin Modelling of Ship Power and Propulsion Systems: Application of the Open Simulation Platform (OSP). *IEEE International Symposium on Industrial Electronics,* 1265–1270. https://doi.org/10.1109/ISIE45063.2020.9152218

PierNext. (2020). Digital twins for safer and more efficient port decisions. *PierNext Technology*. Retrieved from https://piernext.portdebarcelona.cat/en/technology/ports-digital-twins/

Port of Rotterdam. (2018). Innovation takes the port into a new era. *Port of Rotterdam News*. Retrieved from https://www.portofrotterdam.com/en/news-and-press-releases/innovation-takes-the-port-into-a-new-era

Port of Rotterdam. (2019). Digitisation initiatives. *Control & Management*. Retrieved from https://www.portofrotterdam.com/en/doing-business/port-of-the-future/digitisation/control-management

Port of Rotterdam. (2019). Rotterdam sends hyper-smart container on trip around the world. *Port of Rotterdam News*. Retrieved from https://www.portofrotterdam.com/en/news-and-press-releases/rotterdam-sends-hyper-smart-container-on-trip-around-the-world

Port Technology. (2018). Singapore to Develop Digital Twin Tech. *Port Technology News*. Retrieved from https://www.porttechnology.org/news/singapore_to_develop_digital_twin_tech/

Qi, Q., & Tao, F. (2018). Digital Twin and Big Data Towards Smart Manufacturing and Industry 4.0: 360 Degree Comparison. *IEEE Access: Practical Innovations, Open Solutions*, *6*, 3585–3593. doi:10.1109/ACCESS.2018.2793265

Rodseth, O. J., & Berre, A. J. (2018). *From digital twin to maritime data space: Transparent ownership and use of ship information.* Paper presented at the AMIA Conference, Berlin, Germany.

Rosen, R., Boschert, S., & Sohr, A. (2018). Next Generation Digital Twin. *Atp Magazin*, *60*(10), 86. doi:10.17560/atp.v60i10.2371

Rosen, R., Von Wichert, G., Lo, G., & Bettenhausen, K. D. (2015). About the importance of autonomy and digital twins for the future of manufacturing. *IFAC-PapersOnLine*, *28*(3), 567–572. doi:10.1016/j.ifacol.2015.06.141

Schleich, B., Anwer, N., Mathieu, L., & Wartzack, S. (2017). Shaping the digital twin for design and production engineering. *CIRP Annals - Manufacturing Technology*, *66*(1), 141–144. https://doi.org/ doi:10.1016/j.cirp.2017.04.040

Selin, A., & Santos, V. (2018). An Architecture for a Viable Information System. *Trends and Advances in Information Systems and Technologies,* 1175-1189. https://doi.org/ doi:10.1007/978-3-319-77703-0_114

Shafto, M., Conroy, M., Doyle, R., & Glaessgen, E., Kemp, C., LeMoigne, J., & Wang, L. (2010). *NASA Technology Roadmap*. DRAFT Modeling, Simulation, Information Technology & Processing Roadmap Technology Area 11.

Singh, A., & Hess, T. (2017). How chief digital officers promote the digital transformation of their companies. *MIS Quarterly Executive*, *16*(1), 1–17. doi:10.4324/9780429286797-9

Smogeli, Ø. (2017). Digital twins at work in maritime and energy. *DNV-GL Feature*, (February), 1–7.

Solmaz, M. S., & Koray, M. (2020). Blockchain Technology in Maritime Transportation and Management. Handbook of Research on the Applications of International Transportation and Logistics for World Trade, 483-499. DOI: doi:10.4018/978-1-7998-1397-2.ch026

Stark, R., Kind, S., & Neumeyer, S. (2017). Innovations in digital modelling for next generation manufacturing system design. *CIRP Annals - Manufacturing Technology*, *66*(1), 169–172. https://doi.org/ doi:10.1016/j.cirp.2017.04.045

Stopford, M. (2009). *Maritime economics*. Routledge.

Syafrudin, M., Alfian, G., Fitriyani, N. L., & Rhee, J. (2018). Performance analysis of IoT-based sensor, big data processing, and machine learning model for real-time monitoring system in automotive manufacturing. *Sensors (Switzerland), 18*(9). Advance online publication. doi:10.339018092946

Tanniru, M. R., Xi, Y., & Sandhu, K. (2020). Leadership to Advance Innovation for Digital Healthcare Transformation. *Leadership, Management, and Adoption Techniques for Digital Service Innovation,* 1-24. https://doi.org/ doi:10.4018/978-1-7998-2799-3.ch001

Tao, F., Cheng, J., Qi, Q., Zhang, M., Zhang, H., & Sui, F. (2018). Digital twin-driven product design, manufacturing and service with big data. *International Journal of Advanced Manufacturing Technology, 94*(9–12), 3563–3576. doi:10.100700170-017-0233-1

Tao, F., Zhang, H., Liu, A., & Nee, A. Y. C. (2019). Digital Twin in Industry: State-of-the-Art. *IEEE Transactions on Industrial Informatics, 15*(4), 2405–2415. doi:10.1109/TII.2018.2873186

Taylor, N., Human, C., Kruger, K., Bekker, A., & Basson, A. (2019). Comparison of Digital Twin Development in Manufacturing and Maritime Domains. In *International Workshop on Service Orientation in Holonic and Multi-Agent Manufacturing.* Springer.

United Nations Conference on Trade and Development (UNCTAD). (2017). Retrieved from https://unctad.org/system/files/official-document/rmt2017_en.pdf

Vial, G. (2019). Understanding digital transformation: A review and a research agenda. *The Journal of Strategic Information Systems, 28*(2), 118–144. doi:10.1016/j.jsis.2019.01.003

Von Leipzig, T., Gamp, M., Manz, D., Schöttle, K., Ohlhausen, P., Oosthuizen, G., & … . (2017). Initialising customer-orientated digital transformation in enterprises. *Procedia Manufacturing, 8*, 517–524. doi:10.1016/j.promfg.2017.02.066

Weare42. (n.d.). The smartest container this planet has even seen. *We are 42.* Retrieved from https://weare42.io/about/

Weill, P., & Woerner, S. L. (2018). Is your company ready for a digital future? *MIT Sloan Management Review, 59*(2), 21–25. https://sloanreview.mit.edu/article/is-your-company-ready-for-a-digital-future/

World Ocean Review. (2014). *Oil and Gas from the sea.* Retrieved from http://worldoceanreview.com/en/wor-3-overview/oil-and-gas/

KEY TERMS AND DEFINITIONS

Digital Transformation: Transformation from classical systems to digital systems in a way that all functions of a business can be carried out on digital media.

Digital Twin Technology: Technology used to make transactions on complex systems more easily by creating digital twins of them.

Internet of Things (IOT): Internet network of smart objects connected to the internet.

Ship Operations and Management: The section of the maritime sector directly related to the operation of ships.

Supply Chain Management: The planning and management of the process from the time the logistics company takes cargo to delivery in maritime transport.

Chapter 6
Semantic Interoperability in Internet of Things:
Architecture, Protocols, and Research Challenges

Kamalendu Pal
https://orcid.org/0000-0001-7158-6481
City, University of London, UK

ABSTRACT

The industry's internet of things (IoT) applications have drawn significant research attention in recent decades. IoT is a technology in which intelligent objects with sensors-enabled RFID tags, actuators, and processors communicate information to cater to a meaningful purpose in the industry. This way, IoT technology aims to simplify the distributed data collection in industrial practice, sharing and processing information and knowledge across many collaborating partners using suitable enterprise information systems. This chapter describes new methods with grounded knowledge representation techniques to address the needs of formal information modeling and reasoning for web-based services. The chapter presents a framework, apparel business decentralized data integration (ABDDI), which uses knowledge representation methods and formal languages (e.g., description logics – DLs) to annotate necessary business activities. This type of web service requires increased interoperability in service management operations.

DOI: 10.4018/978-1-7998-7793-6.ch006

Copyright © 2022, IGI Global. Copying or distributing in print or electronic forms without written permission of IGI Global is prohibited.

INTRODUCTION

Humanity dwells on mother earth with ambitious goals demanding unprecedented social, economic, and environmental challenges. Science, technology, and innovation are playing an enormous role in realizing these ambitious goals. The process of creative destruction started by technological progress can help change economies and improve living conditions by increasing productivity, reducing production costs and prices, and helping to raise real wages. One of the essential ingredients to create a better world is using technology to move forward and unprecedented change in its scope and pace of daily life.

This way, harnessing the frontier of technologies help to mitigate the persistent gaps among developed and developing nations in getting and using existing technologies. It also creates and delivers innovations (including non-technological and new forms of social innovation), could be transformative in creating sustainable development goals and producing more prosperous, inclusive, and healthy societies. They provide the prospect of solutions and opportunities for sustainable development that are better, cheaper, faster, scalable, and easy to use. The extent of technological advances' development impact has already ushered in the transformative implications of information and communication technologies (ICTs) in many countries worldwide. However, these new technologies are often threatening to outpace the ability of societies and policymakers to adapt to the changes they can create, giving rise to widespread anxiety and ambivalence or hostility to some technological advances.

The question of where ideas come from is on the mind of a researcher visiting a research laboratory, a painter's workshop, or an inventor's experiment laboratory. It is the secret human society hope to see – the magic that happens when new things are born. Even in environments geared for creativity like the discovery of millimeter radio wave by Professor Jagadish Chandra Bose. The world is witnessing the tremendous influence of wireless communication technology on daily working activities. The modern wireless telecommunication is heavily influenced by three great scientific minds – James Clerk Maxwell (Mahon, 2004), Jagadish Chandra Bose (Sarkar et al., 2006), and Tim Berners-Lee (Berners-Lee, 2000). James Clerk Maxwell provided the theoretical foundation of electromagnetic wave propagation; Jagadish Chandra Bose showed to his colleagues the transmission of millimeter waves by transmitting this new type of waves in Presidency College (Calcutta, India) laboratory, and Tim Berners-Lee created the World Wide Web at CERN (Geneva, Switzerland). Today's computer data communication network is at once intangible and in a constant state of mutation, growing larger and more complex with each passing second. A large portion of the world business community is using this incredible network of networks for day to day works.

The advent of development and adoption of new technologies in recent decades is likely to continue, and this continuation is driven by: (i) the cumulative nature of technological change; (ii) the exponential nature of technologies such as microchips that are doubled in power every two years for more than half a century; (iii) the convergence of technologies into new combinations; (iv) drastic reduction in costs; (v) the emergence of digital "platforms of platforms" – most prominently the Internet; and (v) declining entry costs.

Different emerging technologies are presenting the promising potential to improve human society's day-to-day living experiences. Extensive data analysis is opening a new horizon for the scientific community. It can help manage or resolve critical global issues, create new scientific breakthroughs, advance human health-related decision-making by providing real-time streams of categorical information. This way, big data technologies have already made some eye-catching impact in fields related to healthcare, the medical diagnosis from imaging data in medicine, quantifying lifestyle data in the fitness industry, to mention a few. The Internet of Things (IoT) considers the condition and actions of related connected intelligent machines and objects to be monitored and managed and allows more effective monitoring of the natural world, animals, and people. These two technologies have critical applications in healthcare, agriculture, manufacturing, energy, and water management systems.

Artificial intelligence now includes image recognition, problem-solving, and logical reasoning that sometimes exceed humans. Artificial intelligence, particularly robotics, can transform production processes and business activities, especially healthcare and manufacturing. Big data technologies are opening new opportunities and enable breakthroughs related to, among the others, healthcare data analytics addressing different perspectives: (i) descriptive to answer what happened, (ii) diagnostic to answer the reason why it happened, (iii) predictive to understand what will happen and (iv) prescriptive to detect how we can make it happen.

Without any doubt, the potential impact big data technology can bring on technology, economy and society are relevant, boosting innovations in organizations and leading to the improvement of business models. Besides, today the Internet has become ubiquitous, has touched almost every corner of the world, and affects human life in unimaginable ways. However, the journey is far from over. Human society is now entering an era of even more pervasive connectivity where many service applications will be connected to the Web. Human society is entering an era of the IoT. Different academics and practitioners have defined this term in many ways. The IoT is a things-connected network that is wirelessly connected via smart sensors; IoT can interact without human intervention. Some preliminary IoT applications have been already developed in the healthcare, transportation, and automotive industries (He et al., 2014) (Pretz, 2013). The development of IoT involves many issues such as infrastructure, communications, interfaces, protocols, and standards. The IoT refers to a new world where almost all the devices and appliances are connected to a network. Industrial application service providers can use them collaboratively to achieve complex tasks that require a high degree of intelligence.

IoT devices are geared with embedded sensors, actuators, processors, and transceivers for this intelligence and interconnection. IoT is not a single technology; instead, it is an agglomeration of various technologies that work together in tandem. In simple, sensors and actuators are devices that help in interacting with the physical environment. The data collected by the sensors must be stored and processed intelligently to derive valuable inferences from it. This chapter broadly defines the term *sensor*; a handheld mobile phone or even a microwave oven can count as a sensor if it provides inputs about its current state (internal state + environment). An *actuator* is a device used to effect a change in the environment, such as the temperature controller of an air conditioner.

Data storage and processing can be done on the network's edge or on a server located in a different place. If any preprocessing of data is done, it simply happens at either some other proximate device or sensor. In the end, data is then typically sent to a remote server after processing. An IoT object's storage and processing capabilities are also restricted by the available resources, which are often very constrained due to size, energy, power, and computational capability limitations. Consequently, the central research challenge is to make sure that users can get the appropriate type of data at the desired level of correctness.

In addition to data collection and handling challenges, there are also challenges in processed data communication to the relevant service entities. The collaboration and communication between IoT devices are generally wireless in nature because these devices are simply installed at different work locations. The wireless communication channels are often suffering from high rates of disturbance. This way, reliably communicating data without too many retransmissions is a central research issue.

Moreover, after processing the received data, some actions are needed to be taken based on the derived inferences. The nature of action can be diverse. One can directly modify the physical world through actuators. Alternatively, one may do something virtually. For example, one may send some raw data and information to other smart objects.

The process of creating a change in the physical world is simply dependent on its state now. The is called *context-awareness*. Each action is taken, considering the context and why an application can behave differently in separate business contexts. For example, an office member may not like messages from office colleagues to interrupt when that individual is on vacation.

Sensors, actuators, computer servers, and the communication network form the core infrastructure of an IoT framework. However, many software aspects need to be considered. First, one needs a middleware that can be used to connect and manage all these heterogeneous components. This way, the IoT industry needs much standardization to connect many different devices. This chapter discusses methods to exchange information and prevailing standards in a later section.

IoT is the network of associations between those Internet-connected objects (smart devices) that can exchange information using an agreed method and data schema. The IoT based innovative technology finds various applications in healthcare, fitness, education, entertainment, social life, energy conservation, environmental monitoring, home automation, and industrial applications (e.g., supply chain management, transport systems). In the later part of this chapter, an IoT based supply chain management example has been described.

Recent progress on IoT deployments has given a solid push for the IoT to be considered one of the important emerging technologies today. However, the conceptual realization of IoT is far from achieving a full deployment of converged IoT services and technology. Current information technology and communication (ITC) research focuses on providing integrated solutions, primarily on the feature that enables convergence or "*interoperability*". Interoperability can be simplified as the feature for providing a seamless exchange of information to personalize services automatically or simply exchanging information so that other systems can use it to improve performance, enable and create services, and control operations information processing. This type of scenario requires increased interoperability in service management operations.

This chapter reviews the recent trends and challenges on interoperability in the IoT domain, discuss physical versus virtual sensors, and while addressing technology interoperability challenges in parallel, discuss how, with the growing importance of data understanding and processing, semantic web technologies, frameworks and information models can support interoperability in the design of services in the industrial information system design. This chapter aims to identify relevant issues and challenges that need to be considered in the coming and future information system projects.

The remainder of this chapter is described as follows. Section 2 presents the background of IoT-based industrial applications. Section 3 reviews some of the representative research works on semantic modelling methods for general IoT-based applications. Section 4 describes the background knowledge about the proposed system. Section 5 presents the knowledge representation and reasoning approach. Section 6 explains some of the mathematical concepts using a business case and includes a concept similarity assessment. Section 7 put the ideas of future research work forwards. Section 8 concludes the chapter by discussing relevant research issues.

BACKGROUND KNOWLEDGE OF IOT ARCHITECTURE

There is no unique consensus on architecture for IoT, which is agreed universally. Different researchers have proposed different architectures.

Three-Layer and Five-Layer Architectures

The simplest architecture is a three-layer architecture (Mashal et al., 2015) (Said & Masud, 2013) (Wu et al., 2010), as shown in Figure 1. The presented layered IoT-system are initially applied to the entities of the Mobile Business Architecture (MBA). Then, Mobile Internet Technical Architecture (MITA) fundamentals are mapped to these principles and concept models for MIBA and MITA.

Figure 1. Layered architectures of IoT system

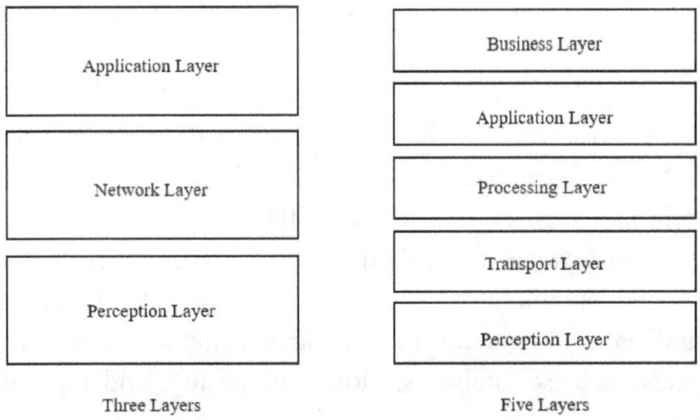

In digital Mobile Internet Technical Architecture, the middleware layer has been named the Network Layer, as illustrated in Figure 1 (Three Layers) model. The above three-element layers are used for each of the MIBA segments and their elements. An interaction between the elements is provided with protocols and content delivery within the payloads of the protocols.

This three-layer architecture was introduced in the early stage of research in this area. It has got three layers, namely, the perception, network, and finally, application layers.

1. The *perception layer* is basically the physical layer, with sensors for sensing and gathering data and creating information about the business operating environment. It senses physical arguments or identifies other smart objects in the business environment.

2. The *network layer* is the sole authority for making other smart objects (e.g., servers, network devices, and physical servers). Its characteristics are also used for transmitting and processing sensor data.
3. The *application layer* is responsible for providing business-specific services to the user. There are different applications in which the IoT can be deployed, for example, smart cities, smart factories, smart health, and smart homes.

A three-layer architecture defines the main idea of the IoT. However, this is not enough for research on IoT due to its focus on more delicate aspects of the IoT. That is why many more layered architectures are presented in the academic article. One is the five-layer architecture that includes the processing and business layers (Mashal et al., 2015) (Said & Masud, 2013) (Wu et al., 2010) (Khan et el., 2012). The five-layers architecture includes

perception, transport, processing, application, and business layers (please see Figure 1). The purpose of the perception and application layers is the same as the architecture with three layers. This chapter outline the function of the remaining three layers.

1. The *transport layer* transfers the gathered sensor data from the perception layer to the processing layer and vice versa through data communication networks (e.g., wireless, 3G, LAN, Bluetooth, RFID, and NFC).
2. The *processing layer* is also called the middleware layer. It stores, analyses, and processes vast amounts of data that comes from the transport layer. It can control and serve a diverse set of services to the lower layers. It uses many technologies such as databases, cloud computing, and big data processing modules.
3. The *business layer* controls the whole IoT system environment, including applications, profit models, business, and end-users individual privacy. However, the business layer details are out of the scope of this chapter.

Another architecture proposed by Ning and Wang (Ning & Wang, 2011) is influenced by the processing layers in a typical human brain.

The human intelligence characteristics also inspire it (e.g., think, feel, remember, make decisions, and react to the physical environment). It is constituted of three parts. First is the human brain, analogous to the processing and data management unit or the data centre. The second is the spinal cord, analogous to the distributed network of data processing nodes and smart gateways. The third is the network of nerves, which corresponds to the networking components and sensors.

Figure 2. Fog architecture of an innovative IoT gateway

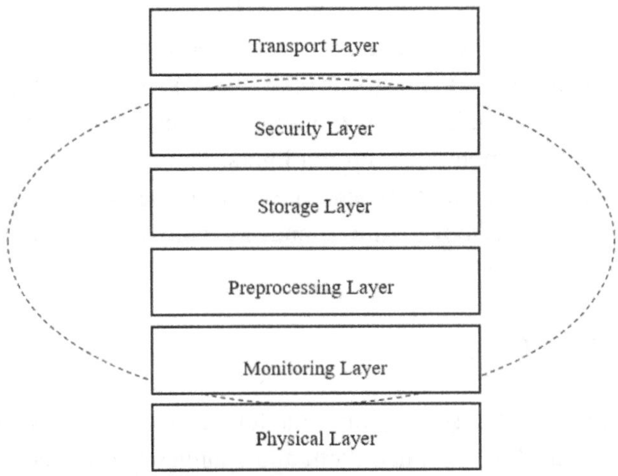

Cloud and Fog Based Architectures

The cloud and fog computing architectures have been playing a significant role in recent years. In some system architectures, cloud computers do the data processing in a significant, centralized fashion. Such a cloud-centric architecture keeps the cloud at the centre, applications above it, and the network of smart things below it (Gubbi et al., 2013). Cloud computing is given main importance because it gives huge scalability and flexibility. It provides services (e.g., platform, core infrastructure, storage, and software). Developers can use their storage tools, software tools, data mining, machine learning, and visualization tools through the cloud.

Lately, there has been a move towards another system architecture, namely, *fog computing* (Bonomi et al., 2014) (Bonomi et al., 2012) (Stojmenovic & Wen, 2014), where the sensors and network gateways do a part of the data processing and analytics. A fog architecture (Aazam & Huh, 2014)is shown in Figure 2, including storage, monitoring, pre-processing, and security layers between the transport and physical layers. The monitoring layer looks after power, resources, responses, and services. The processing layer does the filtering, processing, and analytics of sensor data. The short-time storage layer provides storage functionalities (e.g., data replication, distribution, and storage). Lastly, the security layer uses encryption/decryption and make sure data integrity and privacy. Controlling and pre-processing are done on the edge of the data communication network before sending data to service-oriented computing.

Moreover, the terms "fog computing" and "edge computing" are used interchangeably in a different business context. The latter term relates to the former and is constructed to be more generic. Fog computing, originally called Cisco, refers to smart gateways and smart sensors, whereas edge computing is slightly more penetrative. This paradigm envisions smart data pre-processing capabilities to physical devices such as motors, pumps, or lights. The aim is to do data processing on these devices that are located to be at the *edge* of the network. The diagram is not appreciably different from Figure 2, and this chapter does not describe edge computing details separately.

Basic Components

In a typical commercial IoT setting, this chapter treats the devices and services as bots to set up relationships between them and changes them over time. This will allow the situation to let the devices cooperate and achieve a complex task seamlessly.

To make such a model work, one needs to have many interoperating components. Let us look at some of the significant components in such a system.

- Object Identification (ID): One needs a unique way to identify an object. An ID can be allocated to an object based on traditional parameters such as the MAC ID, IPv6ID, a universal product code, or other custom methods.
- Metainformation: Along with an ID, one needs some extra information about the device that describes its characteristics and operational methods.
- Security Controls: This way, an industrial owner of a device might place restrictions on the kinds of devices that can connect to it. These are referred to as *owner control.*
- Service Discovery: Such a system is like a service cloud, where one needs to store details of devices providing certain kinds of services. It becomes essential to keep these directories up to date such that devices can learn about other devices.
- Relationship management: This module manages relationships information. For example, it also stores the types of devices that a given device should connect with based on the services provided.
- Service Composition: This module takes the IoT model to a new level. The goal of having such a system is to provide better-integrated services to users.

The rest of the chapter presents a manufacturing service integration example with the help of an ontology-concept similarity assessment algorithm.

INDUSTRIAL MANUFACTURING APPLICATIONS

Today, all manufacturing businesses value the consequence of building an effective supply chain as part of enterprise proliferation and profitability (Pal, 2018). There are different industry-specific supply chain types (e.g., automotive, pharmaceutical, apparel, agriculture). Generally, a supply chain consists of a system with organization, people, technology, activity, information, and resource involved in delivering a service or product from suppliers to customers.

Supply chain business activities transform resources into ultimate products and deliver them to customers. The supply chain network is composed of the enterprises and enterprise departments involved in this process. The most important requirements of supply chain operation are minimizing the inventory, creating seamless material and information flow, effective communication among the business partners, market, sale, purchase, manufacturing plan and control, customer delivery service, after-sales service, etc. Therefore, a supply chain is a network of facilities and distribution options that performs material procurement functions, transforming these materials into intermediate and finished products and delivering these finished products to customers. This definition, or a modified version of it, has been used by several researchers (e.g. (Lee & Billington, 1993) (Swaminathan, 2001a) (Keskinocak & Tayur, 2001) (Pal, 2017)). Supply Chain Management (SCM) aims at improving the allocation, management, and control of logistical resources. In this way, manufacturing SCM is a set of synchronized activities for integrating suppliers, manufacturers, transporters, and efficient customer service so that the right product or service is delivered in the right quantities, at the right time, to the right places (Pal, 2020) (Pal & Ul-Haque, 2020).

The ultimate objective of SCM is the efficient management of the end-to-end process, which starts with the design of the product or service and ends with the time when it has been sold, consumed, and finally, discarded by the consumer. This complete process includes product design, procurement, planning and forecasting, production, distribution, fulfilment, after-sales support, and end-of-life disposal. Supply chain management issues can be classified into two broad categories: configuration (design-oriented) issues that relate to the basic infrastructure on which the supply chain executes, coordination (execution-oriented) issues that relate to the actual execution of the supply chain.

Configuration-level issues include the following topics:

1. Procurement and Supplier Decisions: Procurement generally involves making buying decisions under conditions of scarcity. At the same time, the requirements criteria for selecting suppliers and the number of suppliers need to be decided. If sound data is available, it is good practice to use economic analysis methods

such as cost-benefit analysis or cost-utility analysis. Procurement is used to ensure the buyer receives goods, services, or works at the best possible price when aspects such as quality, quantity, time, and location are compared.

2. Production Decisions: This is a multi-criteria decision activity. It includes the decisions regarding production network design (e.g., Where and how many manufacturing sites should be used for production purposes? How much capacity should be installed at each of these sites? What kind of products and services are going to be supported through the supply chain network?).
3. Distribution Decisions: It is mainly based on infrastructure design decisions (e.g., What kind of distribution channels should a manufacturing company have? How many and where should the distribution centres and retail outlets be situated? What types of transportation services and routes should be used? What types of environmental issues does the distribution infrastructure need to be considered?).
4. Information Support Decisions: Managing a manufacturing supply chain involves numerous decisions about the flow of information, product, funds, and coordination. SCM has been instrumental in connecting and smoothing business activities and forming various kinds of business relationships (e.g., Customer Relationship Management, Supplier Relationship Management) among supply chain stakeholders.

Coordination level issues include the following topics:

1. Material Flow Decisions: These decisions include – How much inventory of different product types should be stored to provide the target service levels? Should inventory be carried in finished form or semi-finished form? How often should inventory be replenished? And so many other issues need to be considered.
2. Information Flow Decisions: SCM systems utilize modern Information and Communication Technologies (ICT) to acquire, interpret, retain, and distribute information. The software applications are ready-made packages, usually targeting a set of tasks, e.g., tracking product-related information during the transportation process. These ready-made package-software applications are mass-customized products that ignore the specific requirements of a particular business sector, so they are problematic. The problem of the appropriate IT solutions for supporting collaboration between supply chain business partners is not new, and it has been approached with several standards and protocols implemented in numerous enterprise information systems.

An application like ERP (Enterprise Resource Planning), CRM (Customer Relationship Management), and WMS (Warehouse Management System) contains valuable data that can be utilized by the decision support systems (DSS). Moreover, the digital transformation of business and society presents enormous growth opportunities offered by technologies such as the Internet of Things (IoT), Big Data, advanced manufacturing, blockchain technologies, and artificial intelligence. This digital transformation is characterized by a fusion of advanced technologies and the integration of physical and digital systems, the predominance of innovative business models and new processes, and smart products and services.

The main goal was to reduce inventory levels drastically and regulate the suppliers' interaction with the production line more effectively. It consisted of two distinct flows through the supply chain organizations: material and information. The scope of the supply chain begins with the source of supply and ends at the point of consumption. It extends much further than simply a concern with the physical movement of materials. Equal emphasis is given to supplier management, purchasing, inventory management, manufacturing management, facilities planning, customer service, information flow, transport, and physical distribution. Some of the critical business processes along the supply chain are shown in Figure 3.

Also, the critical challenges in supporting massive heterogeneous data integration in global supply networks are: (i) increasing number of business alliance partners due to globalization of business processes, (ii) different business practice and infrastructure facilities within participating business partners, and (iii) differences in data exchange formats and standards among business-partners. Moreover, data capture and transmission mechanisms (e.g., barcoding, radio frequency identification technique, electronic data interchange, wireless networking infrastructure and protocols, global positioning system's capability) produce vast amounts of supply chain transportation data that, if properly controlled and shared, can enhance performance and agility of global supply chain networks. A single representation data format is essential to harness the value-added service.

Figure 3. Diagrammatic representation of the supply chain business process

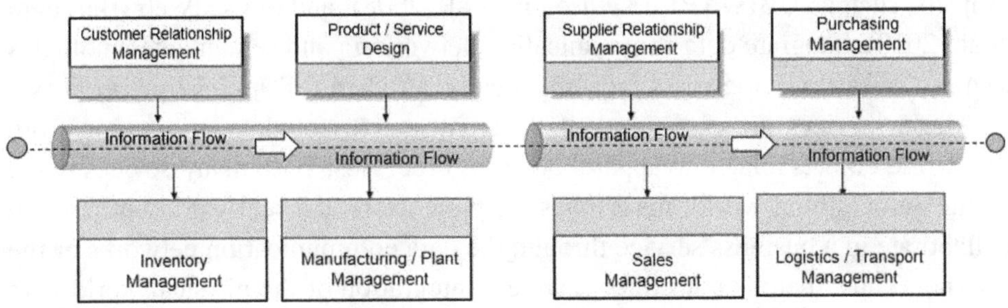

As a result, much global manufacturing (e.g., textile and clothing) businesses invest in new ICT to harness smooth information sharing ability in their supply chain operations (Monteneggro et al., 2007). With the recent progress in Radio Frequency Identification (RFID) technology, low-cost wireless sensor hardwires, and world comprehensive web technologies, the Internet of Things (IoT) advance has attracted attention in connecting global apparel business activities and sharing operational business information. In this context, while IoT technology supports the capability to connect and integrate both digital and physical business entities, enabling the provision of a new type of information system (IS) applications and services. Also, the Semantic Web of Things (SWoT) is ushering a new opportunity in the business community by integrating the Semantic Web and IoT technologies. Its objective is to associate semantically rich and easily accessible information to real-world objects, locations, and events, using inexpensive, disposable, and unobtrusive micro-devices, such as RFID tags and wireless sensors. This opportunity provides new IS applications and services in many apparel business areas (e.g., manufacturing, inventory management, transportation management). In order to facilitate this vision, information technologies and software system frameworks must mitigate with typical pervasive computing application related issues: platform heterogeneity, appropriate resource utilization, intelligent intractability of the user, device volatility, dependence on context, and limitation of device-specific computation power. Hence, the SWoT vision requires pervasive knowledge-based systems with higher degrees of automatic capability in information storage, management, and discovery and transparent access to information sources for processing.

Most IoT technology solutions inherit support from generally stable data communication infrastructures, assistance from centralized brokers for service management, and information discovery. Also, optimization of alternative information provision has been recently getting prominence, for example, 6LoWPAN (IPv6 over Low Power Wireless Personal Area Networks) (Monteneggro et al., 2007) and the Constrained Application Protocol (CoAP) (Colitti et al., 2011). In parallel attempts, ontologies for device and data annotation were presented, for example - OntoSensor (Russomanno et al., 2005) and the SSN-XG ontology of the World Wide Web Consortium for semantic sensor networks (Lefort et al., 2005). Current research projects, such as UBIWARE (Katasonov et al., 2008), and Sense2Web (Barnaghi et al., 2010), integrate data communication networking and semantic technologies to make software frameworks for semantically enriched IoT application services.

These services are composed of different sources of data originating from real-world objects related to apparel business processes. With many devices in the textile and clothing world, many physical parameters and real-world entities can collaborate in a business service through the data communication networks or the Internet. Thus, there is a need for seamless integration of the physical world with the digital world in IoT. Also, the progress in IoT-enabled device abstraction and integration of different data sources in the apparel business is a challenging task. The traditional web service discovery mechanisms are incapable of producing the appropriate result. Also, the heterogeneous nature of IoT generated data requires semantic modelling. Thus, IoT entities need to be formally represented and managed to achieve interoperability.

An essential step towards the vision of IoT-based information systems interoperability is reusing data collected from widely distributed sensor-enabled devices. Ontology-based semantic modelling helps to capture the capability of entities to represent information and its relationships among other entities to enable efficient information exchange. In this way, semantic modelling in conjunction with service-oriented computing and ontology ushers a scalable means of accessing IoT entities. An ontology simply describes a vocabulary modelling a domain of interest and specifying the meaning of terms in that vocabulary. Depending on the accuracies of this specification, the notion of ontology encompasses different data or conceptual models (e.g., classifications). In other words, an ontology is a shared conceptualization, and it is used to represent knowledge as a set of concepts related to each other. The structural part consists of four key components: *classes*, *relations*, *attributes*, and *individuals*. Classes represent the concepts in ontology design, and individuals are the basic, '*ground level*' components or instances of an ontology. Attributes or characteristics represent the features of the classes, and relations describe how the classes and individuals are related to one another.

This chapter presents a semantic knowledge-based for IoT related entities in an apparel manufacturing business. Since most of the IoT data in a textile and clothing industry setting needs to be made available homogeneously to allow integration from a wide variety of sources. A uniðed machine-understandable representation of world knowledge is required to put things into an everyday semantic context. The integrated Apparel Business Decentralised Data Integration (ABDDI) framework uses semantic modelling. Mainly, ontologies are used to form a unified knowledge base to support: (a) semantic definition and representation of IoT entities; (b) dynamic service discovery and matching based on user request; and (c) service composition and orchestration in dynamic environments. This chapter considers ontologies as the key component for automatic service representation, composition, discovery, and orchestration for IoT in dynamic environments. The proposed knowledge base hides the heterogeneity of entities and consequently enables semantic searching and querying capabilities. The presented knowledge base integrates several existing ontologies mainly related to sensor resources and web services and extends them for IoT.

RELATED RESEARCH WORKS

In recent decades automatic identification technologies are gaining more and more attraction for industrial applications. These applications are combined with the technologies of RFID, Electronic Product Code (EPC), and sensor-based data communication networks to share application-specific data. Advances in ICT are bringing into reality the vision of many uniquely identifiable, interconnected objects and things that gather data from diverse physical environments and deliver the information to various innovative applications and services. In this way, the network of objects (e.g., devices, vehicles, machines, containers), embedded with sensors and software, can collect and communicate data over the Internet. The inter-and intra-organizational communication and information exchange are perceived to be facilitated by IoT capability. This, IoT-based technology adoption can be viewed as an additional capability that may add value to the supply chain industries.

While IoT many applications are used in different supply chain industries (Jandl et el., 2019), industrial IoT (IIoT) focuses primarily on industrial usage of IoT devices (Jakl et al., 2018) (Jeschke et al., 2017). Recently, Thomas Moser's research group presented an overview of industrial IoT applications (Jandl et al., 2019) for the smart industry (also known as Industry 4.0). With the advent of the IoT, new opportunities and capabilities emerge in real-time monitoring, management, and optimizing goods distribution and supply chain. As more and more physical objects in supply chain industries are equipped with barcodes, RFID tags or sensors, transport and logistics companies can perform real-time monitoring of the movement of physical objects from one location to another. The goal is to track a product along the entire supply chain, including material management, production, transportation, and distribution (Karakostas, 2013).

The manufacturing companies are changing their IT infrastructure towards the fourth industrial revolution (Lasi et al., 2014). The utilization of artificial intelligence (AI) techniques in cyber-physical systems (CPSs) (Broy et al., 2012) is a typical characteristic of this change (Lee et al., 2014). In this context, flexibility is one of the essential criteria for manufacturing companies, mainly because of ever shorter market launch times and increasing customer demands for individualization (Cheng et al., 2017; Lasi et al., 2014). To conduct industry 4.0 research, researchers are using the factory simulation model because companies are often unwilling to provide data from and access to their production lines for research purposes.

More and more researchers have started concentrating on techniques enabling machines to better intelligently understand IoT data from various sources. In order to use AI applications, contextual operational knowledge must be available in formal and machine-readable representation (Humm et al., 2020). Semantic web services address the issues of automatic discovering, composing, and executing by providing a declarative, ontological framework for describing them. Using AI methods (e.g., automated planning such as (Marrella, 2018) (Marrella & Mecella, 2018), multi-agent systems for decentralized manufacturing control such as (Ciortea et al., 2018), Case-Based Reasoning (CBR) such as Minor et al., 2014) (Muller, 2018)) to enhance flexibility in cyber-physical production workflows (Bordel Sanchez et al., 2018) (Seiger et al., 2018)) inevitably require such semantic annotations.

Much related research work (Puttonen et al., 2010) (Puttonen et al., 2013) exist that already highlight these issues by using semantic web services (SWS). Moreover, the currently available approaches that use semantic web services in the context of Industry 4.0 focusing only on specific aspects and do not consider the entire context of a manufacturing environment. Also, the complex reasoning within the knowledge base makes real-time execution and monitoring of manufacturing processes difficult.

Several research works propose using SWSs for smart manufacturing in Industry 4.0 but focus only on partial aspects and do not consider the entire context of the shop floor. For instance, Puttonen et al. (2013) present an approach to use SWSs for executing manufacturing processes using three software agents represented as web services. One of these agents, called Service Monitor, is a specialized web service that carries out semantic web service composition by using planning techniques concerning a given production goal and the current state of the world provided by a domain ontology. Therefore, they use OWL to describe the state of the production system and OWL-S and SPARQL expressions for semantically describing the available web services that offer production capabilities.

Since modern Cyber-Physical Production Systems (CPPSs) (Monostori, 2014) consist of many different components and therefore many stakeholders are involved in their development process up to the later use in the manufacturing of products, Lobov et al. (2008) investigated the application of SWSs for orchestration of flexible control. They propose OWL for modelling a Process Taxonomy, Product Ontology, Equipment Ontology, and Service Ontology and mainly discuss the responsibilities of involved persons for knowledge acquisition and maintenance rather than present their detailed semantic specification.

Many academic and practitioner work-like Henson et al. (Cory et al., 2009) experiment a semantically enhanced sensor service application, known as SemSOS, having the capability to query both high-level knowledge and low-level environmental reading by sensors. Concerning classical sematic-matchmaking approach, different research groups distinguish among full (subsume), potential (intersection-satisðable) and partial (disjoint) match types to represent the relevant knowledge of different types of entities (Colucci et al., 2007) and (Li & Horrocks, 2004) respectively. Similarly, queries in ubiquitous infrastructure allow only exact matches with facts derived from a support knowledge base. Non-standard inferences like abduction and contraction are needed to support approximate matches, semantic ranking, and explanations of outcomes (Colucci et al., 2007).

This chapter highlights the requirement for a unified semantic knowledge base for automatic service representation, discovery, modelling, and composition in dynamic environments. Different research projects try to address these issues with the use of ontologies in prototype system design. For example, semantic commonalities in the RFID semantic streams project use DLs for system modelling purposes (Ruta et al., 2011). This work is of considerable interest, but so far, it is somewhat sui generis.

All these schemes are worthy of considerable study, and together they represent the wealthiest characterization of knowledge-based approach in pervasive service computing so far produced. Moreover, the systems are implemented and can be shown to generate relevant services using appropriate data streams.

OVERVIEW OF THE FRAMEWORK

The proposed framework uses a model-theoretic semantics modelled in ontologies for IoT generated data modelling purposes. It helps to gather detailed information regarding the characteristics of IoT devices based on their technical requirements. The advantages of this encoding are – (i) interconnecting different classification systems to represent capabilities and properties of constituent parts, (ii) translating characteristics or properties among compound constituent parts, and (iii) aggregating basic properties into complex properties based on the constituents of a superordinate system. Those concepts can be used and adapted for the IoT to enhance the uses of IoT devices in connecting them as a group, create coordination between IoT devices, and improve their interoperability.

One of the main objectives of this framework is to define an IoT architecture, which can also be used for other applications. The design principle in Apparel Business Semantic Data Management (ABDDI) is that any physical/real-world object in the global textile and clothing business can have a virtual representation through a Virtual Object (VO). AVO uses a semantic representation of the functionality and conceals the varied identity of the real-world object. Multiple VOs can be combined to form a Composite Virtual Object (CVO) that provides more compact and reliable services. In simple, CVOs are combined to form a service request. Thus, the ABDDI architecture has three layers: VO, CVO, and Service, as shown in Figure 4.

The functionalities of the three layers are presented below:

1. VO layer: Real-world objects are represented in the digital format as VO. End-users can search semantically and retrieve information from any existing VO. Also, actuation can be done through the VO.

2. CVO layer: In this layer, VOs are combined to form a service request. This layer generally caters functionality to search and query categories of CVOs for service provision semantically.
3. Service layer: This layer gets the request from a user and analyses the service requests to determine the categories of CVOs needed for service accomplishment. This layer also performs service composition and orchestration in a dynamic cloth and textile business environment.

Figure 4. RFID tagging level at different stages in the apparel manufacturing network

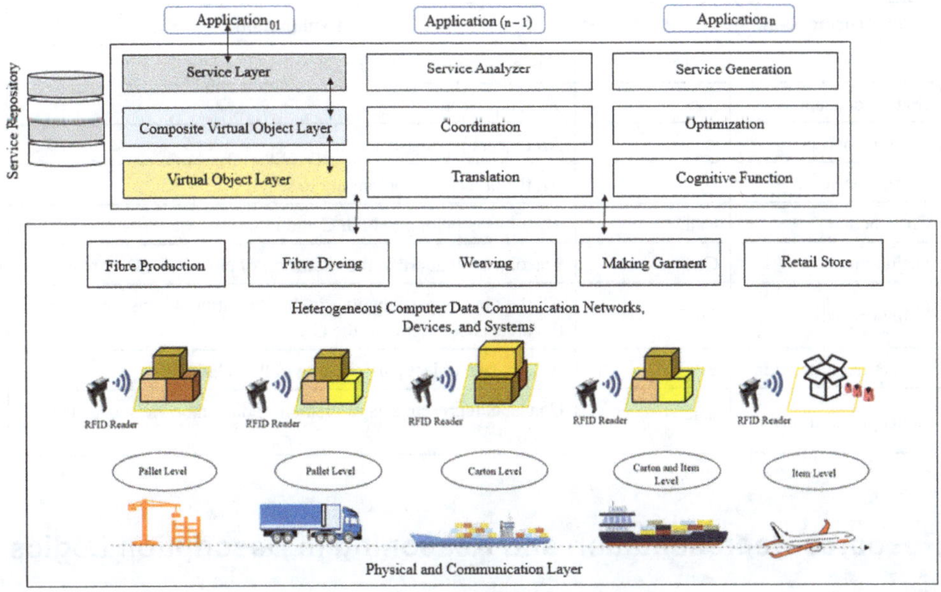

The ABDDI system also has got other components: *registry* and *control unit*. Every layer in this framework has a registry referencing the available VOs, CVOs, and services. These registries provide methods to semantically search and query existing VOs, CVOs, and services. The control unit regulates access to the VOs, CVOs and services based on the level of the end-user requirements.

KNOWLEDGE REPRESENTATION AND REASONING APPROACH

The primary motivation for this chapter stems from the Description Logics (DL) [1] based knowledge representation approach in pervasive computing applications along the global apparel supply chain. This DL based knowledge representation systems play a role very much like Database Management Systems (DBMS). In DL, elementary descriptions are *atomic concepts* and *atomic roles*. Complex descriptions can be built from them inductively with *concept constructors*. In abstract notation, one can use the letters A and B for atomic concepts, R for atomic roles, and C and D for concept descriptions. Possible DL constructors and the related examples are shown in Table 1, and these constructors are used the DLs investigated in this chapter.

Table 1. DLs set of constructors

Constructor Name	Syntax	Explanation
Top concept	⊤	Universal concept. All the objects in the domain.
Bottom concept	⊥	The empty set.
Atomic concept	A	All objects belong to set A.
Atomic negation	¬A	All the objects not belonging to set A.
Conjunction	C⊓D	The objects belong to both C and D sets.
Disjunction	C⊔D	The objects that are in the extension of either C or D or both
Value restriction	∀RC	All the objects participating in the R relation whose rage are all the objects belonging to the C set.
Existential restriction	∃RC	At least one object participating in the relation R.
Concept definition	A ≡ C	Concepts represent sets of elements and can be viewed as unary predicates.

Resource Representation and Reasoning in Description Logics

The most important and well-known service characterizing reasoning in DL checks for specificity hierarchies by determining whether a concept description is more specific than another one or, formally, if there is a *subsumption* relation between them.

Definition 1 (Subsumption): *Give two concept descriptions C and D and a TBox* τ *in a DL L; one can say that D subsumes C* τ ($C \sqsubseteq_\tau D$) *concerning if for every model of* τ, $C^I \subset D^I$. *As a special case, two concepts are equivalent if they subsume each other.*

For example, consider the following concept descriptions, referring to different garments types in an apparel supply chain network: G_1 = *SweaterByGarment* ⊓ ∀ *hasMain.Colour.Red*, and G_2 = *UpperBodyGarment* ⊓ ∀ *hasMain.Colour.Red*. Then using TBox reasoning – the concept inclusion can be achieved, and the output will be

Sweater $\sqsubseteq_T$ *UpperBodyGarment*. Hence, given the model, knowledge expressed by G1 is more specific than the one required by G_2 concerning the reasoning mechanism and the definition G_2 subsumes G_1.

Based on subsumption, new reasoning mechanisms can be defined in DLs. The ABDDI system development uses several non-standard reasoning mechanisms (e.g. Least Common Subsumer – LCS).

Definition 2 (Least Common Subsumer): *Let C_1, ..., C_p be p concept descriptions in a DL L. A Least Common Subsumer (LCS) of C_1, ..., Cp, denoted by LCS (C_1, ..., C_p) is a concept description E in L. state that the following conditions hold: (i) $C_h \sqsubseteq E$ for h = 1, ..., p; (ii) E is the least L–concept description satisfying (iii), i.e., if E' is an L–concept satisfying $C_i \sqsubseteq E'$ for all i = 1, ..., n, then $E \sqsubseteq E'$.*

It is worth showing how to model concept collections formalized in ALN (D) according to a compact lossless representation. Such modelling allows finding commonalities in resource annotations formalized in DL.

Definition 3 (Concept Components): *Let C be a concept described in a DL L, with C formalized as* $C^1 \sqcap \ldots C^m$. *The Concept Components of C are defined as follows: if C^j, with j = 1,..., m is either a concept name, or a negated concept name, or a concrete feature or a number restriction, then C^j is a Concept Component of C; if $C^j = \forall R.E$, with j = 1 ..., m, then $\forall R.E^k$ is a Concept Component of C, for each E^k Concept Component of E.*

Definition 4 (Subsumption): *Give two concept descriptions C and D and a TBox τ in a DL L; one can say that D subsumes C τ* ($C \sqsubseteq_\tau D$) *concerning if for every model of τ, $C^I \subset D^I$. As a particular case, two concepts are equivalent if they subsume each other.*

Definition 5 (Least Common Subsumer): *Let C_1, ..., Cp be p concept descriptions in a DL L. A Least Common Subsumer (LCS) of C_1, ..., Cp, denoted by LCS (C_1, ..., Cp) is a concept description E in L. state that the following conditions hold: (i) $C_h \sqsubseteq E$ for h =* 1, *..., p; (ii) E is the least L–concept description satisfying (iii), i.e., if E' is an L–concept satisfying $C_i \sqsubseteq E'$ for all i = 1, ..., n, then $E \sqsubseteq E'$.*

Definition 6 (r-Common Subsumer, Informative r-Common Subsumers): *Let C_1, ..., Cp be p concept descriptions in a DL L, and let be $k \leq p$. An r-Common Subsumer (r-CS) of C_1, ..., Cp is a concept $D \neq \top$ such that D is an LCS of at least r = k/p concepts among C_1, ..., Cp. One can define a particular case as Informative r-Common Subsumers (IrCS) that specific r-CSS for which r < 1.*

It is worth showing how to model concept collections formalized in ALN (D) according to a compact lossless representation. Such a modelling framework allows finding commonalities in resource annotations formalized in DL.

Definition 7 (Concept Components): *Let C be a concept described in a DL L, with C formalized as* $C^1 \sqcap \ldots C^m$. *The Concept Components of C are defined as follows: if* C^j*, with* $j = 1,\ldots, m$ *is either a concept name, or a negated concept name, or a concrete feature or a number restriction, then* C^j *is a Concept Component of C; if* $C^j = \forall R.E$*, with* $j = 1 \ldots, m$*, then* $\forall R.E^k$ *is a Concept Component of C, for each* E^k *Concept Component of E.*

Definition 8 (Aggregate Collection Matrix): *Let* $S_1, \ldots, S_n$ *be an aggregate collection, with* $S_j = C_{1i}, \ldots, C_{pi}$ *for* $i = 1 \ldots n$. *Let* $D \in \{D_1,\ldots,D_m\}$ *be the Concept Components deriving from all the concepts in the aggregate collection. The Aggregate Subsumers Matrix is defined as* $A = (a_{ij})$*, with* $i = 1 \ldots n$ *and* $j = 1 \ldots m$*, such that for each i,* $a_{ij} = v$*, with* $0 \leq v \leq p_i$*, where v is the number of concept descriptions in* S_i *subsumed by the component* D_j.

Definition 9 (Aggregate Model): *Let* $S_1, \ldots, S_n$ *be an aggregate of concept collections; for* $i = 1 \ldots n$*,* S_i *is a concept collection descriptions* $_{Ski}$ *with* $k = 1 \ldots p_i$*. An Aggregate Model for* $S_1, \ldots, S_n$ *and each of this element consists of the pair of items - <E, G> with the following characteristics: (i) E represents the subsumers matrix deriving from the collection* $C_1,\ldots,C_p = \cup(C_{ki})$*, with* $i = 1 \ldots n$ *and* $k = 1 \ldots p_i$*, whose elements* e_{kj} *are calculated by using prognostications to subsumption; and (ii) G is the collection subsumers matrix deriving from the input collection* $S_1,\ldots,S_n$*, whose elements* a_{ij} *are calculated by using information stored in E. In this computation, each row i in G is related to an aggregate collection* S_i*, defined as a collection of description* C_{ki} *whose subsumption relationship with components deriving from* $S_1,\ldots,$ *Sn is stored in E. To this modelling, values* a_{ij}*, for each component* D_j*, are determined as Concept Component Relative Cardinality* $RC_{D_j}^{S_i}$.

Semantic Similarity Assessment

Before describing the proposed approach's theoretical framework, the employed reasoning services will be shortly recalled in the following subsection to make the chapter self-contained. Furthermore, the proposed algorithmic concept of similarity measurement is presented in this section.

In ABSDM, the similarity between concepts C_i, C_j can be expressed by a number, and its values can fall somewhere between 0 and 1. It may be viewed as a one-directional relation, and its larger values imply a higher similarity between the concepts. The concept similarity is described as follows:

Definition 10 (Concept Similarity): An ontological concept (C) similarity (∂) is considered as a *relation*, and it can be defined as $\partial C \times C \rightarrow [0, 1]$. In simple, it is a function from a pair of concepts to a real number between *zero* and *one* expressing the degree of similarity between two concepts such that:

1. $\forall C_1 \in G, \partial(C_1,C_1) = 1$
2. $\forall C_1,C_2 \in G, 0 \leq \partial(C_1,C_2) \leq 1$
3. $\forall C_1,C_2,C_3 \in G,$ IF $Sim_d(C_1,C_2) > Sim_d(C_1,C_3)$ THEN $\partial(C_1,C_2) < \partial(C_1,C_3)$

The above properties provide the range of semantic similarity function $\partial(C_i,C_j)$. For exactly similar concepts, the similarity is $\partial(C_1,C_2)=1$; when two concepts have nothing in common, their similarity is $\partial(C_1,C_2)=0$. In this way, the output of the similarity function should be in the closed interval [0, 1]. Here Sim_d represents the semantic distance, and (C_1, C_2, C_3) represent three concepts of graph G. In CSIA, the following semantic similarity (∂) function has been used for computation purposes:

$$\partial(C_1,C_2) = \frac{1}{\deg * Sim_d(C_1,C_2)+1}$$

Where C_1 and C_2 represent two concepts, and 'deg' represents the impact of semantic distance on semantic similarity, it should be between $0 < \deg \leq 1$. A weight allocation function is used, as shown below, to compute the semantic similarity between concepts:

$$w(C_m C_n) = \left[\max(depth(C_m)) + \frac{OrderNumber(C_n)}{TNodes(G)+1} + 1 \right]^{-1}$$

Where C_m and C_n represents two nodes directly connected, $\max(depth(C_m))$ represents the maximum depth of the node C_m (the depth of the root node is equal to 0 and 1 for the nodes directly connected to the root node and so on), TNodes(G) and OrderNumber(C_n) represent the total number of nodes in concept graph G and the order number of the node (C_n) between their siblings.

The detailed description of these mathematical formalizations is beyond the scope of this chapter.

Semantic Similarity Assessment

In ABDDI, the similarity between two concepts C_i, C_j can be expressed by a number, and its values can fall somewhere between 0 and 1. It may be viewed as a one-directional relation, and its larger values imply a higher similarity between the concepts. The concept similarity is described as follows:

EXAMPLE OF A BUSINESS SCENARIO

A simple apparel manufacturing scenario is used to present a part of ABDDI algorithmic computation. Semantic IoT-based product flow in a retail outlet is considered. Each product is described using semantic-enhanced IoT as an ALN (D) concept expression in OWL language. As the retail apparel product arrive or depart the shop, they are scanned by the gate RFID readers; reading events, including semantic annotation extracted from tags, are fed to a semantic Data Service Management Service (DSMS), which computes Concept Components and subsumption test through a reasoning mechanism.

Let us consider a situation that allows a user to purchase a sweater from an online business. This example considers how a request is matched with the service advertised for wool garments selling service. An algorithm (i.e., ALGORITHM 1) tries to perform semantic matching for a relevant sweater.

Algorithm 1. *Algorithm for semantic similarity computation*

input: two concepts (C_1, C_2), the root node (root), concepts graph (G)
output: semantic similarity value between two concepts

```
begin
if C_1 and C_2 are same concept then Sim_d = 0
else
    if C_1 and C_2 are directly connected then Sim_d = w (C_1, C_2)
    else
        if idirect path connection exist then
            S_path01 = ShortestPath (G, C_1, Root_N)
            S_path02 = ShortestPath (G, C_2, Root_N)
            Sim_d = w(S_path01) + w(S_path02) - 2*w(CSPath]
        end if
        ∂(C_1,C_2) = 1 / (deg* Sim_d + 1)
    end if
end if
return ∂
end
```

The algorithm takes two ontological concepts, the root node (root), and the concepts graph (G), as input and computes a semantic similarity between the concepts as output. The part of the concept hierarchy used in this example is shown in Figure 5. Each node of this hierarchy represents a concept. The experimental comparison considers semantic similarity among Wool, Shirt, Sweater, Trouser, Cardigan, Pullover, and Jumper.

Figure 5. The hierarchical concept relationships

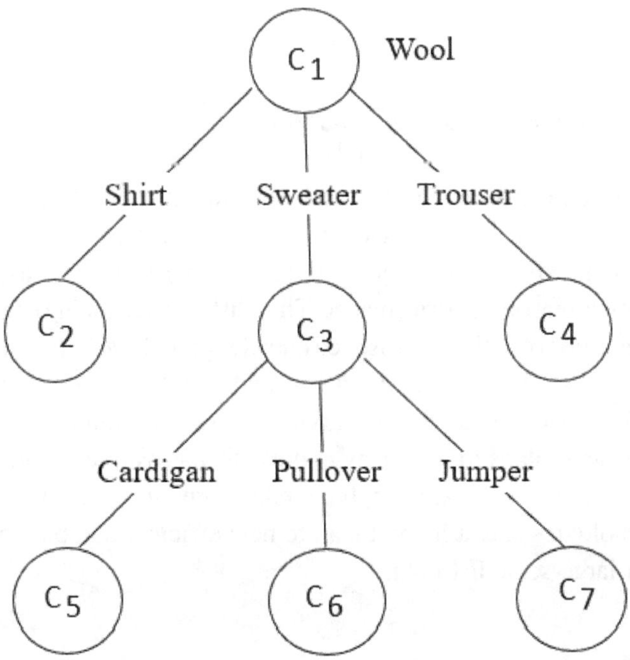

Table 2. The results of various similarity measures

	C_1	C_2	C_3	C_4	C_5
C_1	1.00	0.25	0.50	0.20	0.20
C_2	0.25	1.00	0.50	0.33	0.16
C_3	0.50	0.50	1.00	0.25	0.16
C_4	0.20	0.33	0.25	1.00	0.20
C_5	0.20	0.16	0.16	0.20	1.00

(a) Path similarity

	C_1	C_2	C_3	C_4	C_5
C_1	1.00	0.48	0.65	0.51	0.38
C_2	0.48	1.00	0.65	0.51	0.38
C_3	0.65	0.65	1.00	0.71	0.48
C_4	0.51	0.51	0.71	1.00	0.59
C_5	0.38	0.38	0.48	0.59	1.00

(b) The proposed method

The proposed algorithm (i.e., Algorithm-I) provides semantic similarity between concepts with a high score compared to the path similarity algorithm. In Table 2, (a) is the result of path similarity [18], and (b) tabulates the results of the proposed Algorithm-I used in ABDDI. In ABDDI similarity measure is flexible and customizable, allowing the consideration of user preferences. This refers to two aspects. Firstly, the user may determine some of the similarity assessment parameters' relative importance using the advanced search interface. Second, apart from presenting a single rank for each candidate service, more detailed results may also be provided (e.g., different values for recall, the degree of match) to facilitate the user in identifying the timelier service.

FUTURE RESEARCH DIRECTIONS

Based on the findings, future studies and experiments need to be carried out on semantic reasoning with more diverse information content, complex scenarios, and more detailed contextual knowledge (e.g., rules, other forms). Reasoning engines certainly influence reasoning performance. Thus different reasoning engines should be evaluated. Integration of real-time reasoned knowledge with background knowledge by utilizing federated RDF databases would be valuable, as they can provide background reasoning and knowledge integration services on specific platforms. In the future, the current research plans to use many context scenarios to evaluate the proposed approach's benefit better. Finally, applying edge computing techniques to IoT with semantic technologies can at its best lead to new efficient computing and analysis techniques for large-scale IoT data.

CONCLUSION

This chapter presents some of the uses of IoT technologies (e.g., RFID tag-based technology, sensor) in the manufacturing industry. RFID technology can interact with items (i.e., transport carts, trolleys, keys, and valuable products) without physical contact in the textile and clothing retail industry. Thus, item-level IoT infrastructures provide item handling efficiency and offer a promising way to capture customers' in-store behavioural data and then gain insight into these data using data mining technology. In this way, these sensing objects and things form the Internet of Things (IoT), which are used to automate different manufacturing business processes (e.g., material management, transportation management, and logistics management). IoT applications rely on real-time context data and allow sending information to drive users' behaviours in intelligent supply chain environments.

These IoT-based solutions are mostly tailored for vertical applications and systems, utilizing knowledge only from business areas. In order to realize the full potential of IoT, these specialized silo applications need to be replaced with horizontal collaborative applications, including knowledge acquisition and sharing capabilities.

One of the main challenges in realizing an IoT system lies in dealing with device and data heterogeneities and fostering the interoperability between devices, information, and services built on top of it. Ontologies and semantic description frameworks play an essential role in the IoT. They operate on top of a standardized data interoperability infrastructure and enforce the concept of data uniformity that allows data and data semantics to be described in application-independent ways. In doing so, semantic technologies and ontologies decouple data semantics from application logics, facilitating information exchange, adaptability, and interoperability among tools and systems.

This chapter describes a unified semantic knowledge base (ABDDI) for IoT related technologies in apparel supply chain management. Semantic modelling is a critical component to address issues related to interoperability among different entities to realize the grand vision of IoT. ABDDI's knowledge base comprises ontologies to model different aspects of apparel business (e.g., IoT resources, location information, contextual information, domain knowledge, policies for the dynamic environment and IoT services). Most of the current work focuses on IoT resources and services; however, modelling contextual information in a dynamic environment assists in more accurate knowledge representation for IoT entities.

Real-time data gathering and processing are the main ingredients of current supply chain operations. To further enhance the potential of this promising application, in future, this research will try to propose a unified framework for IoT-based path analytics, which uses both in-store shopping paths and IoT-based purchasing data to mine actionable navigation patterns. In the data preprocessing module, the critical problem of capturing the mainstream shopping path sequences while wiping out redundant and repeated details need to be addressed in detail.

REFERENCES

Aazam, M., & Huh, E. N. (2014). Fog computing and smart gateway based communication for cloud of things. *Proceedings of the 2nd IEEE International Conference on Future Internet of Things and Cloud (FiCloud' 14)*, 464–470. 10.1109/FiCloud.2014.83

Atzori, L., Iera, A., & Morabito, G. (2011). IoT: Giving a social structure to the internet of things. *IEEE Communications Letters, 15*(11), 1193–1195. doi:10.1109/LCOMM.2011.090911.111340

Baader, F., Calvanese, D., McGuinness, D., Nardi, D., & Patel-Schneider, P. (Eds.). (2002). *The Description Logic Handbook.* Cambridge University Press.

Barnaghi, P., Presser, M., & Moessner, K. (2010). Publishing Linked Sensor Data. *Proceedings of the 3rd International Workshop on Semantic Sensor Networks.*

Berners-Lee, T. (2000). *Weaving the Web: The Original Design and Ultimate Design of the World Wide Web by its inventor.* Harper Business.

Bonomi, F., Milito, R., Natarajan, P., & Zhu, J. (2014). *Fog computing: a platform for internet of things and analytics. In Big Data and Internet ofThings: A Road Map for Smart Environments.* Springer.

Bonomi, F., Milito, R., Zhu, J., & Addepalli, S. (2012). Fog computing and its role in the internet of things. *Proceedings of the 1st ACM MCC Workshop on Mobile Cloud Computing*, 13–16. 10.1145/2342509.2342513

Bordel Sánchez, B., Alcarria, R., Sánchez de Rivera, D., & Robles, T. (2018). Process execution in CyberPhysical Systems using cloud and Cyber-Physical Internet services. *The Journal of Supercomputing, 74*(8), 4127–4169. doi:10.100711227-018-2416-4

Broy, M., Cengarle, M. V., & Geisberger, E. (2012). Cyber-Physical Systems: Imminent Challenges. *Large-Scale Complex IT Syst. Dev., Operat. and Manag. - 17th Monterey Workshop*, 7539, 1–28.

Cheng, H., Xue, L., Wang, P., Zeng, P., & Yu, H. (2017). Ontology-based web service integration for flexible manufacturing systems. In *15th Int. Conf. on Ind. Inf.* (pp. 351–356). IEEE. 10.1109/INDIN.2017.8104797

Ciortea, A., Mayer, S., & Michahelles, F. (2018). Repurposing Manufacturing Lines on the Fly with Multi-agent Systems for the Web of Things. In *Proc. of the 17th Int. Conf. on Autonomous Agents and Multi-Agent Systems* (pp. 813–822). ACM.

Colitti, Steenhaut, Caro, & De. (2011). Integrating Wireless Sensor Networks with the Web. *Extending the Internet to Low power and Lossy Networks (IP+SN).*

Colucci, S., Di Noia, T., Pinto, A., Ruta, M., Ragone, A., & Tinelli, E. (2007). A Nonmonotonic Approach to Semantic Matchmaking and Request Refinement in E-Marketplaces. *International Journal of Electronic Commerce, 12*(2), 127–154. doi:10.2753/JEC1086-4415120205

Cory, A., Henson, J., Pschorr, K., Sheth, A. P., & Thirunarayan, K. (2009). SemSOS: Semantic sensor Observation Service. *Proceedings of the International Symposium on Collaborative Technologies and Systems*.

De Virgilio, R., Di Sciascio, E., Ruta, M., Scioscia, F., & Torlone, R. (2011). Semantic-based rfid data management. In *Unique Radio Innovation for the 21st Century* (pp. 111–141). Springer. doi:10.1007/978-3-642-03462-6_6

Gubbi, J., Buyya, R., Marusic, S., & Palaniswami, M. (2013). Internet of Things (IoT): A vision, architectural elements, and future directions. *Future Generation Computer Systems*, *29*(7), 1645–1660.

Jakl, A., Schoffer, L., Husinsky, M., & Wagner, M. (2018). Augmented Reality for Industry 4.0: Architecture and User Experience. *Proceeding of the 11th Forum Media Technology, CER-WS*, 38-42.

Jandl, C., Nurgazina, J., Schoffer, L., Reichl, C., Wagner, M., & Moser, T. (2019). SensiTrack – A Privacy by Design Concept for Industrial IoT Applications. *Proceeding of the 24th IEEE International Conference on Emerging Technologies and Factory Automation*, 1782-1789. 10.1109/ETFA.2019.8869186

Jeschke, S., Brecher, C., Meisen, T., Ozdemir, D., & Eschert, T. (2017). Industrial Internet of Things and Cyber Manufacturing Systems. In Industrial Internet of Things. Springer.

Karakostas, B. (2013). A DNS architecture for the Internet of things: A case study in transport logistics. *Procedia Computer Science*, *19*, 594–601. doi:10.1016/j.procs.2013.06.079

Katasonov, A., Kaykova, O., Khriyenko, O., Nikitin, S., & Terziyan, V. (2008). Smart Semantic Middleware for the Internet of Things. *Proceedings of the 5th International Conference of Informatics in Control, Automation and Robotics*, 11-15.

Keskinock, P., & Tayur, S. (2001). Quantitive analysis of Internet-enabled supply chain. *Interface: a Journal for and About Social Movements*, *31*(2), 70–89. doi:10.1287/inte.31.2.70.10626

Khan, R., Khan, S. U., Zaheer, R., & Khan, S. (2012). Future internet: the internet of things architecture, possible applications and key challenges. *Proceedings of the 10th International Conference on Frontiers of Information Technology (FIT '12)*, 257–260.

Lasi, H., Fettke, P., Kemper, H.-G., Feld, T., & Hoffmann, M. (2014). Industry 4.0. *BISE*, *6*(4), 239–242.

Lastra, J. L. M., & Delamer, I. M. (2006). Semantic Web Services in Factory Automation: Fundamental Insights and Research Roadmap. *IEEE Transactions on Industrial Informatics*, *2*(1), 1–11.

Lee, H. L., & Billington, C. (1992). Managing supply chain inventories: Pitfalls and opportunities. *Sloan Management Review*, *33*(3), 65–77.

Lee, J., Kao, H.-A., & Yang, S. (2014). Service Innovation and Smart Analytics for Industry 4.0 and Big Data Environment. *Procedia CIRP*, *16*, 3–8. doi:10.1016/j.procir.2014.02.001

Lefort, L., Henson, C., Taylor, K., Barnaghi, P., Compton, M., Corcho, O., Garcia-Castro, R., Graybeal, J., Herzog, A., & Janowicz, K. (2005). *Semantic Sensor Network XG Final Report*. W3C Incubator Group Report. http://www.w3.org/2005/Incubator/ssn/XGR-ssn/

Li, L., & Horrocks, I. (2004). A software framework for matchmaking based on semantic web technology. *International Journal of Electronic Commerce*, *8*(4), 39–60. doi:10.1080/10864415.2004.11044307

Lobov, A., Lopez, F. U., Herrera, V. V., Puttonen, J., & Lastra, J. L. M. (2008). Semantic Web Services framework for manufacturing industries. In *Int. Conf. on Rob. and Biomim.*, (pp. 2104–2108). IEEE.

Maass, W., & Filler, A. (2006). Towards an infrastructure for semantically annotated physical products. *INFORMATIK 2006–Informatik für Menschen, 2*(36).

Mahon, B. (2004). *The Man Who Changed Everything: The Life of James Clerk Maxwell*. John Wiley & Sons Ltd.

Marrella, A. (2018). *Automated Planning for Business Process Management*. Academic Press.

Mashal, I., Alsaryrah, O., Chung, T. Y., Yang, C. Z., Kuo, W. H., & Agrawal, D. P. (2015). Choices for interaction with things on Internet and underlying issues. *Ad Hoc Networks*, *28*, 68–90.

Minor, M., Montani, S., & Recio-García, J. A. (2014). Process-oriented Case-based Reasoning. *Information Systems*, *40*, 103–105. doi:10.1016/j.is.2013.06.004

Monostori, L. (2014). Cyber-physical Production Systems: Roots, Expectations and R&D Challenges. *Procedia CIRP*, *17*, 9–13. doi:10.1016/j.procir.2014.03.115

Montenegro, G., Kushalnagar, N., Hui, J., & Culler, D. (2007). Transmission of IPv6 packets over IEEE 802.15.4 networks. Internet proposed standard RFC, 4944.

Müller, G. (2018). *Workflow Modeling Assistance by Casebased Reasoning*. Springer.

Ning, H., & Wang, Z. (2011). Future internet of things architecture: Like mankind neural system or social organization framework? *IEEE Communications Letters*, *15*(4), 461–463.

Ocker, F., Kovalenko, I., Barton, K., Tilbury, D., & VogelHeuser, B. (2019). A Framework for Automatic Initialization of Multi-Agent Production Systems Using Semantic Web Technologies. *IEEE Robotics and Automation Letters*, *4*(4), 4330–4337.

Pal, K. (2017). Supply Chain Coordination Based on Web Services. In H. K. Chan, N. Subramanian, & M. D. Abdulrahman (Eds.), *Supply Chain Management in the Big Data Era* (pp. 137–171). IGI Global Publication. doi:10.4018/978-1-5225-0956-1.ch009

Pal, K. (2018). A Big Data Framework for Decision Making in Supply Chain. IGI Global.

Pal, K. (2020). Information Sharing for Manufacturing Supply Chain Management Based on Blockchain Technology. In Cross-Industry Use of Blockchain Technology and Opportunities for the Future. IGI Global. doi:10.4018/978-1-7998-3632-2.ch001

Pal, K., & Ul-Haque, A. (2000). Internet of Things and Blockchain Technology in Apparel Manufacturing Supply Chain Data Management. *Procedia Computer Science*, 450-457.

Pena-opez, I. (2005). *Internet Report 2005: The Internet of Things*. Academic Press.

Puttonen, J., Lobov, A., & Lastra, J. L. M. (2013). Semantics-Based Composition of Factory Automation Processes Encapsulated by Web Services. *IEEE TII*, *9*(4), 2349–2359. doi:10.1109/TII.2012.2220554

Puttonen, J., Lobov, A., Soto, M. A. C., & Lastra, J. L. M. (2010). A Semantic Web Services-based approach for production systems control. *Advanced Engineering Informatics*, *24*(3), 285–299. doi:10.1016/j.aei.2010.05.012

Russomanno, D. J., Kothari, C. R., & Thomas, O. A. (2005). Building a Sensor Ontology: A Practical Approach Leveraging ISO and OGC Models. *The 2005 International Conference on Artificial Intelligence*, 637-643.

Ruta, M., Colucci, S., Scioscia, F., Di Sciascio, E., & Donini, F. M. (2011). Finding commonalities in RFID semantic streams. *Procedia Computer Science*, *5*, 857–864. doi:10.1016/j.procs.2011.07.118

Said, O., & Masud, M. (2013). Towards internet of things: Survey and future vision. *International Journal of Computer Networks*, *5*(1), 1–17.

Sarkar, T. K., Mailloux, R. J., Oliner, A. A., Salazar-Palma, M., & Sengupta, D. L. (2006). *History of Wireless*. John Wiley & Sons Inc.

Seiger, R., Huber, S., & Schlegel, T. (2018). Toward an execution system for self-healing workflows in cyber-physical systems. *Software & Systems Modeling*, *17*(2), 551–572. doi:10.100710270-016-0551-z

Stojmenovic, I., & Wen, S. (2014). The fog computing paradigm: scenarios and security issues. *Proceedings of the Federated Conference on Computer Science and Information Systems (FedCSIS' 14),* 1–8.

Swaminathan, J. M. (2000). *Supply chain management*. In *International Encyclopedia of the Social and Behavioural Sciences*. Elsevier Sciences.

Varelas, G., Voutsakist, E., Raftopoulout, P., Petrakis, E. G. M., & Milios, E. (2005). Semantic Similarity methods in WordNet and their application to information retrieval on the Web. In *Proceedings of the 7th annual ACM international workshop on web information and data management*. Bremen, Germany: ACM. 10.1145/1097047.1097051

Vermesan, O., Friess, P., & Guillemin, P. (2011). Internet of things strategic research roadmap in Internet of Things. *Global Technological and Societal Trends*, *1*, 9–52.

Weyrich, M., & Ebert, C. (2016). Reference architectures for the internet of things. *IEEE Software*, *33*(1), 112–116.

Wu, M., Lu, T. J., Ling, F. Y., Sun, J., & Du, H. Y. (2010). Research on the architecture of internet of things. *Proceedings of the 3rd International Conference on Advanced Computer Theory and Engineering (ICACTE' 10), 5*, 484-487.

KEY TERMS AND DEFINITIONS

Description Logic: Description logics (DL) are a family of formal knowledge representation languages. Many DLs are more expressive than propositional logic, but less expressive than first-order logic.

EPC: Electronic Product Code (EPC) is a low-cost RFID tag designed for consumer products as a replacement for the universal product code (UPC).

Internet of Things: Internet of things (IoT) means networks of things, software, sensors, network connectivity, and embedded 'things or physical objects. It collects or exchanges data. IoT makes objects sensed or controlled through a network infrastructure, supports integration between physical real world and automated information systems, and brings various effects such as improved productivity or economy in manufacturing industries.

Ontology: Information sharing among supply chain business partners using information systems is an important enabler for supply chain management. There are diverse types of data to be shared across the supply chain, namely – *order, inventory, shipment*, and *customer service*. Consequently, information about these issues needs to be shared to achieve efficiency and effectiveness in supply chain management. In this way, information-sharing activities require that human and / or machine agents agree on common and explicit business-related concepts (the shared conceptualization among hardware / software-agents, customers, and service providers) are known as explicit ontologies; and this help to exchange data and derived knowledge out of the data to achieve collaborative goals of business operations.

RFID Reader: An RFID transceiver, providing real and possible access to RFID tags information.

RFID Tag: An RFID tag (or transponder), typically consisting of an RF coupling element and a microchip that carries identifying data. Tag functionality may range from simple identification to being able to form an ad hoc network.

Semantic Web Service: A Semantic Web Service, like conventional web services, is the server end of a client-server system for machine-to-machine interaction via the Web. Semantic services are a component of the semantic Web because they use mark-up which makes data machine-readable in a detailed and sophisticated way (as compared with human-readable HTML which is usually not easily "understood" by computer programs).

Supply Chain Management: Supply chain management encompasses the planning and management of all activities involved in sourcing, procurement, manufacturing, and distribution. Importantly, it also includes coordination and collaboration with channel partners, which can be suppliers, intermediaries, third-party service providers, and customers. In essence, supply chain management integrates supply and demand management within and across companies.

Web Ontology Language (OWL): The Web Ontology Language (OWL) is a semantic mark-up language for publishing and sharing ontologies on the Web. OWL is developed as a vocabulary extension of RDF (the Resource Description Framework) and is derived from the DAML + OIL Web Ontology Language.

Chapter 7
Relationships and Strategic Implications Among Organizational Culture:
Knowledge, Learning Organizations, and Innovation on Sustainable Organizations

José G. Vargas-Hernández
https://orcid.org/0000-0003-0938-4197
Instituto Tecnológico Mario Molina, Unidad Académica Zapopan, Mexico

ABSTRACT

This study aims to analyze the strategic implications that the organizational culture has on organizational knowledge, learning, and innovation. It begins from the assumption that there is a direct and positive relationship between the organizational culture and knowledge, learning, and innovation in organizations. It also is assumed that organizational culture, knowledge, learning, and innovation are receptive to sustainable organizational practices. The method used is the appreciative inquiry as a collaborative dialogue based on the question of what is the best of and what might be that aims to design and implement innovations in sustainable organizational arrangements and processes. The theoretical framework is based on organizational cultural cognitivism theory and the theory of socio-ecological intergradation. It is concluded that sustainable organization practices require the creation and development of an organizational culture supportive of knowledge, learning, and innovation practices.

DOI: 10.4018/978-1-7998-7793-6.ch007

Copyright © 2022, IGI Global. Copying or distributing in print or electronic forms without written permission of IGI Global is prohibited.

INTRODUCTION

Corporate and organizational culture plays a receptive role to sustainable organizational practices leading to economic growth and efficiency, social inclusion and justice and environmental sustainability. Organizational development is a workplace oriented process integrating knowledge generation, representation, communication and sharing, learning and training management and structuring regulations in achieving results. There is a relationship between the worker's involvement and workplace learning of new sustainable organizational development initiatives and processes. Sustainable organizational development is a pervasive philosophy globally subscribed on the commitment that organizations have to meet the needs of the current generation while not compromising the ability to meet their own needs of the future generations.

Appreciative inquiry is a collaborative dialogue based on the question of what is the best of and what might be that aims to explore, discover, understand, analyze and implement innovations in organizational arrangements and processes.

Old economy based traditional organizations are transforming rapidly into new development path with more informal and creative organizations identified with new economy organizations, more collaborative and participative organizational cultures. Individuals and society that acknowledges the relevance that natural resources, the bio ecosystem and the environment have for human development, they get involved in organizational practices of conservation, maintenance and enhancement of environmental sustainable development. These practices require the creation and development of an organizational culture supportive of knowledge, learning and innovation practices.

The study begins analyzing the components and features of the organizational development in order to continue with the analysis of knowledge transferal, the characteristics and elements of any learning organization and organizational innovation. Finally, the study intends to present a strategic approach of these issues and the concluding remarks.

BACKGROUND

Culture is the set of shared values, vision, assumption, beliefs and norm, which govern organizational policies and people (Bandura, 2002). Organizational culture is a shared understanding and learned way of perceiving, thinking and feeling about problems that are transmitted to members in the organization (Dicle and Okan, 2015). Organizational cultures structure, control and govern individual behaviors through values, rules, norms, and operating procedures.

Organizational cultural cognitivism theory sustains that the focus of learning, power and control is the individual which promote organizational culture and learning coherence (Tomasello, 2010; Thakker and Durrant, 2011). The theory of socio-ecological intergradation using a theory-building approach mimicks natural ecosystems to contribute to the development of sustainable supply chain activities and practices. Socio-ecology intergradation gradually merges the social and ecological system to shift the focus from global to more regional and local supply chain connected operations.

The resource based and the knowledge based views supported by human resource practices, information technology capabilities, environment and organizational culture are issues that have a direct effect on sustainable organizational performance. Human resource management and organizational culture are sources of competitive advantage that make valuable contributions to organizational sustainable development effectiveness. Human resources management practices is related to sustainable organizational development performance although the technology-based staff development may have not significant contributions.

An organizational sustainable system supports a structure to attract and retain human talent and facilitates an organizational culture to promote the greening. Organizational green behavior and green culture may promote motivation and incentives for green practices in designing renewable and efficient-energy products and processes (Gupta, 2008). Personnel motivation and opportunities for feedback supports an effective management performance and organizational goals leading to maximize the achievement of sustainable organizational development. Green training and development motivate and engage human resources to cultivate a sustainable organizational culture, build competencies, to value the organizational environment and solve problems related.

Creation of organizational core competencies as a strategy to enable sustainable organizational development and growth, organizations must identify people and match with positions for a more personalized career development, giving them more specific guidance y expert support in organizational culture and conflict management. Expert and process oriented are two approaches validated by theory most used in different contexts to raise the organizational capacity on consulting the organizations in organizational development. To develop the organizational capacity is required to determine the best approach in consulting the organizations taking into consideration the contextual variables, although the most used is the expert role (Boonstra & Elving, 2009).

Green values teaching and inculcation for the organizational greening is a supportive task of leader involvement (Siebenhüner and Arnold, 2007) which demands competencies and environment-friendly culture and behaviors (Rimanoczy and Pearson, 2010). Green human resource development and training improve awareness and knowledge, build positive and proactive attitudes and develop a culture of competencies toward organizational environmental issues management (Zoogah, 2011). Organizational environment green behaviors can be promoted implementing managerial tools to create and develop a culture, such as the use of financial incentives, green compensation and reward system (Phillips, 2007; Liebowitz, 2010).

Environmental performance in Mexican organizations is positively related to employee empowerment (Daily et al. 2012) forming eco-entrepreneurs, motivated, skilled and ecologically oriented to become involved in greening the organization and environmental activities by organizing natural, human and financial resources to develop a green oriented culture and add value to organizational outcomes (Renwick *et al.*,2013).

Educating, developing and training the workforce on sustainable organizational development for utilizing the knowledge and skills in processes, as well as involvement on organizational ethics, governance, transparency, accountability and compliance, etc., are relevant issues and concerns for organizational culture and management change. Environmental training has effects on sustainable development (Ji et al., 2011), the implementation of an environmental management system and development of an environmentally oriented organizational culture (Teixeira et al., 2012). The organizational culture has an impact on organizational sustainable development.

Organizational culture focuses on the development of workforce cohesion and motivation through the core values of the organization. A diverse workforce may use its competencies to reach the best organizational culture despite that the focus, reasons and execution may vary regarding the resources and how they are used to achieve sustainable organizational development and growth (Bianchi, 2012). The overall organizational culture is tied to the development of the workforce and teamwork through motivating them and focusing on instilling a sense of identity and cohesion amongst the individuals involved to create leadership. Leadership styles have influence in the development of organizational structure and culture and to foster knowledge (Alsabbagh and Khalil, 2016).

Organizational vision and culture must be led by leadership to inspire and guide all the empowered workers to excel in their practices and activities framed by a clear code of conduct in ethical, environmental and safety issues and concerns. Workers use their energies to use their whole self at their work (Moxley 2000, p. 12). Career development for the workers aligned to the vision and incorporated to the values of the organizational culture creates a bond between the organization and workers supported by motivation to attain the organizational goals. A factor for generating organizational sustainable development and growth is the operationalization of the organizational vision and structure while the individual role in a work organization is in guiding through the work environment

Individual reputation in the organization can be enhanced with provision of the right education and knowledge to conduct organizational growth through transfer of knowledge, organizational culture and leadership development, team building activities, etc. All these results of organizational communication have an impact in the development of strategic competences and the creation of organizational competitive advantages. Human resources embed sustainability into the organizational culture to align the vision, values, mission, leadership and strategies to long term sustainable economic, social and environmental results.

The core values of the sustainable organizational developments are embedded in the organizational culture to be developed into processes and procedures. Embedded organizational culture within sustainable organizational strategies shapes the sustainability vision and strategy to be implemented for the sustainable organizational development system aligning all the stakeholders involved. The organizational development process might be complex and turbulent and to avoid the risk of losing touch with the real world (Patton 1997, 26-29), it is recommended an independent internal evaluator to prevent potential bias (Sonnichsen 2000; Love 1991).

However, the involvement of all stakeholders in these actions contribute to the creation of an organizational culture oriented towards more organizational citizenship behaviors in favor of the environment. Appropriate governance mechanisms encourage all the stakeholders involved in the organization to create a culture, value and engage sustainability practices and ensures organizational representation of critical functions.

The organization can create, develop and maintain the organizational culture giving purpose and sense of identity while to work in a cohesive team to improve the environment. The organizational culture requires the management and staff involvement to provide a sense of identity, leadership and reputation, to support innovation, digitalization, environmental sustainability, sustainable organizational growth. Proportions of distribution of workers by demographic indicators referring in majorities and minorities, affect and is affected by organizational culture in terms of stereotypes, bias, etc.

A sustainable work system allows both personal and professional development to workers building on individual and organizational sustainable development. A sustainable work system processes foster to two-way communication and dialogue aimed to improve other organizational factors such as meaningfulness, comprehensibility, and manageability of post-bureaucratic and contemporary work creating the conditions needed for individual and organizational sustainable development (Heckscher, 1994).

A strong organizational culture, management of an organizational brand, analysis of the situation to formulate relevant ideas and backup innovation and possession of core competencies and capabilities such as niche strategic management of brand reputation, have a direct link to organizational sustainable development and growth.

Organizational culture facilitates organizational citizenship behaviors that promote organizational sustainable development (Angelis, 2016). Institutional rules and regulations, organizational culture, procedures and routines, etc., are example of obstacles to fulfill the gender gap equality programs for more resilient sustainable organizational development.

The organizational culture must be innovated, involved and engaged to a code of conduct framed by freedom and guidance. Organizational innovation may have severe intertwined management, institutional setting problems and environmental constraints causing negative operational changes and lack of collaboration influencing the organizational culture.

MAIN FOCUS OF THE CHAPTER

Knowledge Transferal

The organizational capability to facilitate and integrate the knowledge-creation of value in the structure, motivation and communication processes lead to sustainable organizational development and growth. Organizations enable development and enhancement of the organizational knowledge to provide the factors within motivation, communication, cohesion, organizational structure and behavior.

Organizational knowledge is the main factor that contributes to organizational long term core competencies which in turn have a high impact on long term sustainable organizational development and growth. Knowledge human resources development and their retention (Belle, 2016) in organizational learning improves the culture, values, resources, capabilities, processes, mechanisms, etc., becomes a priority of cultural cognitivism in organizational sustainable development (XiaomiAn and Wang, 2010; Csikszentmihalyi, 2015).

Organizational cognition can contribute to improve the computational capacity for organizational knowledge management, problem-solving and decision-making processes supported by the organizational demands and goals (Moon et al., 2017; Staats and Gino 2013). Cognitive factors have an impact on organizational knowledge assets aimed to change the sustainable organizational development (Attwell, 2010) in a motivated environment (Birmingham, 2015) requiring self-actualization (Adcock, 2012).

Organizational knowledge is challenged by the cognitive dissonance theory by exploiting accommodation and assimilation processes at individual knowledge level by introducing and accepting new organizational behaviors (Adcock, 2012).

Knowledge-based (KBV) and resource-based (RBV) theories support the notion that human resources are equally relevant that other organizational resources. Human resource management practices have a relationship with sustainable organizational development innovation and performance. The resource-based theory and knowledge-based theory argue that organizational human resources are equally relevant that other organizational resources to incorporate innovative processes in attaining sustainable organizational development performance.

The human capital theory and the Drucker's knowledge-worker productivity theory sustain that knowledge of individuals in an organization is an asset (Wong, 2012; Adcock, 2012). Investments in human resources development with an emphasis in knowledge and innovation based organizations are crucial in dynamic organizational environments to achieve sustainable organizational development performance.

Knowledge-based organizations under the analysis of knowledge based theory sustains that knowledge innovation has an impact on sustainable organizational development performance leading to the creation of by-products of knowledge capabilities contributing to and organizational competitive advantage, stability, employee satisfaction, etc. Knowledge based innovation from the perspective of resource based view as a mediator for human resource management practices is a key resource for competitive advantage and sustainable organizational development (Lopez-Cabrales, Pérez-Luño, and Cabrera 2009).

The value theory is based on the knowledge obtained from executed projects as a factor that affects the organizational ability to sustain development and growth (Chinta & Kloppenborg's 2010). Organizational knowledge as a tool enables long-term value creation by establishing the sustainable core competencies keeping up with innovation to be created and managed should be differentiating between the organizational and society values to take action leading to sustainable organizational development and growth.

Sustainable human resources management practices should be engaged in sharing intra-organization information and knowledge to attain goals, create value and competitive advantage. Use of organizational communication system enables the exchange and sharing of knowledge and common experiences amongst individuals and groups which leads to organizational effectiveness and sets the foundations for organizational development (Tucker et al., 1996). Organizational communication develops the knowledge required by tasks within the adequate policies creating a community in the organization (Elving, 2005).

Organizational communication allows individuals to share their knowledge and experiences leading to manage its tacit knowledge (Tucker et al., 1996) developed towards the creation of a sustainable organizational competitive advantage (Osterloh & Frey, 2000). Creation of organizational knowledge with the involvement of all the stakeholders holds value through a brand name identified with the potential benefits (Tauber, 1981; Broniarczyk & Alba, 1994) associated to the constructed identity and the connected values such as trust (Keller, 1987).

Organizational knowledge can be created, maintained and efficient transferred through consistent communication across all aspects, structures and hierarchies. Organizations are developing new tools for more viable and efficient organizational communication channels that enable the transferal of knowledge and deliver a sense of efficiency and overall development to all the involved individuals within the organization (Haslam, 1997). Development of open communication channels across all the organizational levels focusing on communicating the purpose of developing sustainable core values and to transfer and disseminate the knowledge.

The organizations value knowledge maintained through communication and an organizational structure and tied to core competencies that enable sustainable organizational development and growth which can be realized if produces more value and benefits (Bianchi, 2012). Organizational communication is prevalent to maintain the sense of an organizational community while still involved with other external communities and develop the networks to facilitate the knowledge transferal with the support of teams.

The organization strives to communicate consistently to transfer knowledge, values and skills to the workforce regarding the processes while maintaining the organizational standards. Sustainable organizational development and growth are connected by the ability to transfer knowledge that creates value and enables the development of core competencies. Consistent transferal of organizational knowledge for sustainable development enables to develop a connection to the overall organizational health and personal development for each one of the workforce, allowing them to communicate with freedom and independence and becoming more motivated.

Organizational development encompasses the core competencies enabling to enhance them and manage the benefits of long term organizational knowledge. The results delivered by an intervention of organizational development are measured in terms of exchange and transfer of organizational knowledge and the impact on individual and organizational performance in terms of the goals achievement.

Any organizational development intervention must promote more that supporting the status quo and accomplish change to renew it. The organizational sustainable development intervention to be fully tailor-made to the organization's developmental needs starting from the current organization's climate and perceived training needs in managerial needs to create and develop an organizational culture where the agendas, purposes and meanings are shared in explicit organizational knowledge involving all the stakeholders (Choo 2000, Järvinen & Poikela 2001).

Organizational knowledge provided by the aptitude and ability to develop projects adds value to the skills and process within the sustainable organizational core competencies (Chinta & Kloppenborg, 2010). Organizational development is a change process that creates and improves the knowledge and skills of all the stakeholders giving them opportunities to be included.

The organizational stakeholders' behaviors need to be properly developed in accordance with the organizational structure, knowledge management and the standardization of benefits (Holbrook & Hirschman, 1982) should be clear to the workforce to enabling the organization to maintain sustainable development and growth. Rotation of the workforce through different organizational practices allows to gain a broad knowledge on the operations and functions of the organization.

Ambidextrous organizations pursue exploration and exploitation of knowledge applied to developmental activities within the organizational structure. Organizational structure and behavior is an emerging theory in some industrial sectors linked to the concepts of power, opportunities and proportions with a delimiting factors (Kanter 2008). Position power changes benefit the organizational development by giving individuals opportunities in a wider range of organizational knowledge in new projects and exposure through the stages to other people in other areas and functions in the organization and value their potentials (Kanter, 2008). Organizational knowledge needs to be shared through all hierarchical levels in all issues and aspects to deliver the improvements and tied to personalized career path plans to much personal motivation, interests, and capabilities.

Motivation of all the workforce enable organizational team and leadership development to further improve as it develops the creation and transference of knowledge, learning, processes, practices and performance. Motivation and communication of the organizational team focused on development of individuals involved with a commitment of knowledge and expertise to continuing growth deliver the organizational performance.

Managerial balance of performance leads to sustainable organizational growth through the continual creation of knowledge and development of standardized competencies. The organizational capability to attain and apply knowledge obtained from projects to create value through the improvement of process used to accomplish the projects lead to sustainable growth (Chinta & Kloppenborg, 2010; Bianchi, 2012). Creation of knowledge combined with experiences of members as an organizational competence create value to achieve overall and long term sustainable growth (Bianchi, 2012; Tucker et al., 1996; Chinta & Kloppenborg, 2010). Continual organizational knowledge development enables sustainable value creation to develop sustainable organizational development and growth.

Organizational change requires information and knowledge based on the performance to design an action plan of intervention to innovate processes, to motivate the need to work cohesively and transfer new knowledge and skills to improve performance. Organizational change must move and transform organizations from consuming to regenerative and upskilling work and resources to have positive results on the individual and organizational sustainable development. Organizational workforce cohesion should focus in the organization´s needs and vision related to the individual´s competencies and knowledge, creating motivation and working as a team with a sense of pride in continual growth and developing expertise.

A motivational program may enable the transferal of organizational knowledge and learning (Osterloh & Frey, 2000) which are considered as intangible competencies to function in a cohesive unit with abilities and skills of the workforce to enable organizational development. In this logics, the tangible competencies are the tangible resources (Schmiedinger et al., 2005). Transferal of organizational knowledge conducted through sharing experiences by the communication system (Tucker, Meyer & Westerman, 1996) in the organizational structure leads to the sustainability of an organization (Roberts & O'Reilly, 1974).

Individuals seek personal development at the workplace having a job that offers this to commit skills, knowledge and abilities to the organization which in turn seeks organizational development through the commitment and efforts to achieve the higher performance output. Organizational knowledge exchange to improve the processes of sustainable organizational strategic development advancement in structures, strategies and policies, motivation, communication and leadership processes, promotes organizational development effectiveness and performance (Cummings & Worley, 2014).

Organizational development focuses on the need to exchange of knowledge and learning with an emphasis of individual and social elements within the organization in reference to concepts such as organizational and work design, group dynamics, leadership, etc. (Cummings & Worley, 2014). Organizational knowledge exchange to improve the processes of sustainable organizational strategic development advancement in structures, strategies and policies, motivation, communication and leadership processes, promotes organizational development effectiveness and performance (Cummings & Worley, 2014).

Organizational design converging with knowledge accumulation based on the principle of self-organization account for measuring the performance of tacit knowledge in a sustainable learning organization model.

The workforce need to be in constant transfer of knowledge through experiential and educational practices to advance their own development to gain broader understanding of processes aligned with the goals, philosophy, culture and outcomes of the organization. The organization needs to expand the expertise and broad knowledge within the workforce by providing education and training, communicating results and engaging them in the process of achieving the best results and outcomes, enhancing the organizational growth. Education and training are try elements necessary to develop individual and team based organizational knowledge, developing common interests across de hierarchical levels to achieve organizational development and growth.

Organizational climate enables organizations the continuous development of a cycle of knowledge transferal through communication among the workers (Elving, 2005). A continuous cycle of organizational communication patterns encompasses a continuous interpersonal relationship to enable transferal of knowledge to develop teams aimed to develop sustainable core competitive advantages as a managerial strategy that leads to sustainable organizational development and growth (Roberts & O'Reilly; Postmes, 2003; Tucker et al., 1996). Organizations engaged in long lasting relationships and dialogue with workers creates corporate branding and fosters sustainable organizational development (Aggerholm, Anderson & Thomsen, 2011).

Transferal of knowledge through organizational communication contributes to develop and manage sustainable competitive advantages (Tucker et al., 1996). Communication patterns enable knowledge transferal which is crucial for the creation, development and management of organizational core competencies and their overall success (Roberts & O'Reilly, 1974; Tucker et al., 1996).

Sustainable organizational health and growth hinge on communication to enable the transferal of knowledge, skills and competencies, as well as the community cohesion that contribute to the innovation and sustainable organizational development. Organizations should develop balanced organizational communication and climate programs enable to structure individual behaviors in organizations enable to provide opportunities to enhance knowledge and learning, to shape organizational structure and to motivate organizational behaviors (Kanter, 2008).

Feedback is a mechanism for acquiring awareness, information and knowledge supporting, self-correcting and ensuring sustainability to organizational development.

Learning Organizations

Organizational learning deals with complexities and uncertainties of sustainable organizational development efforts (Bovaird, 2007). Organizational development involves the implementation, support, and design organizational modifications. Organizational learning for integration of environmental sustainability practices contributes to build a holistic green organization (Kerr, 2006; Siebenhüner and Arnold, 2007). A holistic and constructivist approach to organizational development in accordance to principles are based on standards and regulations workplace oriented, adapted and systematically structured on an organizational learning and knowledge management systems. However, the development initiative processes are complex, uncertain and ambiguous, relying more on ongoing continuous learning processes and evaluation of outcomes.

Sustainability is a fundamental learning principle applied to sustainable circular learning cycle in the concept of sustainable learning organization. The greening of the organizations requires support from top-management support for mutual organizational learning to identify the crucial factors and the integration of green activities, practices and efforts to promote environmentally sustainable organizational behaviors. Top management and project management of the organization are the key players for any initiative on organizational sustainable development.

An interpretive model sustains that organizational learning is a source of cognitive and psychological empowerment of workers for developing their technological and managerial capabilities, involving them in decision-making processes and practices (Rahimian et al., 2014, Thomas and Velthouse, 1990). The learning components has an impact on organizational innovation (Sedighi 2016).

The cognitive learning factors have an impact on the organizational cognition, knowledge and learning management system aimed to improve the effectiveness of sustainable organizational development in any learning organization (Marshall, 2007). Organizational cognition is a systemic discipline concerned with organizational collective learning based on multidisciplinary research (Alhabeeb and Rowley, 2017; Atwood et al., 2010; Belle, 2016) aimed to organize the components of human resources, structure, design, technology, culture and social networks. Organizational sustainable development has managerial research implications for specific environmental and green issues (Commission on Environment and Development 1987; Brundtlandt in Hoverstadt and Bowling, 2005; Baumgartner and Korhonen, 2010; Becker, 2010; Patra, 2009).

The cognitive components of learning, knowledge and structure are very significant factors and contribute with a positive impact towards organizational sustainable development. Organizational cognitive, learning and culture elements are factors that have impact on the Organizational sustainable development. Organizational cognitive factors, behavioral, leadership styles, organizational structure social and contextual elements are relevant for the organizational learning tacit and explicit knowledge and sustainable development.

The organizational cognitive, knowledge and learning perspectives are influenced by factors such as organizational culture, leadership, knowledge, training and development, empowerment, organizational structure and strategy, performance (Alalwan et al., 2016; Adcock, 2012; Coetzer et al., 2017). Trait leadership and organizational cognition theories argue that the cognitive domain is an ability of supportive leadership (Mumford et al., 2016; Dicle and Okan, 2015) that encourages organizational collaborative learning between internal and external environments (Atwood et al., 2010).

Organizational learning and entrepreneurial activities are related with the individual and team. Organizational learning is an individual and organizational dynamic process extending from intuition, interpretation, integration and institutionalization of organizational change (Crossan et al.,1999). There is a positive relationship between dimension of organizational learning and entrepreneurship (Aghajani et al.

2015). Learning organization has a relationship with entrepreneurial performance (Safamansh et al. 2015). Organizational learning capacity has an impact on innovation performance (Gomez and Wojahn 2017).

Organizational change is defined in terms of learning. A learning organization may induce change of learning processes with creativity and innovation as an organizational existential value in a flexible and cohesive structure with the lowest cost and waste of resources (Kouhkan & Mousavi 2015, Gomez & Wojahn 2017, Safamansh et al. 2015, and Hoveida 2007). Creativity has a relationship with learning organization. Less formal and more organic organizational structure promotes more democratic values and organizational learning (Martínez-Leon and Martínez-García, 2011).

Learning and knowledge processes takes into account the individual, group and organizational capabilities and performance (Saadat and Saadat, 2016). The grouping arrangements within the line organization structure can limit organizational mutual learning, knowledge management and idea exchange. The process of organizational learning increases the self-esteem of the involved individuals when gaining experience to achieve their goals (Gomez & Wojahn 2017, Kouhkan & Mousavi 2015, Aghajani et al. 2015, Sedighi 2016, Ehsani Ghodsi & Seyed Abbaszadeh 2012, and Hoveida 2007).

The organizational structure has an impact on the workforce development based on usage of knowledge, communication channels, motivation and cohesion considered as the foundations of core competencies (Han et al. 2010 and Hill & Bowen's (1997). The organic organizational structure is more sustainable providing more organizational learning integrating knowledge in less formal and centralized ways, modularized and combined in processes (Tran and Tian, 2013). A learning organization changes in attitude to favor collective learning to achieve organizational growth and development (Alvani, 2008).

The learning approach to sustainable development requires that project owners get more involved as the leader, sponsor, mentor and critic in accordance with development changes (Van de Ven et al., 2000). Individual and organizational differences have to be turn into benefits to find the common ground for a greater sense of active and shared responsibilities to improve individual and organizational learning and development.

Sustainable organizational development change must take into account the quality work and the continuous organizational learning processes adapted to the new institutional reality and organizational memory (Pfeffer and Sutton 2000) from an emerging thinking and activity levels most suited to the specific current situation.

Institutionalization of strategic change and renewal of sustainable organizational development practices is part of the organization's memory based on founded on organizational learning starting with the steering and guiding the organizational operations and practices (Crossan et al., 1999). Learning institutions identified with higher education institutions that provide educational and academic services which are the base to similar abilities, functions and relationships to become learning organizations whether they are capable to promote and have an impact with organizational innovation.

Appropriate encouragement to continue change to create a learning organization with an institutionalization of a strong organizational culture to facilitate knowledge sharing through communication, fosters creativity and innovation. Institutionalizing strong organizational culture with horizontal structures to facilitate information, communication and knowledge sharing flows are required to create an innovative and creative learning organization. Organizations need to create and develop knowledge and learning units with capabilities to collect information and provide feedback and support the sustainable organizational development (Patton 1998).

The information and knowledge explosion involving information and communication technologies are leading to shorter innovation cycles, continuous individual and organizational learning and knowledge systems and sustainable organizational development. Innovative employees should be attracted to the organization and retained. An implementation of and organizational learning and knowledge system including project principles results in specific experiences related to the standard for management systems, such as the strategies and objectives formulated on customer-based requirements, definition of management, resources, optimization and support processes focused on the optimization and fulfillment of organizations.

Organizational development initiatives play a role in engaging workers by tapping into their efforts for sustainability practices while promoting trust, loyalty and confidence, as well as formalizing knowledge sharing and learning to create organizational responsiveness to internal and external factors. Loyal workers to their organization make them staying at the workplace and committed to develop individual, improve quality of performance and upgrade programs through learning and knowledge infrastructures (Kouhkan & Mousavi 2015; Hoveida 2007).

Organizational learning culture development enhance acquisition, interpretation and distribution of tacit and explicit organizational knowledge (Mehrabi et al., 2013). The explicit organizational knowledge must be systematically structured and documented including all the relevant information on need-oriented processes, procedures, regulations, etc., aimed to promote and improve the sustainable organizational development. Organizational learning and knowledge culture helps to be reused to support organizational living learning environments (Bandura, 2002).

Organizational learning from the best practices will continuously innovate involving the workforce in better opportunities of development created at all levels, engaging, increasing commitment and responsibility.

The rational planning models for managing organizational development and change has some limitations which are being addressed by the perspective of process and learning model on organizational change viewed as an open process of learning and adaptation (March, 1981; Beer et al., 1990; Brulin and Svensson, 2012), or as organizational development (Bennis et al., 1985). Sustainable organizational development is a component of procedural and organizational adaptability and maturity. Planned organizational change is conceptualized as managed learning (Schein, 1996).

Organizational development planning is supported by knowledge, learning and change mechanism. In sustainable organizational development planning emerge knowledge, learning and change dimensions despite that they are not the values, assumptions, strategies and objectives (Friedman et al, 1987). Organizations use to have a high workload of current work processes that may be reduced by targeting the organizational resources to make more rational and efficient use.

Managerialism is an approach to public sector organizations that has rapidly adopted other trends such as learning organizations, strategic human resource and knowledge management (Wiig, 2002) practices in operational task management aimed to achieve sustainable wellbeing and performance and to promote organizational sustainable development.

Evaluations has an impact in assessing the theory of change promoted by learning programs that lead to sustainable organizational development. The organizational process evaluation to use a systematic feedback should be conducted within a comprehensive framework supported by an organizational sustainable development intervention aimed to enhance the organizational capacity building.

Ongoing evaluations aimed to provide confirmation of expectations need to focus more on long-term results of sustainability activities rather than on short term effects questioning action patterns that trigger developmental learning (Schein, 1996; Ellström, 2001). Organizational internal self-evaluation and applied formative developmentative evaluation is needed (Patton 1997, 104 106) as being user and improvement-oriented to be implemented for organizational sustainability development (Patton,1998, 225).

Organizational Innovation

Organizational innovation is an advantageous attribute since the industrial revolution for those organizations that accept new ideas generated within or appropriated from somewhere else, developed and implemented to develop a competitive advantage, to create value and attain benefits.

Organizational innovation means using knowledge, tools, practices and manpower to achieve specific goals through non-recurring strategies. Innovative organizations develop a creative environment where all the stakeholders involved can find motivation to generate new ideas. More of the environmental constraints in a complex system and institutional setting are posed by the institution of the market (Hirschhorn 1988) which helps to understand the limits of organizational innovation priorities. Organizations incorporate innovative practices and processes leading to sustainable organizational innovation performance. Organizational innovation improves corporate practices, methods, intra organizational coordination instruments, and management strategies through structural changes.

Organizational innovations are dependent on the psychological structures of humans involved in organizations (Vansina, 1998) which may be understood in simplistic approaches that do not consider other variables such as participation of workers in the organizational change and innovation. Organization have specific operating conditions to become learning organizations and their potential impacts on organizational innovation.

Organizational innovation mediates between human resource management practices sustainable organizational development performance, which are related to organizational knowledge and environmental sustainability. Human resource management practices are defined as the policies and practices relevant to perform the routines of all personnel for sustainable organizational development performance mediated by organizational innovation (Foss and Lyngsie 2011). Human resources management development enhance organizational innovation emphasizing motivation to encourage competencies which improves the sustainable organizational development outcomes performance.

Organizational innovation and effective performance management are resources to achieve measures of goals in organizational sustainable development performance. The new innovative organizational working mechanisms have effects of the organizational dynamics and are contributing more than the old practices to sustainable organizational development performance.

The components of the learning organization have a relationship with innovation (Kouhkan and Mousavi 2015). The components of learning organization have a significant direct impact on transparency, empowerment and leadership, teamwork, experimentation, reward, etc., and organizational innovation leading to the improvement of organizational performance. Organizational innovation is supported on its core competencies and contributes to create and develop a competitive advantage leading to continue growth (Egbu, 2004). Organizational learning and leadership are factors that promote the use of innovative methods improving the organizational sustainable development (Danish et al., 2015). Leadership abilities are required to influence learning activities to improve the work processes which results in efficiency and organizational sustainable development.

Increasing the organizational ability to deal with emerging environmental needs, demands and changes at the different levels is dependent on the organizational capabilities to innovate, transform and renovate through arrangements of flexible collaboration and relationships of cooperation while the workers are internally committed to the sustainable organizational development.

An organizational change and innovation processes founded on participation need to create internal commitment, responsibility and empowerment of all the involved workers and stakeholders of the organization (Argyris 1998) in organizational practices where the means fit the ends of an organizational sustainable development.

The organizational context is considered a mediating construct of organizational innovation. The academic and research environment influences the organizational innovation and the economic, social, cultural and environmental development (Simao, 2016). Interactive action research is a continuous, joint learning process between the participants and researchers. Organizational resources and infrastructure development are relevant elements to create knowledge and innovativeness in dynamic organizational environments in achieving sustainable organizational performance and development.

The public sector R&D organization in the fields of welfare and health recognize the professionalization of human resources as the most important element to promote ongoing internal organizational sustainable development and organizational learning management (Sharp 2001) through action-oriented as well as outcome-oriented projects (Geertshuis et al. 2002). Transformation of public organizations in a public sector R&D organizations operating in the fields of health and welfare are supported on organizational sustainable development and organizational learning management through internal processes.

Human resource management and staff development influence organizational innovation working mechanisms playing a mediating role for sustainable organizational development performance. Working with innovative mechanisms and improved human resources practices more engaged with staff development are more open to organizational dynamics and more innovation change.

Implementation of human resource management and organizational innovation practices are critical factors to benefit organizations to achieve sustainable organizational development performance. The organizational human resource development and innovation practices promotes creativity and productivity that have a positive relationship to sustainable organizational development performance outcomes. Human capital development is a relevant factor of the staffing creativity assuring high standard employees and organizations.

Sustainable organizational development performance is based on execution of action plans resulting in the positioning of products and services. Organizational human resources practices and organizational innovation are relevant of organizational strategic management aim to attaining sustainable organizational development and performance (Barney, 1991) leading to organizational economic development, working dynamics and firm competiveness.

Systematic customer and worker's involvement in sustainable organizational development in the workplace innovation help to learn about its needs and the potential sources of knowledge for change and innovation. Workers that bring innovation to the organizations have knowledge, skills and expertise in close relationship with the application of staff development techniques, leading to creativity. This close relationship between organizational innovation and staff development influences knowledge, process and product innovation.

Knowledge innovation is related to organizational innovation, to processes, new product and services innovation and development leading to organizational development innovation and sustainable organizational development performance. Organizational knowledge has a close relationship on organizational innovation which begins by recruiting, creating and developing human talent in innovative teams and network for sustainable organizational development.

Organizational values and competencies emphasize the collective team work formed by diverse groups of individuals having cohesion that have to improve unique competencies and set the performance standards. Group problem solving and team work affect the support on organizational innovation.

Organizational knowledge-based innovation has an intervening effect between human resources management practices and their relationships with the sustainable organizational development and performance. Organizational knowledge innovation supported by the resources based theory mediates resources for product and services development outcomes creating sustainable competitive advantage. Innovation and involvement in sustainable development of structure, leadership, and tools innovation lead to brand reputation and business opportunities for sustainable organizational growth.

The organizational management structure not meeting the requirements is leading to low results and efficiency in the economic system. The development of the economic organizational structures requires high institutional quality constantly adapting to technical and social innovations. Boons and Lüdeke-Freund (2013) find that sustainable innovation research neglects the way in which organizations combine value proposition and chain in a financial and business model in the contexts of sustainable organizational, technological and social innovations and propose normative requirements.

Self-organization processes require new intellectual knowledge creatively applied in horizontal cooperation through synergetic processes of a dissipative system between organizations leading to a new development in innovative goods and services and contributing to the growth of the economic system.

Organizational innovation distinguishes between new and old organizational knowledge practices. New ideas that are created, developed and implemented in the organization spans execution and determination for knowledge, processes and product development (Damanpour 1996). Organization change requires information and knowledge based on the performance to design an action plan of intervention to innovate processes, motivate the need to work cohesively and transfer new knowledge and skills to improve performance.

The staff development based on extensive training based on knowledge, skills and experience has a positive effect on organizational innovation.

The consistently organizational innovation through small and incremental changes of its processes contribute to the individual and team development and growth to achieve the goals. New and improved organizational and administrative practices, products and processes innovation are resource mechanisms based on learning and knowledge to benefit employee satisfaction, organizational stability, to create value and attain the organizational advantage and performance (Chowhan 2016; Zehir, Üzmez, and Yıldız 2016).

Organizational change and innovation requires to overcome the difficulties to promote changes in values, business models, procedures, leadership, entrepreneurial strategies and abilities to adapt (Moore & Manring, 2009). Organizations have to adapt continuously to changes and innovations in business models, promote entrepreneurial strategies to achieve the goals (Moore & Manring, 2009).

Knowledge, product and process innovation positively influence sustainable organizational development performance mediated by organizational innovation (Volberda, Van Den Bosch, and Heij, 2013) influenced by human resource management practices (Tsangand Zahra 2008). Organizations accomplish sustainability encouraging organizational knowledge, product and processes innovation and pursuing human resources development.

Strategic Analysis

Strategy plays a relevant role in organizational learning and knowledge which have a significant impact on the organizational sustainable development by guiding the organizational activities by the changing internal and external environment and technological changes. Organizational change is also studied from the learning perspective for strategy (Beer et al., 1990; Mintzberg, 1994). Organizational sustainable strategies and policies consider continues organizational learning, training and development of human resources demanded for organizational strategic continuous change to meet the requirements of the external environment (Crossan and Berdrow, 2011; Morais--Storz and Nguyen, 2017) which need continuous information gathering and processing (Pietrzak and Paliszkiewicz, 2013).

Organizational strategies must focus on the organizational sustainable development considering the strategies for organizational leadership to foster organizational learning (Goodyear et al., 2014). Strategies of organizational structure aim to be more flexible and humanistic enable to empower the workers who in turn have an impact on organizational learning and development (Ahadi, 2011; Martínez-Leon and Martínez-García, 2011).

The institutional setting of organizational sustainable development change corresponds to organizational learning processes and the institutionalization of structures, processes and strategies of transformation. Identifying emerging sustainability trends and learning sustainable development competencies must be the outcome of a collaboration strategy between all the involved stakeholders including local communities and NGOs.

Organizational knowledge enables management to develop strategies and policies to tackle the challenges and to maintain control over its practices and procedures (Hill & Bowen 1997). Bianchi (2016) proposes a conceptual, theoretical and methodological framework on organizational policy to assess and manage organizational sustainable development performance.

Organizational learning and culture strategies harmonize organizational culture and its impact on organizational sustainable development (Jahmurataj, 2015, Danish et al., 2015; Martin, 2014). Knowledge and skills development as a core competency of the organization being its workforce can focus on a strategy of longevity through continuous innovation.

Although the relationship between organizational strategies and organizational learning is not very clear (Hotho et al., 2015), both seem to be moderated and mediated by support of leadership, organizational culture, structure and technology (Goodyear et al., 2014) since they are related to activities carried out and linked to the organizational goals. Leadership commitment and sense of belonging with capabilities affect the organizational creativity and innovation. A motivation and reward system with an experimentation component affects the organizational ability to innovation.

Evaluating the outcomes in relation to the goals set, organizational strategies can be adjusted depending upon the internal and external environmental changes in such a way that this practice has a strong links with organizational learning, knowledge management and sustainable organizational development.

FINDINGS AND CONCLUDING REMARKS

There are strategic implications that the organizational culture has on organizational transfer of knowledge, learning organizations and organizational innovation. Organizational sustainable development must be supported by and organizational culture, organizational knowledge and learning management to conduct organizational change interventions and should be a focal goal in its strategic organizational development planning. Organizations need to develop a culture of organizational learning and knowledge sharing management to enhance the organizational competitive advantage and performance leading to improve the organizational sustainable development.

The components of the learning organization have a direct impact on organizational innovation. Organizational knowledge transfer creates a competitive advantage as resources of learning organizations have an effect on change organizational culture towards a more oriented organizational innovation.

Learning organization and organizational innovation are two components of organizations needed to develop a transparent vision of organizational change to all the stakeholders increasing their commitment and accountability and to accelerate and improve their goals. Organizations must adapt and implement management systems and well-structured regulations in learning and knowledge systems based on the constructivist theory and supported by information technology, involving all the stakeholders in knowledge sharing to improve the corporate learning culture in the workplace for securing a sustainable organizational development.

Organizational leadership must provide the appropriate motivational, spiritual and material rewards to creative and innovative ideas as well as the empowerment of individuals and teams through applied knowledge sharing, development, increase of intellectual capital, training and staffing creativity and innovation. Appropriate motivational rewards, fair promotion and pay systems are factors that stimulate organizational creativity and innovation.

Networking contributes to link cooperation to facilitate learning, knowledge and innovation, share resources and economic, technical and social solutions increasing the potential for the implementation y coordination of sustainable organizational development initiatives. Organizational development leads to resources consumption in consuming work while in regenerative work, resources become regenerated and growth, thus creating a foundation for individual and organizational sustainable development (Docherty et al., 2002). Individuals and organizations can sustainable develop creating resources to deal with future challenges.

FUTURE RESEARCH DIRECTIONS

Future research could discuss the relevance of innovation in sustainable organizations and the strategic implications of organizational culture, knowledge and learning organizations as essential elements for the long-term organizational sustainability, development, and growth. The relationship between organizational culture, learning and knowledge and organizational sustainable innovation remains to be explored for future research. Besides, research must pay more attention to the crucial role these elements are playing to follow the rapid pace and development of markets for the future of the organizations.

Future research should discuss the strategic impact of more specific organizational innovation, culture, knowledge and learning behaviors in specific industries and professions, such as technology and finance. This line of future research can combine multiple research methods and data collection across various periods of time and stages.

It is recommended for future research to conduct more longitudinal studies based on qualitative-oriented approach using in-depth case studies aimed to yield understanding of the relationships of the variables of the construct in the proposed models to test usefulness, applicability, and practicality

REFERENCES

Adcock, A. (2012). Cognitive dissonance in the learning processes. *Encycl. Sci. Learning,* 588–590.

Aggerholm, H. K., Anderson, S. E., & Thomsen, C. (2011). Conceptualising employer branding in sustainable organizations. *Corporate Communication: An International Journal, 16*(2), 105–123. doi:10.1108/13563281111141642

Aghajani, H. A., Samadi Mirakalei, H., & Samadi Myrkalei, H. (2015). The relationship between entrepreneurship and characteristics of a learning organization. *Management Efficiency, 35*(9), 39-64.

Ahadi, S. (2011). *Relationship between empowerment and organizational learning among*. Academic Press.

Alalwan, A. A., Dwivedi, Y. K., Rana, N. P., & Williams, M. D. (2016). Consumer adoption of mobile banking in Jordan: Examining the role of usefulness, ease of use, perceived risk and self-efficacy. *Journal of Enterprise Information Management, 29*(1), 118–139. doi:10.1108/JEIM-04-2015-0035

Alhabeeb, A., & Rowley, J. (2017). Critical success factors for eLearning in Saudi Arabian universities. *International Journal of Educational Management, 31*(2), 131–147. doi:10.1108/IJEM-01-2016-0006

Alsabbagh, M., & Khalil, A. H. (2016). The impact of leadership styles on organizational learning (an empirical study on the education sector in Damascus city). *International Journal of Academic Research in Business & Social Sciences, 6*(5), 197–217. doi:10.6007/IJARBSS/v6-i5/2126

Alvani, S. M. (2008). *Public Administration*. Ney Publications.

Angelis, C. T. (2016). The impact of national culture and knowledge management ongovernmental intelligence. *Journal of Modelling in Management, 11*(1), 240–268. doi:10.1108/JM2-08-2014-0069

Argyris, C. (1998). Organizational behavior: Production of knowledge for action in the world of practice. In J. McKelvey & M. Neufeld (Eds.), *Industrial relations at the dawn of the new millennium* (pp. 54–61). New York State School of Industrial and Labor Relations.

Attwell, G. (2010). Work-based mobile learning environments: Contributing to a socio-cultural ecology of mobile learning. *International Journal of Mobile and Blended Learning, 2*(4), 19–34. doi:10.4018/jmbl.2010100102

Atwood, M. A., Mora, J. W., & Kaplan, A. W. (2010). Learning to lead: Evaluating leadershipand organizational learning. *Leadership and Organization Development Journal, 31*(7), 576–595. doi:10.1108/01437731011079637

Bandura, A. (2002). Social cognitive theory in cultural context. *Applied Psychology, 51*(2), 269–290. doi:10.1111/1464-0597.00092

Barney, J. (1991). Firm resources and sustained competitive advantage. *Journal of Management, 17*(1), 99–120. doi:10.1177/014920639101700108

Baumgartner, R. J., & Korhonen, J. (2010). Strategic thinking for sustainable development. International Sustainable Development Research Society, 18, 71-75.

Becker, J. (2010). Use of backcasting to integrate indicators with principles of sustainability. *International Journal of Sustainable Development World, 17*(3), 189–197. doi:10.1080/13504501003726974

Beer, M., Eisenstat, R. A., & Spector, B. (1990). *The Critical Path to Corporate Renewal*. Harvard Business School Press.

Belle, S. (2016). Organizational Learning? Look Again. *The Learning Organization, 23*(5), 332–341. doi:10.1108/TLO-01-2016-0007

Bennis, W., Benne, K., & Chin, R. (1985). *The Planning of Change*. International Thompson Publishing.

Bianchi, C. (2012). Enhancing performance management and sustainable organizational growth through system-dynamics modelling. In *Systemic management for intelligent organizations* (pp. 143–161). Springer Berlin Heidelberg. doi:10.1007/978-3-642-29244-6_8

Bianchi, C. (2016). Fostering Sustainable Organizational Development Through Dynamic Performance Management. In *Dynamic Performance Management. System Dynamics for Performance Management* (Vol. 1). Springer. doi:10.1007/978-3-319-31845-5_3

Birmingham, U. o. (2015). *Learning Theories, Stages and Styles*. University of Birmingham.

Boons, F., & Lüdeke-Freund, F. (2013). Business models for sustainable innovation: State-of-the-art and steps towards a research agenda. *Journal of Cleaner Production, 45*(April), 9–19. doi:10.1016/j.jclepro.2012.07.007

Boonstra, J. J., & Elving, W. J. L. (2009) Veranderen als kunstje, kunde of kunst. In Communicatiemanagement in praktisch perspectief. Assen: Van Gorcum. Blz.

Bovaird, T. (2007). Beyond engagement and participation: User and community coproduction of public services. *Public Administration Review, 67*(5), 846–860. doi:10.1111/j.1540-6210.2007.00773.x

Broniarczyk, S. M., & Alba, J. W. (1994). The importance of the brand in brand extension. *JMR, Journal of Marketing Research, 31*(2), 214–228. doi:10.1177/002224379403100206

Brulin, G., & Svensson, L. (2012). *Managing Sustainable Development Programmes: A Learning Approach to Change*. Gower Publishing.

Chinta, R., & Kloppenborg, T. J. (2010). Projects and processes for sustainable organizational growth. *S.A.M. Advanced Management Journal, 75*(2), 22.

Choo, C. W. (2001). Knowing Organization as Learning Organization. *Education + Training, 43*(4/5), 197-205.

Chowhan, J. (2016). Unpacking the black box: Understanding the relation-ship between strategy, HRM practices, innovation and organizational performance. *Human Resource Management Journal*, *26*(2), 112–133. doi:10.1111/1748-8583.12097

Coetzer, A., Kock, H., & Wallo, A. (2017). Distinctive characteristics of small businesses assites for informal learning. *Human Resource Development Review*, 18–32.

Commission on Environment and Development. (1987). *World Commission on Environment and Development* (Brundtland Report). Available from: http://www.ace.mmu.ac.uk/ eae/Sustainability/Older/Brundtland_Report.html

Crossan, M., Lane, H. W., & White, R. E. (1999). An organizational learning framework: From intuition to institution. *Academy of Management Review*, *24*(3), 522–537. doi:10.2307/259140

Crossan, M. M., & Berdrow, I. (2011). Organizational learning and strategic renewal. *Strategic Management Journal*, *24*(11), 1087–1105. doi:10.1002mj.342

Csikszentmihalyi, M., (2015). Society, culture, and person: a systems view of creativity. *Syst. Model Creativity,* 47–61.

Cummings, T. G., & Worley, C. G. (2014*). Organization development and change*. Cengage Learning.

Daily, B. F., Bishop, J. W., & Massoud, J. A. (2012). The role of training and empowerment in environmental performance: A study of the Mexican maquiladora industry. *International Journal of Operations & Production Management*, *32*(5).

Damanpour, F. (1996). Organizational Complexity and Innovation Developing and Testing Multiple Contingency Models. *Management Science*, *42*, 693–716.

Danish, R. Q., Munir, Y., Kausar, A., Jabbar, M., & Munawar, N. (2015). Impact of change, culture and organizational politics on organizational learning. *Rev. Contemp. Bus.Res*, *3*(1), 115–126.

Dicle, Ü., & Okan, R.Y. (2015). The relationship between organizational structure andorganizational learning in Turkish automotive R&D companies. *Int. J. Manag. Stud. Res.*, 62–71.

Docherty, P., Forslin, J., Shani, A. B., & Kira, M. (2002) Emerging Work Systems: From Intensive to Sustainable? In Creating Sustainable Work Systems: Perspectives and Practices. London: Routledge.

Egbu, C. O. (2004). Managing knowledge and intellectual capital for improved organizational innovations in the construction industry: An examination of critical success factors. *Engineering, Construction, and Architectural Management, 11*(5), 301–315. doi:10.1108/09699980410558494

Ehsani Ghods, H., & Sayed Abbas Zadeh, M. M. (2012). Relationship between learning organization with creativity and innovation, a high school teacher and colleges, *Journal-Research New Approaches in Educational Administration. Islamic Azad University of Shiraz, 4*, 12–21.

Ellström, P.-E. (2001). Integrating learning and work: Conceptual issues and critical conditions. *Human Resource Development Quarterly, 12*(4), 421–435.

Elving, W. J. (2005). The role of communication in organisational change. *Corporate Communications, 10*(2), 129–138. doi:10.1108/13563280510596943

Foss, N. J., & Lyngsie, J. (2011). *The Emerging Strategic Entrepreneurship Field: Origins*. Academic Press.

Friedman, S., Scholink, E., & Cocking, R. (1987). *Blue prints for thinking: The role of planning in cognitive development*. Cambridge Univ. Press.

Geertshuis, S., Holmes, M., Geertshuis, H., Clancy, D., & Bristol, A. (2002). Evaluation of workplace learning. *Journal of Workplace Learning, 14*(1), 11–18.

Gomes, G., & Wojahn, R. M. (2017). Organizational learning capability, innovation and performance. *Revista ADM, 52*, 163–175.

Goodyear, M., Ames-Oliver, K., & Russell, K. (2014). *Organizational Strategies for Fostering a Culture of Learning*. University of Kansas.

Gupta, A. (2008). Earth on ðre: Implications for corporate responsibility. *American Journal of Business, 23*(1), 3–4.

Han, S. H., Kim, D. Y., Jang, H. S., & Choi, S. (2010). Strategies for contractors to sustain growth in the global construction market. *Habitat International, 34*(1), 1–10. doi:10.1016/j.habitatint.2009.04.003

Han, Y. J., Nunes, J. C., & Dreze, X. (2010). Signaling status *with* luxury goods*: The* role *of* brand prominence. *Journal of Marketing, 74*(4), 15–30. doi:10.1509/jmkg.74.4.015

Haslam, S. A. (1997). Stereotyping and social influence: Foundations of stereotype consensus. In R. Spears, P. J. Oakes, N. Ellemers, & S. A. Haslam (Eds.), *The social psychology of stereotyping and group life* (pp. 119–143). Blackwell.

Heckscher, Ch. (1994). *Defining the post-bureaucratic type*. Sage.

Hill, R. C., & Bowen, P. A. (1997). Sustainable construction: Principles and a framework for attainment. *Construction Management and Economics*, *15*(3), 223–239. doi:10.1080/014461997372971

Hirschhorn, L. (1988). *The workplace within: Psychodynamics of organizational life*. The Mit Press. doi:10.7551/mitpress/7306.001.0001

Holbrook, M. B., & Hirschman, E. C. (1982). The experiential aspects of consumption: Consumer fantasies, feelings, and fun. *The Journal of Consumer Research*, *9*(2), 132–140. doi:10.1086/208906

Hotho, J.J., Lyles, M.A., & Smith, M. (2015). The mutual impact of global strategy and organizational learning: current themes and future directions. *Glob. Strat. J.*, 85–112.

Hoveida, R. (2007). *Investigating the relationship between learning the components of the organization and improving the quality of education the door* (Master's thesis). Governmental Universities of Isfahan Province and Presentation of Student University Model, University of Isfahan.

Hoverstadt, P., & Bowling, D. (2005). Organisational Viability as a factor in Sustainable. *International Journal of Technology*, *4*(2), 131–146.

Jahmurataj, V. (2015). Impact of Culture on Organizational Development: Case Study Kosovo. *Academic Journal of Interdisciplinary Studies*, *4*(2), 206–210. doi:10.5901/ajis.2015.v4n2s1p206

Järvinen, A., & Poikela, E. (2001). Modelling Reflective and Contextual Learning at Work. *Journal of Workplace Learning, 13*(7/8), 282-289.

Ji, L., Huang, J., Liu, Z., Zhu, H., & Cai, Z. (2011). The effects of employee training on the relationship between environmental attitude and ðrms' performance in sustainable development. *International Journal of Human Resource Management*, *23*(14), 2995–3008. doi:10.1080/09585192.2011.637072

Kanter, R. M. (2008). *Men and women of the corporation: New edition*. Basic books.

Keller, K. L. (1987). Memory factors in advertising: The effect of advertising retrieval cues on brand evaluations. *The Journal of Consumer Research*, *14*(3), 316–333. doi:10.1086/209116

Kerr, I.R. (2006). Leadership strategies for sustainable SME operation. *Business Strategy and the Environment*, *15*(1), 30-39.

Kouhkan, A., & Mousavi, S. A. (2015). Review the relationship between the components of the organization Learner and Organizational innovation) Case study: (FreeUniversity of Mazandaran). *First International Conference on Economics, Management, Accounting, Social Sciences*.

Liebowitz, J. (2010). The role of HR in achieving a sustainability culture. *Journal of Sustainable Development, 3*(4), 50-57.

Lopez-Cabrales, A., Pérez-Luño, A., & Cabrera, R.V. (2009). Knowledge as amediator between HRM practices and innovative activity. *Hum Resour Manage.*, *48*(4), 485–503. doi:48:4113 doi:10.1002/hrm.v

Love, A. (1991). *Internal evaluation. Building organizations from within.* Sage.

March, J. G. (1981). Footnotes to organizational change. *Administrative Science Quarterly, 26*(4), 563–577. doi:10.2307/2392340

Marshall, N. (2007). Cognitive and practice-based theories of organisational knowing and learning: Incompatible or complementary? In *Proceedings of OLKC Learning Fusion*. University of Brighton.

Martínez-Leon, I. M., & Martínez-García, J. A. (2011). The influence of organizational structure on organizational learning. *International Journal of Manpower, 32*(5), 537–566. doi:10.1108/01437721111158198

Mehrabi, J., Soltani, I., Alemzadeh, M., & Jadidi, M. (2013). Explaining the relationship between organizational structure and dimensions of learning organizations (case study: Education organization in Boroojerd county and the related departments). *International Journal of Academic Research in Business & Social Sciences*, 116–129.

Mintzberg, H. (1994). *The Rise and Fall of Strategic Planning: Reconceiving Roles for Planning, Plans, Planners*. The Free Press.

Moon, H., Ruona, W., & Valentine, T. (2017). Organizational strategic learning capability: Exploring the dimensions. *European Journal of Training and Development, 41*(3), 222–240. doi:10.1108/EJTD-08-2016-0061

Moore, S. B., & Manring, S. L. (2009). Strategy development in small and medium sized enterprises for sustainability and increased value creation. *Journal of Cleaner Production, 17*(2), 276–282. doi:10.1016/j.jclepro.2008.06.004

Morais-Storz, M., & Nguyen, N. (2017). The role of unlearning in metamorphosis andstrategic resilience. *The Learning Organization, 24*(2), 93–106. doi:10.1108/TLO-12-2016-0091

Mumford, M. D., Michelle, E., Higgs, T. C., & McIntosh, T. (2017). Cognitive skills andleadership performance: The nine critical skills. *The Leadership Quarterly*, *28*(1), 24–39. doi:10.1016/j.leaqua.2016.10.012

Osterloh, M., & Frey, B. S. (2000). Motivation, knowledge transfer, and organizational forms. *Organization Science*, *11*(5), 538–550. doi:10.1287/orsc.11.5.538.15204

Patra, R. (2008). Vaastu Shastra: Towards sustainable development. *Sustainable Development Journal*, *17*(4), 244–256. doi:10.1002d.388

Patton, M. (1997). *Utilization-focused Evaluation*. Sage.

Patton, M. (1998). Discovering Process Use. *Evaluation, 4*(2), 225-233.

Pfeffer, J. (2010). Building sustainable organizations: The human factor. *The Academy of Management Perspectives*, *24*(1), 34–45.

Phillips, L. (2007). Go green to gain the edge over rivals. *People Management*. Available at: www2.cipd.co.uk/pm/peoplemanagement/b/weblog/archive/2013/01/29/gogreentogaintheedgeoverrivals-2007-08.aspx

Pietrzak, M., & Paliszkiewicz, J. (2013). *Framework of Strategic Learning: The PDCA Cycle*. Warsaw University of Life Sciences.

Postmes, T. (2003). A social identity approach to communication in organizations. *Social identity at work: Developing theory for organizational practice*, *81*, 191-203.

Rahimian, H., Zamaneh, M. P., Ahmadpour, M., & Piri, M. (2014). A study of the relationship between empowerment and organizational learning among employees of gas transmission company. *J. Life Sci. Biomed*, *4*(6), 550–556.

Renwick, D., Redman, T., & Maguire, S. (2013). Green human resource management: A review, process model, and research agenda. *International Journal of Management Reviews*, *15*(1), 1–14. doi:10.1111/j.1468-2370.2011.00328.x

Rimanoczy, I., & Pearson, T. (2010). Role of HR in the new world of sustainability. *Industrial and Commercial Training*, *42*(1), 11–17. doi:10.1108/00197851011013661

Roberts, K. H., & O'Reilly, C. A. (1974). Failures in upward communication in organizations: Three possible culprits. *Academy of Management Journal*, *17*(2), 205–215.

Saadat, V., & Saadat, Z. (2016). Organizational learning as a key role of organizational success. *Procedia: Social and Behavioral Sciences*, *230*(12), 219–225. doi:10.1016/j.sbspro.2016.09.028

Schein, E. (1996). Kurt Lewin's Change Theory in the field and in the classroom: Notes toward a model of managed learning. *Systems Practice*, *9*(1), 27–47. doi:10.1007/BF02173417

Schmiedinger, B., Valentin, K., & Stephan, E. (2005). Competence based business development-organizational competencies as basis for successful companies. *Journal of Universal Knowledge Management*, *1*, 13–20.

Sedighi, M. (2016). Application of word co-occurrence analysis method in mapping of the scientific fields (case study: The field of the *field* of Informetrics). *Computer Science. Library Review*. Advance online publication. doi:10.1108/LR-07-2015-0075

Sharp, C. (2001). *Evaluation of Organizational learning intervention and Communities of Practice.* Paper presented in Australasian Evaluation Society Conference, Canberra, Australia.

Siebenhüner, B., & Arnold, M. (2007). Organizational learning to manage sustainable development. *Business Strategy and the Environment*, *16*(5), 339–353. doi:10.1002/bse.579

Simao, L. B. (2016). External relationships in the organizational innovation. *RAI Revista de Administração e Inovação*, *13*(3), 156–165. doi:10.1016/j.rai.2016.06.002

Sonnichsen, R. (2000). *High Impact Internal Evaluation. A Practitioner's Guide to Evaluating and Consulting Inside Organizations*. Sage. doi:10.4135/9781483328485

Tauber, E. M. (1981). Brand franchise extension: New product benefits from existing brand names. *Business Horizons*, *24*(2), 36–41. doi:10.1016/0007-6813(81)90144-0

Teixeira, A. A., Jabbour, C. J. C., & de Sousa Jabbour, A. B. L. (2012). Relationship between green management and environmental training in companies located in Brazil: A theoretical framework and case studies. *International Journal of Production Economics*, *140*(1), 318–329. doi:10.1016/j.ijpe.2012.01.009

Thakker, D. R. (2011). Culture and cognitive theory: Toward a reformulation. *Cult. Cog. Psychopathol*, *3*, 53–71.

Thomas, K. W., & Velthouse, B. A. (1990). Cognitive elements of empowerment: An "interpretive" model of intrinsic task motivation. *Academy of Management Review*, *15*(4), 666–681.

Tomasello, M. (2010). *Culture and Cognitive Development*. Institute of Evolutionary Anthropology.

Tran, Q., & Tian, Y. (2013). Organizational structure: Influencing factors and impact on afirm. *Am. J. Ind. Bus. Manag*, *3*(02), 229–236. doi:10.4236/ajibm.2013.32028

Tucker, M. L., Meyer, G. D., & Westerman, J. W. (1996). Organizational communication: Development of internal strategic competitive advantage. *The Journal of Business Communication*, *33*(1), 51-69.

Van de Ven, A. H., Angle, H. L., & Poole, M. S. (Eds.). (2000). *Research on the Management of Innovation: The Minnesota Studies*. Oxford University Press.

Vansina, L. (1988). The general manager and organizational leadership. In M. Lambrechts (Ed.), *Corporate revival: Managing into the nineties*. University Press.

Volberda, H. W., Van Den Bosch, F. A., & Heij, C. V. (2013). Management innovation: Management as fertile ground for innovation. *European Management Review*, *10*(1), 1–15. doi:10.1111/emre.12007

Wiig, K. (2002). Knowledge management in Public Administration. *Journal of Knowledge Management*, *6*(3), 224-239.

Wong, P. S. (2012). *Drucker's Knowledge-Worker Productivity Theory: A Practitioner's Approach to Integrating Organisational Work Processes with Drucker's Six Major Factors Determining Knowledge-Worker Productivity*. Southern Cross University.

Xiaomi, A., & Wang, W. (2010). Knowledge management technologies and applications: aliterature review. IEEE.

Zehir, C., Üzmez, A., & Yıldız, H. (2016). The effect of SHRM practices oninnovation performance: The mediating role of global capabilities. *Procedia: Social and Behavioral Sciences*, *235*, 797–806. doi:10.1016/j.sbspro.2016.11.088

Zoogah, D. B. (2011). The dynamics of green HRM behaviors: a cognitive social information processing approach. *Zeitschrift Für Personalforschung/German Journal of Research in Human Resource Management*, *25*(2), 117-139.

KEY TERMS AND DEFINITIONS

Innovation: Is to use knowledge to build a new one.

Knowledge Transfer: Knowledge transfer (TC) is the set of activities aimed at the dissemination of knowledge, experience, and skills in order to facilitate the use, application and exploitation of knowledge and R&D capabilities of the university outside the scope academic by other institutions.

Learning Organizations: Is one that facilitates learning for all its members, sharing information globally and undergoing continuous transformation in itself. The learning company changes the culture of the company, whatever its activity or structure.

Organizational Culture: It is the set of beliefs, habits, values, attitudes, and traditions of the members of a company.

Strategy: It is the direction or orientation that is given to the internal resources of an organization depending on the demands of its environment and surroundings to develop a competitive advantage that allows it to survive, lead, etc.

Sustainable Organizational Development: Sustainable organizational development focuses on value creation, environmental management, environmentally friendly production systems and the formation of human capital, social responsibility is linked to transparency, dialogue with stakeholders and care for the environment and the social inclusion.

Chapter 8
Renewable Energies and Urban Environment in Spain

María Jesús García García
University of Valencia, Spain

ABSTRACT

Sustainable development is a type of development that advocates first of all the harmonization between economic development and environmental protection, adding social progress; it would therefore be a development in which high and stable growth in the production of goods and services is compatible with widespread social progress, environmental protection, and prudent and efficient use of natural resources. Among the different sectoral areas transferred by the idea of sustainable development is undoubtedly the field of urban planning and housing. The activity generated in cities has an important environmental impact, so it is necessary to orient urban structures, homes, and buildings under premises that are as respectful as possible with the environment, also taking advantage of its economic potential and its effect on the social fabric that inhabits it. It is about promoting integrated actions in the urban environment that are in tune with the objectives.

INTRODUCTION

The idea of sustainable development has to relate to other concepts and ideas within the framework of which it finds its justification and its content. We cannot talk about sustainable development without first placing it in a broader context from which it owes. In this sense, a reference to the principle of sustainable development, energy efficiency and the idea of urban renovation is necessary. These are generic concepts

DOI: 10.4018/978-1-7998-7793-6.ch008

Copyright © 2022, IGI Global. Copying or distributing in print or electronic forms without written permission of IGI Global is prohibited.

within the framework of which energy renovation is framed and which also lend its justification and reason for being.

The first term to which it is necessary to allude to explain the idea of energy renovation has to do with the concept of sustainable development, which for some time now has been used in our domestic legislation and whose legal implementation has been carried out mainly through Law 2/2011, of 4 March, on Sustainable Economy.

Sustainable development is a concept that combines three interrelated elements and has traditionally been treated differently in Spanish legislation. Perhaps that is why it can be said that in our legal system the concept is relatively new in that it interrelates different objectives that converge in the different sectoral areas, emphasizing the interdependence between them rather than in their singular treatment (Chu, Steven, and Arun Majumdar 2012). These three elements or pillars that converge in the concept of sustainable development are: social, economic and environmental. "Sustainable development is a type of development that advocates first of all the harmonization between economic development and environmental protection, adding social progress; it would therefore be development in which high and stable growth in the production of goods and services is compatible with widespread social progress, environmental protection and prudent and efficient use of natural resources."; it is therefore a delicate building supported by three main pillars: social, economic and environmental in which none of them prevails over the others ".

Accordingly, sustainability has an integrated character, preceded as it is by the objectives of economic recovery, environmental sustainability and social cohesion. It is a general principle with transversal or horizontal projection, capable of crossing different and varied sectoral areas, as many as are relevant to achieve its integrating objectives (Curry, Nathan, and Pragasen Pillay, 2012).

Among the different sectoral areas transferred by the idea of sustainable development is undoubtedly the field of urban planning and housing. The activity generated in cities has an important environmental impact, so it is necessary to orient urban structures, homes and buildings under premises that are as respectful as possible with the environment, also taking advantage of its economic potential and its effect on the social fabric that inhabits it. It is about promoting integrated actions in the urban environment that are in tune with the objectives also integrating sustainable development.

Since sustainable development is an integrative concept, its influence on the urban and housing sector could not fail to have these same connotations, insofar as sustainable urbanism is nothing but a projection of sustained development in a specific area. Urban planning must respond to the requirements of sustainable development, minimizing its commitment to growth and betting on the regeneration of the existing city in order to achieve a sustainable and inclusive urban model, environmentally, socially and economically that improves the quality of life of citizens in urban spaces. In short, we are talking about the integrated objectives of sustainability applied to urban planning, in which the duty of conservation plays a fundamental role.

Spanish Constitution is devoid of explicit references to sustainable development, since it is a relatively new concept in our domestic law. However, the relationship between this principle and certain constitutional rights is evident, since the idea of sustainable urbanism advocates the preservation of urban spaces and buildings in which the constitutional right to decent housing and an adequate environment can be realized. From the perspective of the principle of sustainability, urban planning must be oriented towards renovation in order to comply with article 45 of the Constitution, since renovation does not consume land and makes it possible to exploit and use, rather to reuse, the existing heritage. In this sense, the implications between sustainable development and protection and the right to an adequate environment that guarantees the quality of life are fully established. Sustainable urban development would comply with article 45 of the Constitution in its two aspects: as a requirement imposed on the public authorities to ensure their protection and as the right of citizens to enjoy an adequate environment in order to ensure a certain quality of life. The observation that the urban environment is also the environment, or in other words, that the environment is also integrated by the urban environment, is clearly deduced from this and other recently adopted laws in our legal system. Thus, article 1 of Royal Legislative Decree 7/2015, of 30 October, approving the revised text of the Land Law, when defining its object, shows that the actions that are carried out try to ensure citizens an adequate quality of life, and the effectiveness of their right to enjoy a decent and adequate housing. Article 5 of the Act also establishes the rights of the citizen to whose satisfaction the act is subject, including the right to enjoy a decent, adequate and accessible home that is free of noise or other polluting emissions, as well as the right to enjoy an environment and a suitable landscape (Droege, Peter, ed., 2008)).

On the other hand, Law 7/85 of 2 April, regulating the bases of local regime, in its most recent amendment, also highlighted this point when it speaks in its article 25 of the competence of the municipalities in matters relating to the urban environment.

The connections with the constitutional right to housing are also clear in the extent maintaining the housing in proper condition for use, ensuring the maintenance of the existing population in a way that promotes the social and economic texture of this urban area.

In short, this is indicative that the actions of renovation, renewal and regeneration referred to from the point of view of sustainable development has its legal basis in articles 45 and 46 of the Constitution, without denying the implications that such a treatment of environmental protection will have on the economic and social aspects, such as the revival of economic activity, among others.

And precisely with this integrative purpose, the Law on renovation, renovation and urban regeneration is enacted, which combines the treatment of urban development actions in the urban environment and actions on housing and the architectural park from the point of view of the umbrella of sustainability. The point of view from which this Law rushing to the processing of such sectoral domains was certainly novel, as if, until then, we were accustomed to witness the treatment sector of the subjects on the basis of its consideration of the substantive, that is, as a sectoral domains where the material determined the content of the Law, in the case of the mentioned norm, the unifying element of the different precepts contained in it is not the substantive scope or material one, but the principle under which this treatment acted as an element of cohesion of the different precepts. We refer to the principle of sustainability, which justified that we found regulated under the umbrella of the same law sectoral areas as varied as urban legislation, precepts on urban renovation, urban leasing legislation or horizontal property. Nothing new if we take into account Law 2/2011 of 4 March, Sustainable Economy. The Real Decreto Legislativo 7/2015, de 30 October, approving the revised text of the Land Law and Urban Renovation serves now to a more specific, as it regulates subjects with a greater connection to each other that are all grouped under the generic concept of "urban", or more accurately, "urban environment". The content of this Law seems to consider the regulation of urban planning, as it affects consolidated urban land, susceptible to renovation, regeneration or renovation actions or new urbanization actions. But the truth is that the Law seems to be aimed at regulating urban development actions based on the principle of sustainable development.

BACKGROUND

Obviously, within this perspective of environmental sustainability present in the idea of sustainable urbanism one of the most relevant aspects from the point of view of its impact on the environment is that it has to do with the use and exploitation of energy and the use of certain forms of energy that maximize their consumption causing the minimum environmental impact. And focused as sustainable urbanism is on the idea of maintenance and conservation of the already made city and the existing buildings, this objective is to accommodate the buildings and the existing real estate park to these new energy demands. That is why we talk about energy renovation, meaning a set of actions in the urban environment and in existing buildings and homes that try to adapt the pre-existing elements (housing, but not only this, but also endowments, services and equipment) to the principles of efficiency and energy saving in accordance with the legal framework provided by Law 38/1999, of 5 November, on Building Planning and Royal Decree 314/2006, of 17 March, Technical Building Code.

Directive 2012/27 / EU states that buildings represent 40% of energy consumption in the European Union, so it becomes clear the need to influence the building sector and improve its energy performance (Lund, Peter, 2012).

These objectives, we find in article 3 of Royal Legislative Decree 7/2015, of 30 October, consolidated text of the Law of Soil and Urban Renovation, which speaks of minimizing polluting emissions and greenhouse gases, water and energy consumption and waste production. Also in paragraph i) of the same article these objectives are highlighted, when the Law refers to the need to prioritize renewable energies over the use of fossil energy sources and combat energy poverty with measures in favor of efficiency and energy saving. And finally, subparagraph (h) refers to the need to promote the protection of the atmosphere and the use of clean materials, products and technologies that reduce pollutant emissions and greenhouse gases from the construction sector, as well as reused and recycled materials that contribute to improving resource efficiency.

Energy efficiency is therefore one of the goals to be achieved in the urban environment aimed at achieving the objectives of environmental sustainability that underlie the generic concept of sustainable urban development. Thus, when article 3 of Royal Legislative Decree 7/2015, of 30 October, refers to the purposes to which public policies will tend in the urban environment, it bets on a concept of sustainability from the economic, social, environmental point of view that promotes the rational use of natural resources and energy efficiency. The Law seems to understand that energy efficiency is capable of promoting sustainable environmental conditions by itself and contributing to economic sustainability by generating jobs and employment, which is why its treatment is singled out as an emerging sector with great potential, not only environmental, but also economic.

To this end, energy efficiency must also be accompanied by a policy of diversifying the sources used in energy production, which opens the door to the use, promotion and use of renewable energies. The much discussed energy efficiency cannot consist only of measures aimed at saving and containing demand, but also requires the regulation and management of supply that promotes the introduction of renewable energy sources, which is in turn clean energy given its low level of emissions into the atmosphere (Purohit, Ishan, Pallav Purohit, and Sashaank Shekhar,2013).

In accordance with the above, energy renovation, based on the principle of energy efficiency, would be aimed at:

- Prioritize renewable energies.
- Promote energy savings.

- Reduce pollutant emissions and waste production.

ENERGY EFFICIENCY IN THE CONTEXT OF EUROPEAN UNION REGULATIONS.

It should not be forgotten that European legislation sets specific targets for energy efficiency and emission reductions. In this sense it is necessary to make reference to the Directive 2010/31/EU of the European Parliament and of the Council of 19 may 2010 on the energy performance of buildings (object transposition part in the Royal Decree 235/2013 of April 5) and Directive 2012/27/EU of the European Parliament and of the Council of 25 October 2012 on energy efficiency, which aims to update the community legal order in the context of the general objective of the Europe 2020 Strategy, this implies the objectives of a 20% reduction in greenhouse gas emissions, an increase in the contribution of renewable energies by 20% and a 20% improvement in energy efficiency. The Directive also sets more ambitious targets for 2050 aimed at reducing the level of CO2 emissions by 80-90% compared with 1990 levels. The measures identified by the said Directive concern key areas and sectors for achieving energy efficiency targets, such as building renovation. In this context, the Directive requires not only a significant percentage of central Government buildings to be renovated annually in order to improve their energy efficiency, but also that Member States also establish a strategy to mobilize investment in the renovation of residential buildings in order to improve the energy efficiency of the entire housing stock. The formulas to achieve these objectives are through the control of demand, promoting actions aimed at ensuring savings measures, but also through actions of management and regulation of supply, which includes its diversification, prioritizing the use of renewable energies for energy production over the use of fossil energies.

In this context, the Renewable Energy Plan (PER) 2011-2020 has been approved by resolution of the Council of Ministers of November 11, 2011, setting objectives that are in line with Directive 2009/28/EC of the European Parliament and of the Council of 23 April 2009 on the promotion of the use of energy from renewable sources, and in response to the mandates of the Royal Decree 661/2007, which regulates the activity of electricity production under the special regime and the Law 2/2011 of 4 march, Sustainable Economy. The PER has the objective of achieving, as indicated by the Community Directive, that in the year 2020 at least 20% of the gross final consumption of energy in Spain comes from the use of renewable sources.

Law 8/2013 of 26 June on urban renovation, regeneration and renewal served these purposes by partially transposing Directive 2012/27/EU, on energy efficiency, so that the principle of energy rationality is one of the pillars of the standard. The aforementioned standard established among its objectives those of minimizing the consumption of energy in homes constituting habitual residence and prioritizing renewable energies with measures in favor of efficiency and energy saving. This applies not only to new buildings and installations, but also to existing ones that are the subject of intervention, as we shall see below. As we already know, the content of this rule has become part of the Royal Legislative Decree 7/2015, of 30 October, consolidated text of the Land and Urban Renovation Law. In this context, the urban duty of conservation is considered as an instrument at the service of energy renovation, to the extent that its content is divided into a series of strata that support actions aimed at adapting the existing real estate to the demands of energy efficiency that the rules that regulate the building are demanding.

Some Clarifications on the Concept of Renovation in the Current Regulations

Law 8/2013, of 26 June, established a new nomenclature when formulating actions in the urban environment that differs from the nomenclature used in previous legislation, where the concept of urban renovation was comprehensive of a set of isolated or integrated actions that could even involve the demolition of buildings and urban elements incompatible with actions of sanitation or urban regeneration. Thus, two types of renovation were distinguished: isolated renovation and integrated renovation. The first considered the real estate in its own individuality, without implications or connections with the surrounding elements. On the contrary, integrated renovation considered the affected heritage as part of a larger space in which it was integrated. Integrated renovation consisted of the renovation of urban spaces, which without dispensing with the renovation of individual elements, transcended their effects to project on other elements of the environment, considering it as a whole.

According to the new nomenclature introduced by Law 8/2013, of 26 June, renovation is the term that refers to singular actions in buildings, while those that affect the urban fabric is called regeneration or urban renewal, according to entail the demolition of any of the elements of urban pre-existing. Based on this distinction, article 2 of Royal Legislative Decree 7/2015 of 30 October, establishes possible actions to be carried out in the urban environment, differentiating between renovation of buildings and regeneration and urban renewal. According to the cited article, performances on the urban environment are those that are intended to perform renovation work, when there are situations of failure or degradation of the basic requirements of functionality, safety and habitability of buildings, and the regeneration and urban renewal will be those that affect, both buildings as urban structure, including works of new building in the replacement of buildings previously demolished.

With reference to the basic requirements of functionality, safety, and livability, the idea of renovation of building is spacious and accommodates works and activities related to energy efficiency of the buildings, which introduces the concept of energy renovation, which involves performing actions on the real estate existing in a situation of failure or degradation in relation to the basic requirements of the building to adapt it to the demands of efficiency and energy savings.

Efficiency and Energy Renovation Within the Framework of the Urban Duty of Conservation and the Use of Renewable Energies

Both the renovation of buildings and the integrated actions of urban renewal and regeneration are actions of urban significance, so on these actions must be projected the urban instruments and techniques that affect the situation of buildings and homes. So what sets the Real Decreto legislativo 7/2015, de 30 October, which in its article 2.1 states that all of these actions will apply to the statutory scheme basic duties and charges to which they are entitled in accordance with the performance of urban transformation or building that behave, in accordance with the provisions of article 7.

One of these duties is the duty of urban conservation, whose content is integrated by reference to Law 38/1999, of 5 November, on Building Planning, which in turn refers to Royal Decree 314/2006, of 17 March, which approves the Technical Building Code. The requirements of energy efficiency are incorporated into the duty of conservation through the regulation made in the Technical Building Code in its reference to living conditions, since they are applicable not only to new buildings, but also to existing ones when they are the subject of some intervention. Among these requirements are those related to the use of renewable energies.

But in addition, the Building Planning Law configures the duty of conservation in open terms by reference to the regulations that may be applicable in each case. The Act points to the Technical Building Code may be supplemented with the requirements of other regulations issued by the competent Authorities and is regularly updated according to the evolution of technology and the demand of the society, which emphasizes the open-ended character of the setting of the duty of conservation.

The Content of the Duty of Conservation: The Three Levels

The duty of urban conservation is regulated in article 15 of the consolidated text of the Law on Land and Urban Renovation, article that reformulates the wording of the duty of conservation established by Royal Legislative Decree 2/2008, of 20 June in the terms in which it was drafted after Law 8/2013, of 26 June of urban renovation, regeneration and renewal.

The aforementioned precept establishes different duties and burdens that configure the urban content of the property right, among which is, as we say, the duty of conservation. According to the statement of reasons of the Law on urban renovation, regeneration and renovation, of which the aforementioned article 15 brings cause, the duty of conservation is articulated in three levels depending on the content that results from it for the owner.

At its basic level, the duty of conservation entails the duty to allocate the buildings to uses compatible with territorial and urban planning and the need to guarantee the safety, health, accessibility and decoration of the real estate. In this way, the duty of conservation includes the three basic requirements of the building, referring to functionality, safety and habitability. So far the duty of conservation coincides with its traditional formulation. However, the Law of renovation, regeneration and renewing urban added to article 9 of the Consolidated Text of the Land Act, Royal legislative Decree 2/2008 20 June, a new section under which the duty of conservation also includes the realization of the work and the necessary works in order to satisfy, in general, the basic requirements of the building set forth in article 3.1 of the Law 38/1999, de 5 de November on building renovation. This explicit reference to the previous Law is no longer included in article 15 of Royal Legislative Decree 7/2015 of 30 October, but is implicit in said article insofar as the aforementioned precept establishes the duty to preserve buildings in the legal conditions of safety, health, universal accessibility, ornament and the others required by the laws to serve as support for the uses for which they are intended and are compatible with territorial and urban planning, from which an implicit reference to the Building Planning Law and the Technical Building Code is inferred.

A second level, in which the duty of conservation includes the works and works necessary to adapt and progressively update the buildings, in particular the facilities, to the legal norms that are explicitly required at all times. Law 8/2013, of June 26, started from the consideration of an open conservation duty, whose content was not delimited by article 9 of Royal Legislative Decree 2/2008, of June 20, consolidated text of the Land Law, but subject to variations or extensions from other subsequent laws. Thus, Article 9, paragraph 2, established the competent administration could impose at any time the realization of works to comply with the legal duty of conservation in accordance with the provisions of the applicable state and autonomous community legislation. This provision, due to its obviousness, is also absent in article 15 of Royal Legislative Decree 7/2015 of 30 October, which does not prevent considering the duty of conservation as a duty of an evolutionary nature and subject to the variation of the technical requirements that are foreseen in the different applicable regulations. In this way, the duty of conservation will also include the necessary works to adapt the buildings and update their facilities to the legal norms that are required at any time, as the regulations of the sector introduce modifications in order to maintain the conditions of use of the buildings. The duty of conservation is thus in open terms, by reference to the regulations that may be applicable in each case.

Finally, a third level includes additional works, carried out for reasons of general interest, in respect of which the Law distinguishes two cases:

- Those carried out for tourist or cultural reasons that constitute an assumption already included in the previous legislation, although under the consideration of improvement and forced renovation works.
- Those carried out for the improvement of the quality and sustainability of the urban environment, assumption that now introduces Law of renovation, regeneration and urban renewal in the modification that makes of the Consolidated Text of the Law of the Land.

Energy Efficiency, Duty of Conservation and Renovation

The Initial Content of the Duty of Conservation: Energy Saving and the Use of Renewable Energy

The preservation of buildings in conditions of safety, health and public decoration constitutes a legal duty imposed on the owner on the basis of the social function of the property in accordance with article 33 of the Constitution. To the duty of the owner to maintain the buildings in the aforementioned conditions, it is now also added that of universal accessibility, and in addition, it is implicitly integrated into the duty of conservation the realization of the works and the works necessary to satisfy in general, the basic requirements of the building established in article 3.1 of Law 38/1999, of 5 November, of Building Planning.

Article 3.1 of the Building Planning Act establishes three basic requirements for buildings aimed at ensuring the safety of people, the welfare of society and the protection of the environment. These are requirements relating to functionality, safety and habitability. And precisely in this last section the measures relating to energy saving and thermal insulation are established so that a rational use of the energy necessary for the proper use of the building is achieved. The efficiency and energy savings are part of the duty of conservation to the extent that this duty entails keeping the buildings in terms of serving to its use, which leads to the need to satisfy the basic requirements of the building, within which are located relative to energy savings, thermal insulation and rational use of energy, and that is conducive to the simultaneous execution of conservation work directed to maintain the buildings in terms of safety, sanitation and beautification works and aimed to enhance the energy efficiency of the same. Therefore, we wanted to take advantage of the realization of conservation works in the most traditional sense of the term to promote the realization of actions related to energy renovation, which are now integrated into the duty of conservation.

The requirements of energy efficiency have been incorporated into the duty of conservation through the regulation carried out by the Technical Building Code, Royal Decree 314/2006, of 17 March. and are applicable not only to newly constructed buildings, but also to those undergoing repair or renovation. The aforementioned Royal Decree is issued in implementation of Law 38/1999 of 5 November, on Building Planning, whose second provision empowers the Government to approve a regulatory norm that establishes the basic requirements that buildings must meet in relation to the requirements relating to safety and habitability listed in paragraphs b) and c) of article 3.1 of the Building Planning Law.

Among the requirements relating to habitability, Article 15 of the said Code regulates the basic requirements of energy saving. These basic requirements apply and must be met both by new buildings and by existing buildings that are subject to modification, reform, extension or renovation and are basic, so that their requirements are mandatory throughout the national territory. The eleventh Final Provision of the Law 8/2013, of June 26, has widened the scope of application of Technical Building Code to modify its article 1 that the basic requirements must be met, as established by the regulations set in the project, the construction, the maintenance, preservation and use of buildings and facilities, as well as in interventions in existing buildings. Likewise, the aforementioned rule has modified Article 2 of the Technical Code, so that its basic requirements will be required not only to new buildings but also to all those existing buildings that are the subject of intervention.

The basic requirements for energy savings set out in the Technical Code are five, namely: limitation of energy demand, performance of thermal installations, energy efficiency of lighting installations, minimum solar contribution of domestic hot water and minimum photovoltaic contribution of electrical energy. The purpose for which it is intended with this energy saving enters into what was formerly defined as energy efficiency, as it is to get a rational and sustainable use of the energy used in the building or home, and also enhance the consumption comes from renewable energy sources.

For this reason, among these basic requirements we must highlight those that refer to solar contributions, and above all, those that refer to the production of domestic hot water, which " have the character of minimums, and can be extended as a result of additional provisions issued by the competent administrations"

And this raises the question of which Administration is competent to regulate this question. Some autonomous communities have adopted their own regulations on renewable energy. This is the case of the Autonomous Community of Andalusia and its Law 2/2007, on the promotion of renewable energies and energy savings and efficiency in Andalusia. The aforementioned Law is developed by Decree 169/2011, of 31 May, whose Chapter II " Basic requirements for the use of renewable energies, savings and energy efficiency", complies with the provisions of the Technical Building Code by adapting these requirements to the energy needs and climatic characteristics of Andalusia. However, the Andalusian regulations do not establish additional requirements of contribution to the minimum contributions of thermal energy required in the state regulations through the Technical Building Code.

By applying the principle of linking negative in the interpretation of the principle of legality, the judgments of the Supreme Court of 22 may 2015 (RJ 2015/2620 and 2015/2016) consider such other competent authorities are, in addition to the autonomous communities, local authorities and that the criteria listed in the Technical Building Code constitute minimum values that the local authorities have to respect, but that can increase.

According to the jurisprudential criterion established after the judgments of the Supreme Court of May 22, 2015 (RJ 2015/2620 and 2015/2016), this reference to the competent administrations, also includes local entities that can thus adapt the state provisions to their own peculiarities and the needs that conform their specific local interests.

Thus, some municipalities, in the context of sustainable urbanism, have adopted ordinances aimed at promoting energy savings and promoting the use of renewable energies such as solar energy based on the competences that local legislation recognizes them in matters such as urbanism and the environment. Such is the case of the municipal Ordinance on the collection and use of solar thermal energy in buildings, of the City of Burgos . Also the Ordinance of the same name of the City of Pamplona as well as the municipal Ordinance of eco-energy efficiency and use of renewable energy in buildings and their facilities, of the City of Zaragoza among others.

The approval of the Technical Building Code, Royal Decree 314/2006, of 17 March, has come to provide the legal authorization whose absence motivated the challenge of the local ordinances on energy use to understand that the Law of Bases of Local Regime did not provide sufficient legal authorization for municipalities to approve ordinances in this sense. The judgments of the Supreme Court of May 22, 2015 (RJ 2015/2620 and 2015/2016) indicate that from the approval of the Technical Building Code the normative coverage of the ordinances relating to the use of solar energy is accommodated in the aforementioned legal text, which has the character of basic legislation

Energy Efficiency as an Additional Content to the Duty of Conservation: The Improvement of Eenergy Efficiency and the Use of Renewable Energy Sources

The duty of conservation will also include the adaptation of the building to the use of renewable energies indirectly when renovation actions are carried out that update the duty of conservation.

The duty to initial conservation is added to the duty to perform additional work for tourism or cultural, or to improve the quality and sustainability of the urban environment, since the distinction between the duty of conservation based on the fulfillment of the social function of property and the duty of conservation based on reasons of general interest has been a constant in the planning legislation that the different laws have been addressed in a different way, but always on the basis of their recognition . The content of these additional works is defined by reference to the Technical Building Code, and may consist of partial or complete adaptation to all or some of the basic requirements established therein. In accordance with this article, the Administration may order the owners to carry out works aimed at improving the quality or sustainability of the urban environment, including works to improve energy efficiency and including those aimed at encouraging the installation of renewable energy sources in buildings.

The attention to renewable energies is framed by both in the works additional ordering the administration to improve the quality and sustainability of the urban environment imposed by reasons of general interest, and is justified in the community legislation and in particular Directive 2012/27/EU, noting that buildings represent 40% of energy consumption in the European Union compels the member states to develop strategies that include the realization of investment in the renovation of residential and commercial buildings . The Directive requires not only the annual renovation of a percentage of public buildings of the central State Administration (thus underlining the exemplary nature of public actions), but also the mobilization of investments aimed at the renovation of buildings for commercial or residential uses with the aim of improving their energy efficiency.

The characteristic of these actions is that the law empowers the public administrations to impose them for reasons of general interest beyond the limits that govern the duty of conservation, in which case, the Law indicates, the ordering Administration will be responsible for the works that exceed this limit to obtain improvements of general interest. We are talking about additional conservation, which involves carrying out additional works and financing measures to improve the energy efficiency of buildings. This implies the renovation of buildings through internal strategies of mobilization of real estate investments where the legal limit for the owner is that of the duty of conservation and the administration has to contribute to the financing of the rest, since they are improvements of general interest. In this case, the duty of conservation goes beyond the particular objective of adaptation of the building in question to identify with a broader objective of general interest focused on the consolidated urban environment where it is located and on the fulfillment of energy efficiency objectives that are deduced from European policies, for which the mobilization of investments aimed at the renovation of residential and commercial buildings is foreseen. The additional content of the duty of conservation must be framed within integral actions and policies of economic, social, environmental regeneration and cohesion of the city as a whole, perspective from which the duty of conservation transcends the individual level to achieve improvements of general interest. And from this perspective, not only building renovation actions are imposed, but also actions that include actions to implement renewable energy not only at the building level, but also through urban development actions in urban fabrics that involve urban regeneration or renewal.

However, article 15 of Royal Legislative Decree 7/2015, of 30 October, does not seem to require any additional requirements for the imposition of such additional conservation works. Since it is an additional duty that transcends the individual plan of the property to which it refers to have an impact on the urban environment, it could be considered consubstantial to the general interest alleged that the property was included in some type of legal instrument of renovation. Well established, for example in the article 111 of the Law of Sustainable Economy, repealed by the Law 8/2013, of June 26, in which it is stated that the competent authority could command, in the form, terms and deadlines set by the applicable law, the execution of works of improvement up to the maximum amount of statutory duty, in addition to for reasons cultural and tourist collected by the applicable legislation, in the course of the construction or the building that were to become affected by a program, plan or any other legal instrument for the renovation of housing approved and in force, and refers to works designed to guarantee the rights recognized by law to individuals, or to be imposed by legal norms supervened for reasons of safety, adequacy of facilities and minimum services, reduction of polluting emissions and emissions of any kind and those necessary to reduce water and energy consumption.

Energy Renovation and the Limit of the Duty of Conservation

The Quantitative Limits of the Duty of Conservation

Law 8/2013, of 26 June, introduced some modifications regarding the limits of the duty of conservation and that were fixed by reference to quantitative criteria. These amendments are now incorporated in article 15 of the consolidated text of the Law on Land and Urban Renovation. In this sense, the limit of the duty of conservation is established at half of the current construction value of a new plant property, equivalent to the original in relation to the constructive characteristics and the useful surface, carried out in the necessary conditions so that its occupation is authorized, or where appropriate, is in a position to be legally destined for its own use. By establishing this limit, the state legislation configures the content of the duty of conservation by reference to an objective criterion, thus preventing the autonomous legislation from establishing its own limits with respect to that duty. Law 8/2013, of June 26, introduced an important novelty in the duty of urban conservation and in the regulation that until now had been carried out of it by the Consolidated Text of the Land Law of 2008, by quantifying the limit of the duty of conservation, which were doing the autonomous regulations in some cases. This modification should be subject to positive evaluation, as in this way, the limit is set up with basic character and binding on the legislator autonomous, so that in accordance with the provisions of article 149.1.1 of the Constitution, defines the legal positions of the owners in relation to their duty of conservation, and imposes rules equal and uniform to all property owners of buildings.

FUTURE RESEARCH DIRECTIONS

The duty of conservation is thus established by reference to an objective limit and individualized by reference to each particular property, which is fixed by reference to a percentage applied on the current value of a new construction of similar functional and structural characteristics and equal useful surface. In short, the Law addresses the value or cost of replacement by taking into account not the value of the damaged building (current value of the building), but a new building whose valuation will serve to contrast the cost of repair works and set the limit of the duty of conservation. The valuation system deals exclusively with the replacement value, that is, the hypothetical value of a construction of the same structure and building typology that allows a use of similar characteristics to that of the construction with respect to which the declaration of ruin is intended. The evaluation of these repairs will have to be carried out based on current techniques and materials that allow to maintain or return to the construction the original functionality. The legislation takes into account the economic profitability of the extension of the useful life of the constructions through the conservation or renovation of the same ones. In this sense, the limit of the profitability of the conservation of the buildings is fixed in the disbursement by the owner of expenses that remain below half of the cost of a new construction with characteristics similar to the existing one.

But the limit of the duty of conservation is solved based on economic criteria where the cost of replacement works is only one of the terms of the equation. The second is related to the content and extent of the works to be made to understand fulfilled the aforementioned duty. In this sense, it should be noted that the conservation works are not merely the works necessary to maintain the property in conditions of safety, health and ornament. We have already indicated in the previous section that the duty of conservation also involves the realization of works necessary to ensure universal accessibility, as well as those others that are necessary to meet the basic requirements of the building established in article 3.1 of Law 38/1999 of 5 November on Building Planning, where interventions related to energy efficiency are registered, including both those that are deduced from the current regulations and those others that are explicitly required to adapt and update their facilities to the standards. In short, this means going to the Technical Building Code, in which the basic requirements of the building are specified, which in terms of energy saving also implies the need to include among these works, those relating to the installation of collection systems, transformation, storage and use of solar energy. In addition, the values derived from this basic requirement will be considered minimum, without prejudice to stricter values that may be established by the competent administrations and that contribute to sustainability according to the characteristics of their location and territorial scope.

It could be thought that since one of the terms of the equation expands with respect to what was the traditional duty of conservation, the logical consequence will be that the limit of the duty of conservation will be easily exceeded by including more demanding actions in the maintenance of buildings that also meet criteria of saving and energy efficiency. However, this possible consequence is remedied if we take into account that the second comparative term focuses on the replacement cost of the property. This clarification is important, since urban planning legislation has not always made use of this criterion to delimit the cessation of the duty of conservation. Thus, for example, article 247 of the Consolidated Text of the Land Act of 1992, when referring to the declaration of ruin (which implied the cessation of the duty of conservation), referred to the present value of the building or plants concerned, excluding the value of the land. This meant taking as a reference the value of the building at the time when it was planned to carry out the repair works on it, which implied valuing the building applying criteria indicative of the depreciation suffered by the property depending on age and state of conservation among others. Obviously, this means that the building is quantified at a lower magnitude easily exceeded by the cost of maintenance and renovation works carried out in it. As we said, the option to include the replacement cost of a similar building of new plant allows to increase quantitatively the second term of the equation.

CONCLUSION

The Law 8/2013 introduced within the duty of urban conservation the realization of additional works that had as a common denominator the fact that its imposition is based on reasons of general interest, and that the Consolidated Text of the Land Law of 2008 considered as works of improvement. Royal Legislative Decree 7/2015, of 30 October, refers to them in article 15.1 c). These additional works include those carried out for tourism and cultural reasons, to which are added those focused on improving the quality and sustainability of the urban environment, introduced by Law 2/2011 of 4 March on Sustainable Economy and where those actions related to energy efficiency are framed. The content of these additional works for the improvement of quality and sustainability is determined as we have indicated, by reference to the Technical Building Code

Well, these works additional to the duty of conservation which now also include those related to the improvement of the quality and sustainability of the urban environment, has a particular legal regime, since the law establishes the possibility for the administration to force the landlord to the realization of the same, even once exceeded the limit of the duty of conservation. In this case, the administration that orders or imposes the realization of such works must pay the economic excess that entails the realization of the same. And this economic excess is fixed by reference to the limit of the duty of conservation referred to above. In this way, the limit of the duty of conservation (half of the current value of construction of a building of a new plant, equivalent to the original in connection with the construction features and the useful surface, taken with the conditions necessary for their occupation is approvable or, in your case is in a position to be legally intended for use by own) it is also the limit of the works to be executed at the expense of the owners when the Administration of the order to the improvement of the quality or sustainability of the urban environment. The Law assumes the criterion of the joint participation of the owner and the Administration in the maintenance of the property, as deduced from article 9.1 of the Land Law after the wording given to it by the Law on urban renovation, regeneration and renovation.

Royal Legislative Decree 7/2015, of 30 October, considers the importance of these renovation actions in the urban environment and the need to adapt them to the limits of the legal duty of conservation through the economic viability report, regulated in article 22. This memory, it is expected not only in cases in which they carry out activities of regeneration and renewal, but also in the case of actions of renovation of building, isolated or included in a scope of work (by areas or spaces), establishing as one of its aims to ensure the least possible impact on the personal wealth of the individuals, adjusted in any case the limits of the duty to bequeath conservation.

REFERENCES

Ahuja & Tatsutani. (2021). *Sustainable energy for developing countries*. https://journals.openedition.org/sapiens/823

Chu, S., & Majumdar, A. (2012). Opportunities and challenges for a sustainable energy future. *Nature*, *488*(August), 294–303. doi:10.1038/nature11475 PMID:22895334

Curry, N., & Pillay, P. (2012). Biogas prediction and design of a food waste to energy system for the urban environment. *Renewable Energy*, *41*(May), 200–209. doi:10.1016/j.renene.2011.10.019

Droege, P. (Ed.). (2008). *Urban Energy Transition: From Fossil Fuels to Renewable Power*. Elsevier Ltd. doi:10.1016/B978-0-08-045341-5.00029-3

Lund, P. (2012). Large-scale urban renewable electricity schemes—Integration and interfacing aspects. *Energy Conversion and Management*, *63*(November), 162–172. doi:10.1016/j.enconman.2012.01.037

Purohit, I., Purohit, P., & Shekhar, S. (2013). Evaluating the potential of concentrating solar power generation in North-western India. *Energy Policy*, *62*, 157–175. doi:10.1016/j.enpol.2013.06.069

UN-HABITAT, Local Governments for Sustainability, and the United Nations Environment Programme. (2009). *Sustainable Urban Energy Planning: A handbook for cities and towns in developing countries*. UNEP.

ADDITIONAL READING

Alfasi, N., & Portugali, J.UN-HABITAT, Local Governments for Sustainability, and the United Nations Environment Programme. (2007). Planning rules for a self-planned city. *Planning Theory*, *6*(2), 164–182. doi:10.1177/1473095207077587

Birkmann, J., Garschagen, M., Kraas, F., & Quang, N.UN-HABITAT, Local Governments for Sustainability, and the United Nations Environment Programme. (2010). Adaptive urban governance: New challenges for the second generation of urban adaptation strategies to climate change. *Sustainability Science*, *5*(2), 185–206. doi:10.100711625-010-0111-3

Chance, T.UN-HABITAT, Local Governments for Sustainability, and the United Nations Environment Programme. (2009). Towards sustainable residential communities; the Beddington zero energy development (BedZED) and beyond. *Environment and Urbanization, 21*(2), 527–544. doi:10.1177/0956247809339007

Donatiello, J. E.UN-HABITAT, Local Governments for Sustainability, and the United Nations Environment Programme. (2015). The world's population: An encyclopedia of critical issues, crises, and ever-growing countries. *Reference and User Services Quarterly, 54*(4), 85. doi:10.5860/rusq.54n4.85b

Freytag, T., Gössling, S., & Mössner, S.UN-HABITAT, Local Governments for Sustainability, and the United Nations Environment Programme. (2019). Living the green city: Freiburg's Solarsiedlung between narratives and practices of sustainable urban development. *Local Environment, 19*(6), 644–659. doi:10.1080/13549839.2013.868872

Kennedy, C., Cuddihy, J., & Engel-Yan, J.UN-HABITAT, Local Governments for Sustainability, and the United Nations Environment Programme. (2020). The changing metabolism of cities. *Journal of Industrial Ecology, 11*(2), 43–59. doi:10.1162/jie.2007.1107

Moroni, S.UN-HABITAT, Local Governments for Sustainability, and the United Nations Environment Programme. (2015). Complexity and the inherent limits of explanation and prediction: Urban codes for self-organising systems. *Planning Theory, 14*(3), 248–267. doi:10.1177/1473095214521104

Roggema, R.UN-HABITAT, Local Governments for Sustainability, and the United Nations Environment Programme. (2014). Towards enhanced resilience in city design: A proposition. *Land (Basel), 3*(2), 460–481. doi:10.3390/land3020460

Roggema, R.UN-HABITAT, Local Governments for Sustainability, and the United Nations Environment Programme. (2015). Three urbanisms in one city: Accommodating the paces of change. *Journal of Environmental Protection, 6*(09), 946–956. doi:10.4236/jep.2015.69084

Searns, R. M.UN-HABITAT, Local Governments for Sustainability, and the United Nations Environment Programme. (1995). The evolution of greenways as an adaptive urban landscape form. *Landscape and Urban Planning, 33*(1), 65–80. doi:10.1016/0169-2046(94)02014-7

Sharifi, A.UN-HABITAT, Local Governments for Sustainability, and the United Nations Environment Programme. (2016). From garden city to eco-urbanism: The quest for sustainable neighborhood development. *Sustainable Cities and Society, 20*, 1–16. doi:10.1016/j.scs.2015.09.002

UN-HABITAT, Local Governments for Sustainability, and the United Nations Environment Programme, Adhya, A., Plowright, P., & Stevens, J. (2011) Defining sustainable urbanism: towards a responsive urban design. In: Proceedings of the conference on sustainability and the built environment. King Saud University, Saudi Arabia. 3–6 January 2010

Allen, C., & Clouth, S.UN-HABITAT, Local Governments for Sustainability, and the United Nations Environment Programme (2012). *A guidebook to the green economy*. UNDESA.

Batty, M.UN-HABITAT, Local Governments for Sustainability, and the United Nations Environment Programme (2013). *A new science of cities*. MIT Press. doi:10.7551/mitpress/9399.001.0001

Cohen, J., & Stewart, I.UN-HABITAT, Local Governments for Sustainability, and the United Nations Environment Programme (1994). *The collapse of chaos: discovering simplicity in a complex world*. Penguin Group Ltd.

De Roo, G., Hillier, J., & van Wezemael, J.UN-HABITAT, Local Governments for Sustainability, and the United Nations Environment Programme (Eds.). (2020). *Complexity and planning: systems, assemblages and simulations*. Ashgate Publishing. doi:10.4337/9781786439185

UN-HABITAT, Local Governments for Sustainability, and the United Nations Environment Programme, & Drury, F. (2019) Enchanting photos of the abandoned village taken over by hippies living in fairytale houses in the Spanish mountains. MailOnline, 1 July 2015. http://www.dailymail.co.uk/news/article-3139295/Enchanting-photos-abandoned-village-taken-Spanish-hippies-living-fairytale-houses-mountains.html. Accessed 5 Sept 2016

Girardet, H.UN-HABITAT, Local Governments for Sustainability, and the United Nations Environment Programme (1996). *The GAIA atlas of cities: new directions for sustainable urban living*. Gaia Books Limited.

UN-HABITAT, Local Governments for Sustainability, and the United Nations Environment Programme, & Habitat, I. I. I. (2016) Revised zero draft of the new urban agenda. https://www.habitat3.org/zerodraft. Accessed 23 June 2016

Kennedy, C., Pincetl, S., & Bunje, P.UN-HABITAT, Local Governments for Sustainability, and the United Nations Environment Programme (2010). The study of urban metabolism and its applications to urban planning and design. *Environmental Pollution*, *159*(8–9), 1965–1973. PMID:21084139

Kreimer, A., Arnold, M., & Carlin, A.UN-HABITAT, Local Governments for Sustainability, and the United Nations Environment Programme (Eds.). (2003). *Building safer cities: the future of disaster risk*. The International Bank for Reconstruction and Development/The World Bank.

UN-HABITAT, Local Governments for Sustainability, and the United Nations Environment Programme, & Roggema, R. (2012a) Swarm planning: the development of a spatial planning methodology to deal with climate adaptation, PhD thesis. Delft University of Technology, Delft

Roggema, R.UN-HABITAT, Local Governments for Sustainability, and the United Nations Environment Programme (2012c). Shifting paradigms. In R. Roggema (Ed.), *The design charrette: ways to envision sustainable futures*. Springer.

Shafiea, F. A., Dasimah, O., & Karuppannanb, S.UN-HABITAT, Local Governments for Sustainability, and the United Nations Environment Programme (2013) Urban metabolism: a research methodology in urban planning and environmental assessment. In: *Proceedings of the 1st international conference on research methodology for built environment and engineering Kuala Lumpur*, Malaysia, 17–18 December 2013

Webster, C., & Lai, L. W. C.UN-HABITAT, Local Governments for Sustainability, and the United Nations Environment Programme (2003). *Property rights, planning and markets*. Edward Elgar.

UN-HABITAT, Local Governments for Sustainability, and the United Nations Environment ProgrammeWorld Commission on Environment and Development. (1987). *Our common future*. Oxford University Press.

Wolman, A.UN-HABITAT, Local Governments for Sustainability, and the United Nations Environment Programme. (1965). The metabolism of cities. *Scientific American, 213*(3), 179–190. doi:10.1038cientificamerican0965-178 PMID:14338520

KEY TERMS AND DEFINITIONS

Duty of Conservation: Urban conservation is concerned with those parts of the built environment that are of architectural or historic significance. This includes buildings (individually or in groups), localities (streets, blocks, environments, or precincts), special gardens or landscapes, and other structures.

Renewable Energy: Renewable energies (or renewables) are ways to generate energy from (theoretically) unlimited natural resources. These resources are either available with no time limit or replenish more quickly than the rate at which they are consumed. Renewable energies are generally spoken of as opposed to fossil fuel energies.

Sustainability: Sustainability is usually defined as the processes and actions through which humankind avoids the depletion of natural resources, in order to keep an ecological balance that doesn't allow the quality of life of modern societies to decrease.

Urban Renewal: Rehabilitation of impoverished urban neighborhoods by large-scale renovation or reconstruction of housing and public works.

Chapter 9
The Effect of Product Modularity on Supplier Integration:
A Multi-Objective Approach

Metehan Feridun Sorkun
Izmir University of Economics, Turkey

Özgür Özpeynirci
Izmir University of Economics, Turkey

ABSTRACT

This chapter seeks to identify the set of conditions under which the mirroring hypothesis holds, proposing that modular product architecture leads to organizational modularity (i.e., supplier disintegration). The contradictory results on the mirroring hypothesis in the extant literature call for a more holistic analysis of the issue. To this end, this chapter develops a multi-objective mathematical model, allowing for the simultaneous examination of potentially influential factors, including those claimed to be neglected by the mirroring hypothesis. The findings reveal that modular product architecture does not necessarily lead to supplier disintegration, but that its effect is contingent on a firm's priorities.

DOI: 10.4018/978-1-7998-7793-6.ch009

Copyright © 2022, IGI Global. Copying or distributing in print or electronic forms without written permission of IGI Global is prohibited.

INTRODUCTION

Operational factors indicating an ideal supplier integration level has been under investigation for a while. Modularity theory (Baldwin, 2008) explains this issue at task level; accordingly, firms should integrate with their suppliers to the extent that their tasks are interdependent with the tasks of their suppliers. Since technical interdependencies across components largely determine the degree of task interdependencies with suppliers, product design architecture is an important determinant of the ideal supplier integration level.

Product modularity (PM) is the design property of products showing the decoupling degree between the product components (Schilling, 2000). Modular product (high PM level) contains few spatial, structural, and material interdependencies across components (Sosa et al., 2003) because each component is responsible for one separate product function (Ulrich, 1995). The standardized interfaces embed the remaining interdependencies across components in the codified form (Sanchez & Mahoney, 1996). In contrast, integral product (low PM level) is composed of tightly coupled components. Components are jointly responsible for implementing each product function. Thus, the design change in one component entails the significant changes in other components (Ulrich, 1995).

Organizational modularity (OM) indicates the decoupling degree between organizational units to perform organizational functions. Colfer and Baldwin (2016) define three analysis levels for OM, which are within-firm, across-firm, and open and community-based projects. The second one, across-firm, refers to the organizational decoupling degree (OM level) when product is developed by at least two firms. Therefore, the decoupling degree between a firm and its suppliers is analyzed at across-firm level. Likewise, many previous studies (Furlan et al., 2014; Sorkun, 2016; Zirpoli & Becker, 2011) used the supplier integration level to measure the OM level at across-firm level. Accordingly, while supplier integration indicates low OM, supplier disintegration indicates high OM.

"The mirroring hypothesis" establishes a positive link between PM and OM (Colfer & Baldwin, 2016). The reduced technical interdependencies in modular products decrease the coordinative needs across firms, enabling them to form modular organizations (high OM) (Cabigiosu & Camuffo, 2012; Sanchez & Mahoney 1996). Fine et al. (2005) show the positive effect of PM on OM in supply chains, stating that modular products tend to be produced by modular supply chains.

However, the mirroring hypothesis has received criticisms because of its overlooking other relevant operational factors. According to the papers assuming critical position, the relationship between PM and OM is not straightforward as hypothesized. Modular product may encourage supplier disintegration for reducing coordination costs but other operational factors such as logistics (Jacobs et al., 2007;

Howard & Squire, 2007), innovation (Lau & Yam, 2005; Sabel & Zeitlin, 2004), and production efficiency (Frigant & Talbot, 2005; Tiwana, 2008) require supplier integration (low OM).

The contradictory findings on the PM-OM relationship require an analysis at a larger scope. The research based on single empirical setting may not be sufficient to make conclusive judgments. This study corroborates the viewpoint that specifying under which conditions the mirroring hypothesis holds is more important than debating whether it holds or not (Burton & Galvin, 2018). This acknowledgement calls for comprehensive analytical studies that show the big picture by considering many contingent factors together (Sorkun & Furlan, 2017). Hence, this chapter aims to uncover the set of conditions that modular product leads to supplier disintegration.

LITERATURE REVIEW

Implications of the Product Modularity Level

The need to synchronize and monitor supplier activities may incur huge coordination costs. To reduce these costs, modular product, by means of its features, encourages firms to form modular supply relationships. First, each module's performing separate product function diminishes the effort needed to synchronize supplier activities. Second, the standardized interfaces with which all interdependencies between modules are specified ex-ante ensure the compatibility and quality of the modules outsourced, decreasing the need for monitoring the supplier activities closely (Hoetker et al., 2007).

Modular product decreases inventory-carrying costs in various ways. Initially, high component carry-over rate in modular product provides the product variety level targeted with the lower number of stock-keeping units compared to integral products (Ulrich, 1995). This eliminates the safety stock held for the reduced stock-keeping-units, diminishing inventory costs. Besides, high PM makes product customization easier by mixing and matching modules (Blecker & Abdelkafi, 2006; Lau, 2011), enabling firms to source modules after they receive customer order. This postponement decreases the inventory kept at the costly final product level (Liao et al., 2013). Last, visible rules in modular products increase the number of sourcing alternatives, reducing supply disruption risk (Kleindorfer & Saad, 2005), therefore, firms can keep lower level of safety stock.

Modular product, permitting parallel work, enables firms to introduce novelties on existing modules quickly (Antonio et al., 2009; Pil & Cohen, 2006). While standardized interfaces provide the ease of modules' re-combinability, these modules' highly decoupled nature leverages the specialization that leads to the extended knowledge search (Ethiraj, 2007). The integration and reconfiguration of these knowledge domains facilitate product innovations (Hao et al., 2017; Henderson & Clark, 1990; Sun & Zhong, 2020).

The effect of PM level on production efficiency is ambiguous due to two contrasting viewpoints. One view asserts that integral products are superior to modular products since they exploit better the synergy between components, giving higher product performance (Schilling, 2000). Additionally, the non-existence of standardized rules in integral products provide cost advantage by minimizing the size and mass of components (Ulrich, 1995).

The other view contrarily argues modular product yields higher production efficiency. First, few interdependencies between modules lead firms to specialize in just their own modules, which provides local product performance advantage (Ulrich, 1995). Second, one-to-one mapping between modules and functions makes easier to identify the supplier responsible for quality problems. This positively affects output control (Tiwana, 2008), which decreases quality problems due to opportunism risk (Hoetker, 2006). Also, the standardization in modular product lowers the unit sourcing cost of components through the economies of scale effect (Jacobs et al., 2007). Their ease of disassembly also increases the components' reusability (Sehnem et al., 2019; Yang et al., 2020).

Why May Modular Product not be Sufficient for Supplier Disintegration?

The criticisms to the mirroring hypothesis do not reject modular products' function to decrease coordination costs. Instead, they highlight various factors that enforce supplier integration (low OM) despite modular product. The first criticism maintains that supplier integration is necessary condition to decrease inventory-carrying costs (Sorkun, 2016) even if firms have modular product. Modular products allow firms to postpone the assembly by sourcing modules from their suppliers after customers make an order (Liao et al., 2013). Nevertheless, if firms do not share the demand information continuously with their suppliers (low OM), they cannot supply the modules on time in case of a significant change in demand (Lee et al., 2000). Thereby, insufficient coordination with suppliers compels firms to hold excessive inventory for providing high customer service level. Lau et al. (2010) support this argument based on their case study, illustrating that the case firm having modular product needs to be in on-going communication with their suppliers to ensure on-time deliveries.

Another criticism asserts that supplier integration (low OM) is essential during both the pre-design and post-design phases of developing innovative modular product (Lau & Yam, 2005). Firms aiming to develop modular products attempt to codify the interdependencies across modules ex-ante to define the standardized interfaces.

However, for innovative modular products, it is more difficult to codify these interdependencies in advance due to the novelty of links (i.e. uncertainties) between modules (Nair & Blomquist, 2021). As a result, innovative modular products entail the collaborative work with suppliers (low OM) (Sun & Zhong, 2020), considering that unexpected interdependencies across modules are more likely to arise in time (Ernst, 2005). Thus, the firm has to act as system integrator in supply chain (Brusoni et al., 2001; Cammarano et al., 2017) to manage the resulting unforeseen interdependencies (Ernst, 2005). Such integration mechanism is also essential for the product research and development activities because the specialization in distinct modules may bring cognitive limits, inhibiting innovations. Instead, supplier integration (low OM) allows firms to harmonize their product architectural knowledge with the component-specific knowledge held by suppliers, resulting in successful innovations (Dias Sant´Ana et al., 2020; Garcia-Piqueres et al., 2020).

The objective of having efficient production also requires supplier integration (low OM) for the advancement of both product performance and cost control (Tarafdar & Qrunfleh, 2017). Since functional interdependency and performance interdependency are different issues, one-to-one mapping between modules and functions in modular products may not be a remedy for performance integration unless there is a good joint work with suppliers. Zirpoli and Becker (2011) remark the need for performance integration in modular products because some global product performance indicators may be the joint outputs of different product functions, such as the speed for automobiles and the display resolution for computers. Respectively, Ethiraj (2007) stresses the performance bottleneck risk for modular products. Some components might have shown much better performance if the suppliers of other components adopted and upgraded their components at the same level.

The decoupling from suppliers (high OM) also affects the cost performance negatively despite modular product. It causes the erosion of the firm's component-specific knowledge over time (Persson et al., 2016; Takeishi, 2002), making the control of suppliers' cost-effectiveness more difficult. This might increase the opportunism risk, implying that suppliers may not do their best to reduce their costs.

Figure 1 illustrates the research model based on the arguments abovementioned. Dashed lines show the direct effects of the PM level on the OM level (i.e. supplier disintegration level), inventory-carrying costs, and innovative outcomes. Straight lines indicate how the positive effect of PM on OM indirectly affects coordination costs, inventory-carrying costs, innovative outcomes, and production efficiency. According to this research model, high PM level has direct positive effects on inventory-carrying costs, and innovative outcomes. However, the direct effect of PM level on production efficiency is not indicated in Figure 1 due to the controversial findings on this relationship. In addition, Figure 1 illustrates that indirect effects occur when high PM leads to high OM. Accordingly, the resulting disintegration (high OM) decreases coordination costs; however, it negatively affects inventory-carrying costs, innovative outcomes, and production efficiency.

Figure 1. Research model

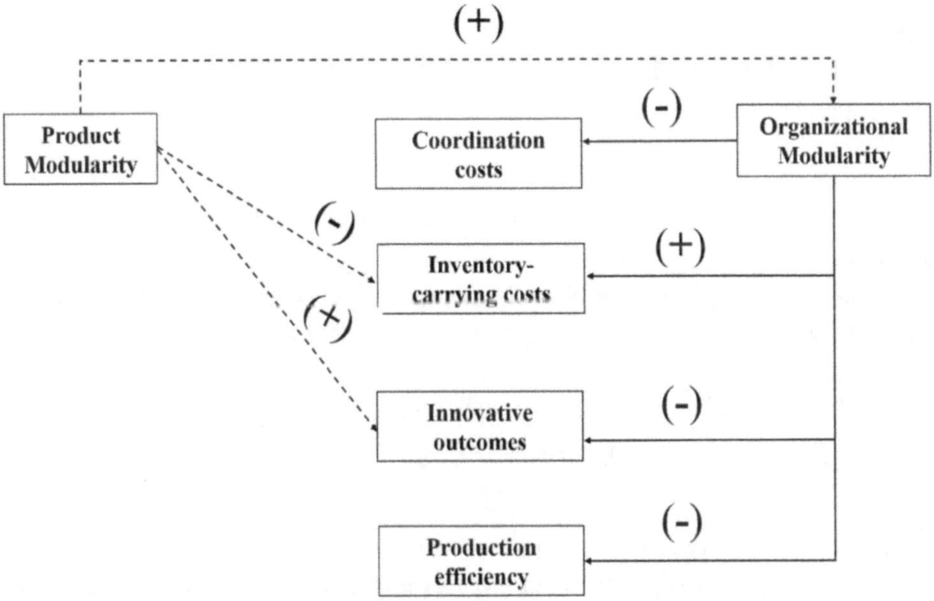

METHODOLOGY AND MODEL

As shown in Figure 1, the understanding of the PM-OM relationship requires the consideration of many objectives, therefore, this research develops a multi-objective mixed integer mathematical model. Since the priorities of these objectives may change in each context, a multi-objective exact algorithm is applied to find Pareto-optimal solutions (nondominated solutions), revealing the conditions for which the mirroring hypothesis holds. Considering the significant effect of suppliers' capabilities on firms' objectives, the supplier selection problem is incorporated into the model to expand the search space for finding a higher number of nondominated solutions. This setting allows exploring the extents of the possible relationship between PM and OM as the weights of model's objectives change.

The model finds the optimal OM level for the given PM level and the objective weight vector. While the model operationalizes the OM level (supplier disintegration) as the inverse measure of the information sharing level with suppliers for the product development and logistics processes (Furlan et al., 2014), it operationalizes the

PM level as the inverse measure of the technical interdependency degrees between modules (Schilling, 2000).

The necessary notation and model is presented as follows.

Notation

Sets

m, h: modules of product; $m, h = 1,\ldots, M$

s: suppliers; $s = 1,\ldots, S$

Parameters

PM: product modularity level, $PM \in [PM_{min,}\ PM_{max}]$ where PM_{min} and PM_{max} are the minimum and maximum values in a range that PM may take respectively.

$Ommax_m$: the maximum supplier disintegration level (maximum OM level) that does not cause any product failure (quality problem) for the module m

$$E_{ms} = \begin{cases} 1, & \text{if supplier } s \text{ is eligible to produce module } m, \\ 0, & \text{otherwise.} \end{cases}$$

$Inform_s$: the quality of the information shared with supplier s

$Homl_s$: The lowest supplier integration level (the highest OM level) where the inventory-carrying cost is at its minimum. Any decrease in the integration level (increase in OM level) deteriorates inventory-carrying cost.

Inv_s: the additional inventory-carrying cost if supplier s is selected

k_1: the direct effect of PM on inventory-carrying costs $k_1 \in [0,1]$ (see Figure 1)

Ic_s: the innovative outcome derived from the selected supplier $s \in S$

k_2: the direct effect of PM on innovative outcomes $k_2 \in [0,1]$ (see Figure 1)

Pe_s: the production efficiency of the selected supplier $s \in S$

$Homp_s$: The lowest supplier integration level (the highest OM level) where the production efficiency is at its maximum. Any decrease in the integration level (increase in OM level) deteriorates production efficiency.

ϵ: a small positive number

B: a large number

The instance specific ϵ and B values are provided in an experimental study.

Binary variables

$$X_{ms} = \begin{cases} 1, & \text{if module } m \text{ is assigned to supplier } s, \\ 0, & \text{otherwise.} \end{cases}$$

$$Y_s = \begin{cases} 1, & \text{if supplier } s \text{ is selected,} \\ 0, & \text{otherwise.} \end{cases}$$

Positive variables

R_s: the *OM* level (the inverse measure of information sharing level) with supplier s, $R_s \in (0,1)$

G_s: the *OM* level indicator used to compute the inventory-carrying costs of suppliers

$$G_s = \begin{cases} R_s, & \text{if } R_s \geq Homl_s, \\ Homl_s, & \text{otherwise.} \end{cases}$$

Q_s: the *OM* level indicator used to compute the production efficiency of suppliers

$$Q_s = \begin{cases} R_s, & \text{if } R_s \geq Homp_s, \\ Homp_s, & \text{otherwise.} \end{cases}$$

$$X_{ms} = \begin{cases} 1, & \text{if module } m \text{ is assigned to supplier } s, \\ 0, & \text{otherwise.} \end{cases}$$

$$Y_s = \begin{cases} 1, & \text{if supplier } s \text{ is selected,} \\ 0, & \text{otherwise.} \end{cases}$$

All three positive continuous variables – R_s, G_s, and Q_s – indicate the optimal *OM* level but in different scopes. While R_s illustrates the optimal *OM* level for the objective function vector, G_s and Q_s link the optimal *OM* level to the specific objective functions; G_s for inventory-carrying costs, and Q_s for production efficiency. This is because the decrease in the *OM* level has no marginal contribution to these objectives beyond some critical point ($Homl_s$ for inventory- carrying costs; $Homp_s$ for production efficiency). Therefore, R_s, G_s, and Q_s are of equal values above these critical points. However, the optimal levels indicated by G_s and Q_s fix respectively to $Homl_s$ and $Homp_s$ when R_s indicates the optimal *OM* level lower than these critical points.

The Mathematical Model

$$\text{Max } Z = (Z_A, -Z_B, Z_C, Z_D) \tag{1}$$

$$Z_A \leq R_S + (\varepsilon \times Inform_S) \quad s \in S \tag{2}$$

$$Z_B = \left[(1-k_1)\times\left(\frac{PM - PM_{min}}{PM_{max} - PM_{min}}\right)\right]\times\left[\sum_{s\in S}\left[Inv_s \times (G_s - Homl_s \times Y_s)\right] - \sum_{s\in S}\left[Inv_s \times (1 - Y_s)\right]\right] \tag{3}$$

$$Z_C = \left[(1+k_2)\times\left(\frac{PM - PM_{min}}{PM_{max} - PM_{min}}\right)\right]\times\sum_{s\in S} Ic_s \times (1 - R_s) \tag{4}$$

$$Z_D = \sum_{s\in S}\left[(Pe_s \times Y_s - Q_s + Homp_s\right] - \sum_{s\in S}(1 - Y_s)\times(Homp_s - 1) + \sum_{s\in S}\varepsilon \times Homp_s \times Y_s \tag{5}$$

The objective function vector (1) maximizes overall utility, regarding four objectives Z_A, Z_B, Z_C and Z_D.

Objective Z_A, i.e. the minimization of coordination costs, maximizes the minimum R_s among the suppliers selected $s \in S$ in equation (2). Z_A could have also been named "the maximization of *OM*" because high *OM* refers to modular supply relationship, leading to lower coordination costs. This is the reason why objective Z_A has a positive sign in the objective function vector in equation (1). Additionally, the multiplier value ϵ in the equation set (2) ensures that when the model is indifferent to select the supplier among the eligible ones with the same R*s* value, it breaks the tie considering the parameter I*nforms* indicating the quality of information shared with supplier.

Objective Z_B minimizes inventory-carrying costs. The second term of equation (3) aims to bring the selected supplier's G_s (*OM* level) down to the level ($Homl_s$) where the inventory-carrying cost is at the minimum possible level. The first term of equation (3) provides that higher PM value decreases the inventory-carrying costs by means of the features of modular product (see Figure 1).

Objective Z_C maximizes the innovative outcomes in equation (4) when R_s (*OM* levels) of the selected suppliers decrease. Integration with suppliers that allows leveraging these suppliers' design and development capabilities increases the number and significance of innovations made. Higher *PM* level has a positive impact on the objective Z_C similar to that on Z_B because modular product provides the ease of re-configurability across components, leading to a rapid set of innovations.

Objective Z_D maximizes the production efficiency in equation (5) as Q_s (*OM* level) comes close to the $Homp_s$ that is the level that further supplier integration does not improve the product's performance and cost. Besides, when more than one supplier provides the same production efficiency, the multiplier value ϵ imposes the model to select the supplier with which the production efficiency is maximized with lower coordination costs (i.e. $Homp_s$ indicates higher OM level).

The constraints of the model are as below:

$$\sum_{s \in S} Y_s = M \tag{6}$$

$$\sum_{s \in S} E_{ms} \times X_{ms} = 1 \quad m \in M \tag{7}$$

$$\sum_{m \in M} X_{ms} = Y_s \quad s \in S \tag{8}$$

The constraint (6) assures that the number of selected suppliers is equal to the number of modules forming a product. The constraint set (7) assigns one supplier $s \in S$ for each module $m \in M$ among the eligible suppliers. The constraint set (8) links the decision variables X_{ms} and Y_s, therefore, it warrants that a supplier $s \in S$ is an active supplier if the model selects it for a module $m \in M$. Besides, this constraint set (8) guarantees that a supplier $s \in S$ cannot provide more than one module $m \in M$.

$$\epsilon \leq R_s \leq 1 \quad s \in S \tag{9}$$

$$1 - Y_s \leq R_s \quad s \in S \tag{10}$$

$$R_s \leq PM + B \times (1 - Y_s) \quad s \in S \tag{11}$$

$$R_s \leq (1 - Ommax_m) + B \times (1 - X_{ms}) \quad s \in S, m \in M \tag{12}$$

The constraint sets (9) and (10) secure no relationship with non-selected supplier $s \in S$ by fixing their R_s values to 1. For the selected supplier $s \in S$, the constraint set (9) provides that the lower bound of R_s is not zero, but a small positive value ($0 < \varepsilon < 0.001$). The constraint sets (11) and (12) determine the upper bound of R_s for the selected suppliers in accordance with the technical requirements of the product. This upper bound guarantees that the *OM* level does not exceed the *PM* level, eliminating product failure risk due to the lack of coordination. The constraint set (12) relaxes this upper bound for non-selected suppliers with sufficiently large number B, therefore, the R_s values of the non-selected suppliers are equal to 1. Note that, the setting $B \geq 1$ is sufficient for the model.

AN EXPERIMENTAL STUDY

This numerical example assumes an Original Equipment Manufacturer (OEM) having a role similar to the one described in the "modular consortium" production system (Frigant & Lung, 2002). Hence, OEM does not produce any module by itself, but outsources them to suppliers and just coordinates these suppliers' tasks.

The product consists of four modules in this instance. *PM* formula aligns with the definition of Schilling (2000), according to which *PM* level increases as there are fewer technical interdependencies $\alpha_{m,h}$ between modules $m,h \in M$. To ensure that an extreme technical interdependency between any of two modules does not manipulate the PM level, the formula also regards the highest technical dependency of each module $m \in M$ to other modules, $maxi_m = \max_{h \in M} \{\alpha_{m,h}\}$. The formula is as below:

$$PM = 1 - \left[\frac{\sum_{h,m \in M} \alpha_{m,h}}{|M| \times (|M| - 1)} + \frac{\sum \max_h i\, \alpha_{mh}}{[M]} \right] / 2$$

where $\alpha_{mh} \sim$ Uniform (0.001, 0.5)

OEM needs to exchange information with their suppliers to manage the technical interdependencies between modules. Accordingly, the *OM* level inversely indicates the information sharing level between the OEM and its suppliers to provide the level of coordination required. As noted previously, the *OM* level with supplier cannot exceed the highest technical interdependency of the respective outsourced module because of the assumption that insufficient information sharing causes a product failure (quality problems).

It is necessary to keep the *PM* level sufficiently high in experiments because this research's aim is to investigate whether modular products lead to modular supply relationships. Besides, high *PM* level enables observing the full extent of downward deviation of the *OM* level from the *PM* level. Thus, the uniform distribution U (0.001, 0.5) assigned to the technical interdependencies across product modules provides sufficiently high *PM* level (ranges between 0.509 and 0.853).

In experiments, the algorithm of Özpeynirci and Köksalan (2010) is applied to find all extreme supported nondominated points. To capture the effect of *PM* on *OM*, the algorithm is implemented for different 12 *PM* levels. The comparison of the nondominated points across these 12 PM levels show the changes in the *OM* level as a consequences of the changes in the *PM* level.

The numerical example measures the values of objective functions with the capability scores of suppliers selected. For the capability scores, this example uses the dataset of Narasimhan et al. (2001) that lists the capability scores of 23 suppliers in 11 criteria. However, not all these 11 criteria are relevant to the four objectives of this research. Instead, their values are the functions of the different subsets of 11 criteria (e.g. the innovation outcome depends on the design and development capability). This makes many of the 23 suppliers dominated by other suppliers regarding this research's numerical example. Since the inclusion of dominated suppliers would not expand the search space to find more Pareto-optimal solutions, it is sufficient for this study to consider only nondominated suppliers with respect to the four objectives. Moreover, the numerical example keeps the number of nondominated suppliers included into analysis at reasonable level to reduce computational effort, which still provides many supplier alternatives for each module. Thus, this numerical example considers 8 of 23 suppliers in Narasimhan et al. (2001) marked with numbers 6, 10, 11, 12, 23, 29, 31, and 35. These suppliers are assigned to modules (in Table 1), ensuring that no supplier dominates any other supplier eligible to provide the same module. Note that although a supplier may be eligible to produce more than one module in this experimental setting, the model assigns at most one module to a supplier.

Table 1. Eligibility list of suppliers for each module

Supplier #	6	10	11	12	23	29	31	35
Module 1	-	✓	✓	✓	✓	✓	-	-
Module 2	✓	-	✓	✓	✓	-	-	-
Module 3	✓	-	-	-	-	✓	✓	-
Module 4	✓	-	-	-	-	✓	✓	✓

OEM selects one supplier for each module among the eligible subset of eight suppliers based on their capabilities (Table 2). The value of each objective is the function of the selected suppliers' capabilities in relevant criteria. For instance, a supplier's on-time delivery capability affects inventory-carrying costs. If a supplier is always punctual on delivery, OEM can keep lower inventory levels, reducing its inventory-carrying costs. Nevertheless, the same supplier's lack of capability in design and development may have negative effect on other objective, innovative outcomes. Taking into account the trade-offs among the four objectives as exemplified above,

OEM selects the suppliers whose capabilities maximize its composite objective function. While Table 2 lists the supplier selection criteria, Table 3 shows the capability scores of suppliers on each of these criteria.

Table 2. Description of the criteria for supplier selection

Criteria	Description
Man	Management capability
Otd	On-time delivery performance
Ddc	Design and development capability
Pmc	Process and manufacturing capability
Crc	Cost reduction capability
Qmp	Quality management practices indicator
Sa	Self-auditing indicator

Table 3. Capability scores of the suppliers

Supplier #	Man	Otd	Ddc	Pmc	Crc	Qmp	Sa
6	0.9607	0.9661	0.9661	0.952	1.1402	1.1272	1.0438
10	1.0808	1.0466	1.0466	0.9376	0.9422	0.9877	1.0438
11	0.9607	1.256	1.256	1.0385	1.0768	0.8051	0.8351
12	1.0208	1.0627	1.0627	1.1251	1.0096	1.1809	1.0438
23	1.0808	1.1593	1.1593	1.1251	1.2115	1.0662	1.0438
29	0.9007	1.1593	1.1593	1.1251	0.9422	1.0735	1.0438
31	1.0808	0.6762	0.6762	1.1251	1.1442	1.0735	1.0438
35	1.0172	0.8695	0.8695	1.0385	1.0768	1.0735	1.0438

Table 4 illustrates how the supplier capabilities listed in Table 2 are used to proxy the mathematical model's parameters. It also shows the quantification of each parameter based on the capability scores in Table 3.

The scalars k_1 and k_2 denote the direct positive effect of PM on inventory carrying costs and innovative outcomes respectively. An improvement of 25% is assumed in both of these objectives when the *PM* level increases from 0.5 to 1. For the lower increases, the contribution of the increased *PM* level decreases proportionally.

Similarly, modular product is assumed to increase the auto-control mechanism (Ac_s) of suppliers because one-to-one mapping between modules and product functions makes easy to identify the supplier responsible for the performance and quality problems. Thus, the OM level (supplier integration level) needed to maximize production efficiency ($Homp_s$) is higher with modular product (i.e. the level of information sharing needed to control suppliers is less). This experimental study assumes that $Homp_s$ improves by 25% as the PM level increases from 0.5 to 1. For lower increases, the contribution of the increased PM level decreases proportionally. In order to align the $Homp_s$ values with those of OM (R_s), i.e. to normalize them, each Ac_s is divided to the highest Ac_s in the supplier data set, and multiplied with the constant 0.2

Table 4. The definition and quantification of parameters based on supplier capabilities

***Inform$_s$*:**	The better-managed supplier (Man_s) increases the quality of the information shared with supplier s. $Inform_s = Man_s$
***Homl$_s$*:**	The better-managed supplier (Man_s) provides more efficient communication, enabling to attain the minimum feasible inventory-carrying cost with less information sharing (higher $Homl_s$). To align the $Homl_s$ values with those of OM (R_s), each $Homl_s$ is multiplied with the constant 0.2. $Homl_s = 0.2 \times Man_s$
***Inv$_s$*:**	On-time delivery capability of supplier (Otd_s) reduces the level of safety stock needed to hedge the stock-out risk, which lowers the inventory-carrying costs. $Inv_s = 1 / Otd_s$
***Ic$_s$*:**	The supplier having more design and development capability (Ddc_s) provides a more innovative outcome. $Ic_s = Ddc_s$
***Pe$_s$*:**	The supplier capabilities – process and manufacturing (Pmc_s), and cost reduction (Crc_s) – increase the production efficiency (product performance and cost). $Pe_s = (Pmc_s + Crc_s) / 2$
***Homp$_s$*:**	Quality management practices (Qmp_s), and self-audit (Sa_s) indicate that suppliers have auto-control mechanism. Therefore, the production efficiency can go up to the maximum feasible level (higher $Homp_s$) with less information sharing. $Homp_s = \left(0.2 \times \frac{Ac_s}{Ac_s^*}\right) \times \left((1+0.25) \times \left(\frac{PM-0.5}{1-0.5}\right)\right)$ where $Ac_s = (Qmp_s + Sa_s)/2 \quad Ac_s^* = \max_s Ac_s$

COMPUTATIONAL RESULTS

The number of extreme supported nondominated points identified is 621. Their corresponding PM and OM values are shown in Figure 2. The straight line, on the top of Figure 2, represents the hypothesized mirroring effect, i.e. the perfect positive correlation between PM and OM. The positions of nondominated points indicate a contrary evidence for the mirroring effect between PM and OM. The group of points moving in parallel to the line representing the mirroring effect in Figure 2 provides an evidence for the validity of the mirroring hypothesis. However, the other groups of points, lining up respectively at the middle of graph and just over the x-axis, provides a contrary evidence.

Figure 2. The corresponding PM and OM levels of the nondominated points

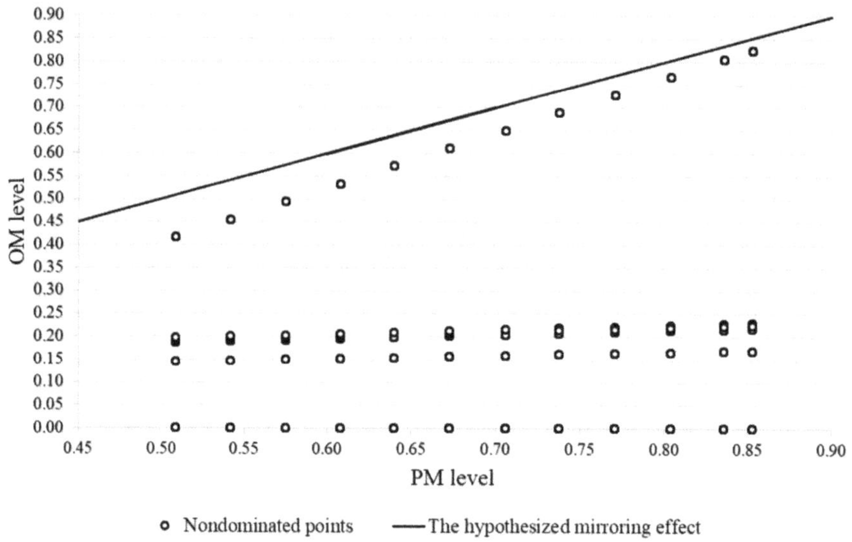

Figures 3, 4, 5, and 6 below graph the nondominated points shown in Figure 2; however, they additionally illustrate the weights of each objective corresponding to each nondominated solution by size. If the size of a point in one chart is large, its size must be relatively smaller in other three charts because the sum of weights in four charts must be equal to 100%. It is also noteworthy that some points encapsulate other points. These interwoven points indicate different nondominated solutions for the same OM level. In other words, although they indicate the same optimal OM level (supplier disintegration level), their weight vectors are different. Note that the nondominated points on the x-axis in Figure 2 do not appear in Figure 3 because the weight of coordination costs at these points is close to zero.

The results show the positive effect of PM on OM when the weight of coordination costs exceeds 41%. In these cases, the reduction of coordination costs is either primary objective or equally important with the inventory-carrying costs when their weights range between 45-47%. Another remarkable result is that as PM level increases, the nondominated points get closer to the mirroring effect line. This is because high PM makes improvement in inventory-carrying costs and innovative outcomes -, therefore, it decreases these objectives' deterioration caused by the lack of integration with suppliers.

Figure 3. The changes in the weight of Z_A

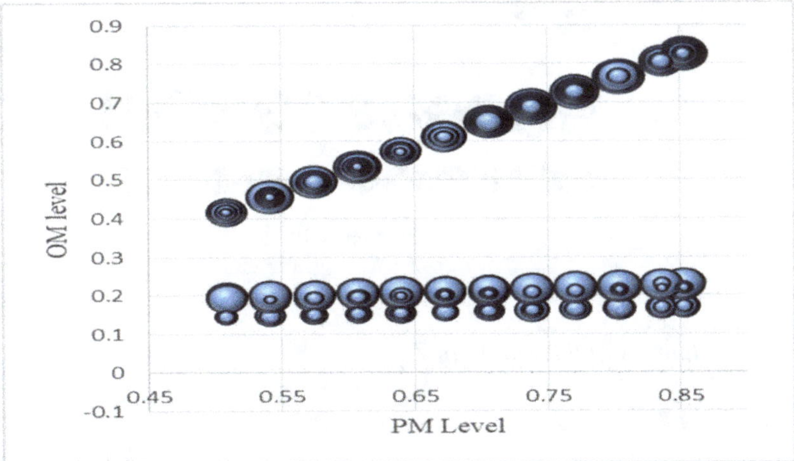

Figure 4. The changes in the weight of Z_B

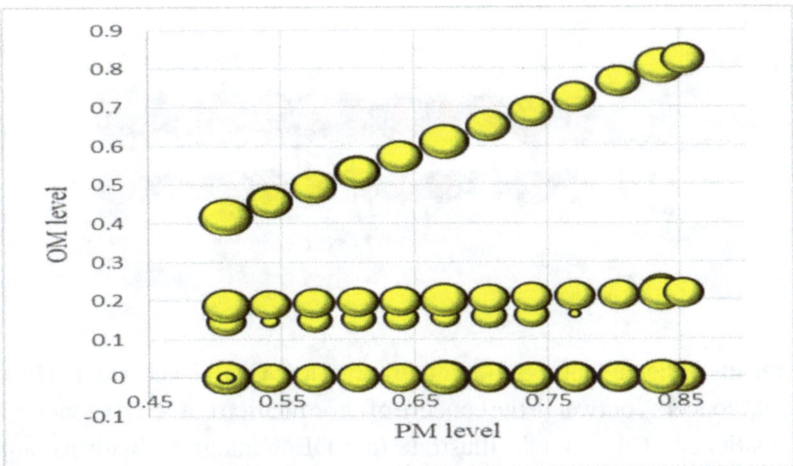

Figure 5. The changes in the weight of Z_C

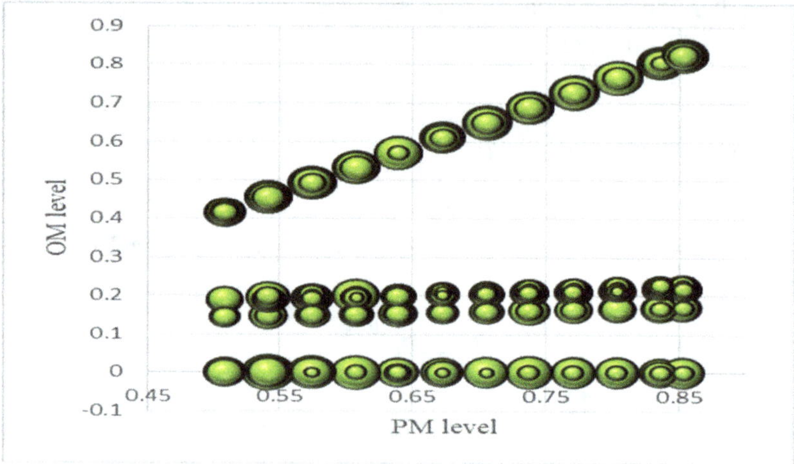

Figure 6. The changes in the weight of Z_D

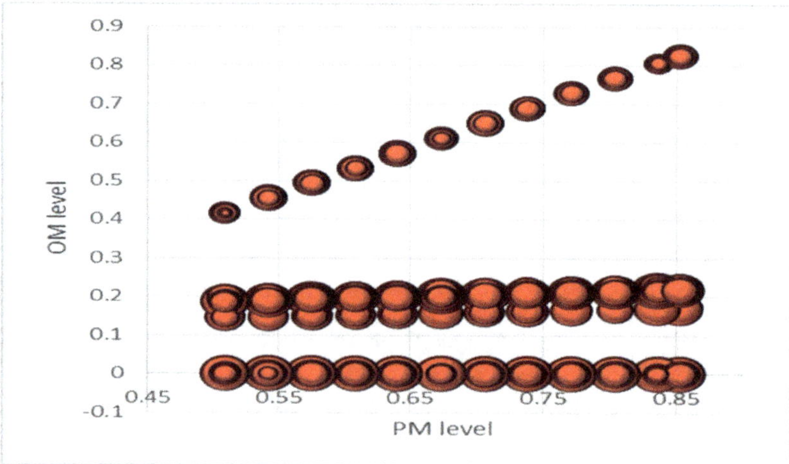

The results indicate that supplier integration (low OM) is necessary when other operational concerns outweigh the concern of coordination costs. The nondominated points positioned at the middle illustrate that OEM integrates with its suppliers where OM level is between 0.144 and 0.228. Note that these levels approximate the inventory-carrying costs to its minimum and the production efficiency to its maximum with respect to this research's experimental design. The higher PM level slightly increases these points' OM levels, since high PM relatively compensates the negative effect of high OM on inventory-carrying costs and innovative outcomes.

The nondominated points just over x-axis refer to full supplier integration, implying that collaborative work with suppliers is crucial to make innovation. Full supplier integration is the optimal relationship not only when innovation is the primary objective. Some of the points over x-axis show that full supplier integration is optimal when the sum of the weights of inventory-carrying costs and production efficiency exceed 80%, and the coordination cost is the out of concern (i.e. its weight is close to zero).

Sensitivity Analysis

Considering that the use of one dataset may make difficult to arrive decisive conclusions, sensitivity analysis is performed on various input parameters of the model. Accordingly, this analysis compares the results by changing the parameter values of Man_s, Otd_s, Ddc_s and Pe_s one by one (– 80%, – 60%, – 40%, – 20%, +20%, +40%, +60%, +80%, +100%) while keeping other parameters at their original value. The PM level in this analysis is fixed to 0.853 that is the highest PM level used in the experiments. This PM level enables a larger range of possibilities for the OM level since the OM level should be less than the PM level in the model. Besides, the objective weight vector in this analysis is specified as [1/2, 1/6, 1/6, 1/6] corresponding to four objective functions. This weight vector provides that the weight of coordination cost favoring high OM is equal to the sum of the weights of other three objectives favoring low OM.

Figure 7 shows the changes in the OM level as a result of the changes in the values of parameters (Man_s, Otd_s, Ddc_s and Pe_s). Whereas the changes in Pe_s do not have any effect on the OM level, the changes in other three parameters cause the OM level to shift considerably. The pattern of these shifts supports the previous findings. In other words, although the parameter values and the objective weights change, nondominated points may indicate different optimal OM levels for the same PM level.

DISCUSSION AND CONCLUSION

The main contribution of this chapter is its comprehensive modelling that examines many contingent factors for the PM-OM relationship. Gunasekaran et al. (2015) remark that the existence of contradictory findings on the mirroring hypothesis over long time has resulted from the lack of this type of mathematical studies that are capable of exploring the nuanced relationship between PM and OM. The authors of this chapter believe that this research's mathematical model fills this gap by showing the larger extent of the relationship between PM and OM. The findings verify that the PM-OM relationship is not straightforward as hypothesized.

Figure 7. The optimal OM level for different values of input parameters
PM level = 0.853 and the objective weight vector = [1/2, 1/6, 1/6, 1/6].

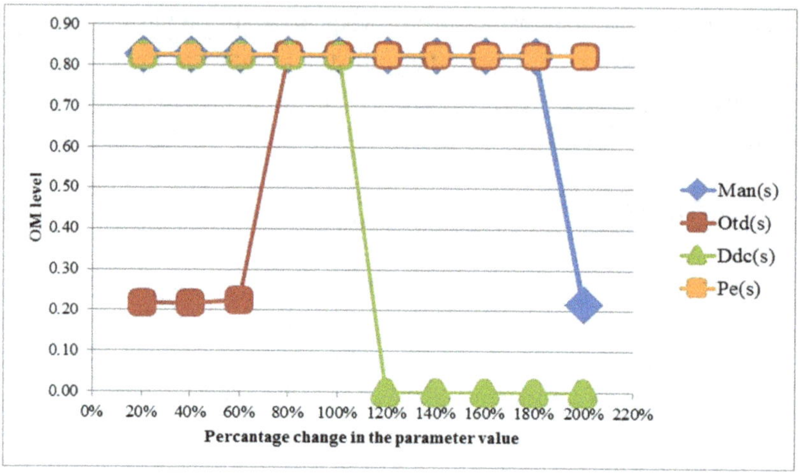

The analysis of this chapter makes further step by jointly analyzing many possible influential factors on the PM-OM relationship at across-firm level. The previous studies have also attempted to explain to the degree that PM leads to supplier disintegration. However, each of these studies narrows its focus and shows why product modularity does not necessarily lead to supplier disintegration due to the specific factor. For example, Furlan et al. (2014) find that the positive effect of PM on OM at across-firm level is up to the technological change rate of the modules sourced. According to this study, the mirroring hypothesis does not hold if the technological change rates of modules are high. Likewise, the findings of Lau and Yam (2005) indicate that supplier disintegration might provide cost advantage for conventional modular products. However, the authors argue that firms should keep integrated with their suppliers regardless of the PM level to reduce inventory costs, and to enhance quality conformance. Hence, each of these studies draws stand-alone boundaries for the validity of the mirroring hypothesis. However, it is not clear whether the boundaries drawn by these studies overlap or some of these boundaries remain non-binding when they are jointly considered.

There are also comprehensive studies (Burton & Galvin, 2018; Lau et al., 2010; Sorkun & Furlan, 2017) that attempt to reveal all contingent factors moderating the relationship between PM and OM, e.g. component technological change and diversity, capability dispersion along the supply network, and logistics costs. Nonetheless, they discuss the effects of these contingent factors separately, keeping other factors under control. Although, these endeavors are invaluable to understand the power of mirroring hypothesis, they are not sufficient to show the exact boundaries of mirroring hypothesis. At this point, this chapter examines the effect of product modularity on supplier integration when many contingent factors are jointly considered. This allows coming closer to defining the exact boundaries for the validity of mirroring hypothesis.

Practical Implications

This chapter helps managers find the ideal supplier integration level considering their firm's priorities and product design architecture. In practice, it may be difficult or even not possible for a firm to change the integration level with its suppliers. In such a case, managers can use the proposed model in an inverse manner to find the optimal PM level for the current supplier integration level. This enables managers to optimize their R&D activities and new product development processes for the given nature of supplier relations. For example, a firm may need to supply its module from one specific supplier due to economic reasons, resource scarcity, or lack of alternatives. A possible cultural misalignment with such supplier might escalate coordination costs too much. In these circumstances, managers may attempt to design a modular product to minimize the required amount of coordination. Alternatively, if a firm works with its suppliers for a long-time based on trust relationship, engineering managers may be willing to develop an integral product assumed to give higher performance (Schilling, 2000), because coordination with these suppliers would not be a difficult task for the firm. At this point, the proposed model helps them find the best product architecture design considering existing supplier relationships.

Limitations and Avenues for Future Research

This research has some limitations that can provide avenues for future studies. First, the number of contingent factors in this chapter is limited to four. Future research may augment the model by including additional contingencies. Besides, this chapter's mathematical model assumes that the differences in the importance of product modules are not significant, which influence the level of integration with suppliers with respect to the importance of the module sourced. Thus, future studies can increase the generalizability of this research's model by distinguishing modules with respect to their features.

Future studies may also make some changes in research design to validate this research's findings. This research measures supplier integration with the amount of information sharing. However, the quality of information shared with suppliers is also important; therefore, it can be considered by future studies to measure supplier integration level. Next, this research builds its model using linear programming; however, modelling the problem in a non-linear and dynamic ways might capture the different aspects of the PM-OM relationship. In addition, this research needed a dataset to conduct an experimental study; therefore, used the supplier dataset of Narasimhan et al. (2001). Future studies may use alternative measures and supplier datasets to validate the results presented in this chapter.

ACKNOWLEDGMENT

This research received no specific grant from any funding agency in the public, commercial, or not-for-profit sectors.

REFERENCES

Antonio, K. L., Richard, C. Y., & Tang, E. (2009). The complementarity of internal integration and product modularity: An empirical study of their interaction effect on competitive capabilities. *Journal of Engineering and Technology Management*, *26*(4), 305–326.

Baldwin, C. Y. (2008). Where do transactions come from? Modularity, transactions, and the boundaries of firms. *Industrial and Corporate Change*, *17*(1), 155–195. doi:10.1093/icc/dtm036

Blecker, T., & Abdelkafi, N. (2006). Complexity and variety in mass customization systems: Analysis and recommendations. *Management Decision*, *44*(7), 908–929. doi:10.1108/00251740610680596

Brusoni, S., & Prencipe, A. (2001). Unpacking the black box of modularity: Technologies, products and organizations. *Industrial and Corporate Change*, *10*(1), 179–205. doi:10.1093/icc/10.1.179

Brusoni, S., Prencipe, A., & Pavitt, K. (2001). Knowledge specialization, organizational coupling, and the boundaries of the firm: Why do firms know more than they make? *Administrative Science Quarterly*, *46*(4), 597–621. doi:10.2307/3094825

Burton, N., & Galvin, P. (2018). When do product architectures mirror organisational architectures? The combined role of product complexity and the rate of technological change. *Technology Analysis and Strategic Management*, *30*(9), 1057–1069. doi:10.1080/09537325.2018.1437259

Cabigiosu, A., & Camuffo, A. (2012). Beyond the "mirroring" hypothesis: Product modularity and interorganizational relations in the air conditioning industry. *Organization Science*, *23*(3), 686–703. doi:10.1287/orsc.1110.0655

Cammarano, A., Michelino, F., & Caputo, M. (2019). Open innovation practices for knowledge acquisition and their effects on innovation output. *Technology Analysis and Strategic Management, 31*(11), 1297–1313. doi:10.1080/09537325.2019.1606420

Colfer, L., & Baldwin, C. Y. (2016). The mirroring hypothesis: Theory, evidence and exceptions. *Industrial and Corporate Change, 25*(5), 709–738. doi:10.1093/icc/dtw027

Dias Sant'Ana, T., de Souza Bermejo, P. H., Moreira, M. F., & de Souza, W. V. B. (2020). The structure of an innovation ecosystem: Foundations for future research. *Management Decision, 58*(12), 2725–2742. doi:10.1108/MD-03-2019-0383

Ernst, D. (2005). Limits to modularity: Reflections on recent developments in chip design. *Industry and Innovation, 12*(3), 303–335. doi:10.1080/13662710500195918

Ethiraj, S. K. (2007). Allocation of inventive effort in complex product systems. *Strategic Management Journal, 28*(6), 563–584. doi:10.1002mj.622

Fine, C. H., Golany, B., & Naseraldin, H. (2005). Modeling tradeoffs in three-dimensional concurrent engineering: A goal programming approach. *Journal of Operations Management, 23*(3), 389–403. doi:10.1016/j.jom.2004.09.005

Frigant, V., & Lung, Y. (2002). Geographical proximity and supplying relationships in modular production. *International Journal of Urban and Regional Research, 26*(4), 742–755. doi:10.1111/1468-2427.00415

Frigant, V., & Talbot, D. (2005). Technological determinism and modularity: Lessons from a comparison between aircraft and auto industries in Europe. *Industry and Innovation, 12*(3), 337–355. doi:10.1080/13662710500195934

Furlan, A., Cabigiosu, A., & Camuffo, A. (2014). When the mirror gets misted up: Modularity and technological change. *Strategic Management Journal, 35*(6), 789–807. doi:10.1002mj.2138

García-Piqueres, G., Serrano-Bedia, A. M., López-Fernández, M. C., & Pérez-Pérez, M. (2020). Relatedness in the adoption of different innovation types: Product, process, organisational and commercial innovations. *Technology Analysis and Strategic Management, 32*(1), 44–57. doi:10.1080/09537325.2019.1632822

Gunasekaran, A., Irani, Z., Choy, K. L., Filippi, L., & Papadopoulos, T. (2015). Performance measures and metrics in outsourcing decisions: A review for research and applications. *International Journal of Production Economics, 161*, 153–166. doi:10.1016/j.ijpe.2014.12.021

Hao, B., Feng, Y., & Frigant, V. (2017). Rethinking the 'mirroring'hypothesis: Implications for technological modularity, tacit coordination, and radical innovation. *R & D Management*, *47*(1), 3–16. doi:10.1111/radm.12106

Henderson, R. M., & Clark, K. B. (1990). Architectural innovation: The reconfiguration of existing product technologies and the failure of established firms. *Administrative Science Quarterly*, *35*(1), 9–30. doi:10.2307/2393549

Hoetker, G. (2006). Do modular products lead to modular organizations? *Strategic Management Journal*, *27*(6), 501–518. doi:10.1002mj.528

Hoetker, G., Swaminathan, A., & Mitchell, W. (2007). Modularity and the impact of buyer–supplier relationships on the survival of suppliers. *Management Science*, *53*(2), 178–191. doi:10.1287/mnsc.1060.0630

Howard, M., & Squire, B. (2007). Modularization and the impact on supply relationships. *International Journal of Operations & Production Management*, *27*(11), 1192–1212. doi:10.1108/01443570710830593

Jacobs, M., Vickery, S. K., & Droge, C. (2007). The effects of product modularity on competitive performance: Do integration strategies mediate the relationship? *International Journal of Operations & Production Management*, *27*(10), 1046–1068. doi:10.1108/01443570710820620

Kleindorfer, P. R., & Saad, G. H. (2005). Managing disruption risks in supply chains. *Production and Operations Management*, *14*(1), 53–68. doi:10.1111/j.1937-5956.2005.tb00009.x

Lau, A. K. (2011). Critical success factors in managing modular production design: Six company case studies in Hong Kong, China, and Singapore. *Journal of Engineering and Technology Management*, *28*(3), 168–183. doi:10.1016/j.jengtecman.2011.03.004

Lau, A. K., Yam, R. C., Tang, E. P., & Sun, H. Y. (2010). Factors influencing the relationship between product modularity and supply chain integration. *International Journal of Operations & Production Management*, *30*(9), 951–977. doi:10.1108/01443571011075065

Lau, A. K. W., & Yam, R. C. M. (2005). A case study of product modularization on supply chain design and coordination in Hong Kong and China. *Journal of Manufacturing Technology Management*, *16*(4), 432–446. doi:10.1108/17410380510594516

Lee, H.L., So, K.C., & Tang, C.S. (2000). The value of information sharing in a two-level supply chain. *Management Science, 46*(5), 626-643. doi:10.1287/mnsc.46.5.626.12047

Liao, K., Deng, X., & Marsillac, E. (2013). Factors that influence Chinese automotive suppliers' mass customization capabilities. *International Journal of Production Economics*, *146*(1), 25–36. doi:10.1016/j.ijpe.2013.01.014

Nair, S., & Blomquist, T. (2021). Business model design in the case of complex innovations: A conceptual model. *Technology Analysis and Strategic Management*, *33*(2), 176–187. doi:10.1080/09537325.2020.1805103

Narasimhan, R., Talluri, S., & Mendez, D. (2001). Supplier evaluation and rationalization via data envelopment analysis: An empirical examination. *The Journal of Supply Chain Management*, *37*(2), 28–37. doi:10.1111/j.1745-493X.2001.tb00103.x

Özpeynirci, Ö., & Köksalan, M. (2010). An exact algorithm for finding extreme supported nondominated points of multiobjective mixed integer programs. *Management Science*, *56*(12), 2302–2315. doi:10.1287/mnsc.1100.1248

Persson, M., Eklind, M. J., & Winroth, M. (2016). Coordinating external manufacturing of product modules. *Decision Sciences*, *47*(6), 1178–1202. doi:10.1111/deci.12197

Pil, F. K., & Cohen, S. K. (2006). Modularity: Implications for imitation, innovation, and sustained advantage. *Academy of Management Review*, *31*(4), 995–1011. doi:10.5465/amr.2006.22528166

Sabel, C. F., & Zeitlin, J. (2004). Neither modularity nor relational contracting: Inter-firm collaboration in the new economy. *Enterprise and Society*, *5*(3), 388–403. doi:10.1093/es/khh057

Sanchez, R., & Mahoney, J. T. (1996). Modularity, flexibility, and knowledge management in product and organization design. *Strategic Management Journal*, *17*(S2), 63–76. doi:10.1002mj.4250171107

Schilling, M. A. (2000). Toward a general modular systems theory and its application to interfirm product modularity. *Academy of Management Review*, *25*(2), 312–334. doi:10.2307/259016

Sehnem, S., Campos, L. M. S., Julkovski, D. J., & Cazella, C. F. (2019). Circular business models: Level of maturity. *Management Decision*, *57*(4), 1043–1066. doi:10.1108/MD-07-2018-0844

Sorkun, M. F. (2016). Contrary evidence: Product modularity and supplier integration. *International Journal of Integrated Supply Management, 10*(3-4), 283–308. doi:10.1504/IJISM.2016.081278

Sorkun, M. F., & Furlan, A. (2017). Product and Organizational Modularity: A Contingent View of the Mirroring Hypothesis. *European Management Review, 14*(2), 205–224. doi:10.1111/emre.12101

Sosa, M. E., Eppinger, S. D., & Rowles, C. M. (2003). Identifying modular and integrative systems and their impact on design team interactions. *Journal of Mechanical Design, 125*(2), 240–252. doi:10.1115/1.1564074

Sun, Y., & Zhong, Q. (2020). How modularity influences product innovation: The mediating role of module suppliers' relationship-specific investments. *Management Decision, 58*(12), 2743–2761. doi:10.1108/MD-06-2019-0837

Takeishi, A. (2002). Knowledge partitioning in the interfirm division of labor: The case of automotive product development. *Organization Science, 13*(3), 321–338. doi:10.1287/orsc.13.3.321.2779

Tarafdar, M., & Qrunfleh, S. (2017). Agile supply chain strategy and supply chain performance: Complementary roles of supply chain practices and information systems capability for agility. *International Journal of Production Research, 55*(4), 925–938. doi:10.1080/00207543.2016.1203079

Tiwana, A. (2008). Does technological modularity substitute for control? A study of alliance performance in software outsourcing. *Strategic Management Journal, 29*(7), 769–780. doi:10.1002mj.673

Ulrich, K. (1995). The role of product architecture in the manufacturing firm. *Research Policy, 24*(3), 419–440. doi:10.1016/0048-7333(94)00775-3

Yang, M. G., Roh, J. J., & Kang, M. (2020). The role of strategic environmental orientation in environmental design practices. *Management Decision, 59*(2), 341–357. doi:10.1108/MD-07-2019-0865

Zirpoli, F., & Becker, M. C. (2011). The limits of design and engineering outsourcing: Performance integration and the unfulfilled promises of modularity. *R & D Management, 41*(1), 21–43. doi:10.1111/j.1467-9310.2010.00629.x

KEY TERMS AND DEFINITIONS

Experimental Study: A quantitative research method that allows to see the effects of changes in the variables of interest by keeping other relevant variables under control.

Mirroring Hypothesis: A theoretical proposition claiming that the design architecture of organizations mirrors the design architecture of products developed by them.

Modularity: A system design feature that shows the degree to which the system components are reconfigurable and decomposable owing to standardized interfaces.

Multi-Criteria Decision Making: A set of analytical techniques that support decisions for which multiple criteria need to be considered.

Multi-Objective Optimization: A mathematical method that aims to find the optimal solution for problems involving multiple objectives.

Nondominated Solutions: A set of solution points identified in multi-criteria decision-making problems that are not less preferable than other solution points at least in one criterion.

Supplier Integration: The degree to which firms are collaborating with their suppliers, such as in idea generation, product concept development, new product development, market testing, and large-scale production.

Chapter 10
Growing Pains:
Shifting From a Traditional Business Model – A Case Study

Marisa R. Ferreira
CIICESI, ESTG, Politécnico do Porto, Portugal

Carina Silva
CIICESI, ESTG, Politécnico do Porto, Portugal

Beatriz Casais
https://orcid.org/0000-0002-7626-0509
School of Economics and Management, CICS.NOVA, University of Minho, Portugal

ABSTRACT

Today's ever-changing business environment is very demanding for companies, particularly those of modest dimensions and operating in more traditional formats. There is an imperative change happening in market and consumer behavior – a need for digital transformation or digital complement to the traditional business model, aiming at improving the lives of individuals, groups, and society as a whole. A Portuguese small company that manufactures cookies and biscuits has identified a need to move forward and revitalize its traditional business format, preserving its traditional origins but seeking to reframe its business in a more digital context. The main goals of the case study are to understand (1) this brand's evolution, (2) its primary difficulties, and (3) strengths, and the authors also indicate possible future paths that can be replicated in other similar businesses.

DOI: 10.4018/978-1-7998-7793-6.ch010

Copyright © 2022, IGI Global. Copying or distributing in print or electronic forms without written permission of IGI Global is prohibited.

INTRODUCTION

Most entrepreneurs, by heading innovations and generating competition, contribute to economic and social development (Krueger, Reilly, & Carsrud, 2000; Nishimura & Tristán, 2011). The dynamic and active atmosphere where companies operate is very challenging. At the same time, in the second half of the 20th century, we witnessed a nostalgia boom, a concept known as a shared and collective phenomenon of growing awareness and fascination with the past. Consumers are increasingly looking for new experiences that can take them back to happier times, oftentimes symbolized in childhood reminisced. In fact, nostalgia for a perceived happier past can be particularly prominent in turbulent and anxious times (Reisenwitz, Iyer, & Cutler, 2004).

Our case study focuses on a longstanding Portuguese brand of cookies and biscuits founded in 1874 and which has been recently taking advantage of the emergent demand for vintage Portuguese products. A nostalgic aura of history, antiquity and tradition envelope this brand (Santos, 2012) of its humble origin seems to be a plus in a heavily disputed and highly competitive market, where a revival of old ways seeks to establish a new order of knowledge, production and consumption, incorporating traditions with reality.

In 2012, the brand initiated a process of expansion of its selling points to reduce its dependence on the final consumer market and avoid the issue of potential non-payment by its resellers. Currently, the technology used by the company merges the authenticity its old equipment with the efficiency of modern machinery, thus ensuring high-quality products. Central to achieving this quality is the artisanal manufacture, which is still quite evident in the packaging processes, with the cookies and biscuits being selected and paired in different packages (Rebelo, 2020). Our case study analyzes different management tools (SWOT and PESTEL analysis) in order to understand (i) this brand's evolution, its (ii) main difficulties and (iii) strengths, and we also indicate possible future paths that can be replicated to other analogous businesses.

The company of our case study believes in and advocates the continuity of tradition, which can be seen in the preservation of the same recipes, i.e., the original recipes — more than a century old —, as well as the general communication strategy and package design of the cookies and biscuits. The brand's assortment packaging underwent a rebranding in 2012 and the packaging is currently the same as the Paupério tin boxes sold in the 40's and 50's, with their blue and white colors reminiscent of the traditional Portuguese tiles. This is a very economical option in terms of design and packaging, and is proof of the brand's authenticity, history and originality in the eyes of consumers (Santos, 2012). The raw materials for manufacture undergo a rigorous selection, and their quality is central to implement the ancestral recipes.

The company's success arose from improving its facilities, promoting employee training of and enforcing strict food control systems. However, the company feels the need to constantly reinvent its business model, overcoming different political regimes, financial crises and internal difficulties.

The PESTEL analysis is particularly valuable to understand how the external ecosystem influences the brand, by considering the political, economic, social, technological and ecological factors, and in general we will observe that the company faces several opportunities that may serve to strengthen its future strategy, since the current market demands impose a fast pace on the sector. The SWOT analysis is also essential for a better understanding of the company's characteristics, and both tools can provide a better analysis of the current moment and help prepare for the future.

Our case study presents a practical approach to cookies and biscuits, particularly in the context of local and traditional production. We present a description of the case and a discussion of the application of management tools. We explore and indicate possibilities of growth in terms of marketplace, specifically in the digital environment, as e-marketplaces sharing the gourmet premium positioning and revival trend.

BACKGROUND

Traditional Businesses

Today, European consumers are increasingly concerned about leading a healthy lifestyle, they are more demanding about quality and freshness and continue to enjoy trying new foods. On the one hand, if bread and/or derivatives producers identify this market opportunity, seeing it as a challenge to meet the needs and new European tastes, on the other hand, the daily hustle can awaken consumers' desire to reconnect with products and/or brands that present themselves as a safe path. The role of tradition plays a very important role in these dynamics, even when we create new products or solutions, as it allows us to move forward and work from an existing reference.

There is a growing interest of in literature on how traditional food products (TFP) are evaluated by consumers and what explains consumers' preferences, attitudes and consumption (Kristbergsson & Oliveira, 2016). There are several attributes inherent to the construct of TFP, such as: they are products normally associated with festive, specific occasions or products that are frequently consumed (Olsen, Skallerud, & Heide, 2021), they contain traditional ingredients and must be processed according to traditional recipes (Verbeke, Guerrero, Almli, Vanhonacker, & Hersleth, 2016), and have their roots in a specific locality, region, country or geographical area (Guerrero et al., 2010).

A relevant feature of TFP is their relationship with the past, as they often constitute a gastronomic heritage, associated with food preferences and particular emotions across generations (Olsen et al., 2021). The brand's history is a good example, it allows consumers to remember some point in the past, or it simply strengthens the importance it exerts in the market over time. In addition to tradition, recognition is another characteristic commonly associated with nostalgia, when we recognize the importance of some past experience. Therefore, nostalgia allows a critical mediation between the past and the present, and plays an important role in creating new identities (Anderson, 2016).

In a world of uncertainties — such as the one we are now experiencing with the COVID-19 pandemic —, consumers prefer brands and products that are more familiar to them and transmit them a guarantee of service or product quality, as a sort of affective memory — the nostalgia market. In fact, the literature in the area (Almli, Verbeke, Vanhonacker, Næs, & Hersleth, 2011; Pieniak, Verbeke, Vanhonacker, Guerrero, & Hersleth, 2009) demonstrates that attitudes and familiarity are the antecedents that have the most impact on traditional food consumption.

According to a Chinese proverb mentioned by Silvertown (2017), "food is enjoyed three times: in anticipation, in its consumption, and its remembrance", thus demonstrating the importance of food memory to the physical and emotional well-being of individuals. The term 'comfort foods' is considered by several authors (Soffin & Batsell, 2019) to describe those foods linked to nostalgia and which, when consumed, provide a psychological and emotional effect in addition to the physical effect (Locher, Yoels, Maurer, & van Ells, 2005), with nostalgic persons being clearly those who show a greater preference for pleasurable foods (Wang, Keh, & Chao, 2018).

Similarly, to the digital market, the nostalgia market presents itself as a market trend that has been gaining momentum and is seen as a promising path to achieve positive business results. However, the attribute of "traditional" is generally linked to the past, while the attribute "online" environment is associated to the present and the future. This opposition can generate a contradiction in consumers' minds between the two concepts, which may frame TFP as not being compatible with the online environment, thus demonstrating the necessity of consolidating their position in the digital market, and trying to find a balance between the old and the new, between the taste of food that lingers across generations and new lifestyles.

The Digital Market

The growing use of the internet has implied significant changes in consumer behavior, from product research to purchase through electronic devices (Mathews, Bianchi, Perks, Healy, & Wickramasekera, 2016). This growth derives from the existence of electronic commerce. The digital channels allow the consumers to make purchases in private brand's online stores, where only products referring to that associated brand/store are sold; or through e-marketplaces, which are digital platforms that offer consumers the possibility of searching for the desired products among several suppliers; and, through the tools available on the platform, be assisted regarding their search, selection, comparison, final purchase of products and post-purchase experience — with the e-marketplace assuming itself as a virtual shopping mall (Casais, 2020). The interactivity enabled by the internet provides many tools to increase the efficiency of digital retail, as it facilitates access to information on products, price comparison, and reduction of user search costs, and the convenience it offers its users override traditional trade (Alba et al., 1997). Amazon at a global level or Dott at a national level are examples of digital e-marketplaces that allow the expansion of sales in digital environments without the requirement of developing an online store – which is particularly convenient for small companies with low brand awareness and/or weak digital skills or logistic conditions to operate an e-commerce site on their own (Casais, 2020).

The fact that a growing number of product categories have been adapting to this new behavior of purchasing online, offering complementary services to assist the consumer decision-making process (Oliveira, Alhinho, Rita, & Dhillon, 2017), also accelerates the evolution of e-commerce, not only in terms of the number of users, but also in its financial return (Chaparro-Peláez, Agudo-Peregrina, & Pascual-Miguel, 2016). Through digital growth and globalization, companies adapt their business models and take advantage of opportunities to increase their brand awareness and generate consumer traffic on their digital platforms.

With the opening of new markets due to new technologies and globalization, more opportunities arise for doing business in the international context, fostering increased operational efficiency within their value chain (Cockayne, 2016). The globalization of markets, combined with high technological and digital changes, requires companies to adapt quickly to maintain or increase their presence in the main markets and even penetrate new markets. This fact highlights the need for the digital transformation of companies to adapt to the characteristics of a global and digital society. One reason for companies to accelerate their digital transformation process is the pressure exerted by increasing competition in a widely globalized world focused on digitization (von Leipzig et al., 2017), predominantly due to the emergence of small startups that disturb already established companies in the sector (Crittenden, Crittenden, & Crittenden, 2019; Tekic & Koroteev, 2019). More than a current trend, digitization is the guarantee of success for a company to survive and prosper in the global market (Tekic & Koroteev, 2019).

The presence of traditional and artisanal products in e-commerce with the purpose of achieving global brand recognition and expand markets may result in a paradox. On the one hand, gourmet and artisanal characteristics are connected with selective and exclusive brand attributes; on the other hand, digital purchasing habits require adaptation to e-commerce environments. This paradox has been extensively researched in the literature (Balasyan & Casais, 2018) and implicates the adaptation of online environments to brand attributes, marketing product exclusivity through product design and presentation, and by a selective choice of e-marketplaces to target niche segments (Casais, 2020). Unique Flavours is an example of a niche e-marketplace, a gourmet e-marketplace that only sells Portuguese food brands and targets consumers who look for particular products from a region, or particular producers who do not have enough production to sell in mass market retailers. In this sense, the expansion of a handicraft brand in digital marketplaces consists in a challenge that requires a marketing strategy regarding targeting procedures and the choice of selective digital e-marketplaces.

PAUPÉRIO AND COMPANHIA: THE CASE STUDY ANALYSIS

The company Paupério & Companhia, better known as Paupério, was founded in 1874 in Valongo, a small town in the north of Portugal, and mainly manufactures and markets cookies and biscuits.

Its values include high quality and continuous improvement for consumer satisfaction, as well as a strong commitment to valuing the quality of life of its workforce, promoting trust, ethical behaviors and mutual respect with its partners, and always bearing in mind the most pressing social concerns. Its production is essentially traditional in nature, a trait that characterizes the brand as a whole.

Paupério's mission is to provide its customers and friends with the best regional cookies and biscuits in the world, boasting an unmistakably traditional flavor and capable of satisfying the most demanding consumer tastes.

The brand's product portfolio has three product lines: cookies and biscuits; marmalades and jellies; and cakes. The most diverse product line is cookies and biscuits, with forty different varieties. The brand is also known for its sponge cake, *bolo-rei* (the traditional Portuguese Christmas cake), and marmalades and jellies, all of which are especially popular during the festive seasons, although their production is not seasonal. There have been ups and downs in over 140 years of activity, but the company is still in the hands of the founding family and is currently experiencing one of its strongest trading periods, exporting directly to Macau, besides its presence in e-marketplaces such as Unique Flavours, which allows internationalization by e-commerce.

The brand chose to target its segment to a public that values quality and bet on the concept of fine grocery, thus reaffirming its position in the market. Its main target audiences are traditional and revivalist. Traditional consumers are adults focused on quality and trust in an experienced brand; revivalists are young adults and adults, lovers of Portuguese products, whose purchase motivation is the current trend of revivalism, more than quality itself; the fashion factor strongly influences the choices of this consumer group, and this segment's critical success factors are the products' vintage/retro component and patriotism. However, this premise does not prevent Paupério from turning its back on large-scale distribution, as the company is increasingly open to the idea of introducing small producers in its stores. Hence the double dimension of the brand: Paupério is selling its products in several multi-brand stores, and in its own shops (in the factory and in one shopping mall in Porto) have products from other small producers of traditional products. Paupério shops are important points of sale and advertising.

PESTEL Analysis

The PESTEL analysis is a strategic tool that can be used to assess how the macro/external environment influences an organization and its products, allowing the identification of opportunities and threats to the business, through the following elements: political and legal, economic, social, technological and environmental. By applying this analysis to the case of Paupério, we present the most important external factors influencing the company's performance.

SWOT Analysis

SWOT analysis is a management tool increasingly used by companies. It helps to do a strategic diagnosis, it allows synthesizing external and internal analysis, making the company's sales forecast considering its abilities, planning strategic options by striking a balance between risks and problems, as well as between advantages and opportunities, and also allows establishing priorities for action via the identification of key aspects for the company's management (Achrol & Kotler, 2012; Dobson, Starkey, & Richards, 2004).

Table 1. PESTEL analysis applied to Paupério

PESTEL elements	General approach	Paupério
Political and legal	The European Union provides access to funds in the context of economic, social and territorial development policy. In Portugal, there are several operational components, namely Portugal 2020.	The company is implementing an internationalization program within the framework of Portugal 2020, and aims to penetrate new markets (France, Switzerland, Luxembourg, Japan, Macau, and Canada).
	Exporting to new markets may bring additional costs – customs fees and taxes.	The company will move out progressively, initially through local distributors in the target markets and by placing its products in specific distribution points (e.g., specialty stores).
	Food producers are subject to national food safety and health regulations, as well as to regulations in export destination countries. One of Paupério's main raw materials is palm oil, which has good characteristics for its purpose (smooth and creamy texture combined with absence of odor, thus maintaining cooking properties). However, palm oil production is increasingly associated with environmental issues (mainly deforestation) and its consumption has more recently been associated with consequences for human health.	By complying with all health and food safety standards, Paupério demonstrates concerns regarding the use of salt and sugar, particularly in products for schools, and thus has been developing recipes with less salt and sugar content. Regarding the use of palm oil, there are still no substitute ingredients, although the company purchases it from a certified supplier (100% sustainable production).
Economic	The evolution of interest and exchange rates has impact on economic activity, either directly on business activity or on the consumption level.	Paupério is exposed to bank debt (2017), so potential changes in interest rates will impact its cost structure. On the other hand, the company's internationalization strategy may bring about an increase in costs or income due to exchange differences.
Social	In recent years, there has been an increase in demand for gourmet/ premium products, associated with the "sense of Portugal" and purchases in prestigious groceries, i.e., the return to vintage is also a trend; the segment of prestigious cookies and biscuits is marked by seasonality (e.g., sales increase strongly during festive seasons such as Christmas or Easter); there is also an increase in tourism influx in Portugal during such festive seasons.	Paupério's current strategic orientation is the gourmet market, adopting the concept of prestigious and traditional grocery in its own stores. The opening of its own stores is part of this concept, albeit also related to tourism. Paupério has benefited from the increase in sales volumes resulting from placing its products at Portuguese airports, having developed specific products for this purpose. Considering seasonality, Paupério has developed specific festive packaging.
Technological	The production process in this sector is highly standardized, oriented towards mass production; in line with the growing trend for gourmet products, consumers (especially the younger segment) use technology as an ally in their purchases; therefore, the digitization of forms of communication (social networks) and online sales are major consumption trends.	Paupério's product portfolio is quite diversified, which requires high investment in equipment; Paupério is present on social networks, but it is developing a more advanced and mature online sales platform. Additionally, the brand is present in e-marketplaces, such as Dott and Unique Flavours.
Environmental	The use of plastic is almost omnipresent in our daily lives, in spite of its heavy impact on the environment; there is growing legislative awareness regarding this matter; the cookies and biscuits production industry makes massive use of plastic in packaging, mainly for food preservation reasons.	There are no good alternative solutions for safe and long-lasting packaging of cookies and biscuits. However, Paupério is attentive both to legislative developments regarding this matter and to the search for packaging alternatives.

Table 2. SWOT analysis applied to Paupério

SWOT	Paupério
Strengths	• Packaging: designed cans and packaging adapted to festive seasons or allusive to cities (e.g., Porto, Lisbon); the design of cans and packaging is developed internally • Wide and complementary product range • Its products use less butter than its competitors
Weaknesses	• Limitations in terms of production equipment due to its life cycle: the company creates different products, but its maintenance is difficult • Small-scale factory • Factory building located in a residential and historic area, which makes it difficult to receive raw materials
Opportunities	• Applying for international investment programs • Growth of tourism in Portugal • Internationalization process • Growth in online sales
Threats	• Legal and environmental issues (e.g., plastics in packaging) • Competition (not with the same product but with substitute or alternative products)

LESSONS LEARNED: DISCUSSION AND CHALLENGES

The PESTEL analysis was very useful to give us the perception of how the external environment influences the brand. Taking into account the political, economic, social, technological and ecological factors, we observe that Paupério faces several challenges, namely the new wave of internationalization that the brand is currently starting and all the logistical and customs constraints that internationalization implies. At the same time, the constant market changes and demands regarding health and food safety standards mean that there is a constant concern to meet these points without changing the product. It was also noted that Paupério is exposed to bank debt, and so changes in interest rates may impact the cost structure program. On the one hand, regarding the technological aspect, it is fair to say that the company benefits from the standardization of production, which is a typical characteristic of this sector. On the other hand, online sales are being initiated. Lastly, the environmental factor is expected to be one of the brand's biggest challenges in the future, as it is already being manifest. Alternatives are being studied regarding the reduction of plastic use, as this element is at present essential for the conservation of products and provide a guarantee of quality when the products leave the factory.

The SWOT analysis was also central for understanding the brand's strengths and weaknesses, as well as potential opportunities and threats. The products' iconic packaging, which is carefully scrutinized and reinvented via minor improvements, was clearly identified as the company's greatest asset, although it boasts other strengths too, such as product differentiation with its various assortment combinations. Unlike other assortments available on the market, all the cookies and biscuits from the Paupério assortments have a different flavor. The antiquity of the machinery will be the company's biggest weakness, and the restriction regarding the use of plastic is its biggest threat. However, the growth of tourism and the nostalgia market are opportunities that the company is already embracing.

Considering our study's main goals — to understand (i) the brand's evolution, its main (ii) difficulties and (iii) strengths — in recent years, Paupério has been expanding its own store network. This expansion began in 2010 with the opening of a point of sale in Rio Tinto, and in 2012 the company opened another store, this time in Ermesinde, with new openings expected in the Porto district. Thus, in the midst of an economic and pandemic crisis, this brand strategy can be considered audacious, and is well complemented by the growth of its online presence, not without growing pains, since the main difficulties are adequate distribution of online channels and respective costs, regular online communication and actualization, as well as environmental restrictions and impositions. At the same time, Paupério's most important strengths suggest that the company uses a focused differentiation strategy, which is appealing for a distinct product, and a range of premium products, with a premium price, but the product and the price are perceived by consumers as special and deserving this extra cost.

FUTURE RESEARCH DIRECTIONS

The Covid-19 global pandemic has driven digital commerce transformation when most of the physical shops closed. It was a major turning point in e-commerce history, and B2C and B2B companies relied on digital channels to make acquisitions. This change definitely amplified online behaviors, but, more prominently, it shaped new ones. While all this enthusiasm means new potentials, it also brings challenges, thus opening space for future research. Therefore, some potential areas of interest related to digital commerce regard (i) the sales channel and (ii) consistent customer experience (Almeida, Santos, & Monteiro, 2020; Bijmolt et al., 2021). Regarding the sales channel, it is important to note that digital commerce goes beyond the sales channel and must consider customer expectations, as well as market trends. At the same time, constructing a consistent and reliable customer experience transversely to all touchpoints and understanding the customer connections throughout those touchpoints is fundamental to keep customers engaged through their lifecycle. One of the biggest challenges in digital commerce is to empower the organization to interconnect and coordinate all channels to build satisfactory customer experiences across all channels, without generating too much internal complexity.

Another important direction for future research, somewhat linked with the digital commerce context, is segmentation. The company's present strategic orientation is the gourmet market, so it would be interesting to investigate the possibilities of adding new potential segments that might emerge with these new channels.

So, roughly, future research should include a wide-ranging and open discussion about what digital commerce represents, and the transformative developments being accepted under its auspices; particularly, future research should look at the specificities of businesses similar to our case study and comprehend their internal and external advantages and disadvantages. Another important area for future research is sustainability; more precisely, future research should look at the idiosyncrasies of local traditional businesses and their growth needs, which are often imposed by the market and may cause the growing pains mentioned in the title of this chapter.

CONCLUSION

This chapter focuses on Paupério, a regional and traditional Portuguese company that decided to intensify its presence in the market. The challenges are discussed and extrapolated for international and digital markets.

The foods we eat have a significant place in our lives and affect our health. At the same time, there are many interactions between food, the environment, and human health. The demand for better and more quality food and the need for a global well-being strategy that is emerging in society have pushed the idea of shifting from a more traditional business model to this company. Within this framework, a diversity of stakeholders — such as producers, manufacturers, distributors, and consumers — are involved and make market-based decisions that are also influenced by the context, so it is crucial both to expand our understanding of each of these mechanisms and adopt a more integrated perspective if we want to reach more innovative solutions and manage food consumption in a more global way.

In parallel, we should consider the importance of the nostalgia market. Some research shows associations between our brain and how we perceive and remember certain foods and beverages, so nostalgia brings back reminiscences of sentimental times, feelings of belonging and close relationships. Generally, consumers appreciate nostalgic products, but it is important to understand consumers, since target markets are a key factor for companies.

This case study presents a practical approach to discuss two management tools – PESTEL and SWOT — applied to traditional products, particularly in the context of local and traditional production. The current pandemic context led to a growing demand for more direct sales from producers to consumers, and this is a fundamental change and an important sign for business growth through digital channels. We present a description of the case and a discussion of the application of the management tools. Furthermore, we explore and indicate opportunities of growth, presenting the benefits and central challenges from their application. This chapter is based on the case of a regional Portuguese company, but the challenges presented here may be extrapolated to an international environment.

ACKNOWLEDGMENT

The authors gratefully acknowledge Paupério's CEO.

Marisa R. Ferreira and Carina Silva gratefully acknowledges financial support from FCT – Fundação para a Ciência e Tecnologia (Portugal), national funding through project UIDB/04728/2020.

REFERENCES

Achrol, R. S., & Kotler, P. (2012). Frontiers of the Marketing Paradigm in the Third Millennium. *Journal of the Academy of Marketing Science*, *40*(1), 35–52. doi:10.100711747-011-0255-4

Alba, J., Lynch, J., Weitz, B., Janiszewski, C., Lutz, R., Sawyer, A., & Wood, S. (1997). Interactive Home Shopping: Consumer, Retailer, and Manufacturer Incentives to Participate in Electronic Marketplaces. *Journal of Marketing*, *61*(3), 38–53. doi:10.1177/002224299706100303

Almeida, F., Santos, J., & Monteiro, J. (2020). The Challenges and Opportunities in the Digitalization of Companies in a Post-COVID-19 World. *IEEE Engineering Management Review*, *48*(3), 97–103. doi:10.1109/EMR.2020.3013206

Almli, V. L., Verbeke, W., Vanhonacker, F., Næs, T., & Hersleth, M. (2011). General image and attribute perceptions of traditional food in six European countries. *Food Quality and Preference*, *22*(1), 129–138. doi:10.1016/j.foodqual.2010.08.008

Anderson, L. (2016). Cooking up the Past: Culinary Nostalgia and Gender Critique in Cuéntame cómo pasó. *Hispanic Research Journal*, *17*(1), 34–48. doi:10.1080/14682737.2015.1125103

Balasyan, I., & Casais, B. (2018). Keeping Exclusivity in An E-Commerce Environment: The case of Farfetch.com and the market of luxury clothes. *International Journal of Marketing. Communication and New Media*, *0*(4), 6–27.

Bijmolt, T. H. A., Broekhuis, M., de Leeuw, S., Hirche, C., Rooderkerk, R. P., Sousa, R., & Zhu, S. X. (2021). Challenges at the marketing–operations interface in omni-channel retail environments. *Journal of Business Research*, *122*, 864–874. doi:10.1016/j.jbusres.2019.11.034

Casais, B. (2020). *Gestão da Distribuição em e-Marketplaces*. Retrieved from http://e-agroinnovation.agrocluster.com/uploads/AGROCLUSTER_Ebooks - E-Marketplaces.pdf

Chaparro-Peláez, J., Agudo-Peregrina, Á. F., & Pascual-Miguel, F. J. (2016). Conjoint analysis of drivers and inhibitors of e-commerce adoption. *Journal of Business Research*, *69*(4), 1277–1282. doi:10.1016/j.jbusres.2015.10.092

Cockayne, D. (2016). Redefining B2B relationship marketing: Insight from postmodern Alibaba. *Journal of Customer Behaviour*, *15*(1), 49–66. doi:10.1362/147539216X14594362873497

Crittenden, A. B., Crittenden, V. L., & Crittenden, W. F. (2019). The digitalization triumvirate: How incumbents survive. *Business Horizons*, *62*(2), 259–266. doi:10.1016/j.bushor.2018.11.005

Dobson, P., Starkey, K., & Richards, J. (2004). *Strategic Management* (2nd ed.)., doi:10.4135/9781446216446

Guerrero, L., Claret, A., Verbeke, W., Enderli, G., Zakowska-Biemans, S., Vanhonacker, F., Issanchou, S., Sajdakowska, M., Granli, B. S., Scalvedi, L., Contel, M., & Hersleth, M. (2010). Perception of traditional food products in six European regions using free word association. *Food Quality and Preference*, *21*(2), 225–233. doi:10.1016/j.foodqual.2009.06.003

Kristbergsson, K., & Oliveira, J. (Eds.). (2016). *Traditional Foods*. Springer. doi:10.1007/978-1-4899-7648-2

Krueger, N. F. Jr, Reilly, M. D., & Carsrud, A. L. (2000). Competing models of entrepreneurial intentions. *Journal of Business Venturing*, *15*(5–6), 411–432. doi:10.1016/S0883-9026(98)00033-0

Locher, J. L., Yoels, W. C., Maurer, D., & van Ells, J. (2005). Comfort Foods: An Exploratory Journey Into The Social and Emotional Significance of Food. *Food & Foodways*, *13*(4), 273–297. doi:10.1080/07409710500334509

Mathews, S., Bianchi, C., Perks, K. J., Healy, M., & Wickramasekera, R. (2016). Internet marketing capabilities and international market growth. *International Business Review*, *25*(4), 820–830. doi:10.1016/j.ibusrev.2015.10.007

Nishimura, J. S., & Tristán, O. M. (2011). Using the theory of planned behavior to predict nascent entrepreneurship. *Academia (Caracas)*, *46*, 55–71.

Oliveira, T., Alhinho, M., Rita, P., & Dhillon, G. (2017). Modelling and testing consumer trust dimensions in e-commerce. *Computers in Human Behavior*, *71*, 153–164. doi:10.1016/j.chb.2017.01.050

Olsen, S. O., Skallerud, K., & Heide, M. (2021). Consumers' evaluation and intention to buy traditional seafood: The role of vintage, uniqueness, nostalgia and involvement in luxury. *Appetite*, *157*, 104994. doi:10.1016/j.appet.2020.104994 PMID:33080331

Pieniak, Z., Verbeke, W., Vanhonacker, F., Guerrero, L., & Hersleth, M. (2009). Association between traditional food consumption and motives for food choice in six European countries. *Appetite*, *53*(1), 101–108. doi:10.1016/j.appet.2009.05.019 PMID:19500626

Rebelo, H. (2020). *A Sucesssão nas Empresas Familiares - estudo longitudinal da empresa Paupério*. Faculdade de Economia - Universidade do Porto.

Reisenwitz, T. H., Iyer, R., & Cutler, B. (2004). Nostalgia Advertising and the Influence of Nostalgia Proneness. *Marketing Management Journal*, *14*, 55–66.

Santos, Í. (2012). *Plano de Comunicação de Marketing Integrad (IMC): marca Paupério*. Universidade do Porto.

Silvertown, J. (2017). *A La Mesa Con Darwin:tras las huellas de la evolucion en nuestros alimentos*. Ariel Mexico.

Soffin, M. T., & Batsell, W. Jr. (2019). Towards a situational taxonomy of comfort foods: A retrospective analysis. *Appetite*, *137*, 152–162. doi:10.1016/j.appet.2019.02.018 PMID:30836119

Tekic, Z., & Koroteev, D. (2019). From disruptively digital to proudly analog: A holistic typology of digital transformation strategies. *Business Horizons*, *62*(6), 683–693. doi:10.1016/j.bushor.2019.07.002

Verbeke, W., Guerrero, L., Almli, V., Vanhonacker, F., & Hersleth, M. (2016). European Consumers' Definition and Perception of Traditional Foods. In K. Kristbergsson & J. Oliveira (Eds.), *Traditional foods* (pp. 3–16)., doi:10.1007/978-1-4899-7648-2_1 von Leipzig, T., Gamp, M., Manz, D., Schöttle, K., Ohlhausen, P., Oosthuizen, G., Palm, D., & von Leipzig, K. (2017). Initialising Customer-orientated Digital Transformation in Enterprises. *Procedia Manufacturing*, *8*, 517–524. doi:10.1016/j.promfg.2017.02.066

Wang, X., Keh, H. T., & Chao, C.-H. (2018). Nostalgia and consumer preference for indulgent foods: The role of social connectedness. *International Journal of Consumer Studies*, *42*(3), 316–326. doi:10.1111/ijcs.12419

Zeng, Y., Jia, F., Wan, L., & Guo, H. (2017). E-commerce in agri-food sector: A systematic literature review. *The International Food and Agribusiness Management Review*, *20*(4), 439–459. doi:10.22434/IFAMR2016.0156

ADDITIONAL READING

Gammon, S., & Ramshaw, G. (2021). Distancing from the Present: Nostalgia and Leisure in Lockdown. *Leisure Sciences*, *43*(1–2), 131–137. doi:10.1080/01490400.2020.1773993

Hofacker, C., Golgeci, I., Pillai, K. G., & Gligor, D. M. (2020). Digital marketing and business-to-business relationships: A close look at the interface and a roadmap for the future. *European Journal of Marketing*, *54*(6), 1161–1179. doi:10.1108/EJM-04-2020-0247

Matarazzo, M., Penco, L., Profumo, G., & Quaglia, R. (2021). Digital transformation and customer value creation in Made in Italy SMEs: A dynamic capabilities perspective. *Journal of Business Research*, *123*, 642–656. doi:10.1016/j.jbusres.2020.10.033

Rana, S., Raut, S. K., Prashar, S., & Hamid, A. B. A. (2021). Promoting through Consumer Nostalgia: A Conceptual Framework and Future Research Agenda. *Journal of Promotion Management*, *27*(2), 211–249. doi:10.1080/10496491.2020.1829773

Singh, R., Sharma, Y., & Kumar, J. (2021). A road less traveled in nostalgia marketing: Impact of spiritual well-being on effects of nostalgic advertisements. *Journal of Marketing Theory and Practice*, *29*(3), 289–307. doi:10.1080/10696679.2020.1836975

Soto-Acosta, P. (2020). COVID-19 Pandemic: Shifting Digital Transformation to a High-Speed Gear. *Information Systems Management*, *37*(4), 260–266. doi:10.1080/10580530.2020.1814461

KEY TERMS AND DEFINITIONS

Brand: An intangible marketing or business conception that helps people identify a company, product, service or individual.

Lifestyle: The way in which a person lives.

Nostalgia: A sentimentality for the past, usually for a period or place with happy individual and distinctive associations.

Traditional Business: Setup has, normally, a physical presence, and it serves people locally by providing services or products.

Traditional Food Products (TFP): Food products produced in a specific area at national, regional or local level, with traditional ingredients and/or production process and genuine in their recipe, and part of a certain gastronomic heritage.

Chapter 11
Addressing the Business Issues Through Open Innovation Initiatives

N. Raghavendra Rao
FINAIT Consultancy Services, India

ABSTRACT

Many concepts are emerging in the disciplines of management and information and communication technology. One needs to identify the concepts that are useful in designing and developing the business models for addressing the business issues of an enterprise. This chapter gives an overview of the various concepts in the disciplines of management and information technology. In the present business scenario, interdisciplinary concepts are needed to develop business models under open innovation environment. An enterprise has to choose the relevant concepts from the two disciplines as per their requirements in designing business models for their open innovation initiatives.

INTRODUCTION

In business, world change has become the norm. The steady predictable growth till the last century has given way to global market competition, radical technical innovation, and a major shift in approach towards business. Business activities have become more complex due to frequent changes in the market. Due to these changes, the type and quantum of information required by business enterprises are also increasing. Hence it has become important that one should use one's wisdom to convert information into knowledge in the present scenario of the business world.

DOI: 10.4018/978-1-7998-7793-6.ch011

Copyright © 2022, IGI Global. Copying or distributing in print or electronic forms without written permission of IGI Global is prohibited.

Now proven ways of applying knowledge in business are known as "Open Innovation Management". Knowledge is ultimately the foundation of an innovation economy.

The overall challenge that many enterprises face today is identifying where the knowledge resides and how to leverage it for their innovative purposes. Efforts to create innovative thinking among the employees in enterprises have been gaining importance. Over the last few years, there has been a growing interest in the field of innovation management. Now more than ever in the present economic uncertainty, constrained resources, more and more organizations are turning to open innovation management as a source of new solutions and renewed inspiration.

One may wonder what makes the need for open innovation different in the present-day context. The business world is in the middle of a significant transition. Three factors are playing important role in the present transition period. The three factors are information and communication technology, expanding world, and the demands of customers. Managing knowledge in respect of the above factors as well as the innovative process is the way to remain competitive in the changing business scenario. The following are the essential elements of open innovation management in an enterprise.

1. Identifying which knowledge is a unique and valuable resource.
2. Identifying which knowledge process represents unique and valuable capabilities.
3. Identifying the above resources and capabilities support the firm's products or services and market positions.

Interdisciplinary concepts will facilitate to development of business models in the open innovation environment for addressing business issues. This approach is discussed in the four case illustrations in this chapter.

BACKGROUND

The existing ways of doing business are constantly changing, due to rapid changes in the global economy. It may be noted that market conditions determine the options available and competitive advantage stems from business to its environment. It has become a necessity for business enterprises to respond quickly to these changes. Many business enterprises have started realizing that managing knowledge as an innovative process is a way to remain competitive in the changing business scenario. It is generally perceived by many enterprises that knowledge management is a technology for preserving and enhancing the knowledge base of an organization. But after a close observation at their organization, they may find many elements related to knowledge management are available in their organization itself. In reality, they need to make use of the elements of knowledge sources in their organization for creating a knowledge management system. The geography of the information is not like a map of a city. Information exists in a variety of domains. Some information is further away and harder to access. Some are closer and easily accessible. It is required to draw a map describing the geography of information, charting the zones or domains in which the knowledge resides. The overall challenge that many enterprises face today is identifying where the knowledge resides and leveraging it across to their organization. Despite heavy investment in information technology infrastructure business enterprises seem to think that they are fighting a losing battle. Business success lies in converting the information in their systems into knowledge. Now it has become important that one should use one's wisdom to convert information into knowledge. In the present scenario of the business world business enterprises seem to think that "Intellectual capital" and "Knowledge management" are the same. In knowledge management indicates a process whereas intellectual capital is an entity and asset.

Historical Background of Knowledge Management

The concept of knowledge management is not new. The focus and approach has been changing over some time. One may observe from the literature on the history of information and knowledge that the basic patterns of behavior remained constant over centuries concerning the role of information and knowledge. History provides many examples. Emperors in the olden days surrounded themselves with advisors who were scholars first and politicians second. Roman emperors like the ancient Greeks consulted educated priests to gain an insight into the possible future. Indian kings seemed to be concerned with the creation of knowledge among people by allocating places for schools and libraries. Julius Cesar used innovative construction methods and advancements in ammunitions to achieve military success. Napoleon made use of the advancements in artillery to defeat his opponents. Cornelius Vander Bilt had taken advantage of the advancements in railroad wheels and brakes to create a vast commercial empire. J.P. Morgan made a huge fortune and revolutionized the financial system by developing modern investment banking practices. Tipu Sultan used a war rocket in some of the battles he fought against the British soldiers in India. This earned universal fame as "innovator of the world's first war rocket". It was his victories against the British forces that ranked Tipu Sultan high among the few Indian rulers who have defeated the British.

In the preindustrial era agriculture was the basis of a nation's economy then the concentration was to learn more about farming. In the post-industrial era manufacturing became the basis of a nation's economy then the concentration was to learn more about manufacturing techniques. In the present globalization scenario, the focus is towards adopting innovation and process speed in business enterprises. The knowledge base in business organizations is an extension of knowledge-sharing systems. Business success lies in making use of knowledge-sharing systems for innovation. In today's business scenario the use of sophisticated knowledge base systems depends on the skill with which executives in business enterprises arrive at their findings from their analysis for framing strategy for their organization. Further business executives can draw insights from the large information stored in their systems. Conclusions drawn from these analyses will help the business executives to involve in innovation.

Trends in Management Concepts

One can find from the analysis of trends in management in every decade. New concepts have been emerging. The moment it emerges, it is considered as "next big thing" or "next important concept". In the 1950s "Brainstorming" concept has become popular. It was considered to be a very important factor in involving the employees in business enterprises to generate new ideas. In the 1960s and 1970s sensitivity groups have played an important role in business enterprises. The group leaders of this group have been considered to be "Gurus". They used to lead group managers. Then it was practice, "Gurus" would make brief opening remarks and they would wait for a response from the group managers. Then the "Gurus" would facilitate them to express and try to clarify. It was a hope that "Inner Manager" would emerge. It was expected that more research would follow in their deliberations. The era '80s was considered as the age of quality management. During this period quality control, quality circles, six sigma, and other related approaches were followed for enhancing workers' performance. The quality-related approaches have been continuing for a long time. In the recent past, the need for knowledge management has been felt very much by globalization. In the present era, the concept of " Open Innovation" is becoming the ultimate goal of enterprises to face the complex global economy.

OBJECTIVES OF THIS CHAPTER

The interdisciplinary development process is becoming important because no science in itself answers all the prerequisites that exist in an implementation expanding field. This is true of the sciences at large as well as the perspectives of the particular application. The concepts such as open innovation, virtual reality, knowledge harvesting, social media, and business process reengineering facilitate design models in addressing the business issues. This chapter consists of explaining the significant features of the above concepts and relates the case illustrations in the context of the above concepts.

Invention Innovation and Creativity

The terms invention and innovation are used interchangeably. These are separate and distinct concepts. Invention means designing and creating something which has never been modeled before. The classic examples are the invention of the light bulb by Thomas Edison, and the invention of telephones by Alexander Graham Bell. Louis Pasteur came up with vaccines. Innovation deals with bringing in new methods and ideas resulting in required changes in an enterprise. In the present business context, innovation is taking interesting ideas and transforming, them into usable business solutions (Erbe-2014).

Creativity can be defined as the discovery of a new idea or connection. Many ideas already exist somewhere in the world. Creativity is to identify these ideas and connect them in a new way. But innovation is much more than just identifying and connecting these creative ideas. It is about strategy and action bringing value to the enterprise through the implementation of these creative and strategic ideas. Innovation can therefore be interpreted as the profitable implementation of strategic creativity (Mathur, Singh & Ashutosh,2013).

History of Innovation

Innovation has always been part of mankind. Since the discovery of fire by rubbing two stones together, human beings have been innovating. Innovation is probably the oldest known process. In other words, innovation is an extension of a person's creativity. Human beings have been using their inner skills to create many new things to help mankind.

Open Innovation

Shortened business cycles and rapid technological changes are forcing organizations to adopt open innovation concepts for their business activities. The open innovation concept mainly stresses making use of external power by companies for their innovations. Some companies are even ready to open up their ideas and technologies to be used by other companies and even competitors. If one closely observes within one's organization, they can find brainpower for the innovation already available in their organization. Experience has shown that human-centered resources are the most valuable asset for any organization. Some studies have indicated that only a small portion of corporate knowledge is in shareable form. The majority is in their employees' brains and it is not shareable form. Business enterprises should provide opportunities to their human-centered assets for applying the concept of open innovation for their business activities.

If enterprises expect their employee to come up with ideas that would work, the employees need to know the business problems faced by their organization. It is the practice of many enterprises that their organization's information is considered important and is also kept as secret. It is meant for the management view only. The environment in enterprises must be friendly instead of closed. Then only the employees will associate themselves with their organization. This would facilitate them to integrate creativity in their approach in open innovation initiatives. It may be observed executives in enterprises are under the impression that open innovation is associated with new products, new technology, and research development activity. This view is too narrow in the present business scenario. Open innovation can be applied broadly across all aspects of an enterprise such as existing products, services, business processes, and business models (Rangaraju & Kennedy, 2013).

Concept of Virtual Reality

The concept of virtual reality facilitates in visualizing new ideas for business purposes. The element constituting virtual reality are audio voice, graphics, images, sound, and motion sensing. These elements along with numerical and textual data facilitate the creation of real-time simulation. Business enterprises have choices to evaluate their new ideas by making use of the concept of virtual reality. Simulated outputs resulting from virtual reality application programs help to visualize the proposed ideas of business enterprises. These outputs help to visualize hypothetical cases in business and interact with the applications developed under the virtual reality concept. It may be noted that the concept of multimedia is required in virtual reality applications. The concept of virtual reality is the seed of innovation for developing business models.

Virtual Reality

Virtual reality refers to the presentation of system-generated data made available in such a way that those who use it perceive the information at their disposal as having similar or enhanced characteristics in business models. The line dividing simulated tasks and their real-world counterparts is very thin. The ability to get real-world perceptions interactively through computer systems explains the interest associated with three-dimensional graphics in virtual reality. The synergy between real and simulated facts yields real effectiveness. It will be more effective if the system and its artifacts are to be active rather than a passive display. The essential element of virtual reality is that interactive simulation with navigation among widely scattered heterogeneous databases. This results in logical, numerical processing and a wide range of visualization functions. The virtual reality concept helps to unlock innovative thinking in enterprises for carrying out incremental and radical innovation in their organization. The virtual reality concept helps enterprises to accomplish their ambitious goals with innovation improvements initiatives. The new initiatives help to generate alternative ideas by taking inputs from different sources and structuring them through virtual reality applications. The virtual reality concept will increase the chances of successfully diffusing knowledge, technology, and process. It will provide scope for innovation to emerge (Linowes, 2015).

Real-Time Simulation Approach

The data relating to enterprises' performance as well as market reactions to their products are available in their database. The data in their databases are to be analyzed in understanding the patterns of change. Accordingly, the management's action is to be planned in response to the changes in the market for their products. Interactive modeling is better than the traditional business analysis process. The technology they would prefer helps to produce better products at lower costs and assists in getting them to the market quicker, reducing the time to market. Both require real-time thinking which is possible through modeling and feature-based simulation. Such an approach makes it possible to understand the variable-driven design of complex products. Real-time simulation and visualization are gaining the competitive benefits they provide. The components required for this type of venture are software and hardware that integrate modeling and interpretation. Further, it facilitates steady operational testing over a computer system. Enterprises who are ready to learn and adapt the real-time simulation approach can achieve their goals in the market for their products (Semalstieg & Holler, 2016).

Knowledge Harvesting

The creation of knowledge management about one's organization is not given much importance by an enterprise. Most of the top management in organizations are under the impression that these systems will be misused by their employees. Some of the organizations fear that there is every likelihood hood of their employees after updating their knowledge from their system they may leave their organization to better their prospects. It would be better for the top management in an organization need to be open and transparent for creating knowledge management systems. This approach will help employees to make use of the knowledge management systems. By making use of these systems, employees will be able to create a knowledge harvesting system. Knowledge harvesting system will facilitate them to create open innovation environment. The involvement of employees in open innovation environment makes them take professional pride and feel they are the backbone of their organization.

Concept of Knowledge Harvesting

In agriculture, the cultivable land is made use of growing a crop. Depending on the season a particular type of crop is grown in the same land. Manure is used to increase the output of the crop from the cultivable land. The cultivable land remains the same. The agriculture output from the same land depends on the season and manure used.

Similarly, the knowledge harvesting system is similar to agricultural land in an organization. Data and information from the knowledge management are made use depending on the wisdom of each employee. This approach is known as the knowledge harvesting initiative. The method followed by each employee inferring and interpreting the information varies depending on his/her experience and business knowledge. This can be compared to using a different type of manure for the different types of crop output from a cultivable land. A group of employees can form as a team and think jointly to address a problem/issue or form a strategy. This will facilitate them to think innovatively. This innovative thinking leads to creating a knowledge harvesting system for open innovation initiatives (Olia S & Yestrom, 2016).

Comparison of Knowledge Harvesting System and Agricultural Harvesting

Information is the main base in knowledge harvesting. Cultivable land is the main base in agricultural harvesting. Knowledge and wisdom are important elements in knowledge harvesting. They can be considered as an equal and to manure. Manure and the latest cultivation techniques play an important role in agricultural harvesting.

Codification of knowledge

It may be interesting to note that a major portion of corporate knowledge is in employees' brains and documents. They are not easily shareable. The knowledge harvesting process is needed for making it shareable. The output of knowledge harvesting is a codification of human-centered assets.

Social Media

Social media has become a powerful persuasive tool for staying in the business. Social media is the collective of online communication channels dedicated to community-based input for collaboration. Social media tools empower all the stakeholders in the different sectors to benefit from one another. Various functions in a sector could integrate most of the activities within social media programs. Sectors referred here are business, education, health care, government, and non-government organizations. The activities cover research, marketing, product design, and consultancy services. Forums and message boards on social media channels facilitate sharing knowledge. Social media use web-based technology to quickly disseminate knowledge and information to a large number of users. Facebook, Twitter, and other related social networking sites are collectively referred to as social media (Ragaghavendra Rao N, 2017).

Business Process Re-Engineering

The essence of business process re-engineering is the fundamental rethinking and radical redesign of business processes in organizations. Further, it emphasizes giving the decision-making power to employees and teams at the workplace. This concept is more apt for developing business models in an open innovation initiative (Vysas, 2014).

Case Illustration related to Virtual Reality

An Indian-based Roa Motor Bikes Limited has been manufacturing motorbikes for Indian and global markets. They have been in the market for over two decades. Their market share has been encouraging. Due to globalization policy followed by many countries the global market is now open to many players across the globe. Roa Motor Bikes Limited has started losing hold on the market due to globalization. Roa Motor Bikes Limited has decided to develop new methods and business processes in the product design and marketing of their bikes.

They have decided to hire the services of domain experts who have rich experience in developing the product design and business process in the global motorbikes sector. They have identified the domain experts who live in France and Korea. It has been agreed among them that the domain experts and their team members would operate from their respective countries. Their role is to design the motorbikes models and suggest the components with ISO standards required for the models suggested by them. The domain experts are expected to guide the employees of Roa Motor Bikes Limited in India for the implementation of the design of the bikes given by them.

Further, the vendors who would supply the components as per the ISO standards would be given access to the bills of materials module for knowing the number of materials and date of supply by them. Engineering design of components would be made available through the system wherever it is needed. It has been decided to make use of the advanced concepts in information and collaborative technologies for developing their models.

Macro-Level Design for Engineering Design and Bill of Materials

Software such as CAD/CAM, multimedia, and virtual reality are required to create a motorbike model for the design and bill of materials module. The hardware and software resources from India are made available to domain experts. The domain experts have taken advantage of time differences in the respective countries. The time differences enabled minimizing of capital expenditure and operational expenses through cloud computing.

Multimedia concepts are applied in the conceptual design of a motorbike. A motorbike for the global market is simulated by domain experts in a virtual reality environment. A group of evaluators in the domain expert's team will test the functionalities and features of the simulated motorbike. Once the simulated motorbike meets the product specification, the next step will be to design the bike by using CAD/CAM software. The enormous competitive pressure in the motorbike sector can get most engineering designs and the requirements of components for less turnaround time from domain experts from any part of the world by making use of the cloud computing concepts.

Virtual Reality in Cloud Computing Environment

The domain experts have developed a model that considers real-world requirements for which parameters are created based on their requirements. A simulated version of a motorbike has been designed, and experiments have been carried out in the computer systems in the cloud computing environment. The domain expert's team members have immersed themselves in every aspect of design and testing in front of a large screen of a computer which has given a sense of actually testing a motorbike in a real-world situation. The concept of virtual reality has helped them to look from the real-world situation. The Cloud computing environment has made it possible for domain experts to make use of the virtual reality concept.

Vendors Role in the Business Model

The domain experts made use of computer-aided design (CAD) software designing proto-type components needed for the proposed motorbike model. The drawings of these components generated by using CAD software are made available to the vendors by giving access to the bills of materials in the module of the ROA Motor Bikes Limited system.

Social Media and Conceptual Design Method

The domain experts felt that it would be better to interact with young automobile engineers in their respective countries who have a passion to do something different. The domain experts have created a site in the social media channel exclusively for young automobile engineers. They have been invited to express their views and suggestions on the existing motorbike models manufactured by ROA Motor Bikes Limited in the social media site created exclusively for them. The views and suggestions discussed by them among themselves are posted on social media sites. The domain experts downloaded the postings from the social media site and stored them in the database created in the cloud computing environment by ROA Motor Bikes Limited. The domain experts have analyzed and considered the feasible features from the above data. They have designed a motorbike from their professional experience along with the feasible features suggested by the young automobile engineers. Their design has taken care of real-world requirements. A simulated version of a motorbike has been tested and experiments have been carried on the computer systems. The domain expert team members have immersed themselves in every aspect of design and testing. Working in front of a large screen of a computer system has given me a sense of being testing a bike in real-world perception. The concept of virtual reality has helped them to look from the real-world situation.

Later the domain experts have posted an invitation on the social media site inviting the young automobile engineers to the motorbike created under virtual reality concept at their office. Some of them have tested the motorbike on the large screen of a computer system at the domain expert's office. This testing has given them a sense of being riding a motorbike in the real world.

This experience induced them to interact with their friends. Further, they persuaded them to visit the domain expert's office to experience themselves. Many more automobile engineers have tested the simulated bike. They have also given their feedback to the domain experts. Some fine-tuning has been carried out based on their feedback. After this, the final design of the motorbike has been given to ROA Motor Bikes Limited. Similar types of testing by automobile engineers have taken place in India before the design has been frozen. It may be noted that the resources of Roa Motor Bikes Limited have been made use of by the domain experts from their respective countries. The use of software such as CAD/CAM, Multimedia, and virtual reality has become possible because of the cloud computing environment. An exclusive social media site created for the young automobile engineers has helped the domain experts to think in an innovative way (Zimmerman J & Deborg N G, 2014).

Developing a New Product Under Open Innovation Approach

ROA Motor Bikes Limited model proves that a new product can be jointly designed by domain experts in a global virtual team through a process of continuous exchange of ideas between stakeholders dispersed across the globe. This process helps in generating alternative ideas by taking inputs from different sources and structuring them through virtual reality applications. This model provides an idea for the creation of a global open innovation model. Further, it helps to organize the workflow by visualizing the various phases of the development of a motorbike. Customers' tastes are becoming more homogeneous around the globe. Customer tastes are becoming more homogeneous. Consequently Roa Motor Bikes Limited can provide a significantly good motorbike through the economies of scale with common design. Roa Motor Bikes model can increase the chances of successfully diffusing knowledge, technology, and process. Advanced telecommunications technologies have drastically changed business operations, providing new services and creating an interconnected worldwide community (Goel, 2016).

Observation Related to Case Illustration on Virtual Reality

Till recently the standard model of innovation has been a linear process from research through design, development, and then manufacturing. In the case of the Roa Motor Bikes model, many of these processes are carried out concurrently and collaborating through the concepts of virtual reality, cloud computing, and the software tools such as CAD/CAM. The management of Roa Motor Bikes Limited has hired the services of domain experts from France and Korea. The employees of Roa Motor Bikes Limited and domain experts with their team members have formed a virtual team to develop the Roa Motor Bikes model. It is interesting to note that domain experts could involve the young automobile engineers in their respective countries for testing the conceptual motorbike model on the computer system. Social media and the concept of virtual reality facilitated their open innovation approach. Another important aspect of this approach is making the vendors a part of the core team for the development of motorbikes models.

In today's knowledge-rich development, business enterprises can no longer afford to rely entirely on their ideas to advance their business, nor can they restrict their innovations to a single path to market. As a result, the traditional model for innovation which has been largely internally focused or a "closed one" has become obsolete. Emerging in its place is a new paradigm "Open Innovation" (Wadhwa, & Harper,2015). This strategically leverages internal and external sources of an idea take them to market through multiple paths. Global enterprises can take advantage of unique knowledge and resource wherever they are located. Information and communication technology has increased virtualization in business activities and ways of working. The term 'virtual' is now appearing in many forms. Roa Motor Bikes model gives an overview of adopting an open innovation approach in designing and developing new products by business enterprises. Roa Motor Bikes Limited has proved that the concept of virtual organization facilitates to share the common resources for computing power and accessing data across the globe.

Case Illustration Related to Knowledge Harvesting

Coimbatore is a textile town in South India. This town is known as Manchester of South India. There are many textile units in this town producing yarn, cloth, and dress materials. The first generation of people in this town has either started their units after getting a formal training or inherited the textile units. Most of them have basic education only. They have started their units with small capital. Most of the units were established in the middle of the last century. It was because of the favorable market conditions; many units made profits and expanded their business activities. Most of the units have created a brand image for their textile products. The people who start a textile unit is known as mill owner. Even though many of them have more than one textile unit, still they are known as mill owners. Generally, they are never referred to as industrialists.

3 G textile mill was started in the mid-1950s by a textile mill owner. He has rich experience and good knowledge about the textile business. He has basic schooling only. His interest and passion for the textile business have helped him to create a name for his textile products. He has trained a group of employees for his business. They are loyal to him. They take pride in being associated with him for a long period. Most of them have either formal or no basic education. The mill owner alone thinks of business strategies. He never involves the group trained by him for designing business strategies. He expects them to carry out his instructions only.

Mill Owner's Method of Working

Cotton is a very important raw material for manufacturing yarn. Cloth material is manufactured based on the quality of yarn used. The selection of cotton mix is an important element for the production of yarn. He updates himself with the latest information about technical aspects and markets for his textile business. He is confident of himself because of his rich experience in the technical process of manufacturing yarn and cloth material.

The mill owner has identified a large room in his mill's premises for selecting cotton for the production of yarn. Samples of cotton are brought by the different cotton merchants and kept on a big table in the room. Brief details of sample cotton are kept along with it. The details mostly cover the information about the year of production name of the country type of cotton has been grown along with the rate of cotton per bale. The mill owner makes use of his both hands for testing the strength of the cotton. He can select the cotton from his manual method. He does not believe in using any equipment for testing and selecting the cotton for the production of yearning. Further, he decides the mix of cotton from his experience. His decision is based on the percentage of imported cotton to be mixed with the cotton produced in India. While mentally he thinks of the mixture of the cotton par alley he visualizes the color of dyes to be used. He also works out mentally the cost of yarn per spindle. He also decides the price at which the yarn is to be sold. While deciding the type of cloth is to be produced, he keeps in mind the prospective customers' tastes and trends in the market. He also interacts with the suppliers and makes inquiries about the welfare of their families. He feels that this interaction with them is required for maintaining a good relationship with the suppliers. Later he gives instructions to his support staff for placing the orders. He has been following the above procedure from the day he started his business activities.

The next generation from his family is not interested in the management of the mills. They prefer to pursue their professional interests. He has not forced his sons to take over the management of the mills. He has realized that he did not make effects to create interest among his sons for the textile business. Further, he felt bad that he did not give the opportunities to his loyal staff for involving the decision process. He did not encourage them to express their views and strategic planning for the business. He decided to share his concerns with his granddaughter who has got a master's degree in computer science. His granddaughter felt it would be advisable to help her grandfather in the business. She started going along with her grandfather to their textile mill daily. She observed that her grandfather is involved in every activity in the mills. Everyone takes instructions from him. Some of them are not clear about technical and business processes.

She has decided with the consultation of the grandfather to create a database. Grandfather has explained every aspect of the business. He also explained how he makes use of knowledge and experience in the areas of production of textile products, marketing, pricing, and costing.

Based on the inputs provided by her grandfather, she created a database. This database mainly contains the procedures followed by him. After analyzing his procedures, she has designed another database with different modules. Various modules contain all the required information relating to cotton, supplier, types of dyes, tastes of customers, market trends, and cost. This database provides the selection process of cotton, the color combination of dyes. Production planning details of yarn and cloth are also stored. This database is known as the textile knowledge harvesting system. This knowledge harvesting system facilitates their employees to learn the process of selection of cotton and mix of cotton. Further, it helps to decide the mix of yarn for the production of cloth material. She has been interacting with her grandfather for guidance. She added many features that would be of use for their business.

She has started conducting orientation courses for employees who have evinced in making use of the textile knowledge harvesting system. She also encouraged them to provide their ideas for fine-tuning the knowledge harvesting system. They are also allowed to think differently. They can also suggest changes in the business process of the textile business.

Observation Related to Case Illustration on Knowledge Harvesting

The existing employees with took interest in making use of the knowledge harvesting system have retired from the organization. The granddaughter has started recruiting young talents with experience to assist her in business activities. She encourages every member of her team to make use of the knowledge harvesting system created by her. She has weekly meetings with them. She is open to suggestions from them. In one of the meetings a group of young executives who joined the textile mill recently, have expressed to suggest an innovative way for designing textile products. They have indicated that the textile mill is not making use of multimedia concepts in the design of a cloth and dress material. They are given the freedom to design the textile mill products with their ideas. They have designed samples with various color combinations with multimedia concepts. They have invited selected priority customers to their office during office hours to view the design on the computer screen at their office. Some of the customers have expressed their views and gave suggestions to the design shown to them. The executives have taken note of their views and suggestions. These inputs are discussed with the granddaughter. After analyzing the inputs they have decided to carry out the changes wherever is feasible. These interactions helped them to know the latest tastes of the group of customers. This helped them to redesign their products. The sale of their products is likely to increase. Open innovation initiative with the knowledge harvesting system approach by the young executives has widened their knowledge in designing textile products. Their talents al

Case Illustration Related to Social Media

A group of senior citizens in India who had a successful career in the manufacturing, finance, and information technology sectors has created social media sites for sharing their professional experience and their thoughts related to various aspects of economic activity in India. They have rich experience in their profession.

Their interactions on their social media site have led them to make use of their professional knowledge for the benefit of small-scale units. From their experience, they know that many small-scale units in India cannot afford in engaging the services of consultancy firms for their advice. Senior citizens felt they are financially well off. They can venture into offering their services to small-scale units.

They have created business guidance software. Their software tool provides technical guidance in the area of production. They have confined themselves to the sectors such as metallurgy, electrical, and automobile components. They have included the costing and marketing aspects of the above sectors. Anything given free has no value. They have decided to collect bare minimum charges for their efforts.

They have created an exclusive social media site for marketing their business guidance software (Golden M, 2011). Responses to their efforts are encouraging. Even some units hired their services also for consultation in the production process. Their interactions with the owners of the small-scale units provided an opportunity to get new ideas in the production process. This has resulted in designing a new innovative production process in the sectors they are consulted. At the request of small-scale industrial units senior citizens, they have given video lectures on the benefits of their employees in the areas such as communication skills, team building, and innovation (Bencsika,2017).

Observation Related to Case Illustration on Social Media

It is interesting to note that the enthusiasm of senior citizens has helped them to form a group. They have created a social media site for sharing their thoughts. This has provided them a scope to open innovation initiative thinking. They have made use of their rich knowledge and experience for the benefit of small-scale units (Buck, 2012). They can create an impact on the small-scale industrial sector through social media sites.

Case illustration Related to Business Process Re-engineering

An automobile manufacturer in India initially was manufacturing all the components required for the production of their cars. Due to the growth of their business and industrial activities, the demand for passenger cars has been in increased. The management of the automobile manufacturer has decided some of the components required for their cars are to be outsourced. The automobile manufacturer has identified the small-scale units that have the required infrastructure and technical knowledge to manufacturer the components as per their specification for their cars. The small-scale units have agreed to produce the components provided they are assured by the automobile manufacturer that later would provide the procurement schedule and delivery dates. Further, the small-scale units have to send delivery receipts along with the components sent to the automobile manufacturer. An invoice for the supplies made during a calendar month would be sent to the automobile manufacturer on the first day of the succeeding month for the payment. The procedure at the automobile manufacturer is to receive the components as per the delivery receipts and record them in the materials inward register. The components will be tested for quality by the quality inspection department. The components approved by the quality inspection department are taken into stock. The rejected components with the rejection slips are given to the suppliers at the end of the month. Due to various components received from the different suppliers, the quality inspection department use to take their time for quality inspection and deciding about the approved quantity

Most of the small-scale units are solely dependent on the automobile unit for the payments towards their supplies made to them. The automobile manufacturer pays for the components approved by their quality inspection department. Small scale units would find it very difficult to manage their finance. It is because the amounts received by them less than their invoice amount. This has resulted in some small-scale units finding it extremely difficult to maintain their production schedule. Consequent to this the automobile manufacturer's production of their passenger is affected. There used to be frequent meetings between the purchasing department of the automobile manufacturer and the owners of the small-scale units. There has not been a concrete outcome from these meetings.

A Solution to the Above Case Illustration:

A group of executives from the departments of purchase, production, quality inspection, and finance at the automobile manufacturer formed as a core team to study and find a solution for receiving the components as per their standard. Further, they wanted to find a way that the small scale units would not struggle for the flow of money for their business.`

They have discussed among themselves the various aspects related to the issue. After a lot of deliberations, they have decided to change the procedure followed by them in their company. They have agreed to create a separate group in the quality inspection department to test the quality of the components received from the small-scale units. They need to send the accepted quantity

information through e-mail to the concerned small-scale unit. The small-scale unit could raise an invoice for the accepted quantity based on the e-mail advice. The quality inspection department would send goods accepted notes to the finance department. This will be a printed form. The idea behind a printed form is to help the finance department to relate with the copy of invoice received by them. In this process, the small-scale units have an option either to rectify the rejected components or to produce the additional components. This procedure has solved the issue of the small-scale units. Further, it has helped the automobile manufacturer to solve the bottlenecks in their production schedule (Tsai, 2013).

The deliberations among the stake at the automobile manufacturer have resulted in acceptable and working solutions for both parties. The automobile manufacturer can maintain their production schedule. Small scale units have also succeeded in managing their finance and also improved their quality procedures.

FUTURE RESEARCH DIRECTIONS

In the present globalization scenario, interdisciplinary concepts play an important role in developing business models. The concepts such as business intelligence with the open innovation approach can simulate enterprises in developing business models in addressing business issues. Many concepts are emerging in the disciplines of management and information and communication technology. One needs to identify the concepts that are useful in designing and developing the business models for addressing the business issues of an enterprise (King & Lakhani, 2013). There is also good scope for making use of the concepts such as artificial intelligence, machine learning, and data science for designing and developing business models for addressing the business issues (Christensen C M, Bartman T, Vanbelver, 2016).

CONCLUSION

Case illustrations discussed in this chapter provide insight into the organizations in addressing the business issues. Involving employees and making use of an interdisciplinary approach facilitated the organizations to find solutions for their business issues. Another important point is to be noted is that employees should be provided with opportunities to understand the cross-functional areas in their organization. This will facilitate them in understanding the issues faced by their organization. It will help them in suggesting solutions to the issues in their organization. Further, it will lead to an open innovation initiative for handling difficult situations. In a rapidly changing competitive environment for products and services quickly become obsolete. Static competitive positions are rapidly overtaken. Open innovation management makes an organization respondconsistently to the changing market scenario.

REFERENCES

Bencsika. (2017). *Knowledge Management Initiatives and Strategies in Small and Medium Enterprises*. IGI Global.

Buck. (2012). *The Talent Wave*. London: Kogan Page.

Christensen, C. M., Bartman, T., & Vanbelver, D. (2016, September). The Hard Truth About Business Model. *MIT Sloan Management Review*.

Erbe. (2014). *Approaches to Managing Organizational Diversity and Innovation*. Global.IGI

Goel. (2016). *Product Innovation through Management and Social Media Strategies*. IGI Global.

Golden, M. (2011). *Social Media Strategies for Professionals and Their Firms*. Wiley and Sons.

King & Lakhani. (2013). Using Open Innovation to Identify the Best Ideas. *MIT Sloan Management Review*.

Linowes. (2015). *Virtual Reality Projects*. Packt.

Mathur, Singh, & Ashutosh. (2013). *Creating Value through Innovation*. Shree Publishers and Distributors.

Olia, S., & Yestrom, A. (2016). An Innovation into the Role of Open Innovation Collaboration Managers. *R & D Management*.

Raghavendra Rao, N. (2017). *Social Media Listening and Monitoring for Business Applications*. IGI Global.

Rangaraju & Kennedy. (2013). *Innovation in Management –Challenges and Opportunities in the Next Decade*. Allied Publishers Private Limited.

Semalstieg & Holler. (2016). *Augmented Virtual Reality*. IGI Global.

Tsai. (2013). *Information Technology and Business Process Re-Engineering*. Praeger.

Vysas. (2014). *Business Process Transformation*. Regal Publishers.

Wadhwa & Harper. (2015). *Technology, Innovation, and Enterprise Transformation*. IGI Global.

Zimmerman, J., & Deborg, N. G. (2014). *Social Media All-in-One for Dummies*. Wiley India Private Limited.

KEY TERMS AND DEFINITIONS

Business Process Re-Engineering: The essence of business process re-engineering is the fundamental rethinking and radical redesign of business processes in organizations.

Knowledge Harvesting: Data and information from the acknowledgment system are made use of depending on the wisdom of each employee. This approach is known as knowledge harvesting.

Knowledge Management: This involves collecting, categorizing, and disseminating knowledge.

Innovation: Innovation deals with bringing in new methods and ideas resulting in required changes in an enterprise.

Social Media: It uses web-based technology to quickly disseminate knowledge and information to a large number of users.

Virtual Reality: Virtual reality provides an opportunity to simulate the tasks for the creation of their real-world counterparts.

Chapter 12
Product Innovation and Personalization via Social Media:
Learnings From the Phenomenal Success of BYJUs

Rajiv Ranjan
Alliance University, India

ABSTRACT

Innovation of products continually, customization, and personalization are the strategies to gain sustainable competitive advantage for companies operating in Industry 4.0 era. Corporations tend to turn to the new social media for access to customer data. How much big data in terms of variety, veracity, velocity, and volume the corporation has determines its prediction architecture and hence customer satisfaction. This is reflected both in terms of inflecting revenues as well as investment from the venture capitalists (VCs), who then see great potential in the business, whether it be a start-up, an established organization, or its spin-off. This chapter explains this new management strategy for corporate sustainability through application of social media to acquire personal consumer and customer data. This is to devise customised products, personalize experience, and innovate for the two. The chapter takes exceptional growth story of BYJU's an educational technology company, as an example to elucidate the theory, concepts, and ideas discussed.

DOI: 10.4018/978-1-7998-7793-6.ch012

Copyright © 2022, IGI Global. Copying or distributing in print or electronic forms without written permission of IGI Global is prohibited.

INTRODUCTION

This chapter on management strategies for sustainability focusses on two themes of technological product innovation and utilizing new media for personalization and product customization in Industry 4.0. From the historical and disciplinary lens of strategic management as an academic discipline and a field of practice in the business world, acquiring resources, keeping in control the internal and the external environment through appropriate Human Resource policies, marketing and advertising strategies, mergers, acquisitions and partnerships, ensure flow of finances through both bootstrapping and Venture Capital funds in case of start-ups and debt and equities in case of established organizations and finally upkeeping with and leading technological change are some of the ways in which sustainable competitive advantage can be achieved (Barney, 1991). While all these are important, this chapter focusses on the two themes of customized product innovation and personalization via the use of social media.

These two themes of technological innovation and personalization are discussed keeping in mind the micro and macro foundations of strategy and the firm's internal as well as the external environment. Resource-based view, Knowledge-based view, Behavioural strategy, Transaction cost economics, Agency theory, Industrial organization, Institutional approach and Entrepreneurship-based approach (Guerras-Martín, Madhok, & Montoro-Sánchez, 2014) are the lenses through which these themes are discussed to give a theoretically rooted understanding of the concept to the reader. To provide contemporary evidence and a deep dive into empiricism the case of educational technology firm BYJU'S in the Indian context is utilized as a case example to illustrate the theory, concepts and ideas discussed. This way the chapter is a rich blend of classic theories, contemporary evidence and new knowledge and insights brought by the author through the empirical evidences and their discussion.

The example of the phenomenal growth story of BYJU'S as a case is used for analysis to discuss upon the facets of strategies for sustainability, innovation for new knowledge creation and personalized products and services creation. BYJU'S is an exceptional case of meritocratic and phenomenal rise of a company in the educational technology industry in particular and Indian start-up space in general. What strategies they adopted to garner initial resources and seed funds, how they utilized that to appeal to the customers in the K-12 education and retain them before diversifying across levels vertically and spreading across streams horizontally. How they kept themselves ahead with the emergent competition both with entering of technically and far more academically networked competitors from the global market and local players with deeper expertise in certain segments? These are some of the questions which can help enlighten the reader especially on the theme of how companies through technological advancement and personalized product and service offerings gain advantage in contemporary 21st century.

BACKGROUND

Managing Sustainable Competitive Advantage in Technology Advanced 21st Century

Strategy making and implementation especially in the context of business have always been the managerial practice of maintaining sustainability and competitive advantage (Freedman, 2015). Innovation (Kline & Rosenberg, 2010) for new knowledge creation (Nonaka & Toyama, 2015), maintaining its secrecy through obtaining Intellectual Property Rights and Patents (Granstrand, 1999) have always been a key driver of sustainable competitive advantage (Barney, 1991). Technological advancements, keeping pace with the change and leading the change is another important driver for companies and businesses which have turned out to be successful in their respective markets, sectors and segments (Porter, 1985).

Strategy making is not only about what ones chooses to do but it is also about what one chooses to not get into (Porter, 1996). It is about defining the boundaries within which the firm or business will operate. This kind of a boundary setting gives clarity on what the firm or business would like to achieve and henceforth facilitates planning. The implementation of the plan in a structured manner with a feedback loop attached to the set goals acts as a yardstick for the strategy process.

In the 21st century especially two factors and their utilization for gaining competitive advantage by firms are very crucial viz., social media to gain personalized information and moving into a digital world from a physical world in a seemingly fast-paced manner.

Recent Fast Paced Technological Advancements: The Emergence of New Media

The technological advancement in the past two to three decades has been so fast paced that companies which has either kept abreast with this change or led this change are the ones which are ruling the roost in terms of financial gains and are at the top of the charts in any business rankings be it the elite Forbes list, Fortune 500 or Economic Times Ranking and so on. This includes companies like Facebook, Google, Microsoft, Amazon, Tesla etc. to name a few.

Data is the new oil (Humby, 2006) in the 21st century when transition has already to Fourth Industrial Revolution (Lee et. Al., 2018) or Industry 4.0. has already taken place. With personalized data readily available to companies and firms, 'personalized products and services' is the new normal. It has its own set of advantages and disadvantages. Say for example, YouTube's feature of suggesting personalised songs to individuals based on their song listening history is an example and it is highly likely that most individuals would prefer this feature, given it has a choice option as well.

Companies which have invested heavily on technology and have left no stone unturned to introduce best in-class technology features in their products or their service offerings are the ones in the current era which have rode the competition in the last two decades. As, newer generation i.e. Generation Z have become and are becoming more tech-savvy, living fast-paced lives, their screen time on mobile devices have increased and their lives have become more virtual than real. Companies in the name of personalization are also adopting strategies for their competitive advantage whose ethical motives can be questionable (Zuboff, 2019).

The Strategy to Succeed for Corporations in the Personalization Race During Industry 4.0. Era

The core to personalized and customized product development and innovation (Bruns & Stalker, 1961) is building up of a prediction architecture for which a company or corporation needs a database and access to consumer and customer data on a regular basis. It is how big data the corporation has and how deep the prediction architecture is determines its economic and financial success in the Industry 4.0. which is also called as an era of "Surveillance Capitalism" (Zuboff, 2019). The big data characteristics are determined by its volume, variety, velocity and veracity. The prediction architecture characteristics can be determined by the quality of modelling and learning models both supervised and unsupervised.

The prediction architecture has three facets: the data extraction architecture, the data modelling architecture and finally the data execution architecture. The first takes us to the issues of data privacy (Ranjan & Saket, 2017), which has started being regulated. Corporations run the risk of getting entangled into legal issues if they do not frame their privacy policies well and hence need to hire experts on these issues as part of their core team.

The creation of an online data extraction architecture seems to be an easy task but is not so. Companies with deep technology expertise, deeper technology architecture, search engines like Google, Facebook, Microsoft etc. are too far ahead in this game and other companies have to depend on them but one has to understand that finally it is the trust factor that counts in customer acquisition, retention, satisfaction and delight. Hence, small companies must try and create a twin strategy of operating in the online mode, joining global networks and following global benchmarks in terms of product quality and services but in terms of customer acquisition there strategy must be a mixed-mode i.e. digital and offline both because that is where global companies still struggle. Small-scale start-ups can add a major value to their local communities by adopting this kind of an approach.

CONNECTING THE DOTS: LEARNING FROM THE PHENOMENAL RISE OF BYJU'S

BYJU'S[1] has been a phenomenal case of meritocratic rise of a company from scratch to a valuation of $16.5 billion in a small period of ten years. There have been myriad of reasons for BYJU'S success like venturing into right markets at the right time, mergers and/or acquisitions with top players in various sub-domains, their ability to garner funding support from top funders, their strategy of subscription based selling especially for the K-12 market, the emergence of COVID-19[2] at the time when they were at the tipping point of their technological advancement for various markets among other host of factors.

The co-founder of BYJU'S, Byju Raveendran have been forthright in acknowledging the contributions of his wife, Divya Gokulnath for her contributions in building the start-up who also is an equal partner in the enterprise (Holla & Mitra, 2020) in terms of participation and belonginess. This is shying away from the false social categories in terms of gender.

BYJU'S success pitted against a host of competitors both from the international market like Coursera, edX, Udemy, Khan Academy etc. and from the local market like Unacademy, upGrad, Vedantu, Toppr, Simplilearn etc. can give insight into the strategy for the 21st century for the education technology industry in particular (Sahu & Abhishek, 2018) but the chapter would written with a generalist orientation taking this case in point. It will not be restricted to a particular industry, i.e. Education Technology.

"Who is an entrepreneur?" is a wrong question (Gartner, 1988), but a question worth asking (Carland & Carland, 1988) especially in the context of Byju Raveendran and Divya Gokulnath of BYJU'S i.e. Think and Learn India Pvt Ltd. It is the passion and an attitude to bring about change that has helped him rise from scratch to set up the education technology company of any start-up entrepreneur's dream, which not only joined the Unicorn club (Anupam, 2018) but have phenomenally grown in the COVID19 period which has given boost to the educational technology market and industry. It is the never say dying attitude of the person, built through habitual practice and then complemented by acquisition of skills and knowledge that has led to this meritocratic rise. How he kept identifying the emerging new business opportunities and connecting the dots (Baron, 2006), this is key to his entrepreneurial strategy and a very important question to ask and understand.

Innovation, personalization, customization has been the mantra for success and with more customer base this ability further enhances and it acts as a feedback loop. BYJU's has brought about technology innovation which helps visualization through animation and facilitates text reading through audio conversion. It is called to be the "Mouse House" of education (Tripathy & Devarapalli, 2021) i.e. one aspect of its innovation is adding entertainment and removing drudgery from learning experiences. It has also made learning self-paced and personalized in line with educational principle, theories, philosophies and recommendations (Sruthi & Mukherjee, 2020). BYJU'S makes easy availability of knowledge and its accessibility at the doorstep just at the click of a mouse without going through the rigorous process of school and college search makes it a popular platform (Sinha & Pandey, 2019), which is true for any Massive online open courses (MOOCs) platform for that matter. Because of these reasons of innovation and personalization, there is good response in the student community with regards to the BYJU'S app (Chavan & Shukla, 2019). Thus, the goal of consumer delight is achieved and which leads to business and company growth and enhancement.

The technological advancement in the past two to three decades has been so fast paced that to keep pace with that one needs to learn from others and makes it a part of one's organizational strategy. In the management of innovation (Bruns & Stalker, 1961), open innovation acts as a very important strategy (Chesbrough & Appleyard, 2007). His acquisition of Akash Educational Services (Shah & Alnoor, 2021) in the Medical Coaching market, partnership with Disney for the Early Learning stages (Roy, 2020) and several other top players in other markets like WhiteHat Jr (Arun, 2020) in early childhood education are testimony of that.

A comparison and strategic analysis of online tutoring platforms (Challa & Anute, 2020) why BYJU'S was able to rule the roost among its other competitors. In the BYJU'S versus Unacademy (Sharma, 2020) competitive race, the advantage with BYJU'S was that it started with school students first so the flow of students which goes from lower class to higher one and hence the database and in informatics terminology "big data" was with BYJU's than Unacademy and hence the competitive advantage. In this age of data, where data is the new oil (Humby, 2006) company sustain competitive advantage on the basis of better prediction architectures and Big Data – "Volume, Veracity, Velocity and Variety". The strategies of mergers, acquisitions and partnerships like partnership with Disney for the Early Learning stages (Roy, 2020), acquisition of Akash Educational Services (Shah & Alnoor, 2021) etc. taken by BYJU's again enhance their data architecture whilst companies like

Unacademy are relying on old techniques of creating databases like Webinars by top people in the area. In that conext, BYJU's aggressive advertising and business strategy (Francina & Aarthi, 2020) is to push their one product which hits the sentiment of the parents and their aspiration. If we see WhiteHat Jr (Arun, 2020) which is at the early learning stage is being advertised by successful professional from different fields. The deeper strategy is to get hold of the data and there is a data extraction architecture at work and that is the deeper strategy that needs to be understood.

The COVID19 outbreak gave a push to online education and BYJU'S took full benefit of the opportunity and its subscription based strategy (Sathyan, 2021) brought it funds from both the customers and also from the investors who saw great earning potential in company's shares. A Bain Report (Sheth, A., Krishnan, S., & Samyukktha, T. (2020) on venture capital in India how BYJU'S was able to capture the attention of the Venture Capitalists and the major chunk of the investments in general and especially of the Education Technology (Edtech) sector and it was the top funded start-up in the Indian entrepreneurial space. Zukerberg inversting in BYJU's was a big push (Zuckerberg, 2016), which happened long back and gave impetus to the company.

As the paradigm is evolving from mass production to mass customization (Hu, 2013), new taxonomies of personalization (Blom, 2000) are being created by corporations. Marketing using personalization and customization which affects choice and enhances purchase (Arora, Dreze, Ghose, Hess, Iyengar, Jing, ... & Zhang, 2008) is becoming commonplace and prediction architectures are being built around them as we usher into a new era of where private governments (Anderson, 2017) rules our lives and human freedom is at risk (Beck, 2009) and is mythical (Harari, 2018).

SOLUTIONS AND RECOMMENDATIONS

There is evidence globally that entrepreneurship causes inequality and does not reduce it (Bruton, Sutter & Lenz, 2021). When the Indian government is looking at start-ups not only as engines of economic growth but also to solve socio-economic issues that lurk before the country and across the world in the 21st century. Inequality being the biggest threats to the human society the pursuit of management as accumulation (Tsoukas, 1994) is not going to take us to far and the profession finds it at cross roads (Ranjan, 2021a). There need to be evolvement of strategies of businesses in real sense and they need to move from the chase of sustainable competitive advantage to how they can contribute to sustainable development endeavour. Change in corporate elite philosophies (Ranjan, 2021b) and new business models need to be evolved in that regard.

BYJU'S choice of serving the US market (Kim & Tahilyani, 2017) and other developed markets than those in need in the underserved Indian context is simply a blind case of chase for money, profits and the bottom line. In such a scenario, multiple bottom lines beyond profits have been recommended for businesses (Jain, Mendiratta & Kashiramka, 2021) but the problem is not that simple. It is part of a deeply seated agenda of the top 1% (Carney & Nason, 2018) against the bottom 99% (OXFAM, 2018) under a false notion of possession (Ranjan 2021c). In spite of getting prises from the World Bank, on their work and how their product innovation and personalization provides deep conceptual understanding (Casanova, 2018), Indian governmental expectations and National Education Policy formulation, BYJU'S chose to remain in the chase for money and profits and did not understand that strategy can also be about creating social value given the sector they are in. One must ask the question that "should education systems build societies or vice-versa?" as the consumerism trends shoots in (Gupta, Verma, Jain, Narshimha, & Nanda, 2019) and e-learning becomes a pervasive trend in the post-COVID world (Ray, 2020). It also becomes a societal responsibility for organizations. When people are willing (Weale, 2018) to cede their privacy (Ranjan & Saket, 2017) in the name of product customization, personalization and innovation, organizations also need to take responsibility of data, their privacy and lives. In this false chase for fictional realities (Harari, 2014), even people at the top of the socio-economic pyramid get caught in false chase for power and possession leading to wastage of natural resources and detrimental human relations.

FUTURE RESEARCH DIRECTIONS

The COVID crisis made palpable the sorry state of Business-society relationship, when people at the bottom of the socio-economic strata suffered and bore the real brunt of the crisis (Parwez, & Ranjan, 2021a). Ecological imbalances and decline has been an outcome of this undesirable relationship (Ranjan, 2021d: 2021e). In the post-COVID era, when business-society scholars, educators and researchers (Bapuji, de Bakker, Brown, Higgins, Rehbein & Spicer, 2020; de Bakker, Matten, Spence, & Wickert, 2020) look into the future of a discipline which is in a broken, fragmented and sad state (Caruana, Crane, Gold & LeBaron, 2020) due to the wrongdoings of the strategies followed in the past and the chase for profit and the bottom-line for the 1% owning family businesses (Carney, M., & Nason, R. S. (2018) and keeping the bottom 99% of them at their helm (OXFAM., 2018). Time is ripe to raise some fundamental questions with regards to public value creation through various institutions including businesses.

Management education and profession finds itself at crossroads because the very philosophical, epistemological and ontological basis needs a revamp from "accumulation" to "co-habitation" (Ranjan, 2021a,d) and the corporate elite need to change the philosophy (Ranjan, 2021b).

Management education seems to be under the traps of "Fictional Conditioning" and "Surveillance Panopticon" in Industry 4.0. era (Ranjan, 2021d). Thus, the research possibilities are the following. *Firstly*, given now businesses also address societal issues the philosophical, epistemological and ontological basis of management education need to be debated and revamped taking a normative lens. *Secondly*, new models of corporate participation in public realm need to be developed. *Thirdly*, the concept of possession from a individual, managerial, corporation and societal point of view needs to be developed (Ranjan, 2021d). *Lastly*, new theories of sociality for interaction in political-economic realms need to be developed (Parwez & Ranjan, 2021c).

CONCLUSION

Artificial Intelligence technologies have the capability of bringing to life personalization and self-paced learning to life (Roy, 2020). However the larger question remains that how these will be used in the political-economic interaction spaces i.e. for furthering the cause of "Surveillance Capitalism" (Zuboff, 2019) or emancipation (Gulenc & Ariturk, 2016). This needs to be actively debated and the right direction for human race needs to be pursued. As pursuits of technology and science are nothing but "ideological choices" taken by societies (Habermas, 1970). It is the time to ask what choice as humanity we would like to take as the purpose of education is nothing but emancipation, renunciation and living with a spirit of detachment attachment in all cultures and societies worldwide. Are we ready to take that forward step!

REFERENCES

Anderson, E. (2017). *Private Government How Employers Rule Our Lives (and Why We Don't Talk about It)*. Princeton University Press.

Anupam, S. (2018). *The Rise Of India's Billion-Dollar Club: Edtech Startup BYJU'S Turns Unicorn.* Inc42 Media.

Arora, N., Dreze, X., Ghose, A., Hess, J. D., Iyengar, R., Jing, B., Joshi, Y., Kumar, V., Lurie, N., Neslin, S., Sajeesh, S., Su, M., Syam, N., Thomas, J., & Zhang, Z. J. (2008). Putting one-to-one marketing to work: Personalization, customization, and choice. *Marketing Letters, 19*(3), 305–321. doi:10.100711002-008-9056-z

Arun, M. (2020). Ed Tech Whitehat Jr. *Indian Innovation: Journal of Startups, 2*(2).

Bapuji, H., de Bakker, F., Brown, J., Higgins, C., Rehbein, K., & Spicer, A. (2020). Business and society research in the times of the corona crisis. *Business & Society, 59*(6), 1067–1078. doi:10.1177/0007650320921172

Barney, J. (1991). Competitive Advantage. *Journal of Management, 17*(1), 99–120. doi:10.1177/014920639101700108

Baron, R. A. (2006). Opportunity recognition as pattern recognition: How entrepreneurs "connect the dots" to identify new business opportunities. *The Academy of Management Perspectives, 20*(1), 104–119. doi:10.5465/amp.2006.19873412

Beck, U. (2009). *World at risk.* Polity Press.

Blom, J. (2000). Personalization: a taxonomy. In CHI'00 extended abstracts on Human factors in computing systems (pp. 313-314). doi:10.1145/633292.633483

Bruns, T., & Stalker, G. M. (1961). *The management of innovation.* Tavistock.

Bruton, G., Sutter, C., & Lenz, A. K. (2021). Economic inequality–Is entrepreneurship the cause or the solution? A review and research agenda for emerging economies. *Journal of Business Venturing, 36*(3), 106095. doi:10.1016/j.jbusvent.2021.106095

Carland, J. W., Hoy, F., & Carland, J. A. C. (1988). "Who is an entrepreneur?" is a question worth asking. *American Journal of Small Business, 12*(4), 33–39. doi:10.1177/104225878801200402

Carney, M., & Nason, R. S. (2018). Family business and the 1%. *Business & Society, 57*(6), 1191–1215. doi:10.1177/0007650316661165

Caruana, R., Crane, A., Gold, S., & LeBaron, G. (2020). Modern slavery in business: The sad and sorry state of a non-field. *Business & Society.*

Casanova, A. M. (2018). BYJU's: How a learning app is promoting deep conceptual understanding that is improving educational outcomes in India (No. 125923). The World Bank.

Challa, A., & Anute, N. (2020). *Strategic analysis of emerging online tutoring platforms in India.* Academic Press.

Chavan, R. R., & Shukla, A. (2019). New Generation E-entrepreneurship-A Case study of BYJU's. *Sumedha Journal of Management, 8*(3), 228–232.

Chesbrough, H. W., & Appleyard, M. M. (2007). Open innovation and strategy. *California Management Review, 50*(1), 57–76. doi:10.2307/41166416

de Bakker, F. G., Matten, D., Spence, L. J., & Wickert, C. (2020). *The elephant in the room: The nascent research agenda on corporations, social responsibility, and capitalism.* Academic Press.

Francina, V. J., & Aarthi, K. (2020). Advertising and Business Strategy of an Indian Edu Tech Giant-Byju's. *Journal of Media and Corporate Management, 3*(2).

Freedman, L. (2015). *Strategy: A history.* Oxford University Press.

Gartner, W. B. (1988). "Who is an entrepreneur?" is the wrong question. *American Journal of Small Business, 12*(4), 11–32. doi:10.1177/104225878801200401

Granstrand, O. (1999). *The economics and management of intellectual property.* Books.

Guerras-Martín, L. Á., Madhok, A., & Montoro-Sánchez, Á. (2014). The evolution of strategic management research: Recent trends and current directions. *BRQ Business Research Quarterly, 17*(2), 69–76. doi:10.1016/j.brq.2014.03.001

Gulenc, K., & Ariturk, M. H. (2016). Is human emancipation through technology possible? *Synthesis Philosophica, 31*(1), 83–103. doi:10.21464p31106

Gupta, S., Verma, A., Jain, U., Narshimha, A., & Nanda, N. (2019). Consumer megatrends: Reshaping the Indian marketplace. *Journal of Critical Reviews, 6*(6), 103–114.

Habermas, J. (1970). Technology and science as "ideology". In J. Habermas (Ed.), *Toward a rational society: Student protest, science, and politics* (pp. 81–122). Beacon Press.

Harari, Y. N. (2014). *Sapiens. A Brief History of Humankind.* Academic Press.

Harari, Y. N. (2018). Yuval Noah Harari: the myth of freedom. *Guardian.* Accessed on August 23, 2021 from https://www.theguardian.com/books/2018/sep/14/yuval-noah-harari-the-new-threat-to-liberal-democracy

Holla, N., & Mitra, A. (2020). *Pushing the Boundaries of Indian Tech.* Observer Research Foundation Online Publications. Accessed on August 27, 2021 from https://www.orfonline.org/wp-content/uploads/2020/10/ORF-Women-in-Tech-report.pdf

Hu, S. J. (2013). Evolving paradigms of manufacturing: From mass production to mass customization and personalization. *Procedia CIRP*, *7*, 3–8. doi:10.1016/j.procir.2013.05.002

Humby, C. (2006). Data is the new oil. *Proc. ANA Sr. Marketer's Summit.*

Jain, A., Mendiratta, P., & Kashiramka, S. (2021). 10 Triple Bottom Line During Pandemic. *Strategic Management During a Pandemic.*

Kaplan, R. (2014). Who has been regulating whom, business or society? The mid-20th century institutionalization of 'corporate responsibility' in the USA. *Socio-Economic Review*, *13*(1), 125–155. doi:10.1093er/mwu031

Kim, J. J. H., & Tahilyani, R. (2017). BYJU'S The Learning App. *Harvard Business School Case*, 317-048.

Kline, S. J., & Rosenberg, N. (2010). An overview of innovation. *Studies on science and the innovation process: Selected works of Nathan Rosenberg*, 173-203.

Lee, M., Yun, J. J., Pyka, A., Won, D., Kodama, F., Schiuma, G., Park, H. S., Jeon, J., Park, K. B., Jung, K. H., Yan, M.-R., Lee, S. Y., & Zhao, X. (2018). How to respond to the fourth industrial revolution, or the second information technology revolution? Dynamic new combinations between technology, market, and society through open innovation. *Journal of Open Innovation*, *4*(3), 21. doi:10.3390/joitmc4030021

Nonaka, I., & Toyama, R. (2015). The knowledge-creating theory revisited: knowledge creation as a synthesizing process. In *The essentials of knowledge management* (pp. 95–110). Palgrave Macmillan. doi:10.1057/9781137552105_4

OXFAM. (2018). *An economy for the 99%.* Accessed on August 22, 2021 from https://www.oxfam.org/sites/www.oxfam.org/files/file_attachments/bp-economy-for-99-percent-160117-summ-en.pdf

Parwez, S., & Ranjan, R. (2021a). The platform economy and the precarisation of food delivery work in the COVID-19 pandemic: Evidence from India. *Work Organisation, Labour & Globalisation*, *15*(1), 11–30. doi:10.13169/workorgalaboglob.15.1.0011

Parwez, S., & Ranjan, R. (2021b). Social Enterprising' Social Change Agenda Co-opted! The Scale, Dependency and Financial Viability Traps. *FIIB Business Review.*

Parwez, S., & Ranjan, R. (2021c). Reinventing the Lost "Public" in Post-COVID Era: Towards a Theory of sociality in political-economy interaction spaces in the 21st century. In 7th *Biennial Conference of the Indian Academy of Management (INDAM.*, IIM Rohtak.

Pfeffer, J., & Sutton, R. I. (2006). *Hard facts, dangerous half-truths and total nonsense: Profiting from evidence-based management*. Harvard Business School Press.

Porter, M. E. (1985). Technology and competitive advantage. *The Journal of Business Strategy*, *5*(3), 60–78. doi:10.1108/eb039075

Porter, M. E. (1996, November-December). What is Strategy? *Harvard Business Review*, 61–78. PMID:10158475

Ranjan, R. (2021a). *Management Education and Profession at Crossroads: Implications of a deeply rooted philosophical assumption*. 8th International Conference on Sustainability, IIM Shillong, India.

Ranjan, R. (2021b). *Corporate elite need to change the Philosophy! A discussion on the Business-Society Relationship in Sustainable Development Context*. 8th Pan IIM World Management Conference, IIM Kozhikode, India.

Ranjan, R. (2021c). *Revisiting Possession in the Oriental and Occidental Traditions: Lessons from a Comparative Study of American Television Series and Pakistani Dramas*. International Conclave on Globalizing Indian Thought, IIM Kozhikode, India.

Ranjan, R. (2021d). *"Management Education" Under Twin Traps of Fictional Conditioning and Surveillance Panopticon in Industry 4.0*. era. International Conference for Markets and Development, IIM Trichy, India.

Ranjan, R. (2021e). *Business and Society/Ecology at the Loggerheads: Understanding from the Adani Experience*. International Society for Data Sciences and Innovation – Global Conference, IIM Nagpur, India.

Ranjan, R., & Saket, S. (2017). *Privacy Cede for "Totalitarian" or "Open Innovation" society?* 5th Pan IIM World Management Conference (WMC), IIML, Lucknow, India.

Ray, A. (2020). E-learning: The new normal in the post-covid world. *International Research Journal of Modernization in Engineering Technology and Science*, *2*(9), 866–876.

Roy, M. (2020). AI Intervention in Education Systems of India: An Analysis. *Solid State Technology*, *63*(2), 1395–1402.

Sahu, A. K., & Abhishek, M. (2018). *A study of ed-tech industry in India, with a focus on the growth of Byju's*. Academic Press.

Sathyan, S. (2021). Byju's Learning App in the COVID-19 Outbreak to Analyze Online Education-A Case Study. *International Journal of Case Studies in Business, IT and Education*, *5*(2), 75–86.

Shah, S., & Alnoor, P. (2021). Byju's acquires Aakash Educational Services in nearly $1-billion deal. *Economic Times*. Accessed on August 30, 2021 from https://economictimes.indiatimes.com/tech/startups/byjus-to-acquire-aakash-educational-services-in-700-million-deal/articleshow/81910598.cms

Sharma, A. (2020). *Comparative Analysis of E-Learning Systems (Byju's un Unacademy) in India*. Academic Press.

Sheth, A., Krishnan, S., & Samyukktha, T. (2020). *India venture capital report 2020*. Accessed on August 28, 2021 from https://ivca.in/wp-content/uploads/2021/03/bain_report_india_venture_capital_2021.pdf

Sinha, A. P., & Pandey, R. K. (2019). A study on accessing the factors leading to the purchase of BYJU'S as a curriculum. *Trans Asian Journal of Marketing & Management Research, 8*(9-10), 44-59.

Sruthi, P., & Mukherjee, S. (2020). Byju's the learning app: An investigative study on the transformation from traditional learning to technology based personalized learning. *International Journal of Scientific and Technology Research*, *9*(3), 5054–5059.

Tripathy, S., & Devarapalli, S. (2021). Emerging trend set by a start-ups on Indian online education system: A case of Byju's. *Journal of Public Affairs*, *21*(1), e2128. doi:10.1002/pa.2128

Tsoukas, H. (1994). What is management? An outline of a metatheory. *British Journal of Management*, *5*(4), 289–301. doi:10.1111/j.1467-8551.1994.tb00080.x

Weale, A. (2018). *The Will of the People*. Polity Press.

Zuboff, S. (2019). *The age of surveillance capitalism: The fight for a human future at the new frontier of power: Barack Obama's books of 2019*. Profile books.

Zuckerberg, M. (2016). *Zuckerberg Facebook Post about Chan Zuckerberg Initiative investing in BYJU's-2016-8-16*. Academic Press.

KEY TERMS AND DEFINITIONS

Big Data: A gargantuan dataset having the feature of high volume, variety, velocity, value, variability, and veracity which is captured through technologies like

Optical Character Readers (OCRs), Smart Cards, Biometrics, Voice Recognition, Magnetic strips, etc.

Fictional Realities: It refers to all the exchange mechanisms like money, bonds, contract etc. which do not have any direct connect to human life but serve as a connecting apparatus for human beings across cultures and geographies through time. It contrasts with absolute reality like food, shelter and clothing which is a primary need for human living.

Industry 4.0: It refers to the fourth Industrial Revolution in which work has started integrating future technologies like Artificial Intelligence (AI) and Machine Learning (ML), etc.

Personalization: Personalization refers to customization of products and services so that the individual can get a unique experience based on individual interests and choices.

Product Innovation: Product innovation means a continual process of revamping the quality, features, forms, facets so that it enhances user experience and causes user delight.

Surveillance Capitalism: It is a new form of capitalism which have evolved in the Industry 4.0 era, i.e., the 4th Industrial Revolution where companies have access to large-scale data and use a predictive architecture to benefit themselves devaluing the privacy cede given by people.

Sustainable Competitive Advantage: It refers to the end goal of corporations in the business environment for survival in the market economy and involves deployment of various kinds of strategies and actions like mergers, acquisitions, partnership, internal and external environment control, etc.

ENDNOTES

1 BYJU'S was started as a tutoring class by Byju Raveendaran and Divya Gokulnath in the offline Common Admission Test (CAT) training space for Indian Institutes of Managements (IIMs) which later grew into and got registered as Think and Learn Pvt. Ltd. popularly known as BYJU'S currently the top player in Indian Educational Technology space having a current valuation of $16.5 billion approximately.

2 COVID19 is a pandemic, having its origins in China in November 2020 and was finally declared so by the World Health Organization (WHO) on March 11, 2021. It is one of the biggest epidemics that has struck the world in the past century and has led to imposition of lockdowns worldwide impacting economies, jobs and especially those from the lower socio-economic strata.

Compilation of References

Aazam, M., & Huh, E. N. (2014). Fog computing and smart gateway based communication for cloud of things. *Proceedings of the 2nd IEEE International Conference on Future Internet of Things and Cloud (FiCloud' 14),* 464–470. 10.1109/FiCloud.2014.83

Acatech, D. A. D. T. (2016). *Kompetenzentwicklungsstudie Industrie 4.0.* https://docplayer.org/24401230-Kompetenzentwicklungsstudie-industrie-4-0.html

Achrol, R. S., & Kotler, P. (2012). Frontiers of the Marketing Paradigm in the Third Millennium. *Journal of the Academy of Marketing Science*, *40*(1), 35–52. doi:10.100711747-011-0255-4

Adams, C. A., & Frost, G. R. (2008). Integrating sustainability reporting into management practices. *Accounting Forum*, *32*(4), 288–302. doi:10.1016/j.accfor.2008.05.002

Adcock, A. (2012). Cognitive dissonance in the learning processes. *Encycl. Sci. Learning,* 588–590.

Adobe. (2015). *Four advantages of a planned approach to digital maturity.* Retrieved from Adobe Systems: Retrieved from https://landing. adobe.com/dam/downloads/whitepapers/192320. en.digital-marketing -survey-report.pdf

Adolph, S., Tisch, M., & Metternich, J. (2014). Challenges and approaches to competency development for future production. *Journal of International Scientific Publications–Educational Alternatives*, *12*(1), 1001–1010.

Agan, Y., Acar, M. F., & Borodin, A. (2013). Drivers of environmental processes and their impact on performance: A study of Turkish SMEs. *Journal of Cleaner Production*, *51*, 23–33. doi:10.1016/j.jclepro.2012.12.043

Agarwal, D. (2019). *Top 5 trends that will rule fashion retail in 2019.* Available at: www. indianretailer. com/article/whats-hot/trends/Top-5-trends-that-will-rule-fashion-retail-in-2019. a6270/

Agarwal, Vempati, & Borar. (2018). *Personalizing similar product recommendations in fashion e-commerce.* arXiv preprint arXiv:1806.11371.

Aggerholm, H. K., Anderson, S. E., & Thomsen, C. (2011). Conceptualising employer branding in sustainable organizations. *Corporate Communication: An International Journal*, *16*(2), 105–123. doi:10.1108/13563281111141642

Aghajani, H. A., Samadi Mirakalei, H., & Samadi Myrkalei, H. (2015). The relationship between entrepreneurship and characteristics of a learning organization. *Management Efficiency, 35*(9), 39-64.

Ahadi, S. (2011). *Relationship between empowerment and organizational learning among*. Academic Press.

Ahuja & Tatsutani. (2021). *Sustainable energy for developing countries.* https://journals.openedition.org/sapiens/823

Al Amoush, A. B., & Sandhu, K. (2020). Digital Transformation of Learning Management Systems at Universities: Case Analysis for Student Perspectives. *Digital Transformation and Innovative Services for Business and Learning,* 41-61. https://doi.org/ doi:10.4018/978-1-7998-5175-2.ch003

Alalwan, A. A., Dwivedi, Y. K., Rana, N. P., & Williams, M. D. (2016). Consumer adoption of mobile banking in Jordan: Examining the role of usefulness, ease of use, perceived risk and self-efficacy. *Journal of Enterprise Information Management, 29*(1), 118–139. doi:10.1108/JEIM-04-2015-0035

Alba, J., Lynch, J., Weitz, B., Janiszewski, C., Lutz, R., Sawyer, A., & Wood, S. (1997). Interactive Home Shopping: Consumer, Retailer, and Manufacturer Incentives to Participate in Electronic Marketplaces. *Journal of Marketing, 61*(3), 38–53. doi:10.1177/002224299706100303

Alhabeeb, A., & Rowley, J. (2017). Critical success factors for eLearning in Saudi Arabian universities. *International Journal of Educational Management, 31*(2), 131–147. doi:10.1108/IJEM-01-2016-0006

Almeida, A. R., Alvarenga, R. A., Sartor, L. B., & Simioni, F. J. (2019). Mitigating environmental impacts using life cycle assessment in Brazilian companies: A stakeholders' perspective. *Journal of Environmental Management, 236,* 291–300. doi:10.1016/j.jenvman.2019.01.094 PMID:30738299

Almeida, F., Santos, J., & Monteiro, J. (2020). The Challenges and Opportunities in the Digitalization of Companies in a Post-COVID-19 World. *IEEE Engineering Management Review, 48*(3), 97–103. doi:10.1109/EMR.2020.3013206

Almli, V. L., Verbeke, W., Vanhonacker, F., Næs, T., & Hersleth, M. (2011). General image and attribute perceptions of traditional food in six European countries. *Food Quality and Preference, 22*(1), 129–138. doi:10.1016/j.foodqual.2010.08.008

Alsabbagh, M., & Khalil, A. H. (2016). The impact of leadership styles on organizational learning (an empirical study on the education sector in Damascus city). *International Journal of Academic Research in Business & Social Sciences, 6*(5), 197–217. doi:10.6007/IJARBSS/v6-i5/2126

Alvani, S. M. (2008). *Public Administration.* Ney Publications.

Anaza, N. A. (2014). Personality antecedents of customer citizenship behaviours in online shopping situations. *Psychology and Marketing, 31*, 251–263.

Anderson, E. (2017). *Private Government How Employers Rule Our Lives (and Why We Don't Talk about It)*. Princeton University Press.

Anderson, L. (2016). Cooking up the Past: Culinary Nostalgia and Gender Critique in Cuéntame cómo pasó. *Hispanic Research Journal, 17*(1), 34–48. doi:10.1080/14682737.2015.1125103

Angelis, C. T. (2016). The impact of national culture and knowledge management ongovernmental intelligence. *Journal of Modelling in Management, 11*(1), 240–268. doi:10.1108/JM2-08-2014-0069

Angst, C. M., & Agarwal, R. (2009). Adoption of electronic health records in the presence of privacy concerns: The elaboration likelihood model and individual persuasion. *Management Information Systems Quarterly, 33*(2), 339–370. doi:10.2307/20650295

Antonio, K. L., Richard, C. Y., & Tang, E. (2009). The complementarity of internal integration and product modularity: An empirical study of their interaction effect on competitive capabilities. *Journal of Engineering and Technology Management, 26*(4), 305–326.

Anupam, S. (2018). *The Rise Of India's Billion-Dollar Club: Edtech Startup BYJU'S Turns Unicorn.* Inc42 Media.

Aragón-Correa, J. A., Hurtado-Torres, N., Sharma, S., & García-Morales, V. J. (2008). Environmental strategy and performance in small firms: A resource-based perspective. *Journal of Environmental Management, 86*(1), 88–103. doi:10.1016/j.jenvman.2006.11.022 PMID:17239519

Argyris, C. (1998). Organizational behavior: Production of knowledge for action in the world of practice. In J. McKelvey & M. Neufeld (Eds.), *Industrial relations at the dawn of the new millennium* (pp. 54–61). New York State School of Industrial and Labor Relations.

Ariker, M., Heller, J., Diaz, A., & Perrey, J. (2015). How marketers can personalize at scale. *Harvard Business Review*. Retrieved from https://hbr.org/ 2015/11/how-marketers-can-personalize-at-scale

Arora, N., Dreze, X., Ghose, A., Hess, J. D., Iyengar, R., Jing, B., Joshi, Y., Kumar, V., Lurie, N., Neslin, S., Sajeesh, S., Su, M., Syam, N., Thomas, J., & Zhang, Z. J. (2008). Putting one-to-one marketing to work: Personalization, customization, and choice. *Marketing Letters, 19*(3), 305–321. doi:10.100711002-008-9056-z

Arun, M. (2020). Ed Tech Whitehat Jr. *Indian Innovation: Journal of Startups, 2*(2).

Assunção, R. R., Luca, M. M. M., & de Vasconcelos, A. C. (2016). Complexity and corporate governance: An analysis of companies listed on the BM & FBOVESPA. *Revista Contabilidade & Finanças, 28*(July), 213–228. doi:10.1590/1808-057x201702660

Atiku, S. O. (Ed.). (2019). *Human capital formation for the fourth industrial revolution* (1st ed.). IGI Global.

Attwell, G. (2010). Work-based mobile learning environments: Contributing to a socio-cultural ecology of mobile learning. *International Journal of Mobile and Blended Learning, 2*(4), 19–34. doi:10.4018/jmbl.2010100102

Atwood, M. A., Mora, J. W., & Kaplan, A. W. (2010). Learning to lead: Evaluating leadershipand organizational learning. *Leadership and Organization Development Journal, 31*(7), 576–595. doi:10.1108/01437731011079637

Atzori, L., Iera, A., & Morabito, G. (2011). IoT: Giving a social structure to the internet of things. *IEEE Communications Letters, 15*(11), 1193–1195. doi:10.1109/LCOMM.2011.090911.111340

Aurier, P., & Guintcheva, G. (2014). Using affect–expectations theory to explain the direction of the impacts of experiential emotions on satisfaction. *Psychology and Marketing, 31*(10), 900–913. doi:10.1002/mar.20742

Baader, F., Calvanese, D., McGuinness, D., Nardi, D., & Patel-Schneider, P. (Eds.). (2002). *The Description Logic Handbook*. Cambridge University Press.

Bagozzi, R. P., Belanche, D., Casaló, L. V., & Flavián, C. (2016). The role of anticipated emotions in purchase intentions. *Psychology and Marketing, 33*(8), 629–645. doi:10.1002/mar.20905

Balasyan, I., & Casais, B. (2018). Keeping Exclusivity in An E-Commerce Environment: The case of Farfetch.com and the market of luxury clothes. *International Journal of Marketing. Communication and New Media, 0*(4), 6–27.

Baldwin, C. Y. (2008). Where do transactions come from? Modularity, transactions, and the boundaries of firms. *Industrial and Corporate Change, 17*(1), 155–195. doi:10.1093/icc/dtm036

Bandura, A. (2002). Social cognitive theory in cultural context. *Applied Psychology, 51*(2), 269–290. doi:10.1111/1464-0597.00092

Bapuji, H., de Bakker, F., Brown, J., Higgins, C., Rehbein, K., & Spicer, A. (2020). Business and society research in the times of the corona crisis. *Business & Society, 59*(6), 1067–1078. doi:10.1177/0007650320921172

Barclay, L. J., & Kiefer, T. (2014). Approach or avoid? Exploring overall justice and the differential effects of positive and negative emotions. *Journal of Management, 40*(7), 1857–1898. doi:10.1177/0149206312441833

Barnaghi, P., Presser, M., & Moessner, K. (2010). Publishing Linked Sensor Data. *Proceedings of the 3rd International Workshop on Semantic Sensor Networks.*

Barney, J. (1991). Firm resources and sustained competitive advantage. *Journal of Management, 17*(1), 99–120. doi:10.1177/014920639101700108

Baron, R. A. (2006). Opportunity recognition as pattern recognition: How entrepreneurs "connect the dots" to identify new business opportunities. *The Academy of Management Perspectives, 20*(1), 104–119. doi:10.5465/amp.2006.19873412

Basole, R. C. (2016). Accelerating digital transformation: Visual insights from the API ecosystem. *IT Professional, 18*, 20–25.

Bassi, L. (2011). Raging debates in HR analytics. *People and Strategy, 34*(2), 14.

Bathla, G., Aggarwal, H., & Rani, R. (2020). A graph-based model to improve social trust and influence for social recommendation. *The Journal of Supercomputing*, *76*(6), 4057–4075. doi:10.100711227-017-2196-2

Baumgartner, R. J., & Korhonen, J. (2010). Strategic thinking for sustainable development. International Sustainable Development Research Society, 18, 71-75.

Baur, C., & Wee, D. (2015). *Industry 4.0 is more than just a flashy catchphrase. A confluence of trends and technologies promises to reshape the way things are made.* https://www.mckinsey.com/business-functions/operations/our-insights/manufacturings-next-act

Beatty, S. E., & Elizabeth Ferrell, M. (1998). Impulse buying: Modeling its precursors. *Journal of Retailing*, *74*(2), 169–191. doi:10.1016/S0022-4359(99)80092-X

Becker, J. (2010). Use of backcasting to integrate indicators with principles of sustainability. *International Journal of Sustainable Development World*, *17*(3), 189–197. doi:10.1080/13504501003726974

Beck, U. (2009). *World at risk*. Polity Press.

Beer, M., Eisenstat, R. A., & Spector, B. (1990). *The Critical Path to Corporate Renewal*. Harvard Business School Press.

Beier, G., Niehoff, S., Ziems, T., & Xue, B. (2017). Sustainability aspects of a digitalized industry – A comparative study from China and Germany. *International Journal of Precision Engineering and Manufacturing-Green Technology*, *4*(2), 227–234. doi:10.1007/s40684-017-0028-8

Belle, S. (2016). Organizational Learning? Look Again. *The Learning Organization*, *23*(5), 332–341. doi:10.1108/TLO-01-2016-0007

Benchmarking: The search for industry best practices that lead to superior performance. (1989). *Choice Reviews Online*, *27*(4), 27-2173-27-2173. doi:10.5860/CHOICE.27-2173

Bencsika. (2017). *Knowledge Management Initiatives and Strategies in Small and Medium Enterprises*. IGI Global.

Benešová, A., & Tupa, J. (2017). Requirements for Education and Qualification of People in Industry 4.0. *Procedia Manufacturing*, *11*, 2195–2202. doi:10.1016/j.promfg.2017.07.366

Bennis, W., Benne, K., & Chin, R. (1985). *The Planning of Change*. International Thompson Publishing.

Berghaus, S., & Back, A. (2016). Stages in Digital Business Transformation: Results of an Empirical Maturity Study. *MCIS 2016 Proceedings*. *22*. Retrieved from http://aisel.aisnet.org/mcis2016/22

Berkovsky, S., Freyne, J., & Oinas-Kukkonen, H. (2012). Influencing individually: Fusing personalization and persuasion. *ACM Transactions on Interactive Intelligent Systems*, *2*(2), 9. doi:10.1145/2209310.2209312

Berners-Lee, T. (2000). *Weaving the Web: The Original Design and Ultimate Design of the World Wide Web by its inventor*. Harper Business.

Bersin, J. (2018, June 18). AI In HR: A Real Killer App. *Forbes*. Available at https://www.forbes.com/sites/joshbersin/2018/06/18/ai-in-hr-a-real-killer-app/#4546756948f1

Beschorner, T. (2013). Creating Shared Value: The One-Trick Pony Approach. *Business Ethics Journal Review*, *1*(17), 106–112. doi:10.12747/bejr2013.01.17

Beyer, M. A., & Laney, D. (2012). *The importance of 'big data': a definition*. Gartner.

Bhattacherjee, A., & Sanford, C. (2006). Influence processes for information technology acceptance: An elaboration likelihood model. *Management Information Systems Quarterly*, *30*(4), 805–825. doi:10.2307/25148755

Bianchi, C. (2012). Enhancing performance management and sustainable organizational growth through system-dynamics modelling. In *Systemic management for intelligent organizations* (pp. 143–161). Springer Berlin Heidelberg. doi:10.1007/978-3-642-29244-6_8

Bianchi, C. (2016). Fostering Sustainable Organizational Development Through Dynamic Performance Management. In *Dynamic Performance Management. System Dynamics for Performance Management* (Vol. 1). Springer. doi:10.1007/978-3-319-31845-5_3

Biernacki, P., & Waldorf, D. (1981). Snowball sampling: Problems and techniques of chain referral sampling. *Sociological Methods & Research*, *10*(2), 141–163. doi:10.1177/004912418101000205

Bijmolt, T. H. A., Broekhuis, M., de Leeuw, S., Hirche, C., Rooderkerk, R. P., Sousa, R., & Zhu, S. X. (2021). Challenges at the marketing–operations interface in omni-channel retail environments. *Journal of Business Research*, *122*, 864–874. doi:10.1016/j.jbusres.2019.11.034

Biondi, V., Frey, M., & Iraldo, F. (2000). Environmental management systems and SMEs. *Greener Management International*, *2000*(29), 55–69. doi:10.9774/GLEAF.3062.2000.sp.00007

Birmingham, U. o. (2015). *Learning Theories, Stages and Styles*. University of Birmingham.

Bjørum, L. O. (2019). *Development of a Digital Twin for Condition Monitoring, Focusing on Electrical Propulsion Systems for Marine Application*. Norwegian University of Science and Technology.

Blecker, T., & Abdelkafi, N. (2006). Complexity and variety in mass customization systems: Analysis and recommendations. *Management Decision*, *44*(7), 908–929. doi:10.1108/00251740610680596

Blom, J. (2000). Personalization: a taxonomy. In CHI'00 extended abstracts on Human factors in computing systems (pp. 313-314). doi:10.1145/633292.633483

Blundel, R., Monaghan, A., & Thomas, C. (2013). SMEs and environmental responsibility: A policy perspective. *Business Ethics (Oxford, England)*, *22*(3), 246–262. doi:10.1111/beer.12020

Boiral, O., Ebrahimi, M., Kuyken, K., & Talbot, D. (2017). Greening remote SMEs: The case of small regional airports. *Journal of Business Ethics*, *154*(3), 813–827. doi:10.100710551-017-3447-0

Bonomi, F., Milito, R., Natarajan, P., & Zhu, J. (2014). *Fog computing: a platform for internet of things and analytics. In Big Data and Internet ofThings: A Road Map for Smart Environments.* Springer.

Bonomi, F., Milito, R., Zhu, J., & Addepalli, S. (2012). Fog computing and its role in the internet of things. *Proceedings of the 1st ACM MCC Workshop on Mobile Cloud Computing*, 13–16. 10.1145/2342509.2342513

Boons, F., & Lüdeke-Freund, F. (2013). Business models for sustainable innovation: State-of-the-art and steps towards a research agenda. *Journal of Cleaner Production*, *45*(April), 9–19. doi:10.1016/j.jclepro.2012.07.007

Boonstra, J. J., & Elving, W. J. L. (2009) Veranderen als kunstje, kunde of kunst. In Communicatiemanagement in praktisch perspectief. Assen: Van Gorcum. Blz.

Bordel Sánchez, B., Alcarria, R., Sánchez de Rivera, D., & Robles, T. (2018). Process execution in CyberPhysical Systems using cloud and Cyber-Physical Internet services. *The Journal of Supercomputing*, *74*(8), 4127–4169. doi:10.100711227-018-2416-4

Bort, J. (2014). *Bill Gates: People don't realise how many jobs will soon be lost to computers.* Retrieved October 10, 2018, from http://www.thejournal.ie/bill-gates-software-automatic-jobs-loss-bots-1363435-Mar2014/

Boudreau, J., & Rice, S. (2015). Bright, Shiny Objects and the Future of HR How Juniper Networks tests and integrates the most valuable new approaches. *Harvard Business Review*, *93*(7-8), 72–78.

Bovaird, T. (2007). Beyond engagement and participation: User and community coproduction of public services. *Public Administration Review*, *67*(5), 846–860. doi:10.1111/j.1540-6210.2007.00773.x

Brammer, S., Hoejmose, S., & Marchant, K. (2011). Environmental management in SMEs in the UK: Practices, pressures and perceived benefits. *Business Strategy and the Environment*, *21*(7), 423–434. doi:10.1002/bse.717

Brammer, S., Jackson, G., & Matten, D. (2012). Corporate social responsibility and institutional theory: New perspectives on private governance. *Socio-economic Review*, *10*(1), 3–28. doi:10.1093er/mwr030

Branco, M. C., & Rodrigues, L. L. (2006). Corporate social responsibility and resource-based perspectives. *Journal of Business Ethics*, *69*(2), 111–132. doi:10.100710551-006-9071-z

Broniarczyk, S. M., & Alba, J. W. (1994). The importance of the brand in brand extension. *JMR, Journal of Marketing Research*, *31*(2), 214–228. doi:10.1177/002224379403100206

Brougham, D., & Haar, J. (2018). Smart Technology, Artificial Intelligence, Robotics, and Algorithms (STARA): Employees' perceptions of our future workplace. *Journal of Management & Organization*, *24*(2), 239–257. doi:10.1017/jmo.2016.55

Brown, B., Chui, M., & Manyika, J. (2011). Are you ready for the era of 'big data'. *The McKinsey Quarterly*, *4*(1), 24–35.

Broy, M., Cengarle, M. V., & Geisberger, E. (2012). Cyber-Physical Systems: Imminent Challenges. *Large-Scale Complex IT Syst. Dev., Operat. and Manag. - 17th Monterey Workshop*, 7539, 1–28.

Brulin, G., & Svensson, L. (2012). *Managing Sustainable Development Programmes: A Learning Approach to Change*. Gower Publishing.

Brunninge, O., Nordqvist, M., & Wiklund, J. (2007). Corporate governance and strategic change in SMEs: The effects of ownership, board composition and top management teams. *Small Business Economics*, *29*(3), 295–308. doi:10.100711187-006-9021-2

Bruns, T., & Stalker, G. M. (1961). *The management of innovation*. Tavistock.

Brusoni, S., & Prencipe, A. (2001). Unpacking the black box of modularity: Technologies, products and organizations. *Industrial and Corporate Change*, *10*(1), 179–205. doi:10.1093/icc/10.1.179

Brusoni, S., Prencipe, A., & Pavitt, K. (2001). Knowledge specialization, organizational coupling, and the boundaries of the firm: Why do firms know more than they make? *Administrative Science Quarterly*, *46*(4), 597–621. doi:10.2307/3094825

Bruton, G., Sutter, C., & Lenz, A. K. (2021). Economic inequality–Is entrepreneurship the cause or the solution? A review and research agenda for emerging economies. *Journal of Business Venturing*, *36*(3), 106095. doi:10.1016/j.jbusvent.2021.106095

Buck. (2012). *The Talent Wave*. London: Kogan Page.

Bui, B., & De Villiers, C. (2017). Management control systems to support sustainability and integrated reporting. In *Sustainability Accounting and Integrated Reporting* (pp. 121–148). Routledge. doi:10.4324/9781315108032-11

Burke, S., & Gaughran, W. F. (2006). Intelligent environmental management for SMEs in manufacturing. *Robotics and Computer-integrated Manufacturing*, *22*(5–6), 566–575. doi:10.1016/j.rcim.2005.11.008

Burton, N., & Galvin, P. (2018). When do product architectures mirror organisational architectures? The combined role of product complexity and the rate of technological change. *Technology Analysis and Strategic Management*, *30*(9), 1057–1069. doi:10.1080/09537325.2018.1437259

Butler, J. B., Henderson, S. C., & Raiborn, C. (2011, Winter). Sustainability and the Balanced Scorecard: Integrating Green Measures into Business Reporting. *Management Accounting Quarterly*, *12*(2), 1–10.

Byrne, B. M. (2016). *Structural equation modeling with AMOS: Basic concepts, applications, and programming*. Routledge/Taylor & Francis. doi:10.4324/9781315757421

Cabigiosu, A., & Camuffo, A. (2012). Beyond the "mirroring" hypothesis: Product modularity and interorganizational relations in the air conditioning industry. *Organization Science*, *23*(3), 686–703. doi:10.1287/orsc.1110.0655

Calogirou, C., Sørensen, S. Y., Bjørn Larsen, P., & Alexopoulou, S. (2010). *SMEs and the Environment in the European Union PLANET SA and Danish Technological Institute for European Commission, DG Enterprise and Industry, Brussels*. Available at: https://op.europa.eu/en/publication-detail/-/publication/aa507ab8-1a2a-4bf1-86de-5a60d14a3977

Cammarano, A., Michelino, F., & Caputo, M. (2019). Open innovation practices for knowledge acquisition and their effects on innovation output. *Technology Analysis and Strategic Management*, *31*(11), 1297–1313. doi:10.1080/09537325.2019.1606420

Cantele, S., & Zardini, A. (2020). What drives small and medium enterprises towards sustainability? Role of interactions between pressures, barriers, and benefits. *Corporate Social Responsibility and Environmental Management*, *27*(1), 126–136. doi:10.1002/csr.1778

Cantoni, F., & Mangia, G. (Eds.). (2019). *Human resource management and digitalization* (1st ed.). Routledge.

Capgemini Research Institute and LinkedIn. (2017). *The Digital Talent Gap: Are Companies Doing Enough?* Available at https://www.capgemini.com/wp-content/uploads/2017/10/Digital-Talent-Gap-Report_Digital.pdf

Carland, J. W., Hoy, F., & Carland, J. A. C. (1988). "Who is an entrepreneur?" is a question worth asking. *American Journal of Small Business*, *12*(4), 33–39. doi:10.1177/104225878801200402

Carney, M., & Nason, R. S. (2018). Family business and the 1%. *Business & Society*, *57*(6), 1191–1215. doi:10.1177/0007650316661165

Carpinetti, L. C., & De Melo, A. M. (2002). What to benchmark? *Benchmarking*, *9*(3), 244–255. doi:10.1108/14635770210429009

Caruana, R., Crane, A., Gold, S., & LeBaron, G. (2020). Modern slavery in business: The sad and sorry state of a non-field. *Business & Society*.

Casais, B. (2020). *Gestão da Distribuição em e-Marketplaces*. Retrieved from http://e-agroinnovation.agrocluster.com/uploads/AGROCLUSTER_Ebooks - E-Marketplaces.pdf

Casanova, A. M. (2018). BYJU's: How a learning app is promoting deep conceptual understanding that is improving educational outcomes in India (No. 125923). The World Bank.

Castiglioni, M., Celli, A., Marchesi, A., & Gatti, N. (2020). Online Bayesian persuasion. *Advances in Neural Information Processing Systems*, 33.

Cesario, J., Grant, H., & Higgins, E. T. (2004). Regulatory fit and persuasion: Transfer from "feeling right.". *Journal of Personality and Social Psychology*, *86*(3), 388–404. doi:10.1037/0022-3514.86.3.388 PMID:15008644

Cesario, J., Higgins, E. T., & Scholer, A. A. (2008). Regulatory fit and persuasion: Basic principles and remaining questions. *Social and Personality Psychology Compass*, *2*(1), 444–463. doi:10.1111/j.1751-9004.2007.00055.x

Challa, A., & Anute, N. (2020). *Strategic analysis of emerging online tutoring platforms in India.* Academic Press.

Chang, E.-C., Lv, Y., Chou, T.-J., He, Q., & Song, Z. (2014). Now or later: Delay's effects on post-consumption emotions and consumer loyalty. *Journal of Business Research*, *67*(7), 1368–1375. doi:10.1016/j.jbusres.2013.08.016

Chang, Y.-T., Yu, H., & Lu, H.-P. (2015). Persuasive messages, popularity cohesion, and message diffusion in social media marketing. *Journal of Business Research*, *68*(4), 777–782. doi:10.1016/j.jbusres.2014.11.027

Chanias, S., Myers, M. D., & Hess, T. (2019). Digital transformation strategy making in pre-digital organizations: The case of a financial services provider. *The Journal of Strategic Information Systems*, *28*(1), 17–33. doi:10.1016/j.jsis.2018.11.003

Chaparro-Peláez, J., Agudo-Peregrina, Á. F., & Pascual-Miguel, F. J. (2016). Conjoint analysis of drivers and inhibitors of e-commerce adoption. *Journal of Business Research*, *69*(4), 1277–1282. doi:10.1016/j.jbusres.2015.10.092

Chattopadhyay, S., Shankar, S., Gangadhar, R. B., & Kasinathan, K. (2018). Applications of artificial intelligence in assessment for learning in schools. In *Handbook of research on digital content, mobile learning, and technology integration models in teacher education* (pp. 185–206). IGI Global. doi:10.4018/978-1-5225-2953-8.ch010

Chavan, R. R., & Shukla, A. (2019). New Generation E-entrepreneurship-A Case study of BYJU's. *Sumedha Journal of Management*, *8*(3), 228–232.

Cheng, H., Xue, L., Wang, P., Zeng, P., & Yu, H. (2017). Ontology-based web service integration for flexible manufacturing systems. In *15th Int. Conf. on Ind. Inf.* (pp. 351–356). IEEE. 10.1109/INDIN.2017.8104797

Chen, L., Gillenson, M. L., & Sherrell, D. L. (2002). Enticing online consumers: An extended technology acceptance perspective. *Information & Management*, *39*(8), 705–719. doi:10.1016/S0378-7206(01)00127-6

Chen, S.-H., & Lee, K.-P. (2008). The role of personality traits and perceived values in persuasion: An elaboration likelihood model perspective on online shopping. *Social Behaviour and Personality: An International Journal*, *36*(10), 1379–1399. doi:10.2224bp.2008.36.10.1379

Chesbrough, H. W., & Appleyard, M. M. (2007). Open innovation and strategy. *California Management Review*, *50*(1), 57–76. doi:10.2307/41166416

Chinta, R., & Kloppenborg, T. J. (2010). Projects and processes for sustainable organizational growth. *S.A.M. Advanced Management Journal*, *75*(2), 22.

Choi, K., Yoo, D., Kim, G., & Suh, Y. (2012). A hybrid online-product recommendation system: Combining implicit rating-based collaborative filtering and sequential pattern analysis. *Electronic Commerce Research and Applications*, *11*(4), 309–317. doi:10.1016/j.elerap.2012.02.004

Choo, C. W. (2001). Knowing Organization as Learning Organization. *Education + Training, 43*(4/5), 197-205.

Chowhan, J. (2016). Unpacking the black box: Understanding the relation-ship between strategy, HRM practices, innovation and organizational performance. *Human Resource Management Journal*, *26*(2), 112–133. doi:10.1111/1748-8583.12097

Christensen, C. M., Bartman, T., & Vanbelver, D. (2016, September). The Hard Truth About Business Model. *MIT Sloan Management Review*.

Christmann, P. (2000). Effects of "Best practices" Of environmental management on cost advantage: The role of complementary assets. *Academy of Management Journal*, *43*(4), 663–680. doi:10.2307/1556360

Chu, S., & Majumdar, A. (2012). Opportunities and challenges for a sustainable energy future. *Nature*, *488*(August), 294–303. doi:10.1038/nature11475 PMID:22895334

Cimini, C., Boffelli, A., Lagorio, A., Kalchschmidt, M., & Pinto, R. (2020). How do industry 4.0 technologies influence organisational change? An empirical analysis of Italian SMEs. *Journal of Manufacturing Technology Management*, *32*(3), 695–721. doi:10.1108/JMTM-04-2019-0135

Ciortea, A., Mayer, S., & Michahelles, F. (2018). Repurposing Manufacturing Lines on the Fly with Multi-agent Systems for the Web of Things. In *Proc. of the 17th Int. Conf. on Autonomous Agents and Multi-Agent Systems* (pp. 813–822). ACM.

Cockayne, D. (2016). Redefining B2B relationship marketing: Insight from postmodern Alibaba. *Journal of Customer Behaviour*, *15*(1), 49–66. doi:10.1362/147539216X14594362873497

Codorniou, J. (2018). *6 Trends Shaping a Future for People in the Workplace*. Available at https://www.entrepreneur.com/article/309804

Coetzer, A., Kock, H., & Wallo, A. (2017). Distinctive characteristics of small businesses assites for informal learning. *Human Resource Development Review*, 18–32.

Colfer, L., & Baldwin, C. Y. (2016). The mirroring hypothesis: Theory, evidence and exceptions. *Industrial and Corporate Change*, *25*(5), 709–738. doi:10.1093/icc/dtw027

Colitti, Steenhaut, Caro, & De. (2011). Integrating Wireless Sensor Networks with the Web. *Extending the Internet to Low power and Lossy Networks (IP+SN).*

Colucci, S., Di Noia, T., Pinto, A., Ruta, M., Ragone, A., & Tinelli, E. (2007). A Nonmonotonic Approach to Semantic Matchmaking and Request Refinement in E-Marketplaces. *International Journal of Electronic Commerce*, *12*(2), 127–154. doi:10.2753/JEC1086-4415120205

Commission on Environment and Development. (1987). *World Commission on Environment and Development* (Brundtland Report). Available from: http://www.ace.mmu.ac.uk/ eae/Sustainability/ Older/Brundtland_Report.html

Coraddu, A., Oneto, L., Baldi, F., Cipollini, F., Atlar, M., & Savio, S. (2019). Data-driven ship digital twin for estimating the speed loss caused by the marine fouling. *Ocean Engineering, 186*(March), 106063. doi:10.1016/j.oceaneng.2019.05.045

Cory, A., Henson, J., Pschorr, K., Sheth, A. P., & Thirunarayan, K. (2009). SemSOS: Semantic sensor Observation Service. *Proceedings of the International Symposium on Collaborative Technologies and Systems.*

Côté, R., Booth, A., & Louis, B. (2006). Eco-efficiency and SMEs in Nova Scotia, Canada. *Journal of Cleaner Production, 14*(6-7), 542–550. doi:10.1016/j.jclepro.2005.07.004

Cotet, G. B., Balgiu, B. A., & Zaleschi, V.-C. (2017). Assessment procedure for the soft skills requested by Industry 4.0. *8th International Conference on Manufacturing Science and Education – MSE 2017 "Trends in New Industrial Revolution,"* 1–8. 10.1051/matecconf/201712107005

Coviello, L., Sohn, Y., Kramer, A. D. I., Marlow, C., Franceschetti, M., Christakis, N. A., & Fowler, J. H. (2014). Detecting emotional contagion in massive social networks. *PLoS One, 9*(3), e90315. doi:10.1371/journal.pone.0090315 PMID:24621792

Cristea, C., & Cristea, M. (2021). KPIs for Operational Performance Assessment in Flexible Packaging Industry. *Sustainability, 13*(6), 3498. doi:10.3390u13063498

Crittenden, A. B., Crittenden, V. L., & Crittenden, W. F. (2019). The digitalization triumvirate: How incumbents survive. *Business Horizons, 62*(2), 259–266. doi:10.1016/j.bushor.2018.11.005

Crossan, M. M., & Berdrow, I. (2011). Organizational learning and strategic renewal. *Strategic Management Journal, 24*(11), 1087–1105. doi:10.1002mj.342

Crossan, M., Lane, H. W., & White, R. E. (1999). An organizational learning framework: From intuition to institution. *Academy of Management Review, 24*(3), 522–537. doi:10.2307/259140

Csikszentmihalyi, M., (2015). Society, culture, and person: a systems view of creativity. *Syst. Model Creativity,* 47–61.

Cui, Z., Xu, X., Fei, X. U. E., Cai, X., Cao, Y., Zhang, W., & Chen, J. (2020). Personalized recommendation system based on collaborative filtering for IoT scenarios. *IEEE Transactions on Services Computing, 13*(4), 685–695. doi:10.1109/TSC.2020.2964552

Cummings, T. G., & Worley, C. G. (2014*). Organization development and change.* Cengage Learning.

Curry, N., & Pillay, P. (2012). Biogas prediction and design of a food waste to energy system for the urban environment. *Renewable Energy, 41*(May), 200–209. doi:10.1016/j.renene.2011.10.019

Daft, R. L. (2015). *Organization theory and design.* Cengage Learning.

Daily, B. F., Bishop, J. W., & Massoud, J. A. (2012). The role of training and empowerment in environmental performance: A study of the Mexican maquiladora industry. *International Journal of Operations & Production Management, 32*(5).

Damanpour, F. (1996). Organizational Complexity and Innovation Developing and Testing Multiple Contingency Models. *Management Science, 42*, 693–716.

Danish, R. Q., Munir, Y., Kausar, A., Jabbar, M., & Munawar, N. (2015). Impact of change, culture and organizational politics on organizational learning. *Rev. Contemp. Bus.Res, 3*(1), 115–126.

Darley, W. K., Blankson, C., & Luethge, D. J. (2010). Toward an integrated framework for online consumer behaviour and decision making process: A review. *Psychology & Marketing, 27*, 94–116.

Dastin, J. (2018, October 10). Amazon scraps secret AI recruiting tool that showed bias against women. *Reuters*. Available at https://www.reuters.com/article/us-amazon-com-jobs-automation-insight/amazon-scraps-secret-airecruiting-tool-that-showed-bias-against-women-idUSKCN1MK08G

Davenport, T. H., Barth, P., & Bean, R. (2012). How'big data'is different. *MIT Sloan Management Review*.

Davenport, T., Guha, A., Grewal, D., & Bressgott, T. (2020). How artificial intelligence will change the future of marketing. *Journal of the Academy of Marketing Science, 48*(1), 24–42. doi:10.100711747-019-00696-0

Davis, F. D. (1989, September). Perceived usefulness, perceived ease of use, and user acceptance of information technology. *Management Information Systems Quarterly, 13*(3), 319–340. doi:10.2307/249008

Dawid, G., Magdalena, K., & Karolina, K. (2019). CSR Practices in Polish and Spanish Stock Listed Companies: A Comparative Analysis. *Sustainability, 11*(4), 1054. doi:10.3390u11041054

de Bakker, F. G., Matten, D., Spence, L. J., & Wickert, C. (2020). *The elephant in the room: The nascent research agenda on corporations, social responsibility, and capitalism*. Academic Press.

De Virgilio, R., Di Sciascio, E., Ruta, M., Scioscia, F., & Torlone, R. (2011). Semantic-based rfid data management. In *Unique Radio Innovation for the 21st Century* (pp. 111–141). Springer. doi:10.1007/978-3-642-03462-6_6

Deloitte. (2018). *The rise of the social enterprise. 2018 Deloitte global human capital trends*. Available at: www2.deloitte.com/content/dam/Deloitte/at/Documents/human-capital/at2018-deloitte-human-capital-trends.pdf

Deng, X., Doll, W. J., Hendrickson, A. R., & Scazzero, J. A. (2005). A multi-group analysis of structural invariance: An illustration using the technology acceptance model. *Information & Management, 42*(5), 745–759. doi:10.1016/j.im.2004.08.001

DeSteno, D., Petty, R. E., Rucker, D. D., Wegener, D. T., & Braverman, J. (2004). Discrete emotions and persuasion: The role of emotion-induced expectancies. *Journal of Personality and Social Psychology*, *86*(1), 43–56. doi:10.1037/0022-3514.86.1.43 PMID:14717627

Dewulf, J., & Van Langenhove, H. (Eds.). (2006). *Renewables-based technology: sustainability assessment.* John Wiley & Sons. doi:10.1002/0470022442

Dias Sant'Ana, T., de Souza Bermejo, P. H., Moreira, M. F., & de Souza, W. V. B. (2020). The structure of an innovation ecosystem: Foundations for future research. *Management Decision*, *58*(12), 2725–2742. doi:10.1108/MD-03-2019-0383

Dicle, Ü., & Okan, R. Y. (2015). The relationship between organizational structure andorganizational learning in Turkish automotive R&D companies. *Int. J. Manag. Stud. Res.*, 62–71.

Docherty, P., Forslin, J., Shani, A. B., & Kira, M. (2002) Emerging Work Systems: From Intensive to Sustainable? In Creating Sustainable Work Systems: Perspectives and Practices. London: Routledge.

Donaldson, C. (2016, December 5). How Microsoft is driving digital HR transformation. *Inside HR.* Available at https://www.insidehr.com.au/microsoft-driving-digital-hr-transformation/

Dreyer, L., Hauschild, M., & Schierbeck, J. (2006). A framework for social life cycle impact assessment (10 pp). *The International Journal of Life Cycle Assessment*, *11*(2), 88–97. doi:10.1065/lca2005.08.223

Droege, P. (Ed.). (2008). *Urban Energy Transition: From Fossil Fuels to Renewable Power.* Elsevier Ltd. doi:10.1016/B978-0-08-045341-5.00029-3

Dumbill, E. (2013). *Making sense of big data.* Academic Press.

Du, S., Yu, K., Bhattacharya, C. B., & Sen, S. (2017). The Business Case for Sustainability Reporting: Evidence from Stock Market Reactions. *Journal of Public Policy & Marketing*, *36*(2), 312–330. doi:10.1509/jppm.16.112

Egbu, C. O. (2004). Managing knowledge and intellectual capital for improved organizational innovations in the construction industry: An examination of critical success factors. *Engineering, Construction, and Architectural Management*, *11*(5), 301–315. doi:10.1108/09699980410558494

Ehsani Ghods, H., & Sayed Abbas Zadeh, M. M. (2012). Relationship between learning organization with creativity and innovation, a high school teacher and colleges, *Journal-Research New Approaches in Educational Administration. Islamic Azad University of Shiraz*, *4*, 12–21.

Eizenberg, E., & Jabareen, Y. (2017). Social Sustainability: A New Conceptual Framework. *Sustainability*, *9*(1), 68. doi:10.3390u9010068

Ejsmont, K. (2021). The Impact of Industry 4.0 on Employees—Insights from Australia. *Sustainability 2021*, *13*(6), 3095. doi:10.3390/su13063095

Eklund, M. A. (2020). Future Prospects in Balanced Scorecard Research: Sustainability Perspective. *Indonesian Journal of Sustainability Accounting and Management*, *4*(2), 192. doi:10.28992/ijsam.v4i2.263

El Baz, J., Laguir, I., Marais, M., & Staglianò, R. (2014). Influence of national institutions on the corporate social responsibility practices of small- and medium-sized enterprises in the food-processing industry: Differences between France and Morocco. *Journal of Business Ethics*, *134*(1), 117–133. doi:10.100710551-014-2417-z

Elkington, J. (1994). Towards the sustainable corporation: win– win–win business strategies for sustainable development. *California Management Review*, *36*(2), 90 – 100. doi:10.2307/41165746

Ellström, P.-E. (2001). Integrating learning and work: Conceptual issues and critical conditions. *Human Resource Development Quarterly*, *12*(4), 421–435.

Elving, W. J. (2005). The role of communication in organisational change. *Corporate Communications*, *10*(2), 129–138. doi:10.1108/13563280510596943

environmental practices a strategical decision for small service companies? Management Decision, 51(1), 41–62. doi:10.1108/00251741311291300

Erbe. (2014). *Approaches to Managing Organizational Diversity and Innovation*. Global.IGI

Ernst, D. (2005). Limits to modularity: Reflections on recent developments in chip design. *Industry and Innovation*, *12*(3), 303–335. doi:10.1080/13662710500195918

Erol, S., Schuhmacher, A., & Sihn, W. (2016). Resource Efficiency for Global Competitiveness. *International Conference on Competitive Manufacturing (COMA)*, 495–500. http://publica.fraunhofer.de/documents/N-382579.html

Erol, S., Jäger, A., Hold, P., Ott, K., & Sihn, W. (2016). Tangible Industry 4.0: A Scenario-Based Approach to Learning for the Future of Production. *Procedia CIRP*, *54*, 13–18. doi:10.1016/j.procir.2016.03.162

Ethiraj, S. K. (2007). Allocation of inventive effort in complex product systems. *Strategic Management Journal*, *28*(6), 563–584. doi:10.1002mj.622

European Commission. (2013). *ESCO European Classification of Skills/Competences, Qualifications and Occupations. The first public release*. doi:10.2767/76494

European Commission. (2021). *A European Green Deal*. Available at: https://ec.europa.eu/info/strategy/priorities-2019-2024/european-green-deal_en

European Commission. (2021a). *ESCO - ESCOpedia*. https://ec.europa.eu/esco/portal/escopedia/Occupations_pillar

European Commission. (2021b). *ESCO - Occupations - Software and applications developers and analysts*. https://ec.europa.eu/esco/portal/occupation?uri=http%3A%2F%2Fdata.europa.eu%2Fesco%2Fisco%2FC251&conceptLanguage=en&full=true#&uri=http://data.europa.eu/esco/isco/C251&treeSelection=C2,C25,C251

Eurostat. (2012). *Population statistics for Mediterranean countries*. Retrieved from https://www.eea.europa.eu/data-and-maps/daviz/sds/population-statistics-for-mediterranean-countries-eurostat/@@view

Eurostat. (2014). *Digital single market-promoting e-commerce for individuals*. Retrieved from http://ec.europa.eu/eurostat/web/products-datasets/ -/isoc_bdek_smi

Falletta, S. (2014). In search of HR intelligence: Evidence-based HR analytics practices in high performing companies. *People and Strategy*, *36*(4), 28.

Felfernig, A., Gula, B., Leitner, G., Maier, M., Melcher, R., & Teppan, E. (2008). Persuasion in Knowledge-Based Recommendation. In H. Oinas-Kukkonen, P. Hasle, M. Harjumaa, K. Segerståhl, & P. Øhrstrøm (Eds.), Lecture Notes in Computer Science: Vol. 5033. *Persuasive Technology. PERSUASIVE 2008*. Springer. doi:10.1007/978-3-540-68504-3_7

Fenton, A., Fletcher, G., & Griffiths, M. (Eds.). (2019). *Strategic digital transformation : a results-driven approach* (1st ed.). Routledge. doi:10.4324/9780429020469

Ferrero-Ferrero, I., Fernández-Izquierdo, M. Á., Muñoz-Torres, M. J., & Bellés-Colomer, L. (2018). Stakeholder engagement in sustainability reporting in higher education. *International Journal of Sustainability in Higher Education*, *19*(2), 313–336. doi:10.1108/IJSHE-06-2016-0116

Figge, F., Hahn, T., Schaltegger, S., & Wagner, M. (2002). The sustainability balanced scorecard - linking sustainability management to business strategy. *Business Strategy and the Environment*, *11*(5), 269–284. doi:10.1002/bse.339

Fine, C. H., Golany, B., & Naseraldin, H. (2005). Modeling tradeoffs in three-dimensional concurrent engineering: A goal programming approach. *Journal of Operations Management*, *23*(3), 389–403. doi:10.1016/j.jom.2004.09.005

Fitsilis, P., Tsoutsa, P., & Gerogiannis, V. (2018). Industry 4.0: Required personnel competences. *Industry 4.0, 3*(3), 130–133.

Fletcher, G., & Griffiths, M. (2020). Digital transformation during a lockdown. *International Journal of Information Management*, *102185*(June). doi:10.1016/j.ijinfomgt.2020.102185

Foley, J. A., DeFries, R., Asner, G. P., Barford, C., Bonan, G., Carpenter, S. R., Chapin, F. S., Coe, M. T., Daily, G. C., Gibbs, H. K., Helkowski, J. H., Holloway, T., Howard, E. A., Kucharik, C. J., Monfreda, C., Patz, J. A., Prentice, I. C., Ramankutty, N., & Snyder, P. K. (2005). Global Consequences of Land Use. *Science*, *309*(5734), 570–574. doi:10.1126cience.1111772 PMID:16040698

Fornell, C., & Larcker, D. F. (1981). Structural equation models with unobservable variables and measurement error: Algebra and statistics. *JMR, Journal of Marketing Research*, *18*(3), 382–388. doi:10.1177/002224378101800313

Forsythe, S., Liu, C., Shannon, D., & Gardner, L. C. (2006). Development of a scale to measure the perceived benefits and risks of online shopping. *Journal of Interactive Marketing*, *20*(2), 55–75. doi:10.1002/dir.20061

Foss, N. J., & Lyngsie, J. (2011). *The Emerging Strategic Entrepreneurship Field: Origins.* Academic Press.

Foutty, J. (2019, January 23). Aspire to Lead in Industry 4.0? Hone Your Soft Skills. *The Wall Street Journal.* https://deloitte.wsj.com/articles/aspire-to-lead-in-industry-4-0-hone-your-soft-skills-01548295337

Francina, V. J., & Aarthi, K. (2020). Advertising and Business Strategy of an Indian Edu Tech Giant-Byju's. *Journal of Media and Corporate Management*, *3*(2).

Franco, M., & Rodrigues, M. (2019). Sustainable practices in SMEs: Reducing the ecological footprint. *The Journal of Business Strategy*, *42*(2), 137–142. doi:10.1108/JBS-07-2019-0136

Frank, A. (2018). *How Artificial Intelligence Will Impact the Future of Work.* Available at https://www.cmswire.com/digital-workplace/how-artificial-intelligence-will-impact-the-future-of-work/

Freedman, L. (2015). *Strategy: A history.* Oxford University Press.

Freeman, R. E. (1994). The politics of stakeholder theory: Some future directions. *Business Ethics Quarterly*, *4*(4), 409–421. doi:10.2307/3857340

Freeman, R. E. (2010). *Strategic Management.* Cambridge University Press. doi:10.1017/CBO9781139192675

Freeman, R. E., Wicks, A. C., & Parmar, B. (2004). Stakeholder theory and "The corporate objective revisited". *Organization Science*, *15*(3), 364–369. doi:10.1287/orsc.1040.0066

Friedman, A. L., & Miles, S. (2002). SMEs and the environment: Evaluating dissemination routes and handholding levels. *Business Strategy and the Environment*, *11*(5), 324–341. doi:10.1002/bse.335

Friedman, S., Scholink, E., & Cocking, R. (1987). *Blue prints for thinking: The role of planning in cognitive development.* Cambridge Univ. Press.

Frigant, V., & Lung, Y. (2002). Geographical proximity and supplying relationships in modular production. *International Journal of Urban and Regional Research*, *26*(4), 742–755. doi:10.1111/1468-2427.00415

Frigant, V., & Talbot, D. (2005). Technological determinism and modularity: Lessons from a comparison between aircraft and auto industries in Europe. *Industry and Innovation*, *12*(3), 337–355. doi:10.1080/13662710500195934

Fu, P. P., Kennedy, J., Tata, J., Yukl, G., Bond, M. H., Peng, T.-K., & Koopman, P. (2004). The impact of societal cultural values and individual social beliefs on the perceived effectiveness of managerial influence strategies: A meso approach. *Journal of International Business Studies*, *35*(4), 284–305. doi:10.1057/palgrave.jibs.8400090

Furlan, A., Cabigiosu, A., & Camuffo, A. (2014). When the mirror gets misted up: Modularity and technological change. *Strategic Management Journal*, *35*(6), 789–807. doi:10.1002mj.2138

Gans, H. J. (2017). The participant-observer as a human being: Observations on the personal aspects of field work. In *Institutions and the Person* (pp. 300–138). Routledge. doi:10.4324/9780203788448-23

Ganu, G., Kakodkar, Y., & Marian, A. (2013). Improving the quality of predictions using textual information in online user reviews. *Information Systems*, *38*(1), 1–15. doi:10.1016/j.is.2012.03.001

García-Piqueres, G., Serrano-Bedia, A. M., López-Fernández, M. C., & Pérez-Pérez, M. (2020). Relatedness in the adoption of different innovation types: Product, process, organisational and commercial innovations. *Technology Analysis and Strategic Management*, *32*(1), 44–57. doi:10.1080/09537325.2019.1632822

Gartner, W. B. (1988). "Who is an entrepreneur?" is the wrong question. *American Journal of Small Business*, *12*(4), 11–32. doi:10.1177/104225878801200401

Gazioğlu, C. (2018). Biodiversity, coastal protection, promotion and applicability investigation of the ocean health index for Turkish seas. *International Journal of Environment and Geoinformatics*, *5*(3), 353–367. doi:10.30897/ijegeo.484067

Gebhardt, J., Flensburg, E.-U., & Neugebauer, L. M. (2015). Developments 4.0 Prospects on future requirements and impacts on work and vocational education. *JOTED*, *3*, 117–133.

Geertshuis, S., Holmes, M., Geertshuis, H., Clancy, D., & Bristol, A. (2002). Evaluation of workplace learning. *Journal of Workplace Learning*, *14*(1), 11–18.

George, G., Haas, M., & Pentland, A. (2014). 'Big data and management'. *Academy of Management Journal*, *57*(2), 321–326. doi:10.5465/amj.2014.4002

Ghasemaghaei, M., Hassanein, K., & Benbasat, I. (2019). Assessing the design choices for online recommendation agents for older adults: Older does not always mean simpler information technology. *Management Information Systems Quarterly*, *43*(1), 329–346. doi:10.25300/MISQ/2019/13947

Goel. (2016). *Product Innovation through Management and Social Media Strategies*. IGI Global.

Golden, M. (2011). *Social Media Strategies for Professionals and Their Firms*. Wiley and Sons.

Gölzer, P., & Fritzsche, A. (2017). Data-driven operations management: Organisational implications of the digital transformation in industrial practice. *Production Planning and Control*, *28*(16), 1332–1343. doi:10.1080/09537287.2017.1375148

Gomes, C. M., Kneipp, J. M., Kruglianskas, I., Rosa, L. A., & Bichueti, R. S. (2015). Management for sustainability: An analysis of the key practices according to the business size. *Ecological Indicators, 52*, 116–127. doi:10.1016/j.ecolind.2014.11.012

Gomes, G., & Wojahn, R. M. (2017). Organizational learning capability, innovation and performance. *Revista ADM, 52*, 163–175.

Goodyear, M., Ames-Oliver, K., & Russell, K. (2014). *Organizational Strategies for Fostering a Culture of Learning*. University of Kansas.

Granstrand, O. (1999). *The economics and management of intellectual property*. Books.

Gray, R. (2006). Social, environmental and sustainability reporting and organisational value creation? *Accounting, Auditing & Accountability Journal, 19*(6), 793–819. doi:10.1108/09513570610709872

Grega, W., & Kornecki, A. J. (2015). Real-time cyber-physical Systems transatlantic engineering curricula framework. *Proceedings of the 2015 Federated Conference on Computer Science and Information Systems, FedCSIS 2015*, 755–762. 10.15439/2015F45

Grenčíková, A., Kordoš, M., & Berkovič, V. (2020). The Impact of Industry 4.0 on Jobs Creation within the Small and Medium-Sized Enterprises and Family Businesses in Slovakia. *Administrative Sciences 2020, 10*(3), 71. doi:10.3390/admsci10030071

Grewal, D., Roggeveen, A. L., & Nordfält, J. (2017). The future of retailing. *Journal of Retailing, 93*(1), 1–6. doi:10.1016/j.jretai.2016.12.008

Grieves, M. (2014). *Digital Twin: Manufacturing Excellence through Virtual Factory Replication*. Academic Press.

Grimheden, M. E., & Törngren, M. (2014, October 12). Towards curricula for Cyber-Physical Systems. *2014 Workshop on Embedded and Cyber-Physical Systems Education, WESE 2014 - Proceedings*. 10.1145/2829957.2829965

Griskevicius, V., Goldstein, N. J., Mortensen, C. R., Sundie, J. M., Cialdini, R. B., & Kenrick, D. T. (2009). Fear and loving in Las Vegas: Evolution, emotion, and persuasion. *JMR, Journal of Marketing Research, 46*(3), 384–395. doi:10.1509/jmkr.46.3.384 PMID:19727416

Griskevicius, V., Shiota, M. N., & Neufeld, S. L. (2010). Influence of different positive emotions on persuasion processing: A functional evolutionary approach. *Emotion (Washington, D.C.), 10*(2), 190–206. doi:10.1037/a0018421 PMID:20364895

Griskevicius, V., Shiota, M. N., & Nowlis, S. M. (2010). The many shades of rose-colored glasses: An evolutionary approach to the influence of different positive emotions. *The Journal of Consumer Research, 37*(2), 238–250. doi:10.1086/651442

Grzelczak, A., Kosacka, M., & Werner-Lewandowska, K. (2017). Employees competences for industry 4.0 in Poland–preliminary research results. *24th International Conference on Production Research, ICPR 2017*, 139–144. 10.12783/dtetr/icpr2017/17598

Gubbi, J., Buyya, R., Marusic, S., & Palaniswami, M. (2013). Internet of Things (IoT): A vision, architectural elements, and future directions. *Future Generation Computer Systems, 29*(7), 1645–1660.

Gudanowska, A. E., Alonso, J. P., & Törmänen, A. (2018). What competencies are needed in the production industry? The case of the Podlaskie Region. *Engineering Management in Production and Services, 10*(1), 65–74. doi:10.1515/emj-2018-0006

Guerras-Martín, L. Á., Madhok, A., & Montoro-Sánchez, Á. (2014). The evolution of strategic management research: Recent trends and current directions. *BRQ Business Research Quarterly, 17*(2), 69–76. doi:10.1016/j.brq.2014.03.001

Guerrero, L., Claret, A., Verbeke, W., Enderli, G., Zakowska-Biemans, S., Vanhonacker, F., Issanchou, S., Sajdakowska, M., Granli, B. S., Scalvedi, L., Contel, M., & Hersleth, M. (2010). Perception of traditional food products in six European regions using free word association. *Food Quality and Preference, 21*(2), 225–233. doi:10.1016/j.foodqual.2009.06.003

Gulenc, K., & Ariturk, M. H. (2016). Is human emancipation through technology possible? *Synthesis Philosophica, 31*(1), 83–103. doi:10.21464p31106

Gunasekaran, A., Irani, Z., Choy, K. L., Filippi, L., & Papadopoulos, T. (2015). Performance measures and metrics in outsourcing decisions: A review for research and applications. *International Journal of Production Economics, 161*, 153–166. doi:10.1016/j.ijpe.2014.12.021

Günther, E., & Kaulich, S. (2005). The EPM-KOMPAS: An instrument to control the environmental performance in small and medium-sized enterprises (SMEs). *Business Strategy and the Environment, 14*(6), 361–371. doi:10.1002/bse.437

Guo, Q. (2015). Learning in a Mixed Reality System in the Context of Industrie 4.0. *Journal of Teacher Education, 3*(2). Advance online publication. doi:10.48513/JOTED.V3I2.60

Gupta, A. (2008). Earth on ðre: Implications for corporate responsibility. *American Journal of Business, 23*(1), 3–4.

Gupta, S., Verma, A., Jain, U., Narshimha, A., & Nanda, N. (2019). Consumer megatrends: Reshaping the Indian marketplace. *Journal of Critical Reviews, 6*(6), 103–114.

Haag, S., & Anderl, R. (2018). Digital twin – Proof of concept. *Manufacturing Letters, 15*, 64–66. doi:10.1016/j.mfglet.2018.02.006

Habermas, J. (1970). Technology and science as "ideology". In J. Habermas (Ed.), *Toward a rational society: Student protest, science, and politics* (pp. 81–122). Beacon Press.

Haddock, G., Maio, G. R., Arnold, K., & Huskinson, T. (2008). Should persuasion be affective or cognitive? The moderating effects of need for affect and need for cognition. *Personality and Social Psychology Bulletin, 34*(6), 769–778. doi:10.1177/0146167208314871 PMID:18344496

Ha, H.-Y., Muthaly, S. K., & Akamavi, R. K. (2010). Alternative explanations of online repurchasing behavioral intentions: A comparison study of Korean and UK young customers. *European Journal of Marketing*, *44*(6), 874–904. doi:10.1108/03090561011032757

Hahn, R., & Kühnen, M. (2013). Determinants of sustainability reporting: A review of results, trends, theory, and opportunities in an expanding field of research. *Journal of Cleaner Production*, *59*, 5–21. doi:10.1016/j.jclepro.2013.07.005

Halila, F. (2007). Networks as a means of supporting the adoption of organizational innovations in SMEs: The case of environmental management systems (EMSs) based on ISO 14001. *Corporate Social Responsibility and Environmental Management*, *14*(3), 167–181. doi:10.1002/csr.127

Hamelin, N., Thaichon, P., Abraham, C., Driver, N., Lipscombe, J., & Pillai, J. (2020). Storytelling, the scale of persuasion and retention: A neuromarketing approach. *Journal of Retailing and Consumer Services*, *55*, 102099. doi:10.1016/j.jretconser.2020.102099

Han, S. H., Kim, D. Y., Jang, H. S., & Choi, S. (2010). Strategies for contractors to sustain growth in the global construction market. *Habitat International*, *34*(1), 1–10. doi:10.1016/j.habitatint.2009.04.003

Hansen, E. G., & Schaltegger, S. (2014). The Sustainability Balanced Scorecard: A Systematic Review of Architectures. *Journal of Business Ethics*, *133*(2), 193–221. doi:10.100710551-014-2340-3

Hansen, E. G., & Schaltegger, S. (2016). Sustainability Balanced Scorecards and their Architectures: Irrelevant or Misunderstood? *Journal of Business Ethics*, *150*(4), 937–952. doi:10.100710551-017-3531-5

Han, Y. J., Nunes, J. C., & Dreze, X. (2010). Signaling status *with* luxury goods*: The* role *of* brand prominence. *Journal of Marketing*, *74*(4), 15–30. doi:10.1509/jmkg.74.4.015

Hao, B., Feng, Y., & Frigant, V. (2017). Rethinking the 'mirroring' hypothesis: Implications for technological modularity, tacit coordination, and radical innovation. *R & D Management*, *47*(1), 3–16. doi:10.1111/radm.12106

Harari, Y. N. (2014). *Sapiens. A Brief History of Humankind.* Academic Press.

Harari, Y. N. (2018). Yuval Noah Harari: the myth of freedom. *Guardian.* Accessed on August 23, 2021 from https://www.theguardian.com/books/2018/sep/14/yuval-noah-harari-the-new-threat-to-liberal-democracy

Hartmann, E. A., & Bovenschulte, M. (2013). Skills Needs Analysis for "Industry 4.0" Based on Roadmaps for Smart Systems. In *Using Technology Foresights for Identifying Future Skills Needs* (pp. 24–37). https://www.bmbf.de/pubRD/Umsetzungsempfehlungen_Industrie4_0.pdf

Hart, S. L. (1995). A natural-resource-Based view of the firm. *Academy of Management Review*, *20*(4), 986–1014. doi:10.5465/amr.1995.9512280033

Haslam, S. A. (1997). Stereotyping and social influence: Foundations of stereotype consensus. In R. Spears, P. J. Oakes, N. Ellemers, & S. A. Haslam (Eds.), *The social psychology of stereotyping and group life* (pp. 119–143). Blackwell.

Hecklau, F., Galeitzke, M., Flachs, S., & Kohl, H. (2016). Holistic approach for human resource management in Industry 4.0. *Procedia CIRP*, *54*, 1–6. doi:10.1016/j.procir.2016.05.102

Heckscher, Ch. (1994). *Defining the post-bureaucratic type.* Sage.

Heilig, L., Lalla-Ruiz, E., & Voß, S. (2017). Digital transformation in maritime ports: Analysis and a game theoretic framework. *NETNOMICS: Economic Research and Electronic Networking*, *18*(2–3), 227–254. doi:10.100711066-017-9122-x

Hellenic Statistical Authority. (2015). *Survey on the use of information and communication technologies by households: 2015.* Retrieved from https://www.statistics.gr/documents/20181/41c9a392-34c6-4250-87e1-0c7858f813e4

Henderson, R. M., & Clark, K. B. (1990). Architectural innovation: The reconfiguration of existing product technologies and the failure of established firms. *Administrative Science Quarterly*, *35*(1), 9–30. doi:10.2307/2393549

Hess, T., Benlian, A., Matt, C., & Wiesböck, F. (2016). Options for formulating a digital transformation strategy. *MIS Quarterly Executive*, *15*(2), 123–139. doi:10.4324/9780429286797-7

Hewitt-Dundas, N. (2006). Resource and capability constraints to innovation in small and large plants. *Small Business Economics*, *26*(3), 257–277. doi:10.100711187-005-2140-3

Higgins, E. T. (2000). Making a good decision: Value from fit. *The American Psychologist*, *55*(11), 1217–1230. doi:10.1037/0003-066X.55.11.1217 PMID:11280936

Higgins, E. T. (2005). Value from regulatory fit. *Current Directions in Psychological Science*, *14*(4), 209–213. doi:10.1111/j.0963-7214.2005.00366.x

Higgins, E. T. (2006). Value from hedonic experience and engagement. *Psychological Review*, *113*(3), 439–460. doi:10.1037/0033-295X.113.3.439 PMID:16802877

Hillary, R. (2004). Environmental management systems and the smaller enterprise. *Journal of Cleaner Production*, *12*(6), 561–569. doi:10.1016/j.jclepro.2003.08.006

Hillary, R. (Ed.). (2017). *Small and Medium-Sized Enterprises and the Environment.* Routledge. doi:10.4324/9781351282840

Hill, R. C., & Bowen, P. A. (1997). Sustainable construction: Principles and a framework for attainment. *Construction Management and Economics*, *15*(3), 223–239. doi:10.1080/014461997372971

Hirschhorn, L. (1988). *The workplace within: Psychodynamics of organizational life*. The Mit Press. doi:10.7551/mitpress/7306.001.0001

Hirsh, J. B., Kang, S. K., & Bodenhausen, G. V. (2012). Personalized persuasion: Tailoring persuasive appeals to recipients' personality traits. *Psychological Science*, *23*(6), 578–581. doi:10.1177/0956797611436349 PMID:22547658

Hoberg, P., Krcmar, H., & Welz, B. (2017). *Skills for Digital Transformation*. Academic Press.

Hoetker, G. (2006). Do modular products lead to modular organizations? *Strategic Management Journal*, *27*(6), 501–518. doi:10.1002mj.528

Hoetker, G., Swaminathan, A., & Mitchell, W. (2007). Modularity and the impact of buyer–supplier relationships on the survival of suppliers. *Management Science*, *53*(2), 178–191. doi:10.1287/mnsc.1060.0630

Holbrook, M. B., & Hirschman, E. C. (1982). The experiential aspects of consumption: Consumer fantasies, feelings, and fun. *The Journal of Consumer Research*, *9*(2), 132–140. doi:10.1086/208906

Holla, N., & Mitra, A. (2020). *Pushing the Boundaries of Indian Tech*. Observer Research Foundation Online Publications. Accessed on August 27, 2021 from https://www.orfonline.org/wp-content/uploads/2020/10/ORF-Women-in-Tech-report.pdf

Holloway, C., & Hand, H. H. (1988). Who's running the store, anyway? Artificial intelligence!!! *Business Horizons*, *31*(2), 70–76. doi:10.1016/0007-6813(88)90084-5

Holzwarth, M., Janiszewski, C., & Neumann, M. M. (2006). The influence of avatars on online consumer shopping behaviour. *Journal of Marketing*, *70*(4), 19–36. doi:10.1509/jmkg.70.4.019

Ho, S. Y., & Bodoff, D. (2014). The effects of web personalization on user attitude and behavior: An integration of the elaboration likelihood model and consumer search theory. *Management Information Systems Quarterly*, *38*(2), 497–520. doi:10.25300/MISQ/2014/38.2.08

Hotho, J. J., Lyles, M. A., & Smith, M. (2015). The mutual impact of global strategy and organizational learning: current themes and future directions. *Glob. Strat. J.*, 85–112.

Hoveida, R. (2007). *Investigating the relationship between learning the components of the organization and improving the quality of education the door* (Master's thesis). Governmental Universities of Isfahan Province and Presentation of Student University Model, University of Isfahan.

Hoverstadt, P., & Bowling, D. (2005). Organisational Viability as a factor in Sustainable. *International Journal of Technology*, *4*(2), 131–146.

Howard, M., & Squire, B. (2007). Modularization and the impact on supply relationships. *International Journal of Operations & Production Management*, *27*(11), 1192–1212. doi:10.1108/01443570710830593

Hristov, I., & Chirico, A. (2019). The Role of Sustainability Key Performance Indicators (KPIs) in Implementing Sustainable Strategies. *Sustainability*, *11*(20), 5742. doi:10.3390u11205742

Hsieh, J.-K., Hsieh, Y.-C., Chiu, H.-C., & Yang, Y.-R. (2014). Customer response to web site atmospherics: Task-relevant cues, situational involvement and PAD. *Journal of Interactive Marketing*, *28*(3), 225–236. doi:10.1016/j.intmar.2014.03.001

Hsu, C., Hu, A. H., Chiou, C., & Chen, T. (2011). Using the FDM and ANP to construct a sustainability balanced scorecard for the semiconductor industry. *Expert Systems with Applications*, *38*(10), 12891–12899. doi:10.1016/j.eswa.2011.04.082

Huang, L. C., Huang, K. S., Huang, H. P., & Jaw, B. S. (2004, June). Applying fuzzy neural network in human resource selection system. In *Fuzzy Information, 2004. Processing NAFIPS'04. IEEE Annual Meeting of the* (Vol. 1, pp. 169-174). IEEE.

Huang, T., Pepper, M., & Bowrey, G. (2014). Implementing a sustainability balanced scorecard to contribute to the process of organisational legitimacy assessment. Australasian Accounting. *Business and Finance Journal*, *8*(2), 15–34. doi:10.14453/aabfj.v8i2.3

Hudson Smith, M., & Smith, D. (2007). Implementing strategically aligned performance measurement in small firms. *International Journal of Production Economics*, *106*(2), 393–408. doi:10.1016/j.ijpe.2006.07.011

Humby, C. (2006). Data is the new oil. *Proc. ANA Sr. Marketer's Summit.*

Hu, S. J. (2013). Evolving paradigms of manufacturing: From mass production to mass customization and personalization. *Procedia CIRP*, *7*, 3–8. doi:10.1016/j.procir.2013.05.002

Huselid, M., & Minbaeva, D. (2018) *Big Data and Human Resource Management*. Academic Press.

Iacobucci, D., Posavac, S. S., Kardes, F. R., Schneider, M., & Popovich, D. (2015). Toward a more nuanced understanding of the statistical properties of a median split. *Journal of Consumer Psychology*, *25*(4), 652–665. doi:10.1016/j.jcps.2014.12.002

Imran, F., & Kantola, J. (2018). Review of Industry 4.0 in the Light of Sociotechnical System Theory and Competence-Based View: A Future Research Agenda for the Evolute Approach. *Advances in Intelligent Systems and Computing*, *783*, 118–128. doi:10.1007/978-3-319-94709-9_12

Industrial Internet Consortium. (2013). *Fact Sheet*. https://www.iiconsortium.org/docs/IIC_FACT_SHEET.pdf

Institute of Chartered Shipbrokers (ICS). (2007). *Port and Terminal Management*. London, UK: Witherbys Publishing Limited.

Intel I. T. Center. (2012). *Big Data analytics. Intel's IT manager survey on how organizations are using big data*. Author.

Jacobs, M., Vickery, S. K., & Droge, C. (2007). The effects of product modularity on competitive performance: Do integration strategies mediate the relationship? *International Journal of Operations & Production Management*, *27*(10), 1046–1068. doi:10.1108/01443570710820620

Jahmurataj, V. (2015). Impact of Culture on Organizational Development: Case Study Kosovo. *Academic Journal of Interdisciplinary Studies*, *4*(2), 206–210. doi:10.5901/ajis.2015.v4n2s1p206

Jain, A., Mendiratta, P., & Kashiramka, S. (2021). 10 Triple Bottom Line During Pandemic. *Strategic Management During a Pandemic.*

Jai, T.-M. C., Burns, L. D., & King, N. J. (2013). The effect of behavioral tracking practices on consumers' shopping evaluations and repurchase intention toward trusted online retailers. *Computers in Human Behavior*, *29*(3), 901–909. doi:10.1016/j.chb.2012.12.021

Jakl, A., Schoffer, L., Husinsky, M., & Wagner, M. (2018). Augmented Reality for Industry 4.0: Architecture and User Experience. *Proceeding of the 11th Forum Media Technology, CER-WS*, 38-42.

Jamali, D., Zanhour, M., & Keshishian, T. (2008). Peculiar strengths and relational attributes of SMEs in the context of CSR. *Journal of Business Ethics*, *87*(3), 355–377. doi:10.100710551-008-9925-7

Jandl, C., Nurgazina, J., Schoffer, L., Reichl, C., Wagner, M., & Moser, T. (2019). SensiTrack – A Privacy by Design Concept for Industrial IoT Applications. *Proceeding of the 24th IEEE International Conference on Emerging Technologies and Factory Automation*, 1782-1789. 10.1109/ETFA.2019.8869186

Jarrahi, M. H. (2018). Artificial intelligence and the future of work: Human-AI symbiosis in organizational decision making. *Business Horizons*, *61*(4), 577–586. doi:10.1016/j.bushor.2018.03.007

Järvinen, A., & Poikela, E. (2001). Modelling Reflective and Contextual Learning at Work. *Journal of Workplace Learning, 13*(7/8), 282-289.

Jaschke, S. (2014). Mobile learning applications for technical vocational and engineering education: The use of competence snippets in laboratory courses and industry 4.0. *Proceedings of 2014 International Conference on Interactive Collaborative Learning, ICL 2014*, 605–608. 10.1109/ICL.2014.7017840

Jassem, S., Zakaria, Z., & Che Azmi, A. (2021). Sustainability balanced scorecard architecture and environmental performance outcomes: a systematic review. *International Journal of Productivity and Performance Management*. doi:10.1108/IJPPM-12-2019-0582

Jeschke, S., Brecher, C., Meisen, T., Ozdemir, D., & Eschert, T. (2017). Industrial Internet of Things and Cyber Manufacturing Systems. In Industrial Internet of Things. Springer.

Jesuthasan, R. (2017). HR's new role: Rethinking and enabling digital engagement. *Strategic HR Review*, *16*(2), 60–65. doi:10.1108/SHR-01-2017-0009

Ji, L., Huang, J., Liu, Z., Zhu, H., & Cai, Z. (2011). The effects of employee training on the relationship between environmental attitude and ðrms' performance in sustainable development. *International Journal of Human Resource Management*, *23*(14), 2995–3008. doi:10.1080/09585192.2011.637072

Johnson, M. P. (2015). Sustainability management and small and medium-sized enterprises: Managers' awareness and implementation of innovative tools. *Corporate Social Responsibility and Environmental Management, 22*(5), 271–285. doi:10.1002/csr.1343

Johnson, M. P., & Schaltegger, S. (2015). Two decades of sustainability management tools for SMEs: How far have we come? *Journal of Small Business Management, 54*(2), 481–505. doi:10.1111/jsbm.12154

Journeault, M., Perron, A., & Vallières, L. (2021). The collaborative roles of stakeholders in supporting the adoption of sustainability in SMEs. *Journal of Environmental Management, 287*, 112349. doi:10.1016/j.jenvman.2021.112349 PMID:33735683

Kachersky, L. (2011). Reduce content or raise price? The impact of persuasion knowledge and unit price increase tactics on retailer and product brand attitudes. *Journal of Retailing, 87*(4), 479–488. doi:10.1016/j.jretai.2011.08.001

Kagermann, H., Wahlster, W., Helbig, J., Hellinger, A., Stumpf, M. A. V., Treugut, L., Blasco, J., Galloway, H., & Findeklee, U. (2013). *Recommendations for implementing the strategic initiative Industrie 4.0: Final report of the Industrie 4.0.* http://alvarestech.com/temp/tcn/CyberPhysicalSystems-Industrial4-0.pdf

Kagermann, Wahlster, & Helbig. (2013). *Recommendations for implementing the strategic initiative Industrie 4.0: Final report of the Industrie 4.0 Working Group.* Acatech. https://doi.org/ doi:10.13140/RG.2.2.14480.20485

Kalyanaraman, S., & Sundar, S. S. (2006). The psychological appeal of personalized content in web portals: Does customization affect attitudes and behaviour? *Journal of Communication, 56*(1), 110–132. doi:10.1111/j.1460-2466.2006.00006.x

Kanter, R. M. (2008). *Men and women of the corporation: New edition.* Basic books.

Kaplan, A. M., & Haenlein, M. (2010). Users of the world, unite! The challenges and opportunities of Social Media. *Business Horizons, 53*(1), 59–68. doi:10.1016/j.bushor.2009.09.003

Kaplan, A., & Haenlein, M. (2018). Siri, Siri, in my hand: Who's the fairest in the land? On the interpretations, illustrations, and implications of artificial intelligence. *Business Horizons.*

Kaplan, R. (2014). Who has been regulating whom, business or society? The mid-20th century institutionalization of 'corporate responsibility' in the USA. *Socio-Economic Review, 13*(1), 125–155. doi:10.1093er/mwu031

Kaplan, R., & Norton, D. (1992). The Balanced Scorecard – measures that drive performance. *Harvard Business Review*, 71–79. PMID:10119714

Kaptein, M., & Eckles, D. (2012). Heterogeneity in the effects of online persuasion. *Journal of Interactive Marketing, 26*(3), 176–188. doi:10.1016/j.intmar.2012.02.002

Kaptein, M., Markopoulos, P., De Ruyter, B., & Aarts, E. (2015). Personalizing persuasive technologies: Explicit and implicit personalization using persuasion profiles. *International Journal of Human-Computer Studies, 77*, 38–51. doi:10.1016/j.ijhcs.2015.01.004

Karakostas, B. (2013). A DNS architecture for the Internet of things: A case study in transport logistics. *Procedia Computer Science, 19*, 594–601. doi:10.1016/j.procs.2013.06.079

Kargas, A., Kiriakidis, M., & Zacharakis, E. (2020). Europe's Economic Crisis: Re - Clustering European Economies. *European Journal of Social Science Education and Research, 7*(1), 41. doi:10.26417/ejser.v7i1.p41-50

Kargas, A., & Tsokos, A. (2020). Employer Branding Implementation and Human Resource Management in Greek Telecommunication Industry. *Administrative Sciences, 10*(1), 17. doi:10.3390/admsci10010017

Kargas, A., & Varoutas, D. (2020). Industry 4.0 in Cultural Industry. A Review on Digital Visualization for VR and AR Applications. In C. M. Bolognesi & S. Cettina (Eds.), *Impact of Industry 4.0 on Architecture and Cultural Heritage* (pp. 1–19). IGI Global. doi:10.4018/978-1-7998-1234-0.ch001

Katasonov, A., Kaykova, O., Khriyenko, O., Nikitin, S., & Terziyan, V. (2008). Smart Semantic Middleware for the Internet of Things. *Proceedings of the 5th International Conference of Informatics in Control, Automation and Robotics*, 11-15.

Kavussanos, M. G., & Visvikis, I. D. (2016). *The international handbook of shipping finance: Theory and practice*. Palgrave Macmillan.

Keller, K. L. (1987). Memory factors in advertising: The effect of advertising retrieval cues on brand evaluations. *The Journal of Consumer Research, 14*(3), 316–333. doi:10.1086/209116

Kergroach, S. (2017). Industry 4.0: New challenges and opportunities for the labour market. *Foresight and STI Governance, 11*(4), 6–8. doi:10.17323/2500-2597.2017.4.6.8

Kerr, I.R. (2006). Leadership strategies for sustainable SME operation. *Business Strategy and the Environment, 15*(1), 30-39.

Keskinock, P., & Tayur, S. (2001). Quantitive analysis of Internet-enabled supply chain. *Interface: a Journal for and About Social Movements, 31*(2), 70–89. doi:10.1287/inte.31.2.70.10626

Khan, R., Khan, S. U., Zaheer, R., & Khan, S. (2012). Future internet: the internet of things architecture, possible applications and key challenges. *Proceedings of the 10th International Conference on Frontiers of Information Technology (FIT '12)*, 257–260.

Kiesel, M., & Wolpers, M. (2015). Educational challenges for employees in project-based Industry 4.0 scenarios. *ACM International Conference Proceeding Series*. 10.1145/2809563.2809602

Kim, J. J. H., & Tahilyani, R. (2017). BYJU'S The Learning App. *Harvard Business School Case*, 317-048.

Kim, D. H., & Sung, Y. (2013). Gucci versus Old Navy: Interplay of brand personality and regulatory focus in advertising persuasion. *Psychology and Marketing*, *30*(12), 1076–1087. doi:10.1002/mar.20668

Kim, D., & Ammeter, T. (2014). Predicting personal information system adoption using an integrated diffusion model. *Information & Management*, *51*(4), 451–464. doi:10.1016/j.im.2014.02.011

Kim, H., & John, D. R. (2008). Consumer response to brand extensions: Construal level as a moderator of the importance of perceived fit. *Journal of Consumer Psychology*, *18*(2), 116–126. doi:10.1016/j.jcps.2008.01.006

Kim, J., Choi, I., & Li, Q. (2021). Customer Satisfaction of Recommender System: Examining Accuracy and Diversity in Several Types of Recommendation Approaches. *Sustainability*, *13*(11), 6165. doi:10.3390u13116165

Kim, J., Kim, H., & Kwon, H. (2019). Corporate Social Responsibility Activity Combinations for Sustainability: A Fuzzy Set Analysis of Korean Firms. *Sustainability*, *11*(24), 7078. doi:10.3390u11247078

King & Lakhani. (2013). Using Open Innovation to Identify the Best Ideas. *MIT Sloan Management Review*.

Kleindorfer, P. R., & Saad, G. H. (2005). Managing disruption risks in supply chains. *Production and Operations Management*, *14*(1), 53–68. doi:10.1111/j.1937-5956.2005.tb00009.x

Kline, S. J., & Rosenberg, N. (2010). An overview of innovation. *Studies on science and the innovation process: Selected works of Nathan Rosenberg*, 173-203.

Klychova, G. S., Ziganshin, B. G., Zakirova, A. R., Valieva, G. R., & Klychova, A. S. (2017). Benchmarking as an efficient tool of social audit development. *Journal of Engineering and Applied Sciences (Asian Research Publishing Network)*, *12*(19), 4958. doi:10.36478/jeasci.2017.4958.4965

Kohan, S. E. (2020). Amazon's sharing of cutting-edge technology may change the way you shop for groceries. *Forbes*. Retrieved April 4, 2020 from https://www.forbes.com/sites/shelleykohan/2020/03/15/amazons-sharing-of-cutting-edge-technology-may-change-the-way-you-shop-for-groceries/

Kolbjørnsrud, V., Amico, R., & Thomas, R. J. (2016). How artificial intelligence will redefine management. *Harvard Business Review*, 2.

Koo, D.-M., & Ju, S.-H. (2010). The interactional effects of atmospherics and perceptual curiosity on emotions and online shopping intention. *Computers in Human Behavior*, *26*(3), 377–388. doi:10.1016/j.chb.2009.11.009

KopninaH.BlewittJ. (2018). *Sustainable business*. doi:10.4324/9781315110172

Koroljova, A., & Voronova, V. (2007). Eco-mapping as a basis for environmental management systems integration at small and medium enterprises. *Management of Environmental Quality*, *18*(5), 542–555. doi:10.1108/14777830710778300

Kortuem, G., Bandara, A. K., Smith, N., Richards, M., & Petre, M. (2013). Educating the Internet-of-Things Generation. *Computer*, *46*(02), 53–61. doi:10.1109/MC.2012.390

Kouhkan, A., & Mousavi, S. A. (2015). Review the relationship between the components of the organization Learner and Organizational innovation) Case study: (FreeUniversity of Mazandaran*).* *First International Conference on Economics, Management, Accounting, Social Sciences.*

KPMG International Cooperative (KPMG). (2011). Integrated Reporting. *Performance insight through Better Business Reporting – Issue 1.* Available from: http://www.kpmg.com/Global/en/IssuesAndInsights/ArticlesPublications/Documents/road- to-integrated-reporting.pdf

Kravcik, M., Wang, X., Ullrich, C., & Igel, C. (2018). Towards Competence Development for Industry 4.0. Lecture Notes in Computer Science, 10948, 442–446. doi:10.1007/978-3-319-93846-2_83

Kristbergsson, K., & Oliveira, J. (Eds.). (2016). *Traditional Foods*. Springer. doi:10.1007/978-1-4899-7648-2

Krotov, V. (2017). The Internet of Things and new business opportunities. *Business Horizons*, *60*(6), 831–841. doi:10.1016/j.bushor.2017.07.009

Krueger, N. F. Jr, Reilly, M. D., & Carsrud, A. L. (2000). Competing models of entrepreneurial intentions. *Journal of Business Venturing*, *15*(5–6), 411–432. doi:10.1016/S0883-9026(98)00033-0

Kumar, M., Syed, D., Ali, A., & Pandey, D. (2020). *How adoption of online resources can help indian smes in improving performance during covid-19 pandemic.* Test Engineering and Management Journal.

Kuo, Y.-F., & Wu, C.-M. (2012). Satisfaction and post-purchase intentions with service recovery of online shopping websites: Perspectives on perceived justice and emotions. *International Journal of Information Management*, *32*(2), 127–138. doi:10.1016/j.ijinfomgt.2011.09.001

Laitsou, E., Kargas, A., & Varoutas, D. (2020). Digital Competitiveness in the European Union Era: The Greek Case. *Economies*, *8*(4), 85. doi:10.3390/economies8040085

Lasi, H., Fettke, P., Kemper, H.-G., Feld, T., & Hoffmann, M. (2014). Industry 4.0. *BISE*, *6*(4), 239–242.

Lastra, J. L. M., & Delamer, I. M. (2006). Semantic Web Services in Factory Automation: Fundamental Insights and Research Roadmap. *IEEE Transactions on Industrial Informatics*, *2*(1), 1–11.

Lau, A. K. (2011). Critical success factors in managing modular production design: Six company case studies in Hong Kong, China, and Singapore. *Journal of Engineering and Technology Management*, *28*(3), 168–183. doi:10.1016/j.jengtecman.2011.03.004

Lau, A. K. W., & Yam, R. C. M. (2005). A case study of product modularization on supply chain design and coordination in Hong Kong and China. *Journal of Manufacturing Technology Management*, *16*(4), 432–446. doi:10.1108/17410380510594516

Lau, A. K., Yam, R. C., Tang, E. P., & Sun, H. Y. (2010). Factors influencing the relationship between product modularity and supply chain integration. *International Journal of Operations & Production Management, 30*(9), 951–977. doi:10.1108/01443571011075065

Lee, H.L., So, K.C., & Tang, C.S. (2000). The value of information sharing in a two-level supply chain. *Management Science, 46*(5), 626-643. doi:10.1287/mnsc.46.5.626.12047

Lee, A. Y., & Aaker, J. L. (2004). Bringing the frame into focus: The influence of regulatory fit on processing fluency and persuasion. *Journal of Personality and Social Psychology, 86*(2), 205–218. doi:10.1037/0022-3514.86.2.205 PMID:14769079

Lee, A. Y., Keller, P. A., & Sternthal, B. (2010). Value from regulatory construal fit: The persuasive impact of fit between consumer goals and message concreteness. *The Journal of Consumer Research, 36*(5), 735–747. doi:10.1086/605591

Lee, E.-S., & Song, D.-W. (2010). Knowledge management for maritime logistics value: Discussing conceptual issues. *Maritime Policy & Management, 37*(6), 563–583. doi:10.1080/03088839.2010.514959

Lee, H. L., & Billington, C. (1992). Managing supply chain inventories: Pitfalls and opportunities. *Sloan Management Review, 33*(3), 65–77.

Lee, I. (2017). Big data: Dimensions, evolution, impacts, and challenges. *Business Horizons, 60*(3), 293–303. doi:10.1016/j.bushor.2017.01.004

Lee, I., & Lee, K. (2015). The Internet of Things (IoT): Applications, investments, and challenges for enterprises. *Business Horizons, 58*(4), 431–440. doi:10.1016/j.bushor.2015.03.008

Lee, J., Kao, H.-A., & Yang, S. (2014). Service Innovation and Smart Analytics for Industry 4.0 and Big Data Environment. *Procedia CIRP, 16*, 3–8. doi:10.1016/j.procir.2014.02.001

Lee, K. C., & Kwon, S. (2008). Online shopping recommendation mechanism and its influence on consumer decisions and behaviours: A causal map approach. *Expert Systems with Applications, 35*(4), 1567–1574. doi:10.1016/j.eswa.2007.08.109

Lee, M.-C. (2009). Factors influencing the adoption of internet banking: An integration of TAM and TPB with perceived risk and perceived benefit. *Electronic Commerce Research and Applications, 8*(3), 130–141. doi:10.1016/j.elerap.2008.11.006

Lee, M., Yun, J. J., Pyka, A., Won, D., Kodama, F., Schiuma, G., Park, H. S., Jeon, J., Park, K. B., Jung, K. H., Yan, M.-R., Lee, S. Y., & Zhao, X. (2018). How to respond to the fourth industrial revolution, or the second information technology revolution? Dynamic new combinations between technology, market, and society through open innovation. *Journal of Open Innovation, 4*(3), 21. doi:10.3390/joitmc4030021

Lefort, L., Henson, C., Taylor, K., Barnaghi, P., Compton, M., Corcho, O., Garcia-Castro, R., Graybeal, J., Herzog, A., & Janowicz, K. (2005). *Semantic Sensor Network XG Final Report.* W3C Incubator Group Report. http://www.w3.org/2005/Incubator/ssn/XGR-ssn/

Lengnick-Hall, M. L., Neely, A. R., & Stone, C. B. (2018). Human Resource Management in the Digital Age: Big Data, HR Analytics and Artificial Intelligence. In P. N. Melo & C. Machado (Eds.), *Managaement and Technological Challenges in the Digital Age* (pp. 1–30). CRC Press. doi:10.1201/9781351238922-1

Li, F. (2020). The digital transformation of business models in the creative industries: A holistic framework and emerging trends. *Technovation, 92–93*(January), 102012. https://doi.org/doi:10.1016/j.technovation.2017.12.004

Liao, K., Deng, X., & Marsillac, E. (2013). Factors that influence Chinese automotive suppliers' mass customization capabilities. *International Journal of Production Economics*, *146*(1), 25–36. doi:10.1016/j.ijpe.2013.01.014

Liboni, L. B., Cezarino, L. O., Jabbour, C. J. C., Oliveira, B. G., & Stefanelli, N. O. (2019). Smart industry and the pathways to HRM 4.0: Implications for SCM. *Supply Chain Management*, *24*(1), 124–146. doi:10.1108/SCM-03-2018-0150

Liebowitz, J. (2010). The role of HR in achieving a sustainability culture. *Journal of Sustainable Development, 3*(4), 50-57.

Li, L., & Horrocks, I. (2004). A software framework for matchmaking based on semantic web technology. *International Journal of Electronic Commerce*, *8*(4), 39–60. doi:10.1080/10864415.2004.11044307

Lind, M., Becha, H., Watson, R. T., Kouwenhoven, N., Zuesongdham, P., & Baldauf, U. (2020). Digital twins for the maritime sector. *Smart Maritime Network*, (August). Advance online publication. doi:10.13140/RG.2.2.27690.24006

Lin, K. Y. H., Zheng, P., & Chen, C. H. (2019). A state-of-the-art survey of Digital Twin: Techniques, engineering product lifecycle management and business innovation perspectives. *Journal of Intelligent Manufacturing*, *31*, 1313–1337. doi:10.100710845-019-01512-w

Linowes. (2015). *Virtual Reality Projects*. Packt.

Liszka, K., Klimkiewicz, K., & Malinowski, P. (2019). Polish foundry engineer with regard to changes carried by the industry 4.0. *Archives of Foundry Engineering*, *19*(1), 103–108. doi:10.24425/AFE.2019.127102

Liu, M., Fang, S., Dong, H., & Xu, C. (2020). Review of digital twin about concepts, technologies, and industrial applications. *Journal of Manufacturing Systems*, (October), 1–16. https://doi.org/doi:10.1016/j.jmsy.2020.06.017

Lobov, A., Lopez, F. U., Herrera, V. V., Puttonen, J., & Lastra, J. L. M. (2008). Semantic Web Services framework for manufacturing industries. In *Int. Conf. on Rob. and Biomim.*, (pp. 2104–2108). IEEE.

Locher, J. L., Yoels, W. C., Maurer, D., & van Ells, J. (2005). Comfort Foods: An Exploratory Journey Into The Social and Emotional Significance of Food. *Food & Foodways*, *13*(4), 273–297. doi:10.1080/07409710500334509

Lopez-Cabrales, A., Pérez-Luño, A., & Cabrera, R.V. (2009). Knowledge as amediator between HRM practices and innovative activity. *Hum Resour Manage., 48*(4), 485–503. doi:48:4113 doi:10.1002/hrm.v

Lorenz, M., Russmann, M., Strack, R., Lasse Lueth, K., & Bolle, M. (2015). *Man and Machine in Industry 4.0: How Will Technology Transform the Industrial Workforce Through 2025?* Academic Press.

Loukis, E., Ferro, E., & Arvanitis, S. (2017). Digital technologies in the Mediterranean region [special section]. *Telematics and Informatics, 34*(5), 694–809. doi:10.1016/j.tele.2016.12.008

Love, A. (1991). *Internal evaluation. Building organizations from within.* Sage.

Lund, P. (2012). Large-scale urban renewable electricity schemes—Integration and interfacing aspects. *Energy Conversion and Management, 63*(November), 162–172. doi:10.1016/j.enconman.2012.01.037

Lynch, C. (2015). *Stephen Hawking on the Future of Capitalism and Inequality.* Available at https://www.counterpunch.org/2015/10/15/stephen-hawkings-on-the-tuture-of-capitalism-and-inequality/

Maass, W., & Filler, A. (2006). Towards an infrastructure for semantically annotated physical products. *INFORMATIK 2006–Informatik für Menschen, 2*(36).

MacKenzie, S. B., & Podsakoff, P. M. (2012). Common method bias in marketing: Causes, mechanisms, and procedural remedies. *Journal of Retailing, 88*(4), 542–555. doi:10.1016/j.jretai.2012.08.001

MacKinnon, D. P., Lockwood, C. M., & Williams, J. (2004). *Confidence limits for the indirect effect: Distribution of the product and resampling methods.* Academic Press.

Mäenpää, H., Tarkoma, S., Varjonen, S., & Vihavainen, A. (2015). Blending problem- and project-based learning in internet of things education: Case greenhouse maintenance. *SIGCSE 2015 - Proceedings of the 46th ACM Technical Symposium on Computer Science Education,* 398–403. doi:10.1145/2676723.2677262

Maggon, M., & Chaudhry, H. (2018). Exploring relationships between customer satisfaction and customer attitude from customer relationship management viewpoint: An empirical study of leisure travellers. *FIIB Business Review, 7*(1), 57–65. doi:10.1177/2319714518766118

Mahon, B. (2004). *The Man Who Changed Everything: The Life of James Clerk Maxwell.* John Wiley & Sons Ltd.

Maisiri, W., Darwish, H., & van Dyk, L. (2019). An investigation of industry 4.0 skills requirements. *South African Journal of Industrial Engineering, 30*(3), 90–105. doi:10.7166/30-3-2230

Mamede, H. (2009). MICEP-A methodology for digital business in SME. *Revista de Ciências da Computação, 4.* https://www.researchgate.net/publication/228758013_MICEP-A_methodology_for_digital_business_in_SME

Manuti, A., & de Palma, P. D. (2018). The Cognitive Technology Revolution: A New Role of HR Practices? In Digital HR (pp. 39-53). Palgrave Macmillan. doi:10.1007/978-3-319-60210-3_3

March, J. G. (1981). Footnotes to organizational change. *Administrative Science Quarterly*, *26*(4), 563–577. doi:10.2307/2392340

Marín, L., & de Maya, S. R. (2013). The role of affiliation, attractiveness and personal connection in consumer-company identification. *European Journal of Marketing*, *47*(3), 655–673. doi:10.1108/03090561311297526

Marrella, A. (2018). *Automated Planning for Business Process Management*. Academic Press.

Marshall, N. (2007). Cognitive and practice-based theories of organisational knowing and learning: Incompatible or complementary? In *Proceedings of OLKC Learning Fusion*. University of Brighton.

Martín, S. S., Camarero, C., & José, R. S. (2011). Does involvement matter in online shopping satisfaction and trust? *Psychology & Marketing, 28*, 145– 167.

Martínez-Leon, I. M., & Martínez-García, J. A. (2011). The influence of organizational structure on organizational learning. *International Journal of Manpower*, *32*(5), 537–566. doi:10.1108/01437721111158198

Mashal, I., Alsaryrah, O., Chung, T. Y., Yang, C. Z., Kuo, W. H., & Agrawal, D. P. (2015). Choices for interaction with things on Internet and underlying issues. *Ad Hoc Networks*, *28*, 68–90.

Mathews, S., Bianchi, C., Perks, K. J., Healy, M., & Wickramasekera, R. (2016). Internet marketing capabilities and international market growth. *International Business Review*, *25*(4), 820–830. doi:10.1016/j.ibusrev.2015.10.007

Mathur, Singh, & Ashutosh. (2013). *Creating Value through Innovation*. Shree Publishers and Distributors.

Matt, C., Hess, T., & Benlian, A. (2015). Digital Transformation Strategies. *Business & Information Systems Engineering*, *57*(5), 339–343. doi:10.100712599-015-0401-5

Matthijs, N., & Radlinski, F. (2011). Personalizing web search using long term browsing history. *Proceedings of the Fourth ACM International Conference on Web search and data mining*. 10.1145/1935826.1935840

Mavrikios, D., Georgoulias, K., & Chryssolouris, G. (2018). The Teaching Factory Paradigm: Developments and Outlook. *Procedia Manufacturing*, *23*, 1–6. doi:10.1016/j.promfg.2018.04.029

McAfee, A., Brynjolfsson, E., Davenport, T. H., Patil, D. J., & Barton, D. (2012). Big data: The management revolution. *Harvard Business Review*, *90*(10), 60–68. PMID:23074865

McGuire, W. J. (1968). Personality and attitude change: An information processing theory. In A. G. Greenwald, T. C. Brock, & T. M. Ostrom (Eds.), *Psychological foundation of attitudes* (pp. 171–196). Academic Press. doi:10.1016/B978-1-4832-3071-9.50013-1

McIver, D., Lengnick-Hall, M. L., & Lengnick-Hall, C. A. (2018). A strategic approach to workforce analytics: Integrating science and agility. *Business Horizons*, *61*(3), 397–407. doi:10.1016/j.bushor.2018.01.005

McKinsey. (2019 a). *A transformation in store*. McKinsey. Retrieved March 16, 2020 from https://www.mckinsey.com/business-functions/operations/our-insights/a-transformation in-store.

McWilliams, A., & Siegel, D. S. (2011). Creating and capturing value: Strategic corporate social responsibility, resource-based theory, and sustainable competitive advantage. *Journal of Management*, *37*(5), 1480–1495. doi:10.1177/0149206310385696

Mehrabi, J., Soltani, I., Alemzadeh, M., & Jadidi, M. (2013). Explaining the relationship between organizational structure and dimensions of learning organizations (case study: Education organization in Boroojerd county and the related departments). *International Journal of Academic Research in Business & Social Sciences*, 116–129.

Mergel, I., Edelmann, N., & Haug, N. (2019). Defining digital transformation: Results from expert interviews. *Government Information Quarterly*, *36*(4), 101385. doi:10.1016/j.giq.2019.06.002

Meyers-Levy, J., & Malaviya, P. (1999). Consumers' processing of persuasive advertisements: An integrative framework of persuasion theories. *Journal of Marketing*, *63*, 45–60.

Milà i Canals, L., Bauer, C., Depestele, J., Dubreuil, A., Freiermuth Knuchel, R., Gaillard, G., Michelsen, O., Müller-Wenk, R., & Rydgren, B. (2006). Key elements in a framework for land use impact assessment within LCA (11 pp). *The International Journal of Life Cycle Assessment*, *12*(1), 5–15. doi:10.1065/lca2006.05.250

Minor, M., Montani, S., & Recio-García, J. A. (2014). Process-oriented Case-based Reasoning. *Information Systems*, *40*, 103–105. doi:10.1016/j.is.2013.06.004

Mintzberg, H. (1994). *The Rise and Fall of Strategic Planning: Reconceiving Roles for Planning, Plans, Planners*. The Free Press.

Mintz, S. M. (2011). Triple Bottom Line Reporting for CPAs. *The CPA Journal*, *81*(12), 26–33.

Miranda, S. M., & Saunders, C. S. (2003). The social construction of meaning: An alternative perspective on information sharing. *Information Systems Research*, *14*(1), 87–106. doi:10.1287/isre.14.1.87.14765

Mishra, B. (2020). *Applying Digital Twin in Shipping and Maritime*. Sea News. Retrieved from https://seanews.co.uk/features/applying-digital-twin-in-shipping-and-maritime/

Monostori, L. (2014). Cyber-physical Production Systems: Roots, Expectations and R&D Challenges. *Procedia CIRP*, *17*, 9–13. doi:10.1016/j.procir.2014.03.115

Montenegro, G., Kushalnagar, N., Hui, J., & Culler, D. (2007). Transmission of IPv6 packets over IEEE 802.15.4 networks. Internet proposed standard RFC, 4944.

Moon, H., Ruona, W., & Valentine, T. (2017). Organizational strategic learning capability: Exploring the dimensions. *European Journal of Training and Development*, *41*(3), 222–240. doi:10.1108/EJTD-08-2016-0061

Moore, S. B., & Manring, S. L. (2009). Strategy development in small and medium sized enterprises for sustainability and increased value creation. *Journal of Cleaner Production*, *17*(2), 276–282. doi:10.1016/j.jclepro.2008.06.004

Morais-Storz, M., & Nguyen, N. (2017). The role of unlearning in metamorphosis andstrategic resilience. *The Learning Organization*, *24*(2), 93–106. doi:10.1108/TLO-12-2016-0091

Mosteller, J., Donthu, N., & Eroglu, S. (2014). The fluent online shopping experience. *Journal of Business Research*, *67*(11), 2486–2493. doi:10.1016/j.jbusres.2014.03.009

Müller, G. (2018). *Workflow Modeling Assistance by Casebased Reasoning*. Springer.

Mumford, M. D., Michelle, E., Higgs, T. C., & McIntosh, T. (2017). Cognitive skills andleadership performance: The nine critical skills. *The Leadership Quarterly*, *28*(1), 24–39. doi:10.1016/j.leaqua.2016.10.012

Nagalakshmi, M., & Kumar, M. (2020). Key Tool of Sustainable Management during COVID-19: WFH and Technology. *PIMT Journal of Research*, *12*(4).

Na, H. J., Lee, K. C., Choi, S. U., & Kim, S. T. (2020). Exploring CEO Messages in Sustainability Management Reports: Applying Sentiment Mining and Sustainability Balanced Scorecard Methods. *Sustainability*, *12*(2), 590. doi:10.3390u12020590

Nair, S., & Blomquist, T. (2021). Business model design in the case of complex innovations: A conceptual model. *Technology Analysis and Strategic Management*, *33*(2), 176–187. doi:10.1080/09537325.2020.1805103

Narasimhan, R., Talluri, S., & Mendez, D. (2001). Supplier evaluation and rationalization via data envelopment analysis: An empirical examination. *The Journal of Supply Chain Management*, *37*(2), 28–37. doi:10.1111/j.1745-493X.2001.tb00103.x

Nassar, N., Jafar, A., & Rahhal, Y. (2020). A novel deep multi-criteria collaborative filtering model for recommendation system. *Knowledge-Based Systems*, *187*, 104811. doi:10.1016/j.knosys.2019.06.019

Ning, H., & Wang, Z. (2011). Future internet of things architecture: Like mankind neural system or social organization framework? *IEEE Communications Letters*, *15*(4), 461–463.

Nishimura, J. S., & Tristán, O. M. (2011). Using the theory of planned behavior to predict nascent entrepreneurship. *Academia (Caracas)*, *46*, 55–71.

Noar, S. M., Benac, C. N., & Harris, M. S. (2007). Does tailoring matter? Metaanalytic review of tailored print health behavior change interventions. *Psychological Bulletin*, *133*(4), 673–693. doi:10.1037/0033-2909.133.4.673 PMID:17592961

Nonaka, I., & Toyama, R. (2015). The knowledge-creating theory revisited: knowledge creation as a synthesizing process. In *The essentials of knowledge management* (pp. 95–110). Palgrave Macmillan. doi:10.1057/9781137552105_4

O'brien, R. M. (2007). A caution regarding rules of thumb for variance inflation factors. *Quality & Quantity, 41*(5), 673–690. doi:10.100711135-006-9018-6

O'Leary, D. E. (2013). Artificial intelligence and big data. *IEEE Intelligent Systems, 28*(2), 96–99. doi:10.1109/MIS.2013.39

Ocker, F., Kovalenko, I., Barton, K., Tilbury, D., & VogelHeuser, B. (2019). A Framework for Automatic Initialization of Multi-Agent Production Systems Using Semantic Web Technologies. *IEEE Robotics and Automation Letters, 4*(4), 4330–4337.

Oinas-Kukkonen, H., & Harjumaa, M. (2009). Persuasive systems design: Key issues, process model, and system features. *Communications of the Association for Information Systems, 24*, 28. doi:10.17705/1CAIS.02428

Olia, S., & Yestrom, A. (2016). An Innovation into the Role of Open Innovation Collaboration Managers. *R & D Management.*

Oliveira, T., Alhinho, M., Rita, P., & Dhillon, G. (2017). Modelling and testing consumer trust dimensions in e-commerce. *Computers in Human Behavior, 71*, 153–164. doi:10.1016/j.chb.2017.01.050

Olsen, S. O., Skallerud, K., & Heide, M. (2021). Consumers' evaluation and intention to buy traditional seafood: The role of vintage, uniqueness, nostalgia and involvement in luxury. *Appetite, 157*, 104994. doi:10.1016/j.appet.2020.104994 PMID:33080331

Orams, M. (1998). *Marine Tourism: Development, Impacts and Management.* Routledge.

Osterloh, M., & Frey, B. S. (2000). Motivation, knowledge transfer, and organizational forms. *Organization Science, 11*(5), 538–550. doi:10.1287/orsc.11.5.538.15204

OXFAM. (2018). *An economy for the 99%.* Accessed on August 22, 2021 from https://www.oxfam.org/sites/www.oxfam.org/files/file_attachments/bp-economy-for-99-percent-160117-summ-en.pdf

Özpeynirci, Ö., & Köksalan, M. (2010). An exact algorithm for finding extreme supported nondominated points of multiobjective mixed integer programs. *Management Science, 56*(12), 2302–2315. doi:10.1287/mnsc.1100.1248

Pal, K. (2018). A Big Data Framework for Decision Making in Supply Chain. IGI Global.

Pal, K. (2020). Information Sharing for Manufacturing Supply Chain Management Based on Blockchain Technology. In Cross-Industry Use of Blockchain Technology and Opportunities for the Future. IGI Global. doi:10.4018/978-1-7998-3632-2.ch001

Pal, K., & Ul-Haque, A. (2000). Internet of Things and Blockchain Technology in Apparel Manufacturing Supply Chain Data Management. *Procedia Computer Science*, 450-457.

Pal, K. (2017). Supply Chain Coordination Based on Web Services. In H. K. Chan, N. Subramanian, & M. D. Abdulrahman (Eds.), *Supply Chain Management in the Big Data Era* (pp. 137–171). IGI Global Publication. doi:10.4018/978-1-5225-0956-1.ch009

Pappas, I. O., Kourouthanassis, P. E., Giannakos, M. N., & Chrissikopoulos, V. (2014). Shiny happy people buying: The role of emotions on personalized e-shopping. *Electronic Markets, 24*(3), 193–206. doi:10.100712525-014-0153-y

Pappas, I. O., Kourouthanassis, P. E., Giannakos, M. N., & Chrissikopoulos, V. (2016). Explaining online shopping behavior with fsQCA: The role of cognitive and affective perceptions. *Journal of Business Research, 69*(2), 794–803. doi:10.1016/j.jbusres.2015.07.010

Pappas, I. O., Kourouthanassis, P. E., Giannakos, M. N., & Lekakos, G. (2017). The interplay of online shopping motivations and experiential factors on personalized e-commerce: A complexity theory approach. *Telematics and Informatics, 34*(5), 730–742. doi:10.1016/j.tele.2016.08.021

Parker, C. M., Redmond, J., & Simpson, M. (2009). A review of interventions to encourage SMEs to make environmental improvements. *Environment and Planning. C, Government & Policy, 27*(2), 279–301. doi:10.1068/c0859b

Parwez, S., & Ranjan, R. (2021c). Reinventing the Lost "Public" in Post-COVID Era: Towards a Theory of sociality in political-economy interaction spaces in the 21st century. In 7th *Biennial Conference of the Indian Academy of Management (INDAM.*, IIM Rohtak.

Parwez, S., & Ranjan, R. (2021a). The platform economy and the precarisation of food delivery work in the COVID-19 pandemic: Evidence from India. *Work Organisation, Labour & Globalisation, 15*(1), 11–30. doi:10.13169/workorgalaboglob.15.1.0011

Parwez, S., & Ranjan, R. (2021b). Social Enterprising' Social Change Agenda Co-opted! The Scale, Dependency and Financial Viability Traps. *FIIB Business Review*.

Pateli, A. G. (2011). E-,M-business status in the Mediterranean region. *International Journal of E-Services and Mobile Applications, 3*, 1–91.

Patma, T. S., Wardana, L. W., Wibowo, A., Narmaditya, B. S., & Akbarina, F. (2021). The impact of social media marketing for Indonesian SMEs sustainability: Lesson from Covid-19 pandemic. *Cogent Business & Management, 8*(1), 1953679. doi:10.1080/23311975.2021.1953679

Patra, R. (2008). Vaastu Shastra: Towards sustainable development. *Sustainable Development Journal, 17*(4), 244–256. doi:10.1002d.388

Patton, M. (1998). Discovering Process Use. *Evaluation, 4*(2), 225-233.

Patton, M. (1997). *Utilization-focused Evaluation*. Sage.

Peck, J., & Wiggins, J. (2006). It just feels good: Customers' affective response to touch and its influence on persuasion. *Journal of Marketing*, *70*, 56–69.

Pedersen, T. A., Glomsrud, J. A., Ruud, E. L., Simonsen, A., Sandrib, J., & Eriksen, B. O. H. (2020). Towards simulation-based verification of autonomous navigation systems. *Safety Science*, *129*(December), 104799. https://doi.org/ doi:10.1016/j.ssci.2020.104799

Pena-opez, I. (2005). *Internet Report 2005: The Internet of Things*. Academic Press.

Perabo, F., Park, D., Zadeh, M. K., Smogeli, O., & Jamt, L. (2020). Digital Twin Modelling of Ship Power and Propulsion Systems: Application of the Open Simulation Platform (OSP). *IEEE International Symposium on Industrial Electronics,* 1265–1270. https://doi.org/10.1109/ISIE45063.2020.9152218

Perini, S., Arena, D., Kiritsis, D., & Taisch, M. (2017). An Ontology-Based Model for Training Evaluation and Skill Classification in an Industry 4.0 Environment. *IFIP Advances in Information and Communication Technology, AICT*, *513*(Part I), 314–321. doi:10.1007/978-3-319-66923-6_37

Persson, M., Eklind, M. J., & Winroth, M. (2016). Coordinating external manufacturing of product modules. *Decision Sciences*, *47*(6), 1178–1202. doi:10.1111/deci.12197

Petrelli, D. (2017). Industry 4.0: Is It Time for Interaction Design Craftsmanship? *The Design Journal*, *20*(sup1), 2735–2745. doi:10.1080/14606925.2017.1352785

Petty, R. E., Fabrigar, L. R., & Wegener, D. T. (2003). Emotional factors in attitudes and persuasion. In R. J. Davidson, K. R. Scherer, & H. H. Goldsmith (Eds.), *Handbook of affective sciences* (pp. 752–772). Series in affective science. Oxford University Press.

Petty, R., & Cacioppo, J. (2012). *Communication and persuasion: Central and peripheral routes to attitude change*. Springer Science & Business Media.

Pfeffer, J. (2010). Building sustainable organizations: The human factor. *The Academy of Management Perspectives*, *24*(1), 34–45.

Pfeffer, J., & Sutton, R. I. (2006). *Hard facts, dangerous half-truths and total nonsense: Profiting from evidence-based management*. Harvard Business School Press.

Phillips, L. (2007). Go green to gain the edge over rivals. *People Management*. Available at: www2.cipd.co.uk/pm/peoplemanagement/b/weblog/archive/2013/01/29/gogreentogaintheedgeoverrivals-2007-08.aspx

Pieniak, Z., Verbeke, W., Vanhonacker, F., Guerrero, L., & Hersleth, M. (2009). Association between traditional food consumption and motives for food choice in six European countries. *Appetite*, *53*(1), 101–108. doi:10.1016/j.appet.2009.05.019 PMID:19500626

PierNext. (2020). Digital twins for safer and more efficient port decisions. *PierNext Technology*. Retrieved from https://piernext.portdebarcelona.cat/en/technology/ports-digital-twins/

Pietrzak, M., & Paliszkiewicz, J. (2013). *Framework of Strategic Learning: The PDCA Cycle*. Warsaw University of Life Sciences.

Pil, F. K., & Cohen, S. K. (2006). Modularity: Implications for imitation, innovation, and sustained advantage. *Academy of Management Review*, *31*(4), 995–1011. doi:10.5465/amr.2006.22528166

Pillai, K. G., & Kumar, V. (2012). Differential effects of value consciousness and coupon proneness on consumers' persuasion knowledge of pricing tactics. *Journal of Retailing*, *88*(1), 20–33. doi:10.1016/j.jretai.2011.03.002

Pimenova, P., & Van der Vorst, R. (2004). The role of support programmes and policies in improving SMEs environmental performance in developed and transition economies. *Journal of Cleaner Production*, *12*(6), 549–559. doi:10.1016/j.jclepro.2003.07.001

Pinzone, M., Fantini, P., Perini, S., Garavaglia, S., Taisch, M., & Miragliotta, G. (2017). Jobs and Skills in Industry 4.0: An Exploratory Research. *IFIP Advances in Information and Communication Technology*, *513*, 282–288. doi:10.1007/978-3-319-66923-6_33

Podsakoff, P. M., MacKenzie, S. B., Lee, J.-Y., & Podsakoff, N. P. (2003). Common method biases in behavioural research: A critical review of the literature and recommended remedies. *The Journal of Applied Psychology*, *88*(5), 879–903. doi:10.1037/0021-9010.88.5.879 PMID:14516251

Port of Rotterdam. (2018). Innovation takes the port into a new era. *Port of Rotterdam News*. Retrieved from https://www.portofrotterdam.com/en/news-and-press-releases/innovation-takes-the-port-into-a-new-era

Port of Rotterdam. (2019). Digitisation initiatives. *Control & Management*. Retrieved from https://www.portofrotterdam.com/en/doing-business/port-of-the-future/digitisation/control-management

Port of Rotterdam. (2019). Rotterdam sends hyper-smart container on trip around the world. *Port of Rotterdam News*. Retrieved from https://www.portofrotterdam.com/en/news-and-press-releases/rotterdam-sends-hyper-smart-container-on-trip-around-the-world

Port Technology. (2018). Singapore to Develop Digital Twin Tech. *Port Technology News*. Retrieved from https://www.porttechnology.org/news/singapore_to_develop_digital_twin_tech/

Porter, M. E. (1985). Technology and competitive advantage. *The Journal of Business Strategy*, *5*(3), 60–78. doi:10.1108/eb039075

Porter, M. E. (1996, November-December). What is Strategy? *Harvard Business Review*, 61–78. PMID:10158475

Postmes, T. (2003). A social identity approach to communication in organizations. *Social identity at work: Developing theory for organizational practice*, *81*, 191-203.

Prifti, L., Knigge, M., Kienegger, H., & Krcmar, H. (2017). A Competency Model for "Industrie 4.0" Employees. *13th International Conference on Wirtschaftsinformatik (WI)*, 44–60.

Psychology. (2010). 6th ed.). Worth Publishers.

Pu, G., Qamruzzaman, M., Mehta, A. M., Naqvi, F. N., & Karim, S. (2021). Innovative Finance, Technological Adaptation and SMEs Sustainability: The Mediating Role of Government Support during COVID-19 Pandemic. *Sustainability, 13*(16), 9218. doi:10.3390u13169218

Purohit, I., Purohit, P., & Shekhar, S. (2013). Evaluating the potential of concentrating solar power generation in North-western India. *Energy Policy, 62*, 157–175. doi:10.1016/j.enpol.2013.06.069

Putrevu, S. (2014). Effects of mood and elaboration on processing and evaluation of goal-framed appeals. *Psychology and Marketing, 31*(2), 134–146. doi:10.1002/mar.20682

Puttonen, J., Lobov, A., & Lastra, J. L. M. (2013). Semantics-Based Composition of Factory Automation Processes Encapsulated by Web Services. *IEEE TII, 9*(4), 2349–2359. doi:10.1109/TII.2012.2220554

Puttonen, J., Lobov, A., Soto, M. A. C., & Lastra, J. L. M. (2010). A Semantic Web Services-based approach for production systems control. *Advanced Engineering Informatics, 24*(3), 285–299. doi:10.1016/j.aei.2010.05.012

PwC. (2015). *Workforce of the future: The competing forces shaping 2030.* Available at https://www.pwc.com/gx/en/services/people-organisation/workforce-of-the-future/workforce-of-the-future-the-competing-forces-shaping-2030-pwc.pdf

Qi, Q., & Tao, F. (2018). Digital Twin and Big Data Towards Smart Manufacturing and Industry 4.0: 360 Degree Comparison. *IEEE Access: Practical Innovations, Open Solutions, 6*, 3585–3593. doi:10.1109/ACCESS.2018.2793265

Raghavendra Rao, N. (2017). *Social Media Listening and Monitoring for Business Applications.* IGI Global.

Rahimian, H., Zamaneh, M. P., Ahmadpour, M., & Piri, M. (2014). A study of the relationship between empowerment and organizational learning among employees of gas transmission company. *J. Life Sci. Biomed, 4*(6), 550–556.

Rangaraju & Kennedy. (2013). *Innovation in Management –Challenges and Opportunities in the Next Decade.* Allied Publishers Private Limited.

Ranjan, R. (2021a). *Management Education and Profession at Crossroads: Implications of a deeply rooted philosophical assumption.* 8th International Conference on Sustainability, IIM Shillong, India.

Ranjan, R. (2021b). *Corporate elite need to change the Philosophy! A discussion on the Business-Society Relationship in Sustainable Development Context.* 8th Pan IIM World Management Conference, IIM Kozhikode, India.

Ranjan, R. (2021c). *Revisiting Possession in the Oriental and Occidental Traditions: Lessons from a Comparative Study of American Television Series and Pakistani Dramas.* International Conclave on Globalizing Indian Thought, IIM Kozhikode, India.

Ranjan, R. (2021d). *"Management Education" Under Twin Traps of Fictional Conditioning and Surveillance Panopticon in Industry 4.0.* era. International Conference for Markets and Development, IIM Trichy, India.

Ranjan, R. (2021e). *Business and Society/Ecology at the Loggerheads: Understanding from the Adani Experience.* International Society for Data Sciences and Innovation – Global Conference, IIM Nagpur, India.

Ranjan, R., & Saket, S. (2017). *Privacy Cede for "Totalitarian" or "Open Innovation" society?* 5th Pan IIM World Management Conference (WMC), IIML, Lucknow, India.

Rasmussen, T., & Ulrich, D. (2015). Learning from practice: How HR analytics avoids being a management fad. *Organizational Dynamics*, *44*(3), 236–242. doi:10.1016/j.orgdyn.2015.05.008

Ray, A. (2020). E-learning: The new normal in the post-covid world. *International Research Journal of Modernization in Engineering Technology and Science*, *2*(9), 866–876.

Reap, J., Roman, F., Duncan, S., & Bras, B. (2008). A survey of unresolved problems in life cycle assessment. *The International Journal of Life Cycle Assessment*, *13*(5), 374–388. doi:10.100711367-008-0009-9

Rebelo, H. (2020). *A Sucesssão nas Empresas Familiares - estudo longitudinal da empresa Paupério*. Faculdade de Economia - Universidade do Porto.

Reisenwitz, T. H., Iyer, R., & Cutler, B. (2004). Nostalgia Advertising and the Influence of Nostalgia Proneness. *Marketing Management Journal*, *14*, 55–66.

Renwick, D., Redman, T., & Maguire, S. (2013). Green human resource management: A review, process model, and research agenda. *International Journal of Management Reviews*, *15*(1), 1–14. doi:10.1111/j.1468-2370.2011.00328.x

Revell, A., & Rutherfoord, R. (2003). UK environmental policy and the small firm: Broadening the focus. *Business Strategy and the Environment*, *12*(1), 26–35. doi:10.1002/bse.347

Richter, A., Heinrich, P., Stocker, A., & Schwabe, G. (2018). Digital work design. *Business & Information Systems Engineering*, *60*(3), 259–264. doi:10.100712599-018-0534-4

Riegger, A. S., Klein, J. F., Merfeld, K., & Henkel, S. (2021). Technology-enabled personalization in retail stores: Understanding drivers and barriers. *Journal of Business Research*, *123*, 140–155. doi:10.1016/j.jbusres.2020.09.039

Rimanoczy, I., & Pearson, T. (2010). Role of HR in the new world of sustainability. *Industrial and Commercial Training*, *42*(1), 11–17. doi:10.1108/00197851011013661

Roberts, K. H., & O'Reilly, C. A. (1974). Failures in upward communication in organizations: Three possible culprits. *Academy of Management Journal*, *17*(2), 205–215.

Rodseth, O. J., & Berre, A. J. (2018). *From digital twin to maritime data space: Transparent ownership and use of ship information.* Paper presented at the AMIA Conference, Berlin, Germany.

Rosen, R., Boschert, S., & Sohr, A. (2018). Next Generation Digital Twin. *Atp Magazin, 60*(10), 86. doi:10.17560/atp.v60i10.2371

Rosen, R., Von Wichert, G., Lo, G., & Bettenhausen, K. D. (2015). About the importance of autonomy and digital twins for the future of manufacturing. *IFAC-PapersOnLine, 28*(3), 567–572. doi:10.1016/j.ifacol.2015.06.141

Roy, M. (2020). AI Intervention in Education Systems of India: An Analysis. *Solid State Technology, 63*(2), 1395–1402.

Russom, P. (2011). Big data analytics. *TDWI Best Practices Report, 19*, 40.

Russomanno, D. J., Kothari, C. R., & Thomas, O. A. (2005). Building a Sensor Ontology: A Practical Approach Leveraging ISO and OGC Models. *The 2005 International Conference on Artificial Intelligence*, 637-643.

Ruta, M., Colucci, S., Scioscia, F., Di Sciascio, E., & Donini, F. M. (2011). Finding commonalities in RFID semantic streams. *Procedia Computer Science, 5*, 857–864. doi:10.1016/j.procs.2011.07.118

Saadat, V., & Saadat, Z. (2016). Organizational learning as a key role of organizational success. *Procedia: Social and Behavioral Sciences, 230*(12), 219–225. doi:10.1016/j.sbspro.2016.09.028

Saarikko, T., Westergren, U. H., & Blomquist, T. (2017). The Internet of Things: Are you ready for what's coming? *Business Horizons, 60*(5), 667–676. doi:10.1016/j.bushor.2017.05.010

Sabel, C. F., & Zeitlin, J. (2004). Neither modularity nor relational contracting: Inter-firm collaboration in the new economy. *Enterprise and Society, 5*(3), 388–403. doi:10.1093/es/khh057

Sackey, S. M., & Bester, A. (2016). Industrial engineering curriculum in industry 4.0 in a South African context. *South African Journal of Industrial Engineering, 27*(4), 101–114. doi:10.7166/27-4-1579

Sahu, A. K., & Abhishek, M. (2018). *A study of ed-tech industry in India, with a focus on the growth of Byju's*. Academic Press.

Said, O., & Masud, M. (2013). Towards internet of things: Survey and future vision. *International Journal of Computer Networks, 5*(1), 1–17.

Sanchez, R., & Mahoney, J. T. (1996). Modularity, flexibility, and knowledge management in product and organization design. *Strategic Management Journal, 17*(S2), 63–76. doi:10.1002mj.4250171107

Santos, Í. (2012). *Plano de Comunicação de Marketing Integrad (IMC): marca Paupério*. Universidade do Porto.

Sarkar, T. K., Mailloux, R. J., Oliner, A. A., Salazar-Palma, M., & Sengupta, D. L. (2006). *History of Wireless*. John Wiley & Sons Inc.

Sathyan, S. (2021). Byju's Learning App in the COVID-19 Outbreak to Analyze Online Education-A Case Study. *International Journal of Case Studies in Business, IT and Education, 5*(2), 75–86.

Schallock, B., Rybski, C., Jochem, R., & Kohl, H. (2018). Learning Factory for Industry 4.0 to provide future skills beyond technical training. *Procedia Manufacturing*, *23*, 27–32. doi:10.1016/j.promfg.2018.03.156

Schaltegger, S., & Wagner, M. (2006). Managing Sustainability Performance Measurement and Reporting in an Integrated Manner. Sustainability Accounting as the Link between the Sustainability Balanced Scorecard and Sustainability Reporting. *Sustainability Accounting and Reporting*, 681–697. doi:10.1007/978-1-4020-4974-3_30

Schein, E. (1996). Kurt Lewin's Change Theory in the field and in the classroom: Notes toward a model of managed learning. *Systems Practice*, *9*(1), 27–47. doi:10.1007/BF02173417

Scherer, K. R., Shuman, V., Fontaine, J. R., & Soriano, C. (2013). The GRID meets the Wheel: Assessing emotional feeling via self-report. In J. R. J. Fontaine, K. R. Scherer, & C. Soriano (Eds.), *Components of Emotional Meaning: A Sourcebook* (pp. 281–298). Oxford University Press. doi:10.1093/acprof:oso/9780199592746.003.0019

Schilling, M. A. (2000). Toward a general modular systems theory and its application to interfirm product modularity. *Academy of Management Review*, *25*(2), 312–334. doi:10.2307/259016

Schleich, B., Anwer, N., Mathieu, L., & Wartzack, S. (2017). Shaping the digital twin for design and production engineering. *CIRP Annals - Manufacturing Technology*, *66*(1), 141–144. https://doi.org/ doi:10.1016/j.cirp.2017.04.040

Schmiedinger, B., Valentin, K., & Stephan, E. (2005). Competence based business development-organizational competencies as basis for successful companies. *Journal of Universal Knowledge Management*, *1*, 13–20.

Schuh, G., Potente, T., Varandani, R., & Schmitz, T. (2014). Global Footprint Design based on genetic algorithms – An "Industry 4.0" perspective. *CIRP Annals*, *63*(1), 433–436. doi:10.1016/j.cirp.2014.03.121

Schumacher, A., Erol, S., & Sihn, W. (2016). A Maturity Model for Assessing Industry 4.0 Readiness and Maturity of Manufacturing Enterprises. *Procedia CIRP*, *52*, 161–166. doi:10.1016/j.procir.2016.07.040

Sedighi, M. (2016). Application of word co-occurrence analysis method in mapping of the scientific fields (case study: The field of the *field* of Informetrics). *Computer Science. Library Review*. Advance online publication. doi:10.1108/LR-07-2015-0075

See, Y. H. M., Petty, R. E., & Fabrigar, L. R. (2008). Affective and cognitive meta-bases of attitudes: Unique effects on information interest and persuasion. *Journal of Personality and Social Psychology*, *94*(6), 938–955. doi:10.1037/0022-3514.94.6.938 PMID:18505310

Sehnem, S., Campos, L. M. S., Julkovski, D. J., & Cazella, C. F. (2019). Circular business models: Level of maturity. *Management Decision*, *57*(4), 1043–1066. doi:10.1108/MD-07-2018-0844

Seiger, R., Huber, S., & Schlegel, T. (2018). Toward an execution system for self-healing workflows in cyber-physical systems. *Software & Systems Modeling*, *17*(2), 551–572. doi:10.100710270-016-0551-z

Selamat, A., Taspir, S. H., Puteh, M., & Alias, R. A. (2017). Higher Education 4.0 Current Status and Readiness in Meeting the Fourth Industrial Revolution Challenges. *Redesigning Higher Education towards Industry, 1*, 23–24. https://pdfcoffee.com/higher-education-40-current-status-and-readiness-in-meeting-the-fourth-industrial-revolution-challenges-1-pdf-free.html

Selin, A., & Santos, V. (2018). An Architecture for a Viable Information System. *Trends and Advances in Information Systems and Technologies,* 1175-1189. https://doi.org/ doi:10.1007/978-3-319-77703-0_114

Semalstieg & Holler. (2016). *Augmented Virtual Reality*. IGI Global.

Sen, S. (2006). The role of corporate social responsibility in strengthening multiple stakeholder relationships: A Field experiment. *Journal of the Academy of Marketing Science*, *34*(2), 158–166. doi:10.1177/0092070305284978

Sen, S., & Cowley, J. (2013). The Relevance of Stakeholder Theory and Social Capital Theory in the Context of CSR in SMEs: An Australian Perspective. *Journal of Business Ethics*, *118*(2), 413–427. doi:10.100710551-012-1598-6

Setia, P., Venkatesh, V., & Joglekar, S. (2013). Leveraging digital technologies: How information quality leads to localized capabilities and customer service performance. *Management Information Systems Quarterly*, *37*(2), 565–590. doi:10.25300/MISQ/2013/37.2.11

Shafto, M., Conroy, M., Doyle, R., & Glaessgen, E., Kemp, C., LeMoigne, J., & Wang, L. (2010). *NASA Technology Roadmap*. DRAFT Modeling, Simulation, Information Technology & Processing Roadmap Technology Area 11.

Shah, S., & Alnoor, P. (2021). Byju's acquires Aakash Educational Services in nearly $1-billion deal. *Economic Times*. Accessed on August 30, 2021 from https://economictimes.indiatimes.com/tech/startups/byjus-to-acquire-aakash-educational-services-in-700-million-deal/articleshow/81910598.cms

Shamim, S., Cang, S., Yu, H., & Li, Y. (2016, July). Management approaches for Industry 4.0: A human resource management perspective. In *Evolutionary Computation (CEC), 2016 IEEE Congress on* (pp. 5309-5316). IEEE.

Shang, R.-A., Chen, Y.-C., & Shen, L. (2005). Extrinsic versus intrinsic motivations for consumers to shop on-line. *Information & Management*, *42*(3), 401–413. doi:10.1016/j.im.2004.01.009

Sharma, A. (2020). *Comparative Analysis of E-Learning Systems (Byju's un Unacademy) in India*. Academic Press.

Sharp, C. (2001). *Evaluation of Organizational learning intervention and Communities of Practice*. Paper presented in Australasian Evaluation Society Conference, Canberra, Australia.

Sheth, A., Krishnan, S., & Samyukktha, T. (2020). *India venture capital report 2020*. Accessed on August 28, 2021 from https://ivca.in/wp-content/uploads/2021/03/bain_report_india_venture_capital_2021.pdf

Shvetsova, O. A., & Kuzmina, A. D. (2018). Development of Engineering Personnel in the Era of the Fourth Industrial Revolution. *Proceedings of the 3rd International Conference Ergo-2018: Human Factors in Complex Technical Systems and Environments, Ergo 2018*, 45–48. 10.1109/ERGO.2018.8443927

Siebenhüner, B., & Arnold, M. (2007). Organizational learning to manage sustainable development. *Business Strategy and the Environment, 16*(5), 339–353. doi:10.1002/bse.579

Silveira, T., Zhang, M., Lin, X., Liu, Y., & Ma, S. (2019). How good your recommender system is? A survey on evaluations in recommendation. *International Journal of Machine Learning and Cybernetics, 10*(5), 813–831. doi:10.100713042-017-0762-9

Silvertown, J. (2017). *A La Mesa Con Darwin:tras las huellas de la evolucion en nuestros alimentos*. Ariel Mexico.

Simao, L. B. (2016). External relationships in the organizational innovation. *RAI Revista de Administração e Inovação, 13*(3), 156–165. doi:10.1016/j.rai.2016.06.002

Singh, A., & Hess, T. (2017). How chief digital officers promote the digital transformation of their companies. *MIS Quarterly Executive, 16*(1), 1–17. doi:10.4324/9780429286797-9

Sinha, A. P., & Pandey, R. K. (2019). A study on accessing the factors leading to the purchase of BYJU'S as a curriculum. *Trans Asian Journal of Marketing & Management Research, 8*(9-10), 44-59.

Sivathanu, B., & Pillai, R. (2018). Smart HR 4.0–how industry 4.0 is disrupting HR. *Human Resource Management International Digest, 26*(4), 7–11. doi:10.1108/HRMID-04-2018-0059

SmitJ.KreutzerS.MöllerC.CarlbergM. (2016). *Industry 4.0*. https://op.europa.eu/en/publication-detail/-/publication/1b970736-9acb-11e6-868c-01aa75ed71a1

Smogeli, Ø. (2017). Digital twins at work in maritime and energy. *DNV-GL Feature*, (February), 1–7.

Soffin, M. T., & Batsell, W. Jr. (2019). Towards a situational taxonomy of comfort foods: A retrospective analysis. *Appetite, 137*, 152–162. doi:10.1016/j.appet.2019.02.018 PMID:30836119

Solmaz, M. S., & Koray, M. (2020). Blockchain Technology in Maritime Transportation and Management. Handbook of Research on the Applications of International Transportation and Logistics for World Trade, 483-499. Doi:10.4018/978-1-7998-1397-2.ch026

Sonnichsen, R. (2000). *High Impact Internal Evaluation. A Practitioner's Guide to Evaluating and Consulting Inside Organizations*. Sage. doi:10.4135/9781483328485

Sorkun, M. F. (2016). Contrary evidence: Product modularity and supplier integration. *International Journal of Integrated Supply Management, 10*(3-4), 283–308. doi:10.1504/IJISM.2016.081278

Sorkun, M. F., & Furlan, A. (2017). Product and Organizational Modularity: A Contingent View of the Mirroring Hypothesis. *European Management Review*, *14*(2), 205–224. doi:10.1111/emre.12101

Sosa, M. E., Eppinger, S. D., & Rowles, C. M. (2003). Identifying modular and integrative systems and their impact on design team interactions. *Journal of Mechanical Design*, *125*(2), 240–252. doi:10.1115/1.1564074

Sruthi, P., & Mukherjee, S. (2020). Byju's the learning app: An investigative study on the transformation from traditional learning to technology based personalized learning. *International Journal of Scientific and Technology Research*, *9*(3), 5054–5059.

Stark, R., Kind, S., & Neumeyer, S. (2017). Innovations in digital modelling for next generation manufacturing system design. *CIRP Annals - Manufacturing Technology*, *66*(1), 169–172. https://doi.org/ doi:10.1016/j.cirp.2017.04.045

Steinmann, S., Mau, G., & Schramm-Klein, H. (2015). Brand communication success in online consumption communities: An experimental analysis of the effects of communication style and brand pictorial representation. *Psychology and Marketing*, *32*(3), 356–371. doi:10.1002/mar.20784

Stephan, M., Uzawa, S., Volini, E., Walsh, B., & Yoshida, R. (2016). Digital HR: Revolution, not evolution. In B. Pelster & J. Schwartz (Eds.), Global Human Capital Trends 2016 - The new organization: Different by design (pp. 97–103). Academic Press.

Stocker, A., Brandl, P., Michalczuk, R., & Rosenberger, M. (2014). Mensch-zentrierte IKT-Lösungen in einer Smart Factory. *Elektrotechnik Und Informationstechnik*, *131*(7), 207–211. doi:10.100700502-014-0215-z

Stojmenovic, I., & Wen, S. (2014). The fog computing paradigm: scenarios and security issues. *Proceedings of the Federated Conference on Computer Science and Information Systems (FedCSIS' 14)*, 1–8.

Stopford, M. (2009). *Maritime economics*. Routledge.

Strack, R., Dyrchs, S., Kotsis, A., & Mingardon, S. (2017). *How to Gain and Develop Digital Talent and Skills*. Boston Consulting Group. Available at https://image-src.bcg.com/Images/BCG-How-to-Gain-and-Develop-Digital-Talent-and-Skills-July-2017_tcm9-165367.pdf

Sun, Y., & Zhong, Q. (2020). How modularity influences product innovation: The mediating role of module suppliers' relationship-specific investments. *Management Decision*, *58*(12), 2743–2761. doi:10.1108/MD-06-2019-0837

Swaminathan, J. M. (2000). *Supply chain management*. In *International Encyclopedia of the Social and Behavioural Sciences*. Elsevier Sciences.

Syafrudin, M., Alfian, G., Fitriyani, N. L., & Rhee, J. (2018). Performance analysis of IoT-based sensor, big data processing, and machine learning model for real-time monitoring system in automotive manufacturing. *Sensors (Switzerland)*, *18*(9). Advance online publication. doi:10.339018092946

Takeishi, A. (2002). Knowledge partitioning in the interfirm division of labor: The case of automotive product development. *Organization Science, 13*(3), 321–338. doi:10.1287/orsc.13.3.321.2779

Tam, K. Y., & Ho, S. Y. (2005). Web personalization as a persuasion strategy: An elaboration likelihood model perspective. *Information Systems Research, 16*(3), 271–291. doi:10.1287/isre.1050.0058

Tam, K. Y., & Ho, S. Y. (2006). Understanding the impact of web personalization on user information processing and decision outcomes. *Management Information Systems Quarterly, 30*(4), 865–890. doi:10.2307/25148757

Tandon, U., Kiran, R., & Sah, A. (2017). Analyzing customer satisfaction: Users perspective towards online shopping. *Nankai Business Review International, 8*(3), 266–288. doi:10.1108/NBRI-04-2016-0012

Tanniru, M. R., Xi, Y., & Sandhu, K. (2020). Leadership to Advance Innovation for Digital Healthcare Transformation. *Leadership, Management, and Adoption Techniques for Digital Service Innovation,* 1-24. https://doi.org/ doi:10.4018/978-1-7998-2799-3.ch001

Tao, F., Cheng, J., Qi, Q., Zhang, M., Zhang, H., & Sui, F. (2018). Digital twin-driven product design, manufacturing and service with big data. *International Journal of Advanced Manufacturing Technology, 94*(9–12), 3563–3576. doi:10.100700170-017-0233-1

Tao, F., Zhang, H., Liu, A., & Nee, A. Y. C. (2019). Digital Twin in Industry: State-of-the-Art. *IEEE Transactions on Industrial Informatics, 15*(4), 2405–2415. doi:10.1109/TII.2018.2873186

Tarafdar, M., & Qrunfleh, S. (2017). Agile supply chain strategy and supply chain performance: Complementary roles of supply chain practices and information systems capability for agility. *International Journal of Production Research, 55*(4), 925–938. doi:10.1080/00207543.2016.1203079

Tauber, E. M. (1981). Brand franchise extension: New product benefits from existing brand names. *Business Horizons, 24*(2), 36–41. doi:10.1016/0007-6813(81)90144-0

Taylor, N., Human, C., Kruger, K., Bekker, A., & Basson, A. (2019). Comparison of Digital Twin Development in Manufacturing and Maritime Domains. In *International Workshop on Service Orientation in Holonic and Multi-Agent Manufacturing*. Springer.

Teeny, J. D., Siev, J. J., Briñol, P., & Petty, R. E. (2021). A review and conceptual framework for understanding personalized matching effects in persuasion. *Journal of Consumer Psychology, 31*(2), 382–414. doi:10.1002/jcpy.1198

Teixeira, A. A., Jabbour, C. J. C., & de Sousa Jabbour, A. B. L. (2012). Relationship between green management and environmental training in companies located in Brazil: A theoretical framework and case studies. *International Journal of Production Economics, 140*(1), 318–329. doi:10.1016/j.ijpe.2012.01.009

Tekic, Z., & Koroteev, D. (2019). From disruptively digital to proudly analog: A holistic typology of digital transformation strategies. *Business Horizons*, *62*(6), 683–693. doi:10.1016/j.bushor.2019.07.002

Temtime, Z. T., & Solomon, G. H. (2002). Total quality management and the planning behavior of SMEs in developing economies. *The TQM Magazine*, *14*(3), 181–191. doi:10.1108/09544780210425900

Testa, F., Boiral, O., & Iraldo, F. (2018). Internalization of environmental practices and institutional complexity: Can stakeholders pressures encourage greenwashing? *Journal of Business Ethics*, *147*(2), 287–307. doi:10.100710551-015-2960-2

Thakker, D. R. (2011). Culture and cognitive theory: Toward a reformulation. *Cult.Cog. Psychopathol*, *3*, 53–71.

Thite, M. (Ed.). (2019). *E-HRM: Digital Approaches, Directions & Applications*. Routledge.

Thomas, K. W., & Velthouse, B. A. (1990). Cognitive elements of empowerment: An "interpretive" model of intrinsic task motivation. *Academy of Management Review*, *15*(4), 666–681.

Thompson, D. V., & Hamilton, R. W. (2006). The effects of information processing mode on consumers' responses to comparative advertising. *The Journal of Consumer Research*, *32*(4), 530–540. doi:10.1086/500483

Thompson, D. V., & Malaviya, P. (2013). Consumer-generated ads: Does awareness of advertising co-creation help or hurt persuasion? *Journal of Marketing*, *77*(3), 33–47. doi:10.1509/jm.11.0403

Thongpapanl, N., & Ashraf, A. R. (2011). Enhancing online performance through website content and personalization. *Journal of Computer Information Systems*, *52*, 3–13.

Tiwana, A. (2008). Does technological modularity substitute for control? A study of alliance performance in software outsourcing. *Strategic Management Journal*, *29*(7), 769–780. doi:10.1002mj.673

Tomasello, M. (2010). *Culture and Cognitive Development*. Institute of Evolutionary Anthropology.

Tran, Q., & Tian, Y. (2013). Organizational structure: Influencing factors and impact on afirm. *Am. J. Ind. Bus. Manag*, *3*(02), 229–236. doi:10.4236/ajibm.2013.32028

Tripathy, S., & Devarapalli, S. (2021). Emerging trend set by a start-ups on Indian online education system: A case of Byju's. *Journal of Public Affairs*, *21*(1), e2128. doi:10.1002/pa.2128

Tsai. (2013). *Information Technology and Business Process Re-Engineering*. Praeger.

Tsoukas, H. (1994). What is management? An outline of a metatheory. *British Journal of Management*, *5*(4), 289–301. doi:10.1111/j.1467-8551.1994.tb00080.x

Tucker, M. L., Meyer, G. D., & Westerman, J. W. (1996). Organizational communication: Development of internal strategic competitive advantage. *The Journal of Business Communication*, *33*(1), 51-69.

Turk, T., Blažic, B. J., & Trkman, P. (2008). Factors and sustainable strategies ˇ fostering the adoption of broadband communications in an enlarged European Union. *Technological Forecasting and Social Change*, *75*(7), 933–951. doi:10.1016/j.techfore.2007.08.004

Turner, M. G., Gardner, R. H., & O'Neill, R. V. (2001). *Landscape ecology in theory and practice: Pattern and process*. Springer Science & Business Media.

Ulrich, D. (1998). A new mandate for human resources. *Harvard Business Review*, *76*, 124–135. PMID:10176915

Ulrich, D., Kryscynski, D., Ulrich, M., & Brockbank, W. (2017). Competencies for HR Professionals Who Deliver Outcomes. *Employment Relations Today*, *44*(2), 37–44. doi:10.1002/ert.21623

Ulrich, D., Younger, J., Brockbank, W., & Ulrich, M. D. (2013). The state of the HR profession. *Human Resource Management*, *52*(3), 457–471. doi:10.1002/hrm.21536

Ulrich, K. (1995). The role of product architecture in the manufacturing firm. *Research Policy*, *24*(3), 419–440. doi:10.1016/0048-7333(94)00775-3

UN-HABITAT, Local Governments for Sustainability, and the United Nations Environment Programme. (2009). *Sustainable Urban Energy Planning: A handbook for cities and towns in developing countries*. UNEP.

United Nations Conference on Trade and Development (UNCTAD). (2017). Retrieved from https://unctad.org/system/files/official-document/rmt2017_en.pdf

Van de Ven, A. H., Angle, H. L., & Poole, M. S. (Eds.). (2000). *Research on the Management of Innovation: The Minnesota Studies*. Oxford University Press.

Van Noort, G., Voorveld, H. A., & Van Reijmersdal, E. A. (2012). Interactivity in brand web sites: Cognitive, affective, and behavioural responses explained by consumers' online flow experience. *Journal of Interactive Marketing*, *26*(4), 223–234. doi:10.1016/j.intmar.2011.11.002

Vansina, L. (1988). The general manager and organizational leadership. In M. Lambrechts (Ed.), *Corporate revival: Managing into the nineties*. University Press.

Varelas, G., Voutsakist, E., Raftopoulout, P., Petrakis, E. G. M., & Milios, E. (2005). Semantic Similarity methods in WordNet and their application to information retrieval on the Web. In *Proceedings of the 7th annual ACM international workshop on web information and data management*. Bremen, Germany: ACM. 10.1145/1097047.1097051

Venkatesh, V., Morris, M. G., Davis, G. B., & Davis, F. D. (2003). User acceptance of information technology: Toward a unified view. *Management Information Systems Quarterly*, *27*(3), 425–478. doi:10.2307/30036540

Verbeke, W., Guerrero, L., Almli, V., Vanhonacker, F., & Hersleth, M. (2016). European Consumers' Definition and Perception of Traditional Foods. In K. Kristbergsson & J. Oliveira (Eds.), *Traditional foods* (pp. 3–16)., doi:10.1007/978-1-4899-7648-2_1

Verhagen, T., & van Dolen, W. (2011). The influence of online store beliefs on consumer online impulse buying: A model and empirical application. *Information & Management, 48*(8), 320–327. doi:10.1016/j.im.2011.08.001

Vermesan, O., Friess, P., & Guillemin, P. (2011). Internet of things strategic research roadmap in Internet of Things. *Global Technological and Societal Trends, 1*, 9–52.

Vial, G. (2019). Understanding digital transformation: A review and a research agenda. *The Journal of Strategic Information Systems, 28*(2), 118–144. doi:10.1016/j.jsis.2019.01.003

Volberda, H. W., Van Den Bosch, F. A., & Heij, C. V. (2013). Management innova-tion: Management as fertile ground for innovation. *European Management Review, 10*(1), 1–15. doi:10.1111/emre.12007

Volini, E., Mazor, A., Schaefer, F., Tsuchida, A., & Walsh, B. (2016). Global human capital trends 2016: HR growing momentum toward a new mandate. Deloitte University Press.

Volini, E., Occean, P., Stephan, M., & Walsh, B. (2017). Digital HR: Platforms, people, and work. In G. Lahiri & D. Singh (Eds.), Global Human Capital Trends 2017: Rewriting the Rules for the Digital Age (pp. 87–93). Academic Press.

Vom Brocke, J., Maaß, W., Buxmann, P., Maedche, A., Leimeister, J. M., & Pecht, G. (2018). Future Work and Enterprise Systems. *Business & Information Systems Engineering*, 1–10.

Von Leipzig, T., Gamp, M., Manz, D., Schöttle, K., Ohlhausen, P., Oosthuizen, G., & … . (2017). Initialising customer-orientated digital transformation in enterprises. *Procedia Manufacturing, 8*, 517–524. doi:10.1016/j.promfg.2017.02.066

Vysas. (2014). *Business Process Transformation.* Regal Publishers.

Wadhwa & Harper. (2015). *Technology, Innovation, and Enterprise Transformation.* IGI Global.

Wahlster, W. (2013). *Industry 4.0: The Semantic Product Memory as a Basis for Cyber-Physical Production Systems.* Recent Trends in Artificial Intelligence and Cognitive Science.

Walsh, G., Shiu, E., Hassan, L. M., Michaelidou, N., & Beatty, S. E. (2011). Emotions, store-environmental cues, store-choice criteria, and marketing outcomes. *Journal of Business Research, 64*(7), 737–744. doi:10.1016/j.jbusres.2010.07.008

Wang, C., Xu, H., & Mao, X. (2012). Construction of hardware curriculum group for transition from network to Internet of Things engineering major. *ICCSE 2012 - Proceedings of 2012 7th International Conference on Computer Science and Education*, 1575–1579. 10.1109/ICCSE.2012.6295364

Wang, X., Keh, H. T., & Chao, C.-H. (2018). Nostalgia and consumer preference for indulgent foods: The role of social connectedness. *International Journal of Consumer Studies, 42*(3), 316–326. doi:10.1111/ijcs.12419

Wang, Y. J., Minor, M. S., & Wei, J. (2011). Aesthetics and the online shopping environment: Understanding consumer responses. *Journal of Retailing*, *87*(1), 46–58. doi:10.1016/j.jretai.2010.09.002

Weale, A. (2018). *The Will of the People*. Polity Press.

Weare42. (n.d.). The smartest container this planet has even seen. *We are 42*. Retrieved from https://weare42.io/about/

Weill, P., & Woerner, S. L. (2018). Is your company ready for a digital future? *MIT Sloan Management Review*, *59*(2), 21–25. https://sloanreview.mit.edu/article/is-your-company-ready-for-a-digital-future/

Weyrich, M., & Ebert, C. (2016). Reference architectures for the internet of things. *IEEE Software*, *33*(1), 112–116.

White, S. K. (2018). *AI's impact on the future of work*. Available at https://www.cio.com/article/3285705/artificial-intelligence/ais-impact-on-the-future-of-work.html

Wiig, K. (2002). Knowledge management in Public Administration. *Journal of Knowledge Management, 6*(3), 224-239.

Wilson, H. J., & Daugherty, P. R. (2018). Collaborative intelligence: Humans and AI are joining forces. *Harvard Business Review*.

Wisskirchen, G., Biacabe, B. T., Bormann, U., Muntz, A., Niehaus, G., Soler, G. J., & von Brauchitsch, B. (2017). *Artificial intelligence and robotics and their impact on the workplace.* International Bar Association Global Employment Institute, April 2017 Report.

Wong, P. S. (2012). *Drucker's Knowledge-Worker Productivity Theory: A Practitioner's Approach to Integrating Organisational Work Processes with Drucker's Six Major Factors Determining Knowledge-Worker Productivity*. Southern Cross University.

World Economic Forum. (2016). *The future of jobs: employment, skills and workforce strategy for the Fourth Industrial Revolution*. World Economic Forum.

World Economic Forum. (2018). *The future of jobs report*. Available at https://www3.weforum.org/docs/WEF_Future_of_Jobs_2018.pdf

World Ocean Review. (2014). *Oil and Gas from the sea*. Retrieved from http://worldoceanreview.com/en/wor-3-overview/oil-and-gas/

Wu, M., Lu, T. J., Ling, F. Y., Sun, J., & Du, H. Y. (2010). Research on the architecture of internet of things. *Proceedings of the 3rd International Conference on Advanced Computer Theory and Engineering (ICACTE' 10), 5*, 484-487.

Wu, H. (2021, February). Application of Collaborative Filtering Personalized Recommendation Algorithms to Website Navigation. *Journal of Physics: Conference Series*, *1813*(1), 012048. doi:10.1088/1742-6596/1813/1/012048

Xia, S. (2011). Training programs for excellent engineers with engineering of Internet of Thing. *ITME 2011 - Proceedings: 2011 IEEE International Symposium on IT in Medicine and Education, 1*, 610–615. 10.1109/ITiME.2011.6130912

Xiaomi, A., & Wang, W. (2010). Knowledge management technologies and applications: aliterature review. IEEE.

Xu, H., Luo, X. R., Carroll, J. M., & Rosson, M. B. (2011). The personalization privacy paradox: An exploratory study of decision making process for location-aware marketing. *Decision Support Systems, 51*(1), 42–52. doi:10.1016/j.dss.2010.11.017

Xu, J. D., Benbasat, I., & Cenfetelli, R. T. (2013). Integrating service quality with system and information quality: An empirical test in the e-service context. *Management Information Systems Quarterly, 37*(3), 777–794. doi:10.25300/MISQ/2013/37.3.05

Yang, M. G., Roh, J. J., & Kang, M. (2020). The role of strategic environmental orientation in environmental design practices. *Management Decision, 59*(2), 341–357. doi:10.1108/MD-07-2019-0865

Yi, Y., & Gong, T. (2013). Customer value co-creation behaviour: Scale development and validation. *Journal of Business Research, 66*(9), 1279–1284. doi:10.1016/j.jbusres.2012.02.026

Zakhem, A., & Palmer, D. E. (2017). Normative Stakeholder Theory. In Stakeholder Management (pp. 49–73). Emerald Publishing Limited. doi:10.1108/S2514-175920170000003

Zehir, C., Üzmez, A., & Yıldız, H. (2016). The effect of SHRM practices oninnovation performance: The mediating role of global capabilities. *Procedia: Social and Behavioral Sciences, 235*, 797–806. doi:10.1016/j.sbspro.2016.11.088

Zeng, Y., Jia, F., Wan, L., & Guo, H. (2017). E-commerce in agri-food sector: A systematic literature review. *The International Food and Agribusiness Management Review, 20*(4), 439–459. doi:10.22434/IFAMR2016.0156

Zhang, L., Wei, Q., Zhang, L., Wang, B., & Ho, W. H. (2020). Diversity balancing for two-stage collaborative filtering in recommender systems. *Applied Sciences (Basel, Switzerland), 10*(4), 1257. doi:10.3390/app10041257

Zimmerman, J., & Deborg, N. G. (2014). *Social Media All-in-One for Dummies*. Wiley India Private Limited.

Zinn, B. (2015). Conditional variables of 'Ausbildung 4.0' – Vocational education for the future. *JOTED, 3*, 1–9.

Zirpoli, F., & Becker, M. C. (2011). The limits of design and engineering outsourcing: Performance integration and the unfulfilled promises of modularity. *R & D Management, 41*(1), 21–43. doi:10.1111/j.1467-9310.2010.00629.x

Zoogah, D. B. (2011). The dynamics of green HRM behaviors: a cognitive social information processing approach. *Zeitschrift Für Personalforschung/German Journal of Research in Human Resource Management, 25*(2), 117-139.

Zuboff, S. (2019). *The age of surveillance capitalism: The fight for a human future at the new frontier of power: Barack Obama's books of 2019.* Profile books.

Zuckerberg, M. (2016). *Zuckerberg Facebook Post about Chan Zuckerberg Initiative investing in BYJU's-2016-8-16.* Academic Press.

About the Contributors

Mirjana Pejić-Bach is a Full Professor at the Department of Informatics at the Faculty of Economics & Business. She graduated at the Faculty of Economics & Business – Zagreb, where she also received her PhD degree in Business, submitting a thesis on "System Dynamics Applications in Business Modelling" in 2003. She is the recipient of the Emerald Literati Network Awards for Excellence 2013 for the paper Influence of strategic approach to BPM on financial and non-financial performance published in Baltic Journal of Management. Mirjana was also educated at MIT Sloan School of Management in the field of System Dynamics Modelling, and at Olivia Group in the field of data mining. She participates in a number of EU FP7 projects and is an Expert for Horizon 2020. Mirjana Pejić-Bach is editor in chief of two journals and serves as the Associate Editor and member of Editorial Board in several other journals, in the field of Information and Management, as well as conferences.

* * *

Cihat Aşan was born İn Istanbul, Turkey in 1970. Served in the Turkish Navy until 2013 and became master (unlimited) and has been serving as a lecturer (Asst. Prof.Dr.) in Piri Reis University/Istanbul since then. Introduction to Navigation, Terrestrial Navigation, International Maritime Conventions, Leadership, Organization and Management, Quality Management System lectures have been treated. Alongside the subject of marine pollution intervention in Istanbul Strait for the thesis of PhD, several studies have been published especially in marine environmental pollution.

Dogan Basar graduated Business Administration from Black Sea Technical University in 2005. He took master degree at Gebze Technical University in 2009. He lived in London in 2007 to study English. He took lessons about business administration at Tomas Bata University, Zlin, Çekya in 2008. He took phd degree at Gebze Technical University in 2016. He has worked at HR departmant at Finance Sector in Turkey. He has worked at Central Bank of The Republic of Turkey since 2020 as HR Executive Director. He also give courses at Universities of Turkey since 2017 about HR and business administration.

Beatriz Casais has a Ph.D. in Business and Management Studies from the University of Porto, MSc in Marketing, with a Bachelor Degree in Communication Sciences. She is the vice-Dean of the School of Economics and Management of the University of Minho, and the head of the executive education unit – UminhoExec. She is currently an Assistant Professor in the fields of Marketing and Strategy, Her research focuses on social marketing, business ethics, and public health advertisement. She has published in Journal of Macromarketing, Tourism Perspectives, Health Marketing Quarterly, Journal of Social Marketing, International Journal of Entrepreneurial Behavior & Research, Journal of Fashion and Marketing Management, Corporate Communications, Journal of Hospitality and Tourism Technology, Journal of Hospitality and Tourism Management, Place Branding and Public Diplomacy, Social Sciences, World Review of Entrepreneurship Management and Sustainable Development, and International Review on Public and Nonprofit Marketing, among others.

Çağlar Doğru, is an Associate Professor of Management and Strategy. He is the advisor to the Rector at Ufuk University, Ankara, Turkey. He completed bachelor's degree at Hacettepe University, department of business administration. He received master's degree in human resources management and doctoral degree in business administration from Gazi University, Ankara, Turkey. He participated in the Stanford University LEAD Business Program. He is a member of Commitee on Publication Ethics. His research interests are concentrated on management, leadership, organization, sustainability, organizational behavior, human resources management, and strategic management. Both having work experience in the prestigious national and international corporations in Turkey as a manager, he has still advising to the leader companies in the industry. He has given lessons in stated research areas, both at bachelor's and master's degrees. He has supervised many master's theses on management and organization as well. Additionally, he has numerous research articles in both national and international journals in the field of management and leadership. Moreover, he has several book chapters in the international publishing houses and he presented numerous studies at many national and international conferences and published at proceedings. He serves as editor at both international books and national/international prestigious journals. Among his hobbies playing piano and swimming come first. He speaks English, French, German and Russian. He is married and has a daughter.

Marisa R. Ferreira has a Ph.D. in Business Sciences – Marketing and Strategy specialization, School of Economics, University of Porto; Master of Science in Economics and Management Sciences in MAICH and graduated in Management in UTAD. Lecturer (associate professor) at School of Technology and Management in the subjects of Business Sciences. As researcher has several publications in the area of Nonprofit Organizations and Social Responsibility and her main topics of interest are marketing, social marketing, corporate social responsibility, sustainability, nonprofit sector.

Iraklis Foukas holds a bachelor's degree in Applied Informatics in Business and Administration from West Technological Institute of Greece, as well as a MSc from the Department of Informatics and Telecommunications in National Kapodistrian University of Athens. His research interests include managerial issues related with technological implementation and digital transformation in bank and telecommunication sectors. He is now working as an Application Development Analyst for Accenture, a multinational company that provides consulting and professional services.

Andreas Giannakis holds a bachelor's degree in economics from University of Piraeus, as well as a master's degree from the department of Informatics & Telecommunications / Economics in National & Kapodistrian University of Athens. He works for a telecommunications provider for 5 and a half years, and the last year has the position of CS Supervisor – CS Team Leader in the Order Fulfillment department.

Daniele Giordino is a PhD student in Business and Management for the University of Turin, Italy. Previous studies include BA(Hons) & MSc in Accounting and Finance at the University of Winchester, UK.

Hasan Aykut Karaboğa recieved his first master's degree from Yıldız Technical University statistics program. He completed his second master's degree in innovation, entrepreneurship, and management at the same university. He received his PhD Degree in statistics from Yıldız Technical University. He works as a research assistant at Amasya University. His areas of interest include statistical methods, machine learning, artificial intelligence, data mining, statistical programming. His articles have been published in various journals.

Tuğba Karaboğa received PhD degree in Management and Organization at Yıldız Technical University Department of Business Administration, Istanbul. Her research interests focus on Institutional Entrepreneurship, Innovation Management, Human Resource Management, Big data and AI in management. She has attended several PhD courses, focusing both on a theoretical and methodological perspective, including Organization Theory, Strategic Management, Organizational Behavior, Organizational Change and Development, Strategic HRM and Advanced Statistical Analysis Techniques in Social Sciences. She is currently focusing on digital transformation of HR and businesses and its effect on organizational performance. She took part into different international conferences and national projects.

Antonios D. Kargas holds a bachelor's degree in economics from National and Kapodistrian University of Athens, as well as a master's degree and a Ph.D. degree from the Department of Informatics and Telecommunications in the same University. His research interests include managerial issues related with technological implementation and digital transformation, as well as cost benefit analysis, technoeconomic analysis, applied economics for the telecommunication sector. He has more than 30 publications in peer reviewed journals / conferences in the field and more than 160 citations, while he serves as reviewer and co-editor in several international editions. Since 2007 he has worked as a research associate for the University of Athens, participating in more than 20 National and European funded projects. He holds significant experience as Economist / Financial Expert, responsible for conducting Cost – Benefit Analysis in several international projects. In 2009 he co-founded "Win to Win, Business Consultants", working in Business Consulting and Evaluating several investment projects. In 2013 he co – founded "Content Management in Culture P.C." (Comic), a private company activated in the field of IT services and serious games' solutions.

Özgür Özpeynirci received his B.S., M.S. and PhD. degrees in Industrial Engineering from Middle East Technical University in 2002, 2004, and 2008, respectively. He worked as a researcher at the Scientific and Technological Research Council of Turkey (TÜBİTAK) between the years 2001 and 2007. In February 2008, he joined Izmir University of Economics. He was a visiting research at Ecole Centrale Paris in 2014 and Université Paris-Saclay in 2019. His research interests include multi-objective decision making, combinatorial optimization and scheduling. He received the Best Doctoral Dissertation Award of the International Society on Multiple Criteria Decision Making, in 2011. His publications appeared in international journals including Management Science, European Journal of Operational Research, Naval Research Logistics, and Journal of the Operational Research Society.

Kamalendu Pal is with the Department of Computer Science, School of Mathematics, Computer Science and Engineering, City University London. Kamalendu received his BSc (Hons) degree in Physics from Calcutta University, India, Postgraduate Diploma in Computer Science from Pune, India; MSc degree in Software Systems Technology from Sheffield University, Postgraduate Diploma in Artificial Intelligence from Kingston University, MPhil degree in Computer Science from University College London, and MBA degree from University of Hull, United Kingdom. He has published dozens of research papers in international journals and conferences. His research interests include knowledge-based systems, decision support systems, computer integrated design, software engineering, and service oriented computing. He is a member of the British Computer Society, the Institution of Engineering and Technology, and the IEEE Computer Society.

Priyadarsini Patnaik is a knowledgeable, experienced & Seasoned Marketing professional with a huge experience in both industry and academics. Currently pursuing Ph.D. in Birla Global University, Bhubaneswar, Odisha, India. Her research area of interest are Artificial Intelligence, Consumer Behaviour, Advertising, Retail Management, Digital Marketing,

Rajiv Ranjan holds a Ph.D. in Public Policy and Management from Indian Institute of Management, Ahmedabad, and B.Tech. in Electronics and Communication Engineering with Distinction from Cochin University of Science and Technology, Kochi. Dr. Rajiv's research expertise, teaching and training interests lie in the field of Public Policies related to health and education, sustainable development, and business & society studies. He is also an adjunct faculty in the Strategy area with Liverpool Business School, UK. He is advisor to Board of several companies and start-ups such as Half-Circles Media Pvt. Ltd., e-Vishwavidyalaya LLP in India and SuMaya AaiT LLC in USA. He has presented, participated and served as a reviewer in conferences of International and National repute such as Academy of Management (AOM) annual meetings, International Humanistic Management Association (IHMA) meetings, Australian Association for research in Education (AARE), Australia and New Zealand Academy of Management (ANZAM), Canadian International Conference on Education (CICE), Harvard Conference, Kobe-Japan, Pan-IIM World Management Conferences (WMC), Indian Academy of Management (INDAM), MARCON, North American Case Research Association (NACRA) etc. He has also worked with a team at IIMA which formulated the Monitoring and Evaluation Framework for Pradhan Mantri Gram Sadak Yojna (PMGSY), NRRDA, Ministry of Rural Development (MoRD), Government of India (GoI). He has also consulted Ministry of Education (erstwhile Ministry of Human Resource Development) on National Education Policy several times and Ministry of Health and Family Welfare, AYUSH Ministry and Ministry of Women and Child Development on several projects. His other important works in area of social policy include "Developing of Monitoring and Evaluation Framework for Pradhan Mantri Gram Sadak Yojna (PMGSY)" – a project of Ministry of Rural Development (MoRD), Government of India and also papers on MGNREGA, 2005 and NFSA, 2013 out of which the first paper is highly appreciated and recommended worldwide with more than 43 thousand reads on ResearchGate. He has several peer-reviewed publications and conference presentations. He has served as reviewer to Journal of Teacher education, International Journal of Emerging Markets, North American Case Research Association (NACRA), IIM World Management Conferences etc. Papers from his thesis titled – "Self-Initiated Teacher Innovations in Rural Government Elementary Schools: Evolution, Impact and Sustainability" has been impactful locally and has been appreciated by researchers from Norway, Sweden, British Educational Research

Association (BERA) etc. when they were presented Infront of them at prestigious peer-review forums like Australian Association for Research in Education (AARE) and Australia and New Zealand Academy of Management (ANZAM). He is also co-author of non-fiction genre on die-hard entrepreneurship – "SMALL BIG BANG". Owing to his wonderful works, he was commemorated with "SOCIAL HERO AWARD" in Bihar Leadership Festival on October 14, 2017, an event organized in memory of late Dr. Rajendra Prasad.

N. Raghavendra Rao is an Advisor to FINAIT Consultancy Services, India. He has a doctorate in the area of Finance. He has a rare distinction of having experience in the combined areas of Information Technology and Business applications. His rich experience in the Industry is matched with a parallel academic experience in Management & IT in Business Schools. He has over two decades of experience in the development of application software related to manufacturing, healthcare and hospitality sectors, financial institutions and business enterprises. He contributes chapters for research reference books. He presents papers related to Information Technology and Management at National and International conferences. He contributes articles on Information Technology in mainstream newspapers and journals. His area of research interest is Mobile Computing, Virtual Technology, and Commerce in Space, Ubiquitous Commerce, Cloud Computing, e-governance, Knowledge Management, and Social Media for Business Applications. He is a member of the Editorial Advisory Board for research reference books published by IGI Global USA. He is also a Review Board Member of International Research Journals. He is the editor for the four research reference books published by IGI Global USA. The books are *Virtual Technologies for Business and Industrial Applications: Innovative and Synergistic Approaches, Enterprise Strategies in the Era of Cloud Computing,* and *Social Media listening and Monitoring for Business Applications, and Global Virtual Enterprises in Cloud Computing Environments.* He is the author of the book titled *Effective Open Innovation Strategies in Modern Business* published by IGI Global USA under Research Insights Category.

Aydın Şıhmantepe (PhD) is an assistant professor of the Maritime Faculty, Piri Reis University. Dr Şıhmantepe does research on maritime related affairs such as oil pollution, risk assessment, maritime accidents and maritime verbal communication. He also has past studies on Foreign policy crisis management and decision-making, International Relations and Foreign Policy.

Carina Silva is an Adjunct Professor of Business Sciences for the School of Technology and Management - Polytechnic Institute of Porto. In 2021, she finished the Doctoral Program in Economic Analysis and Business Strategy the U. of Vigo. Her research interests lie in the intersection of international business, strategy and managerial cognition.

Murat Selçuk Solmaz is an Assistant Professor Doctor at Piri Reis University, Maritime Faculty, Department of Maritime Transportation and Management. He completed his master's program in 2004 and doctoral program in 2012 at Istanbul University, Institute of Marine Sciences and Management. His professional and research experience includes maritime security, maritime safety, port management, and maritime transportation management.

Metehan Feridun Sorkun is an Associate Professor of Operations Management at the Izmir University of Economics. His recent research interests cover topics in the fields of product returns, modularity, logistics service quality, reverse logistics, and waste management. He has publications in the leading academic journals, such as Industrial Marketing Management, Waste Management, International Journal of Physical Distribution & Logistics Management, and European Management Review. He earned his bachelor's degrees in Logistics Management and International Trade and Finance from the Izmir University of Economics in 2010. He was a Visiting Scholar at the University of Greenwich in 2014. He completed the Ph.D. program in management, in 2016, jointly organized by Ca'Foscari University of Venice, the University of Padua, and the University of Verona.

José G. Vargas-Hernández, M.B.A., Ph.D., Member of the National System of Researchers of Mexico and a research professor at Instituto tecnológico Mario Molina, Unidad Acadpemica Zapopan, before at University Center for Economic and Managerial Sciences, University of Guadalajara. Professor Vargas-Hernández has a Ph. D. in Public Administration and a Ph.D. in Organizational Economics. He has undertaken studies in Organisational Behaviour and has a Master of Business Administration, published four books and more than 200 papers in international journals and reviews (some translated to English, French, German, Portuguese, Farsi, Chinese, etc.) and more than 300 essays in national journals and reviews. He has obtained several international Awards and recognition.

Songül Zehir received a Ph.D. in Management at Gebze Technical University, Turkey and Master's degree from Istanbul Ticaret University international business programme. Her research interests cover topics in the field of Strategic Management, Management and Organization, Total Quality Management.

Index

I

K

L

M

N

O

P

R

S

Recommended Reference Books

IGI Global's reference books can now be purchased from three unique pricing formats:
Print Only, E-Book Only, or Print + E-Book.
Shipping fees may apply.

www.igi-global.com

ISBN: 978-1-7998-1048-3
EISBN: 978-1-7998-1049-0
© 2020; 605 pp.
List Price: US$ 285

ISBN: 978-1-5225-8933-4
EISBN: 978-1-5225-8934-1
© 2020; 667 pp.
List Price: US$ 295

ISBN: 978-1-7998-0357-7
EISBN: 978-1-7998-0359-1
© 2020; 451 pp.
List Price: US$ 235

ISBN: 978-1-7998-0070-5
EISBN: 978-1-7998-0071-2
© 2020; 144 pp.
List Price: US$ 175

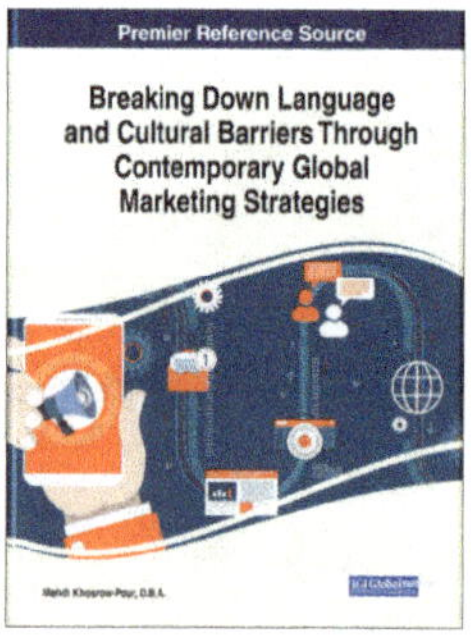

ISBN: 978-1-5225-6980-0
EISBN: 978-1-5225-6981-7
© 2019; 339 pp.
List Price: US$ 235

ISBN: 978-1-5225-5390-8
EISBN: 978-1-5225-5391-5
© 2018; 125 pp.
List Price: US$ 165

Do you want to stay current on the latest research trends, product announcements, news, and special offers?
Join IGI Global's mailing list to receive customized recommendations, exclusive discounts, and more.
Sign up at: **www.igi-global.com/newsletters.**

Publisher of Peer-Reviewed, Timely, and Innovative Academic Research

IGI Global
PUBLISHER of TIMELY KNOWLEDGE

www.igi-global.com Sign up at www.igi-global.com/newsletters facebook.com/igiglobal twitter.com/igiglobal

Ensure Quality Research is Introduced to the Academic Community

Become an Evaluator for IGI Global Authored Book Projects

The overall success of an authored book project is dependent on quality and timely manuscript evaluations.

Applications and Inquiries may be sent to:
development@igi-global.com

Applicants must have a doctorate (or equivalent degree) as well as publishing, research, and reviewing experience. Authored Book Evaluators are appointed for one-year terms and are expected to complete at least three evaluations per term. Upon successful completion of this term, evaluators can be considered for an additional term.

If you have a colleague that may be interested in this opportunity, we encourage you to share this information with them.

IGI Global Author Services

Providing a high-quality, affordable, and expeditious service, IGI Global's Author Services enable authors to streamline their publishing process, increase chance of acceptance, and adhere to IGI Global's publication standards.

Benefits of Author Services:

- **Professional Service:** All our editors, designers, and translators are experts in their field with years of experience and professional certifications.
- **Quality Guarantee & Certificate:** Each order is returned with a quality guarantee and certificate of professional completion.
- **Timeliness:** All editorial orders have a guaranteed return timeframe of 3-5 business days and translation orders are guaranteed in 7-10 business days.
- **Affordable Pricing:** IGI Global Author Services are competitively priced compared to other industry service providers.
- **APC Reimbursement:** IGI Global authors publishing Open Access (OA) will be able to deduct the cost of editing and other IGI Global author services from their OA APC publishing fee.

Author Services Offered:

English Language Copy Editing
Professional, native English language copy editors improve your manuscript's grammar, spelling, punctuation, terminology, semantics, consistency, flow, formatting, and more.

Scientific & Scholarly Editing
A Ph.D. level review for qualities such as originality and significance, interest to researchers, level of methodology and analysis, coverage of literature, organization, quality of writing, and strengths and weaknesses.

Figure, Table, Chart & Equation Conversions
Work with IGI Global's graphic designers before submission to enhance and design all figures and charts to IGI Global's specific standards for clarity.

Translation
Providing 70 language options, including Simplified and Traditional Chinese, Spanish, Arabic, German, French, and more.

Hear What the Experts Are Saying About IGI Global's Author Services

*"Publishing with IGI Global has been **an amazing experience** for me for sharing my research. The **strong academic production** support ensures quality and timely completion."* – **Prof. Margaret Niess, Oregon State University, USA**

*"The service was **very fast, very thorough, and very helpful** in ensuring our chapter meets the criteria and requirements of the book's editors. I was **quite impressed and happy** with your service."* – **Prof. Tom Brinthaupt, Middle Tennessee State University, USA**

Learn More or Get Started Here:

For Questions, Contact IGI Global's Customer Service Team at cust@igi-global.com or 717-533-8845

IGI Global
PUBLISHER of TIMELY KNOWLEDGE
www.igi-global.com

IGI Global
PUBLISHER of TIMELY KNOWLEDGE
www.igi-global.com

Celebrating Over 30 Years of Scholarly Knowledge Creation & Dissemination

InfoSci®-Books

A Database of Nearly 6,000 Reference Books Containing Over 105,000+ Chapters Focusing on Emerging Research

InfoSci®-Books Database

The **InfoSci®-Books** is a database of nearly 6,000 IGI Global single and multi-volume reference books, handbooks of research, and encyclopedias, encompassing groundbreaking research from prominent experts worldwide that spans over 350+ topics in 11 core subject areas including business, computer science, education, science and engineering, social sciences, and more.

Open Access Fee Waiver (Read & Publish) Initiative

For any library that invests in IGI Global's InfoSci-Books and/or InfoSci-Journals (175+ scholarly journals) databases, IGI Global will match the library's investment with a fund of equal value to go toward **subsidizing the OA article processing charges (APCs) for their students, faculty, and staff** at that institution when their work is submitted and accepted under OA into an IGI Global journal.*

INFOSCI® PLATFORM FEATURES

- Unlimited Simultaneous Access
- No DRM
- No Set-Up or Maintenance Fees
- A Guarantee of No More Than a 5% Annual Increase for Subscriptions
- Full-Text HTML and PDF Viewing Options
- Downloadable MARC Records
- COUNTER 5 Compliant Reports
- Formatted Citations With Ability to Export to RefWorks and EasyBib
- No Embargo of Content (Research is Available Months in Advance of the Print Release)

**The fund will be offered on an annual basis and expire at the end of the subscription period. The fund would renew as the subscription is renewed for each year thereafter. The open access fees will be waived after the student, faculty, or staff's paper has been vetted and accepted into an IGI Global journal and the fund can only be used toward publishing OA in an IGI Global journal. Libraries in developing countries will have the match on their investment doubled.*

To Recommend or Request a Free Trial:
www.igi-global.com/infosci-books

eresources@igi-global.com • Toll Free: 1-866-342-6657 ext. 100 • Phone: 717-533-8845 x100

IGI Global
PUBLISHER of TIMELY KNOWLEDGE
www.igi-global.com

www.ingramcontent.com/pod-product-compliance
Lightning Source LLC
LaVergne TN
LVHW081536300926
849161LV00006B/1459